PORTRAYING THE PRESIDENT

PORTRAYING THE PRESIDENT

THE WHITE HOUSE AND THE NEWS MEDIA

Michael Baruch Grossman and Martha Joynt Kumar

The Johns Hopkins University Press

Baltimore and London

Copyright © 1981 by The Johns Hopkins University Press
All rights reserved
Printed in the United States of America

The Johns Hopkins University Press, Baltimore, Maryland 21218
The Johns Hopkins Press Ltd., London

Library of Congress Cataloging in Publication Data
Grossman, Michael Baruch.
    Portraying the President.
    Includes bibliographical references and index.
    1. Presidents—United States—Press conferences.
2. Government and the press—United States. 3. Press
and politics—United States. I. Kumar, Martha Joynt,
joint author. II. Title.
JK518.G76   353.03′5   80-24634
ISBN 0-8018-2375-7
ISBN 0-8018-2537-7 (pbk.)

CONTENTS

PREFACE

I N THIS BOOK we explore the continuities in the relationship between two major political institutions: the evolving White House organization and an increasingly complex news media. To be sure, it is a relationship that profoundly affects the American political system; yet, surprisingly few attempts have been made to analyze in a comprehensive way the functioning of that relationship. Only one outstanding effort exists in the literature—Elmer Cornwell's 1964 book, *Presidential Leadership in Public Opinion*. Other than Cornwell's book, we have literary scrapbooks compiled by former White House officials and reporters. Their pages are filled with sketches of a particular presidency or a particular crowd of journalists. They include some wise insights, but their emphasis is topical and not analytical.

These books by White House correspondents reflect the dissatisfaction that so many of them experience after an assignment to cover the White House. For this and a number of other reasons, they are insufficient in providing us with a complete, clear discussion of the White House–press relationship. Most reporting about American institutions attains eminence only when the individual correspondent develops connections with well-placed persons who are privy to information. For example, the enterprising reporter covering Congress has little difficulty in finding people who not only have something to say but seek out the opportunity to say it. On the other hand, the White House reporter finds himself or herself frustrated by the inability to identify such individuals. Much of the information the White House reporter must use comes from a White House spokesman who can limit a reporter's access to opposing views by creating both physical and psychological impediments on the reporter's activities.

A news organization's expectations also restrict a reporter's ability to cover the White House. Most organizations expect their representatives to follow the physical movements of the President. They want stories that emphasize his personal role, or the role of one of his chief surrogates, in an event. Explanations of how the White House operates as an institution are often regarded as too arcane for a mass audience.

As a result, their books and articles emphasize the more personal characteristics of the relationship between the White House and the media. They examine the president's attitude toward the media as friends or foes of his political career, consider whether he is an open or secretive person, or evaluate his personal relations with reporters. Some journalists use these writings as an opportunity to vent their hostility toward the White House, for what they perceived to be manipulation of their reporting. Others will admit that despite the media's increasing criticism of presidents since Dwight D. Eisenhower, the ability even of unpopular presidents to generate positive images of themselves in the media remains considerable.

On the other side of the presidential–press relationship, White House officials involved in information policy do not provide any more of a complete picture in books and articles they eventually write. They are very much aware of the press's importance to a president who needs to send a favorable message and image to his constituency. Yet most White House officials turned authors have been more concerned with the history of their administration than with trends and issues of interest to other disciplines. To be sure, many of these officials are extremely knowledgeable and proved valuable as sources for this book; yet most of them are slow to elaborate on the insights of their own published work.

Soon after we began the writing of this book, we realized that the scope of our study would require more than an examination of a president and the journalists assigned to cover his activities. At the outset, we intended to write about what we thought to be the central operating unit in the White House, the Office of the Press Secretary. What we found, instead, was that almost every important White House official—and a large proportion of the not so important—was involved in presidential publicity. The White House contains a vast array of presidential strategists who share responsibility for portraying the President to his public throughout the media. Similarly, our examination of the "press" led us to present a more elaborate picture than we first intended. Those who portray the President for the media are editors and producers as well as reporters; cameramen, crew, and columnists as well as print media journalists for the daily press. We had to evaluate what appeared in the media in terms of a journalist's particular medium, a news organization's needs and structure, and the prevailing values among reporters assigned to the White House.

When we began this study in December of 1975, we were admitted to the White House press room through the courtesy of the Ford administration. Similar assistance in gaining access was granted by officials of the Carter administration. Our location at Towson State University, near Baltimore, made it possible for us to attend frequently the daily briefings at the White House and to interview reporters, White House staff, and others in the Washington area who are concerned with the White House–press relationship. In particular, we took advantage of the postelection "lame duck" period of the Ford administration by holding extensive interviews with several prominent members of the White House staff. The relatively easy access to the White House that characterized the first two years of the Carter administration also made our job easier.

We benefitted, too, from many visits to the files of the Roosevelt, Truman, Eisenhower, Kennedy, and Johnson libraries and the Television News Archives at Vanderbilt University. And we pieced together pertinent information about the Nixon administration from some of their files held by congressional committees.

In the course of this project, we received a lot of excellent advice and assistance. Leslie Lichter-Mason, our chief research assistant, provided aid in such areas as interviews, content analysis, and the production of the manuscript. We are deeply grateful to her. Two other assistants, Cecilia Forney and Judith Katz, spent weeks pouring over the *New York Times, Time,* and clips of CBS News.

Among the scholars who provided guidance, advice, and critical assessments of the manuscript were Francis Rourke of Johns Hopkins, Fred Greenstein of Princeton, Leon Sigal of Wesleyan, and Elmer Cornwell of Brown. Michael Nelson of Vanderbilt provided many helpful editorial criticisms. Richard Katz of Johns Hopkins gave time and assistance with the computer work for the content analysis of the three news sources we studied. William Ascher and Matthew Crenson of Johns Hopkins offered helpful suggestions, as did Stephen Wayne of George Washington University, and George Edwards of Texas A & M.

Several journalists spent a good deal of time informing two novices about the workings of the Washington press corps. We wish to offer special thanks to Dom Bonafede of the *National Journal,* James Deakin of the *St. Louis Post Dispatch,* Dennis Farney of the *Wall Street Journal,* James Naughton, now of the *Philadelphia Inquirer,* Martin Tolchin of the *New York Times,* and Frank Cormier of the Associated Press. During the first year of our study, Peter Lisagor of the *Chicago Daily News* was a most generous adviser. We found we admired him as much personally as we did professionally. With his death, the Washington community lost a valuable resource.

Walter Wurfel, former Deputy Press Secretary, now with the Gannett News Service, read the manuscript as did Max Grossman, formerly with the Voice of America. Both Ron Nessen of the Ford administration and Jody Powell of the Carter administration are due our thanks both for their willingness to sit through long sessions of questioning and for their forbearance with two outsiders who demanded entrance to their operations.

Among the many helpful personnel at libraries we would like to thank James Pilkington, director of the Television News Archives at Vanderbilt University, and Claudia Anderson at the Lyndon Baines Johnson Library.

Towson State University provided support from the Faculty Research Committee and by encouraging us to continue. We would like to express particular gratitude to Joseph Cox, vice president for Academic Affairs, and Peter Merani, chairperson of the political science department.

A Ford Foundation grant for the study of the presidency made it possible for us to spend a full year at work on the manuscript. We wish to thank

Louis Winnick and Marcia Bikales who provided continuous assistance and encouragement.

Henry Tom of The Johns Hopkins University Press expressed an early interest in our project as did Michael Aronson, the former editor-in-chief of the Press. We wish to thank them and our copy editor, Jacqueline Wehmueller. Joseph Hollander, of M. E. Sharpe Press, and Henry Herndon also provided useful counsel.

Most of the manuscript was typed from our imperfect drafts by Joanne Hildebrandt; the remainder by Catherine Grover. We wish to thank them both.

Vijayendra Kumar and Gabrielle Grossman read many drafts and listened to many of the ideas that became part of this book. We thank them for this help and for the extra encouragement they elicited from Erica and Michele Grossman and Zal and Vivek Kumar.

We would also like to thank the Baltimore Orioles for their distracting and winning ways that helped to make the bad moments more bearable.

Finally, each of us would like to dedicate this book to scholars and mentors who have provided inspiration to us that was particularly important for this book. Martha Kumar to Marvin Harder of the University of Kansas and Travis Cross, Press Secretary to Governor Mark Hatfield of Oregon. Michael Grossman to Francis Rourke of The Johns Hopkins University.

I
A CRITICAL RELATIONSHIP

T HE WHITE HOUSE and news organizations are involved in a relationship with high stakes for the presidency, the media, and the public.
Although both sides have been under considerable pressure during
recent decades, particularly during the years of Vietnam and Watergate, it
would be a mistake to view the relationship as basically antagonistic. The
adversary elements of the relationship tend to be its most highly visible
aspects. Cooperation and continuity are at its core.

ONE

CONFLICT AND COOPERATION

The Stakes of the Relationship

THE PRESIDENT of the United States ordinarily is brought to you by the news media. Images of the White House produced by strategists who advise the President reach their audience after they are processed in the great news factories and fine craft shops of print, broadcast, and television journalism. Reporters, editors, and producers regularly communicate messages from and about the President to workers, businessmen, farmers, ethnic groups, religious groups, and similar segments of the population—all of whom once received them primarily from their own leaders.

The President, the news media, and the people have an enormous stake in the critical relationship between the White House and news organizations. Both White House officials and reporters work to capture a national audience that demands information about the presidency. Since each uses the other's prestige to add to its own, the relationship between the two sides is often cooperative. Tensions occur because partisans of the President and partisans of the news media compete to gain the most benefits from the relationship. Both argue that their side speaks for the people.

THE STAKES FOR THE PRESIDENT

Newly elected presidents and their advisers know that their ability to acquire political influence often depends on their ability to use the tools of image-building. White House officials learn quickly that using these tools to bolster their reputation in the Washington community, as well as with the larger public, contributes to the success of their administration. "Presidential leadership is as much a matter of intangibles as of tangibles, as much shadow as substance," wrote Patrick Anderson, who has observed the office as chief speechwriter for Jimmy Carter's 1976 presidential campaign, as a national political reporter, and as a White House aide during the Johnson administration. "What a President does may matter less than what the people think he is doing."[1]

A president requires popular support to obtain political influence because his office's constitutional and institutional prerogatives are insufficient for him to achieve many important objectives. Although his powers to command are considerable, effective leadership requires his ability to use a variety of political skills. A president must be able to persuade Congress, the bureaucracy, his political party, lobbyists for interest groups, state and local officials, and an army of influentials in the private sector that it is in their interest to support his programs.[2] In order to influence and persuade these groups, presidents have found it increasingly necessary to demonstrate their effectiveness as leaders of public opinion.[3] The mass media is the principal vehicle through which they influence public opinion.

A president needs news organizations because, as communicator of most of his political messages, they determine his credibility with major public officials and the leaders of the most powerful interest groups. His 600 White House subordinates organize his relations with a long list of crucial individuals including most congressmen, important officials of state and local governments, key figures among the diffuse layers in the domestic and foreign policy bureaucracies, the officers and lobbyists for interest groups, and the leading figures of party organizations. In meetings with them, the President or his aides impart vital specialized information and shape the personal elements in the relationship. Since these contacts take place in a society in which, like the public at large, influential leaders get most of their messages about the White House from the news media, organizing the President's relations with news organizations is an important element of all the relationships. "There is no way to do this job as president if you are not willing to think about the media as part of the process in the same way that Congress is part of the process," Richard Cheney, White House chief of staff for Gerald Ford reflected shortly before that administration left office. "Consciously or unconsciously, the press often becomes an actor in the scenario."[4]

THE STAKES FOR THE MEDIA

News organizations need to cover the President because he represents the focal point in the American political system for their staffs and audience. For many reporters, a White House assignment represents the high point of a career. They know that the stories they prepare are virtually guaranteed a leading position in the daily or weekly editions of their publications or programs. The White House assignment also gives reporters high visibility with the public, which sees their faces, hears their voices, or reads their bylines. For print media editors and broadcast media producers, maintaining a regular correspondent at the White House is an important aspect of the prestige of their publication or programs. They want their organizations to reflect the aura of the presidency.

Because the Chief Executive is an individual, presidential activities can be portrayed more dramatically by the media than can those of Congress or the bureaucracy. The news media presents the President in its columns, telecasts, and broadcasts as an embodiment of national authority. John Herbers, deputy chief of the *New York Times*'s Washington bureau and a former White House correspondent, gave the following explanation for the predictable manner in which the media lavishes time and space to present the President to the public: "It's the way the whole process operates. If you have an institution [the presidency] in which an enormous amount of power is invested, an enormous amount of prestige, an enormous amount of publicity in the past has been centered on, then you get into a situation which is difficult to break out of. . . . It's a matter of habits in people's minds all the way from the reporting staff through the editors. I think it's true of most news organizations. They're conditioned to think in these terms."[5]

News organizations regard themselves as surrogates for the public; this is another reason why they place so much importance on their relationship with the President. This role found support even from a White House official for the Nixon administration, which was not known for expressing such thoughts during the incumbency of its leader. Gerald Warren, deputy press secretary during parts of the Nixon and Ford administrations, provided the unlikely testimonial: "If you don't assume that, then the whole process breaks down. They are the best representatives our system has been able to find. It's an entirely different subject if you want to discuss how well they represent the American people. But what other representatives do the American people have? . . . On a daily basis, the White House press corps must be assumed to be the people's representatives."[6]

Until recently, working correspondents at the White House were reluctant to define their roles as political actors. They maintained that they merely portrayed events for their viewers and readers. They would speak about getting the story for their news organization or, in general terms, of finding out what's going on and reporting it to the public. They tended to resist analysis of their influence by others and did not offer any themselves. Because of the high level of antagonism between the White House and the news media during the Johnson and Nixon administrations, however, and possibly because the media has been attacked from a variety of political positions during recent years, some reporters are now more inclined to reflect on the critical nature of their role in the relationship that connects the people to the government. Peter Lisagor, one of the most widely respected reporters in Washington during his twenty years there, linked the stakes in the relationship for the President, for the public, and for news organizations when he reflected on his reaction to a tense moment that occurred during the Vietnam War: "Once when Dean Rusk got angry at reporters' questions he yelled, 'Who the hell elected you?' Someone shouted back at him, 'Who the hell ever elected you?' What I would have said is that we represent the public interest. Nobody elected us to do this, but since we don't have a parliamentary system in which the President can be questioned on the floor of Congress, the press acquired that role by custom and tradition. We can't make a strong case for it though. We're used to being challenged all the time."[7]

THE STAKES FOR THE PUBLIC

The ultimate significance of the relationship between the White House and news organizations is that most segments of American society depend on what appears in the media for their information about the President. This is true in particular as well as in general. For example, media reports about the President's labor policy and his relations with labor leaders are monitored by union and management officials who are concerned both with what they learn from the stories and with whether they are shown favorably. For most of these individuals what appears in the media will be their only authentic source of information. And the public has a stake in the reliability of this information because it has a stake in labor policy.

The highest stakes involve two major aspects of the political system: first, that the President be able to communicate with the public; second, that the people get an accurate assessment of his conduct and activities. Because the media is the main intermediary between president and public, conflicts occur between White House officials and news organizations over which messages will appear, what information will be available, and which activities reporters will be permitted to cover. The outcome affects whether the public response will be to provide support for the President or to demand that his policies change.

Other important consequences occur when the relationship becomes too cooperative or too competitive. One probable outcome of a cozy relationship is that reporters, editors, or producers will gloss over official mistakes and thus fail to inform the public who was responsible for a bad decision. For example, because many columnists and reporters had close relations with Henry Kissinger, they minimized his role in the protraction of the Vietnam conflict, his ignorance of international economic policy, and his possible involvement in the Nixon administration's use of methods of dubious legality to track down unauthorized leaks of information. They became collaborators with Kissinger in his largely successful efforts to portray himself as a White House official whose involvement in maintaining America's world position was too important to subject him to close scrutiny on these types of questions. As a result, public demands for closer supervision of some of his policies never became widespread.

When news organizations are too sensitive to White House needs, they fail to report important aspects of the character of a president. Most reporters did not report the strange developments that took place in the White House during the final days of both the Johnson and Nixon administrations. Later it was revealed that President Johnson was convinced that his critics were subversives plotting with the country's enemies, while Nixon was so beset by his problems that he was often unable to function as president. Some critics of the media's role during this period believe that because news organizations later did report many stories of this type, public confidence in the President has been undermined, which makes it harder for him to serve public needs. Alternatively, the failure to report this information at the time may have led to the deep suspicions that are currently prevalent in public opinion that the same types of events may be going unreported now.

There are a number of important consequences for the public when the relationship becomes highly competitive. During the past decade, the media made it difficult for the President to transmit important messages to the public; at the same time, the White House used manipulative methods to prevent unfavorable stories from appearing. Each side appeared to assault the other. The public, the President, and the media all have a large stake in a final unraveling of these activities that figured so prominently in recent history.

The Effects of Recent History

The recent history of the office of the President is in large part a history of the expansion of the resources that presidents have to get their message to the public. Even before a large communications apparatus became part of the White House's machinery, officials acquired resources and personnel to aid presidents in the politics of persuasion. In order to enhance both its image and its effectiveness, Franklin Roosevelt's administration created (and its successors expanded) the White House Office and the Executive Office of the President. Since the 1930s the number of staff members with a public relations function in these offices has grown steadily. Early ad hoc operations for conducting publicity campaigns often evolved into permanent institutions for the exercise of presidential leadership. Subsequently, in response to the technical requirements of news organizations representing network radio and television, many temporary arrangements were rationalized, reorganized, or re-created in the form of permanent offices.

Representatives of national, regional, and specialized news organizations argued with White House officials that their needs for access and information required special facilities. So did reporters from the greatly enlarged Washington bureaus of newspapers, especially those of the *Washington Post, New York Times,* and *Los Angeles Times,* whose expansion was in some measure a response to White House publicity activities. Thus the Press Office and the Media Liaison operation were designed in part to assist news organizations in covering the agenda of activities the President and his advisers wished to set before the public; the Office of Public Liaison was created to promote the President and his programs; and other offices assumed the function of planning and coordinating direct press operations, White House promotion, and other political communications. White House officials learned that when they combined the resources of these offices with more traditional avenues of public exposure such as presidential speeches, press conferences, and the regular activities of the press secretary, they had tools that enabled them to deal more effectively with news organizations and thus get the President's message to the appropriate audience.

By the middle decades of the twentieth century the role played by the media had become crucial to the success of the President's efforts to bring about most significant changes in policy or even to administer existing policies. Although news organizations had been of importance to the White House since the late nineteenth century, until relatively recently most policy changes could be negotiated with the interested handful among the few score barons who controlled Congress, bureaucratic empires, regional press kingdoms, political parties, and electoral followings. Much more so then than later, media strategies were optional strategies. Even during the presidency of a traditional Washington "insider" such as Lyndon Johnson, the old politics had to be supplemented by new tactics since most of the old leaders had passed from the scene and their successors did not retain their power to make or keep deals on important matters. The new congressional leaders, bureaucratic chiefs, and private sector influentials no longer had the institutional power of an old-style congressional committee chairman, FBI director, or United Mine Workers chief. They also had far less ability to rally the people or groups they represented except when they were working for some narrowly defined but broadly beneficial economic objective such as higher social security payments or lower taxes.

Groups that fought change seem to have had more success than those that sponsored change. In the diffuse political milieu of post–World War II American politics, the success of the *antis* in forming majority coalitions against change seemed an irresistible trend. If a president was to overcome these forces, he needed the media's help to reach groups and individuals outside the shifting ad hoc alliance of veto groups. A president and his aides had to understand that if they were to succeed in bringing about major changes, they needed support from more leaders of more groups than had their predecessors; they also were in need of the support of the large army of people that had drifted away from its traditional associations and that thus no longer could be assumed to be supportive or quiescent after a deal had been struck with its leaders. These were the people President Nixon referred to as "the silent majority."

ANTAGONISM AND THE "ADVERSARY" RELATIONSHIP

The adversary aspects of the White House–media relationship broke into open conflict during the years 1965 to 1974 (roughly the period between President Johnson's implementation of his decision to send large numbers of troops to Vietnam and President Nixon's resignation). The scar tissue left on the presidency, the media, and even the concept of public interest merits some examination. Consequently, it is useful to review some important developments during this period and in its immediate aftermath.

The claim that the President represents the public interest was one casualty of the internal upheavals that marked American society during the 1960s and 1970s. The reputation of the President as the public's servant was tainted by Johnson's furtive escalation of the unsuccessful intervention in Vietnam and by urban racial disorders that some critics attributed to the dislocations of Great Society social programs. It was the political and constitutional crises of Watergate, however, that convinced many journalists, scholars, and other members of the attentive public to revise their opinions of the presidency. Revelations of criminal activities and other wrongdoing by the Nixon administration led many to the view that the White House often is occupied by mentally unbalanced power seekers and the sycophantic members of their clique who use the office of the President for their own ends. Several widely publicized books by former White House aides, journalists, and historians seem to provide evidence that Johnson, Nixon, and other presidents were beset by personal demons that they tried to exorcise through presidential power.[8] One of the main consequences of the subsequent decline in the credibility of presidents is that presidential invocations of national unity in the post-Watergate period often are greeted with cynicism by important portions of the media and the public.

During the same period the public perception of news organizations changed from that of society's "mirrors and messengers" to one of self-interested participants in the political process. Because they resented the role played by journalists and powerful news organizations as shapers of the reputations of their administrations, many White House officials, as well as other observers of national politics, challenged the media's claim to represent the public interest. Supporters of Lyndon Johnson such as John Roche, and Nixon advocates like Patrick Buchanan, Reed Irvine, and Edith Efron, suggested that the media are controlled by ideological news twisters.[9] Others argued that news organizations are commercial ventures more interested in the competitive advantage gained from antiadministration scandal mongering than in reporting the whole story, and that they are aided by reporters who are more concerned about the rung they have reached on a career ladder than in serving as fact finders for their audience.

Even in less volatile times many White House officials and reporters looked cynically at those who purported to be self-appointed spokesmen for the people. Such views are reinforced by prominent political analysts such as David Truman, who even question the validity of the concept of "the public."[10] They believe that coalitions of powerful and influential special interest groups, some of which have become sophisticated in the use of public relations techniques, try to convince Congress or the President that they represent the public interest. Other writers such as Robert Dahl and Charles Lindbloom suggest that although a number of "publics" represent important societal interests, there are always conflicting interests that have an equally legitimate claim.[11] Nevertheless, even if the notion of a public superior to any individual or group is fictional, interests that are broadly shared throughout the society are important. It is these shared interests that some observers believe were badly damaged during the Johnson and Nixon years.

Vermont Royster, a distinguished former editor of the *Wall Street Journal* whose White House reporting experience began in 1936, lamented to the National Press Club in 1978 that "in those different times we in the press did not think of ourselves as adversaries, enemies even, of our government."[12] By the late 1960s this had changed. The loss of confidence in the believability of White House officials experienced by many reporters during the Johnson and Nixon administrations is reflected in titles of their books about the era: *Anything But the Truth, The Politics of Lying, The Great Coverup, No Thank You, Mr. President.*[13] Former and current officials of the White House Press Office agree that both the tone of the relationship with the media and the scale of White House press operations have changed dramatically since the early 1960s. Reference to "simpler relations of a different era" were made in almost identical language by James Hagerty and Pierre Salinger, who recalled their experiences as press secretaries prior to Vietnam. Ronald Nessen and Jody Powell, who occupied the post after Watergate, made the same point using similar words.[14]

David Halberstam's career as a Vietnam War correspondent epitomized the conflict between reporters and government. His reports on the war subjected him to White House retaliation at the time.[15] Halberstam's expression of his lack of belief in what the administration told the press, the public, and many of its own functionaries provides a good example of the attitudes of many reporters during that time. Referring to the Johnson years, he told us in 1978 that "the White House constantly, constantly lied about what its intentions were. . . . Scotty Reston's phrase 'escalating by stealth' is exactly right. . . . They were lying to their own Bureau of the Budget Director, they were lying to the Council of Economic Advisers, they were lying to everybody. . . . They are liars. That is why they have no credibility."[16]

The administration responded to critics such as Halberstam by providing special briefings and interviews at which President Johnson or his top aides presented their position to reporters from major news organizations. These sessions frequently resulted in important stories for the reporters who attended. According to Joseph Laitin, a deputy press secretary during this period, Johnson described this policy toward the media as "throwing them a piece of meat when they are nipping at your ass."[17] Walt Rostow, President Johnson's national security adviser during the final years of his administration, recalled that there were many meetings with small groups of reporters during this period. The President spoke with "great openness, trying to make them understand something," he told us in 1976. "I would get the *New York Times, Washington Post, Newsweek,* and *Time* people in. . . . Those poor fellows were fascinated. They were late for dinner because the President would get rolling."[18]

Although Nixon administration officials also provided information to friendly and influential reporters, their major tactic was to confront their media critics with charges of bias and distortion. Vice President Agnew's attacks, which aimed to destroy the media's credibility, publicly amplified the latent resentments against news organizations that are felt by many people. Other administration officials explored legal avenues such as antitrust actions and license renewal challenges as a means of threatening hostile broadcasting and publishing enterprises. Illegal wiretaps were placed on the phones of some reporters in order to track down the sources of leaks.[19] During the Watergate crisis bitter-end partisans of the administration charged that news organizations were out to "get" President Nixon for actions they had winked at when committed by those like President Kennedy who were popular with reporters.[20] Nixon's critics accused him of trying to destroy the free press in America.

POST-WATERGATE CHANGES

Although Presidents Ford and Carter made strong efforts to run "open administrations" and establish good relations with the press, continued tensions during both administrations are regarded by some observers as proof that the relationship between the President and the press changed drastically and permanently as a result of the turmoil of the 1960s and 1970s. Ford never completely shook his association with Nixon, especially after he pardoned him. For Carter, however, things were supposed to be different. He and his aides arrived in Washington in January, 1977, intending to end the era of bad feelings between the White House and the news media. "We will be the first administration with the opportunity to make a really clean break with Vietnam and Watergate," Jody Powell told us a week before he was installed in office as President Carter's press secretary. "As much as he wanted to, Ford could not break clean of it because of spillovers. We, hopefully, can."[21]

During its first few months the Carter administration did enjoy a brief period of general acclaim. Tributes to the President's skill as a leader of public opinion were widespread throughout the media. There was even some concern that he was doing too well. In a *Washington Star* article that appeared on April 25, 1977, syndicated columnists Jack Germond and Jules Witcover suggested that reporters were asking such soft questions at presidential press conferences that they ran the risk of "having Carter use them as props in a continuing political exercise."[22] On May 15, 1977, *New York Times Magazine*'s cover presented a cartoon picture of a smiling president controlling the operations of a television studio's console on which all of the pictures were of himself. The headline next to the cartoon described the President as the "Maestro of the Media."[23]

The summer of 1977, however, was the beginning of the decline of public and press esteem for the President. The conflicts between the White House and reporters began with the publication of stories that eventually led to the resignation of Bert Lance, the director of the Office of Management and Budget. Some reporters described White House officials at this time as exhibiting a "siege mentality" toward the press, thus utilizing the same term that had been used to portray the attitude of the Nixon administration.[24] Throughout this period the media were filled with news stories, editorials, and columns that seemed to bring nothing but bad news for the White House. "Is Jimmy Carter suited for the job?" Hugh Sidey asked in his nationally syndicated column on the presidency at the end of August, 1978. "The question is now out on the table for serious and thoughtful debate."[25]

The President's achievement at the Camp David Summit Conference on the Middle East in September, 1978, provided a temporary reprieve from what had seemed to be an unending decline in his status. He improved his public standing (as measured in the polls) and his standing in the media (as expressed in favorable stories, editorials, and comments). Shortly after this boost in the President's position, we asked Jody Powell to reflect on the administration's press relations during the first twenty-one months of its history. Powell admitted that the media had been more antagonistic and abrasive than he had expected. Reporters, he suggested, were still affected by Vietnam and Watergate, whose "wounds will take a lot longer to heal than I anticipated."[26] Even before Carter's decline began, Powell had lost some of his earlier optimism. "The basic relationship between the President and press or the President and Congress has changed over the past decade," he had told a television interviewer. "It will never be what it was."[27]

The legacy of Vietnam and Watergate continued to be most visible at the press secretary's daily press briefing. Efforts by Presidents Ford and Carter to assure the press and the public that they would require their spokesmen to speak with candor did not change the attitudes of some reporters. Many correspondents continued a style of questioning suitable to inquisitors trying to unveil a dark secret. If a White House spokesman announced that the administration had changed its position on an issue, reporters asked both Ronald Nessen and Jody Powell if their earlier answers were now "inoperative," the term used to mock President Nixon's press secretary, Ronald Ziegler, when he admitted that his vehement denials of White House involvement in Watergate were inaccurate. A leading White House correspondent at the time, Helen Thomas of United Press International, displayed the continuing power of memories of the Nixon era when she commented that Jody Powell "can garbage up an answer when he doesn't want you to know what he is saying; he is very Ziegleresque in that respect."[28]

TRADITIONAL INTERPRETATIONS OF THE RELATIONSHIP

The relationship between the White House and the news media since 1965 might appear to demonstrate three points: first, that the relationship is characterized by an underlying antagonism; second, that it is subject to dramatic and unpredictable changes; and third, that it is still affected by the traumas of Watergate and Vietnam. Thus after the Carter administration enjoyed a few months of honeymoon with the press and public, it endured a series of conflicts with the press that led to a long period during which its public standing declined. International achievements and international crises might temporarily restore a higher standing with news organizations and the public. But Carter administration officials felt that the President's inability to establish a positive public assessment of his activities could be attributed to the deep suspicions created by the Johnson and Nixon administrations, when influential reporters became convinced that the leadership could not be trusted.

Yet there are a number of factors idiosyncratic to the events of a particular time, the objectives of an administration, and the personalities of reporters and officials that may be decisive in determining how the President is portrayed to the public. As we have seen, major crises such as Vietnam and Watergate have affected reporters' view of the presidency. Another determining factor may be whether an administration offers programs for significant legislative or administrative change. A third is the attitudes a particular president and his staff have toward the representatives of news organizations and the attitudes that a given set of reporters bring with them to the White House.

These points all seem to substantiate the view, widely held by many White House reporters and officials, that their relationship is subject to too many intangible and unpredictable factors to permit a systematic analysis. For example, some presidents have enjoyed good relations with the media because of their charm, their accessibility, and the skills that they and their staff had in manipulative techniques. Yet an approach that resulted in favorable coverage in one instance might lead in similar circumstances to a major confrontation with the media. In a dramatic description of what he perceived as the amorphous nature of the relationship, Patrick Anderson, in his book *The President's Men,* concluded that ''perhaps the central fact about the relationship between the White House and the press is that no rules govern it. The President and his aides do not have to cooperate with the press; the press does not have to publicize the President. The relationship is based upon mutual need, with hostility never far beneath the surface; it is a no man's land of power and personality, bluff and bluster, experience and expedience.''[29]

The View of This Book: Cooperation and Continuity

Ten years during which respected journalists saw deceit in the White House while partisans of the government believed that the media played a major role in the departure of two Presidents from office have left visible effects on the contemporary relationship between the White House and news organizations. Perhaps the most enduring effect has been a reinforcement of the already heavy emphasis that the news media give to the presidency. In other ways, as well, the ten-year war accelerated rather than ended existing trends. Thus, although newly arrived White House officials and reporters alike in the post-Watergate era may think of themselves as free agents, they invariably follow the routines dictated by the enduring needs of the organizations they work for. What they attempt to do usually is programmed by their organization's expectations, and what they don't or can't do is often a result of organizational constraints. New White House officials find that organizational imperatives dictate the way they can use the media. Newly assigned reporters find that achieving their organization's goals leads them to follow the same routines as the reporters who preceded them to the White House.

So, in contrast to the view that they are adversaries whose relations recently have undergone dramatic change, the argument here is that the White House and the news media are involved in a continuing relationship rooted in permanent factors that affect both sides no matter who is president or who is doing the reporting. Continuing forces shape both sides more than specific incidents, however traumatic, or the impact of particular personalities, however unusual. What's more, the cooperative elements in this relationship are at least as strong as those that are antagonistic, for a fundamental reason: presidents and news people depend on each other in their efforts to do the job for which they are responsible.

Only through news organizations can a president get and keep the attention of the public. Tradition and constitutional proscriptions prohibit him from commandeering the press, except infrequently and with its consent. With the exception of those Pearl Harbor–like crises when the public automatically turns to the White House for explanation and reassurance, the President needs regular assistance from the press to get his message across. Although the White House and news organizations disagree over what and when the public should learn about the character, activities, policies, and decisions of the President, most of what appears about the President in the media is a result of efforts that are at least partly cooperative.

Presidents want the news media to transmit messages to their many constituencies. News organizations must cover the President because his activities represent the single biggest continuing news story that their audience demands they present. The evolution of the present relationship based on the common need to attain these complementary goals began in the late nineteenth and early twentieth centuries, when mass circulation newspapers and magazines were creating a national audience. At that time some presidents and their aides recognized the advantages of establishing a system for the release of news that gave them control over the rules by which reporters gained access to information and individuals at the White House; this enhanced the President's ability to get his unfiltered message across to the public. During the same period Washington became an important center for the press. Reporters assigned to cover national news began to focus on the activities and personalities of presidents, who replaced the Congress as the central interest of their editors and readers.

The current availability of staff and other resources, more than any desire of presidents to make war against the media, accounts for the systematic efforts by recent administrations to coordinate political communications, public information, and publicity policies, although antagonism certainly was an element during the Nixon administration. The larger and wealthier news organizations in turn have developed strategies for covering the President that have made it possible for them to deal on a nearly equal level with White House officials. This rough parity has made some journalists more willing to present critical accounts of White House activity and has led a few, since they are less frightened by the prospect of White House reprisals, to take a stance of almost permanent antagonism. Parity also contributes to the stability of their relationship. Since each side can inflict considerable damage on the other, cooperation suits the needs of both better than an adversary relationship.

Because both the White House and news organizations gain from prominent and even favorable coverage of the activities of the President, senior White House officials and the managers of publishing and broadcasting enterprises try to avoid major conflicts. The public displays of anger and sarcasm at the press secretary's daily briefing are misleading if they are regarded as symptoms of fundamental hostility rather than as an outpouring of personal frustrations and antagonisms reinforced by a physical set-up and organizational structure that provides many opportunities for outbursts. Many observers whose only view of the relationship is at the briefing or at similar events mistakenly label the two sides as adversaries. They are not. They do not always share the same interests, but that is another matter. The evidence, as indicated in the files of the presidential libraries and as substantiated in numerous interviews, indicates that those who lead the major news organizations as well as most of those who serve as senior advisers to the President will go to considerable lengths to attain and maintain cordial relations with each other.

The high intensity with which different versions of reality were presented to the public during Vietnam and Watergate and the attacks by supporters of the President and the press on the credibility of each other have led some observers to believe that the relationship has changed drastically and permanently. In the past when the media published materials the White House considered unfavorable, White House officials blamed political rivals or insubordinate and unhappy underlings for attempting to enhance their own positions by passing harmful information to reporters. More recently, particularly but not exclusively during the Johnson and Nixon administrations, White House officials, including the President, have focused their attention on the media itself. These attacks have ranged beyond presidential anger at individual reporters and news organizations. The media as a whole have been portrayed as independent actors plotting to undermine the political authority of the administration or even destroy public confidence in the presidency.

There is not much evidence that the media have either the organizational unity or the ideological affinity to mount a sustained attack on the President. Nonetheless, the evidence justifies one White House allegation about the role of news organizations. They have become one of the principal forces on the national political scene, influencing the other major forces—the President, Congress, the bureaucracy, the parties, and the pressure groups—and in turn being influenced by them.

II

REPORTERS AND OFFICIALS AT THE WHITE HOUSE

D URING an era of great political pressures and technological changes, those who work for and run the White House publicity apparatus and those who cover the White House for news organizations have adapted to each other in evolutionary ways. Reporters at the White House establish patterns for their professional activity shaped by the type of media for which they work, their particular news organizations, and their own personal notions of how they should get stories. The most important determinant of their behavior, however, is the White House itself. Vast resources exist to help the President conduct his political communications through the media. The most common point of interchange between the news media and the White House is in the Press Office, where the press secretary, the manager of the President's message, plays a number of roles designed to suit the needs of the President, the White House staff, and news organizations.

TWO

A CONTINUING RELATIONSHIP

WHITE HOUSE publicity operations evolved from the organizational world of a White House bureaucracy that had been established to get the President's image and message into the media. The present White House activities of the media, developed in response to the enlarged prominence of the presidency, are possible because of the economic and technological expansion of publishing and broadcasting enterprises. By the late nineteenth century several essential features emerged that continue to affect the relationship between the President and the press: (1) news about the White House was transmitted to the public by independent nonpartisan news organizations; (2) these organizations were heavily dependent on the White House staff for most of the information they received about the President's activities and policies; (3) the transition from an episodic to a regular relationship between the President and the press required the development of procedures to provide reporters with information on a regular basis; (4) the increase in both the amount and the diversity of White House publicity activities made it necessary for the President to seek specialized assistants with skills as promoters and with knowledge of the press.

In the following decades the continuing expansion of the resources of both news organizations and the White House staff made the relationship between president and press a recognizable feature of the Washington landscape. Today several important White House officials administer publicity operations comprising one of the major functions and perhaps the central preoccupation of the President's men and women, while the presidency has become the central concern of major news enterprises and their leading journalists.

Since the 1930s the White House and news organizations have established institutions that function best in an atmosphere of continuity and stability. Self-perpetuating organizational routines, characteristic of complex organizations, have made the relationship less flexible than participants on either side believe it is or wish that it would be. Each side reacted to technical changes by emphasizing patterns of behavior that reinforce the need for continuing cooperation. Consequently, important aspects of the relationship continue over long periods.

This chapter consists of an analysis of factors that perpetuate the continuing relationship. It begins with a description of some of the publicity practices that have been institutionalized in the organizational world of the White House. The second section shows how technological changes such as television have had a powerful impact on the way the staffs of news organizations and the White House behave. The final portion deals with the organizational needs, routines, and activities of news organizations covering the White House.

The Organizational World of the White House

Because publicity is often an inseparable component of policy, many White House officials, especially those who think it is always inseparable, believe that their political power depends on the public perception that the President is providing strong leadership. They believe that his image as an effective leader is as important to the success of his administration as the substantive appeal of his programs. "The universe out there is concerned with how you are projecting," an aide to President Ford reflected.[1] This is a lesson well studied and often exaggerated by many White House officials, including several recent presidents.

White House officials decided to create a structure for news operations in response to the growing organizational and technological complexity of the news media as well as to their own ongoing publicity requirements. In his pioneering work on the subject, *Presidential Leadership of Public Opinion*, Elmer Cornwell described the central importance of communications policy for presidential power.[2] Cornwell demonstrated that since the administration of Theodore Roosevelt, an increasingly important factor in determining the success of a president's communications strategies has been the sophistication with which White House officials approached the job of creating and coordinating White House offices that have responsibilities for communicating the President's image and messages to the public. The roots of these White House offices and the origins of some of these White House publicity activities may be traced back as far as the administration of Grover Cleveland, although a large and effective operation was not introduced until the 1930s.

Thus, over a period of almost a century, the organizational world of the White House evolved in a manner that has made it possible for the President to maintain, stabilize, and at times exploit his relations with the media. During the fifty years beginning with Grover Cleveland's administration and ending at Franklin D. Roosevelt's, the evolving White House institutionalized a number of ad hoc roles performed by the President's secretary and other assistants into the permanent position of press secretary, whose most conspicuous role is as the President's spokesman. In the following years, roughly from 1933 to the present, an expanded White House staff began to provide even more publicity resources for the President. A third development, which began in the late 1960s, involved the establishment of permanent institutions that administer and coordinate administration publicity with White House liaison activities that channel the President's message to Congress and interest groups.

THE PRESIDENT AND HIS SPOKESMAN

Although presidents have always been aware of the impact that newspaper stories can have on administrations, it was not until the final third of the nineteenth century that the President's secretary, his only professional assistant at that time, began to assume regular responsibility for managing the technical details necessary to get his message across to the public. It was not until near the end of the first third of the twentieth century that presidents and their assistants sought to institutionalize their methods of obtaining favorable coverage in the press. Presidential assistants became important to the President and to reporters during the administrations of Theodore Roosevelt and Woodrow Wilson because of these presidents' commitment to the leadership of public opinion; assistants were also important during the term of Grover Cleveland, who disliked personal contacts with reporters and therefore delegated this responsibility to his subordinates.[3] In order to respond to demands placed on them by both press and president, secretaries organized reporters' daily routines at the White House, arranged their contacts with the President and other administration officials, and channeled information from the President through reporters to the public.

Organizing reporters' routines. During Cleveland's administration the White House secretary, Dan Lamont, realized that to reach the public on behalf of the President he had to find ways to provide the press with a continuous flow of news. He needed to supply reporters with appropriate information in time for them to meet their deadlines, and to do so in a way that also would help the President. Lamont provided reporters with routine information on a regular basis and acted as their source on more important White House stories. O. O. Stealey, a veteran reporter of that era, suggested that Lamont "had tact, judgment, knew what to say and how to say it, and what to do and how to do it. He let the 'boys' do most of the talking and guessing, but never allowed them to leave the White House with a wrong impression, or without thinking that they had got about all there was in the story.'"[4]

By the time of the McKinley administration the President's secretary was routinely providing a number of services to reporters. He gave them advance copies of speeches, arranged interviews and conferences with the President, and provided a daily meeting, which may have been the progenitor of the daily briefing by the press secretary. According to a contemporary account by Ida M. Tarbell, a journalist who is remembered for her muckraking stories on the trusts of that era, "Every evening about 10 o'clock [reporters] gather around Secretary Porter for a kind of family talk, he discussing with them whatever of the events of the day he thinks it is wise to discuss.'"[5]

Arranging contacts and channeling information. As both formal and informal contacts between the White House and reporters increased during the years from Theodore to Franklin Roosevelt, the responsibility of White House officials for arranging these contacts and channeling information to reporters also increased. Among the arrangements were presidential press conferences, which began on a regular but informal basis during Theodore Roosevelt's administration and became scheduled events during the Wilson administration.[6] The information included facts about the President's travel, schedules, and appointments. Roosevelt's secretary, William Loeb, Jr., continued the practice of providing "guidance" for reporters by issuing statements and press releases, answering questions at regular but informal meetings, and providing reporters with stories when their deadlines required that they have something. Joseph Tumulty, Wilson's secretary, played an even larger role, according to Cornwell:

It was Tumulty, not the President, one can safely assume, who kept the whole range and pattern of administration publicity and public relations under constant review and who laid the plans for improving them. He held daily conferences of his own with the reporters who frequented the White House and thus kept in touch with their thinking and the issues their queries brought to his attention. He directed the compilation of the "yellow journal" of press clippings and editorial comment which was traditionally prepared in the White House for the President.[7]

The arrival of the press secretary. As presidents became more sensitive to the idea that the press could be used as an instrument of presidential leadership, they sought additional assistance to coordinate the various ways in which they communicated with the public. There was a growing recognition in the 1920s of the need to delegate more press duties to the staff. During the Harding and Coolidge administrations a speechwriter or "literary agent," as he was known by reporters of the time, worked at the White House.[8] But the President was authorized to have on his staff only two professional-level White House assistants. His secretary was responsible for a variety of important activities of which press relations was only one. Tumulty, for example, dealt with patronage.[9] When Hoover was granted a third secretary he appointed George Akerson and limited his responsibilities to making appointments and maintaining press relations. Both Akerson and his successor, Theodore Joslin, handled the service and information functions of the President's relations with the press. They did not have the wider range of responsibilities involving the coordination and management of White House publicity that were taken on by some of their successors. The *Christian Science Monitor*'s Richard Strout, one of the few reporters from this era still active in the 1980s, recalled to some interviewers that "Akerson and Joslin were not spokesmen for the President but were merely giving you information about the activities of the President."[10]

Stephen Early, the secretary appointed by Franklin Roosevelt to handle press relations, quickly made it apparent that he was going to do more than inform reporters about the activities of the President. "The whole administration was a public relations effort, and Early was right in the middle of it,"[11] Richard Strout commented, as did other reporters who observed the White House before, during, and after the New Deal.[12] "Early took charge and ran publicity for the government," observed Bascom Timmons, whose active years spanned administrations from Taft to Lyndon Johnson.[13] "Roosevelt always kept Early informed," Louis Brownlow remembered. "He and Hassett [Early's assistant] always had access to the President."[14] Early played a major role in Roosevelt's decision to hold frequent press conferences, to allow newsreel cameras to film recreations of his radio addresses, and to provide services for the special needs of the larger White House press corps that covered Washington when the New Deal took office.[15] During these years, however, there was still an ad hoc character to most publicity matters. Early and other White House aides established and managed new programs as the situation demanded.

Thus since the 1930s a factor of considerable importance to a president's ability to gain support has been whether the individual he selected to manage his relations with the media could act as a spokesman in a variety of different circumstances. In the Roosevelt administration, when the skills of the President as a communicator became more critical to his success, a press secretary emerged who played an important role as his public relations manager. Since then the President has needed a variety of staff resources in order to achieve his publicity goals.

THE EXPANSION OF THE PRESIDENT'S PUBLICITY RESOURCES

Press relations was Early's major but not exclusive responsibility as one of Roosevelt's four secretaries. Forty years later press operations were a major part of an even larger publicity program. Although many decisions still have to be made on the run, long-range public relations policy often is formulated in settings such as Camp David, where both the Ford and Carter administrations held retreats to deal with their problem in getting their messages and image across. Important publicity decisions also are made in meetings of the President's senior advisers, themselves often institutionalized in the form of the "senior staff." These decisions are implemented by offices that in most cases did not exist a few years ago, such as the Office of the Assistant to the President for Communications, the Office of Public Liaison, and the Media Liaison operation.

The President's chief bureaucratic resource for publicity continues to be the Press Office, which expanded from fewer than ten employees in 1953 to more than thirty during the late 1960s and early 1970s. The Press Office holds briefings, arranges press travel and interviews, provides lists of speeches, and supplies presidential messages to a large army of Washington reporters. It also produces additional materials and provides separate meetings for non-

Washington-based media and the specialty press; mails White House statements to every news organization in the country with a circulation of over
100,000; and prepares a daily summary of what appears in the media for the
President and the White House staff.

Presidents devote much time and attention to trying to determine the best
use of White House publicity resources. Their chief targets include private
and public sector leaders whose support they hope to gain; rivals whose opposition they hope to neutralize; and influential editors, producers, columnists,
and commentators whose news judgments they hope to shape. Although presidents recognize that the use and coordination of these publicity resources is
linked closely to the success of their programs, not all recent presidents have
recognized the extent to which they would have to become involved in planning and implementing specific activities. It was not until after he had been in
office for eighteen months that Jimmy Carter recognized the relationship
between his lack of attention to political communications and his political
weakness. "They were doing substantive things, but it wasn't synthesized
into a message," said Gerald Rafshoon, whose position as assistant to the
President for communications was created to improve Carter's relations with
the official, political, and public constituencies. Rafshoon and Anne Wexler,
the assistant to the President for public liaison, were brought into the White
House after the President and his chief advisers concluded that new personnel
better skilled at coordinating White House communications activities were
required to obtain support for administration programs. The decision was
made after an agonizing reappraisal of his problems by the President, after
which, according to Rafshoon, Carter instigated reforms and participated in
their implementation. "The President has become more personally involved
and more thematic in his approach," he said. "My job is to see that we don't
send out conflicting signals."[16]

Two other presidents of the post-1933 era, Harry Truman and Gerald Ford,
also seemed unaware of the policy-publicity lesson when they took office.
Truman never learned. Ford grasped the lesson once he selected an able group
of assistants to coach him. In contrast, all the other presidents of this era—
Franklin Roosevelt, Dwight Eisenhower, John Kennedy, Lyndon Johnson,
and Richard Nixon—sensed the importance of White House publicity operations. Both Franklin Roosevelt, in Stephen Early, and Dwight Eisenhower,
in James Hagerty, had exceptionally able assistants to coordinate their publicity efforts for them at a time when it was still possible for most publicity
functions to be personally overseen by one individual. During his short term
John Kennedy relied on the institutional innovations of his staff and met with
similar success. All benefited from an intuitive grasp of their own public
relations role.

Although Roosevelt, Eisenhower, and Kennedy directed their publicity
resources to serve personal political goals as well as the broader policy goals
of their administrations (and though each used the cloak of national security to

hide activities that now seem dubious), their attempts to mold public support stirred less public and media criticism than did those of Lyndon Johnson and Richard Nixon, who were often accused of treating publicity as a substitute for policy. It was during the administrations of these two presidents that concern about the possible perversion of the publicity process led many to question whether a highly coordinated and powerful publicity tool is inherently a dangerous instrument to give to a powerful and ambitious president.

Although attempts to exploit publicity resources for narrow partisan advantages were common in prior administrations, it seemed that the staffs of Presidents Johnson and Nixon broke new ground in the use of these powers to punish enemies, win cheap victories over their weaker opponents, and defend policies and activities that would otherwise seem indefensible. In addition to overseeing their well-known and at least temporarily successful campaigns on Vietnam and Watergate, Johnson and Nixon scrutinized the details of their publicity campaigns. Lyndon Johnson asked his staff to prepare a study of his popularity during the terms of his several press secretaries, and also had the staff prepare numerous papers "refuting" what the President thought were unfair stories.[17] President Nixon requested an aide to have letters to the editor sent to *Newsweek* "mentioning the President's tremendous reception in Mississippi and at last Saturday's Miami Dolphin football game," according to a memorandum written by Jeb Stuart Magruder, deputy director of the Office of Communications. Magruder wrote that Nixon also requested "a report on what action was taken concerning Senator Muskie's appearance on 'The Merv Griffin Show.' "[18]

CREATING PERMANENT INSTITUTIONS

Throughout recent decades efforts to obtain a favorable public image in the media for the President that once were performed on an ad hoc basis by members of the White House staff have become part of the assigned responsibilities of a presidential assistant. If these responsibilities are perceived to be of great importance by the President, they become the aide's major responsibility and an office is created to assist the individual. For example, the Kennedy and Johnson administrations saw benefits to the White House in assigning people like Press Secretary Pierre Salinger and Cabinet Secretary Robert Kintner, the former president of NBC, to deal directly with editors, publishers, and columnists, instead of having the media dealt with indirectly through the White House press corps. In the Nixon administration these functions became part of the responsibilities of the newly created Office of Communications. In the revelations that accompanied the Watergate investigation, the Office of Communications was shown to be a major organ of the Nixon administration's efforts to discredit and circumvent the Washington press corps. Jeb Stuart Magruder described its operations during this period:

We also tried to develop positive programs that could get the Administration's case to the people. We were involved in media politics, and we were seeking not only to speak

through the media in the usual fashion—press releases, news conferences—but to
speak *around* the media, much of which we considered hostile, to take our message
directly to the people. . . .

We tried to devise an imaginative, aggressive publicity program. We did the trivia
and the dirty tricks when we had to, but we also tried to explore every possible means
to reach the public with a program that we all believed to be excellent.[19]

When Nixon left office the antagonistic style and exploitative methods of
his underlings left with him, but the basic apparatus remained intact. The
Office of Communications continued to function in the Ford administration;
in 1976, under David Gergen, it was given a major role as a coordinator of
the President's campaign publicity. In the Carter administration Patricia Bario,
one of six major assistants and associates of the press secretary, became the
head of the office now renamed "Media Liaison." Bario set up meetings between President Carter and groups of editors, publishers, and non-Washington-
based reporters two Fridays every month. White House reporters could not
attend these conferences and did not have access to the stenographic transcripts until after the materials first could be used by those who were invited.

Many reporters and White House officials believe that such conferences
provide the President with an opportunity to influence the media in a setting
that is more favorable to him than a press conference with the White House
regulars. James Naughton of the *New York Times* suggested that an arrangement of this sort "gives him [the President] a shot at meeting with media
people who are pleased to be at the White House, are susceptible to his charm,
and are likely to show it in their copy."[20]

White House officials maintain that these conferences offer an entirely
appropriate opportunity for the non-Washington press corps to meet with the
President and for the President to get some exposure to what people outside
of Washington are thinking. "The Washington press corps reflects a highly
rarified and distorted view of America," John Ehrlichman commented,
stating the views of many Washington officials in the Johnson and Nixon
administrations.[21] Walter Wurfel, a deputy press secretary in the Carter
administration, agreed that it was useful for the non-Washington press and
the President to see each other. He added that these meetings are particularly
important for the President because of the limited attention the Washington
press corps pays to the process of explaining an issue. "Take something as
complicated as energy," he said. "We have to keep sending out our message
if we expect people to understand. The Washington press corps will explain
a policy once and then it will feature the politics of the issue."[22]

In any event the Media Liaison operation now regularly schedules meetings
that the White House used to seek on an ad hoc basis. The need that White
House advisers felt to establish contacts with the media outside of Washington
has been institutionalized in an office that enables the President to fulfill this
need as part of his schedule.

Technology and Change

Technical and organizational changes in the media beginning in the late nineteenth and early twentieth centuries made it increasingly important for White House officials to understand the media. Presidents found that their ability to reach an audience directly through radio and television depended on their ability to learn the proper use of these new forms of media. In this regard the personal qualities each president brought to his efforts to communicate directly to the public—his personal appearance, his speaking voice, and his ability to articulate the ideas, symbols, and programs of his administration—all affected his success. The President, like other performers, needed coaching on how to appear and, since the new media changed both the nature and the amount of public exposure a president could receive, advice on when and how often to appear.

For news organizations the technical and organizational changes presented both a new set of decisions about how to use their new resources and a question of how to adapt their relations with the White House to the requirements of the new media. Editors and producers had to decide how to use the new processes that created photojournalism, radio, and the newsreel camera, all of which made it possible to present the President's voice and image directly to the public. After World War II, television, which made possible even more intimate presentations of White House activities, enlarged the appetite of news organizations and the public for information about the President. Since the 1950s the opportunities to use television to communicate with the public has been a central concern of presidents and their White House advisers. That they have these opportunities has been a concern of those who fear they will be tempted to use television to dominate public opinion.

FAST PHOTOGRAPHY, NEWSREELS, AND RADIO

By the 1930s technological developments adapted to journalism made possible the establishment of new media forms with a new set of managers.[23] The most noteworthy developments included fast lenses on portable cameras, which set the stage for the large circulation photojournalism magazines such as *Life* and *Look;* talking newsreel coverage and documentary films; and the opportunities for direct communication with people via radio, an information source nearly every American had access to.

Stephen Early, who worked for a newsreel company before he accepted Roosevelt's appointment as press secretary, recognized that these technical changes presented opportunities for the President. He learned quickly how to take advantage of the transformation of the old, printed-word news media into one with important visual and aural components. He was particularly successful in turning fast-lens photography to Roosevelt's advantage. Photographers got special access to FDR if they played by Early's rules. Acceptance of these rules by photographers, which included the unwritten requirement that they not take pictures that showed the President as a helpless invalid, often resulted in a positive pictorial portrayal of Roosevelt, his family, and his aides in papers whose news columns were controlled by anti-Roosevelt publishers. According to David Kennerly, White House photographer for the Ford administration, some of these special unwritten rules and arrangements still exist. Photographers are sometimes permitted to stay on in meetings after reporters leave if they agree not to report on what they may overhear.[24]

Early also made special arrangements for newsreel and radio coverage of the President. Meetings frequently were held and speeches often given in settings recommended by Early on the basis of their suitability for newsreel coverage. Partial reenactments of these meetings and of the famous fireside chats were staged for the camera. Reporters and camera crews learned that their ability to get good material depended on arrangements provided by White House officials. They also learned that the power of their medium made the White House dependent on them.

Presidential radio broadcasts, though controlled technically by the networks, also were influenced by Early. One recommendation that broadcasters accepted was to turn on the podium microphone several seconds before the President appeared. Early expected that the sound of the waves of applause for the President would create a positive personal reception for him among listeners, even if he could not convince them with his arguments.

THE IMPACT OF TELEVISION

The most conspicuous changes in the relationship between the White House and news organizations since the 1950s can be traced to the growing perception by White House officials that television is the most important medium for the President to dominate. Many of the younger Press Office personnel in the Carter administration have no memory of the pretelevision era. "These people are all members of the Howdy Doody generation," said Walter Rodgers of Associated Press Radio. "It's hard to get them to think about the importance of any other medium."[25] Networks influence both the timing and the nature of the agenda of activities that the White House schedules for public consumption, sometimes demanding that White House events be held at places and times suitable for their needs. At the same time, television correspondents occasionally use the airways to berate the White House for being too responsive to television. When President Carter's departure for the Middle East in March of 1979 was scheduled so that network television could cover it live on the evening news, the White House correspondent for CBS News, Lesley Stahl, said that the schedule was an attempt to manipulate television rather than, as White House officials maintained, to meet its needs.[26] CBS did not exercise its option of not covering the event, however.

The combined efforts of the White House and the networks have made the President the single biggest continuing story on television news. The labor involved in the networks' massive coverage of his activities is equalled by the large-scale efforts of the White House to influence what television portrays. White House aides treat television as their major resource for winning public support for the President and his programs. In no other area do the organizational worlds of the White House and news organizations come together so dramatically. William Greener Jr., deputy press secretary during the Ford administration, described some of the efforts that he and Ronald Nessen, the press secretary, made to get events televised: "Whenever possible, everything was done to take into account the need for coverage. After all, most of the events are done for coverage. Why else are you doing them? I mean you know you don't dedicate the [Dirksen] library in Pekin, Illinois, which we did, and then deny it to television by doing it behind a closed door. You wanted the coverage. For the sake of the library, for the sake of the President, for the memory of Everett Dirksen, for everything else."[27]

The President and his advisers have three ways to use television: they can ask to have the President appear live for a television address; they can "permit" the networks to televise an event such as a speech before Congress or a presidential news conference; and they can try to get him on the news broadcasts, which are edited and produced by the media.[28]

A television address by the President can be his most important direct means of communicating with the public. Barry Jagoda, President Carter's television adviser during the 1976 campaign and the first eighteen months of his administration, remarked that "one of the things television does best is to let people feel they are a part of a national moment."[29] The decision by the White House to allow coverage of events like a press conference provided the President direct contact with the public with reporters as a foil rather than a filter. The benefits of such coverage became apparent to James Hagerty, President Eisenhower's press secretary, after he decided to allow the networks to show films of an Eisenhower press conference. Hagerty had been furious at stories by James Reston and Edward Folliard that indicated that Eisenhower had responded softly to Senator Joseph McCarthy's accusations. He wrote in his diary, "I'm glad we released the tape of the statement to radio, TV, and newsreels. To hell with slanted reporters, we'll go directly to the people who can hear exactly what Pres [Eisenhower] said without reading warped and slanted stories."[30] The benefits of live coverage also were seen by Pierre Salinger, Hagerty's successor. Salinger convinced President Kennedy that it was to his advantage to let the networks transmit press conferences live and without any White House precensorship.

Because a large portion of the public relies on television for news, there has been a built-in incentive for the White House to try to dominate what appears on the networks. The senior staff as well as Press Office officials arrange the President's schedule so that he will have his minute on the evening news. Even the manner of public addresses made by the President has been influenced by television. According to James Fallows, the first chief speechwriter for the Carter administration, the President preferred to deliver two- or three-minute statements in the briefing room rather than the traditional long televised addresses because all "most people hear [of those speeches] is about a minute or two on the news anyway. [That's] the same amount of coverage you get if you go out there and talk for one or two minutes."[31] The implication is that by giving a short statement, the White House is more likely to get what it wants on the news than it would be if editors decided what portion of a longer speech to use.

The Organizational Needs of News Organizations

In the years after Franklin Roosevelt succeeded Herbert Hoover, the changed political situation created by the depression and the war made White House news more important to the press. By this time reporters had become an important force in the politics of Washington policy making. According to Leo Rosten, whose 1937 study *The Washington Correspondents* ranks among the most comprehensive surveys and analyses of Washington reporters, "Their help is sought by persons and organizations trying to publicize an issue; their displeasure is avoided. They are aware, by virtue of the deference paid to them and the importance attached to their dispatches, that they are factors of political consequence."[32]

THE INSTITUTIONALIZATION OF THE MEDIA'S INFLUENCE

White House officials expect that their regulation of the flow of information to the media will provide such benefits to the President as a higher standing in the polls, greater success in his policy initiatives, and reelection. Although the media's need to cover the President tempts White House officials to try to manipulate news organizations into providing large amounts of favorable coverage, the success of these techniques requires that the public perceive the media as credible and independent. Thus the White House also has contributed to the growing national importance of news organizations. Just as the White House influences the way reporters cover the presidency, reporters affect the way the White House governs. In particular, the media's influence has been institutionalized in three areas.

Issues. Because the media has the ability to raise issues, it can alter the agenda the White House has set for itself. President Carter discovered this early in his administration when he was forced to deal with accounts in the *New York Times* and the *Washington Post,* repeated on television, that King Hussein of Jordan was receiving secret funding from the CIA. A representative of the White House told us on a background basis that the President already had decided to discontinue some of the assistance and reevaluate all other secret projects when the stories were published.[33] But because the media brought the issue to public attention before he was ready to act, the President felt forced to defend the existing arrangements. He denied that there had been any improprieties and postponed the examination of the program. Ben Bagdikian, a prominent journalist and student of the media, has suggested that "a news story in a serious and reliable paper can force decisions, sometimes in haste, often with attention out of proportion to importance, and at times under the worst possible circumstances."[34]

Reputation. The news media can bestow a reputation on an individual or institution and thereby influence how seriously other actors in the system respond to his or its objectives. At no time is this more important than during a presidential nomination campaign, when reporters' presentation of "serious" candidates is widely believed to influence who will be regarded as a viable candidate by voters and political leaders. Hamilton Jordan, Carter's political assistant, recognized this early during Carter's own campaign for the nomination. In a memorandum dated November 4, 1972, he wrote to Carter:

Like it or not, there exists in fact an eastern liberal news establishment which has tremendous influence in this country all out of proportion to its actual audience. The views of this small group of opinion-makers in the papers they represent are noted and imitated by other columnists and newspapers throughout the country and the world. Their recognition and acceptance of your candidacy as a viable force with some chance of success could establish you as a serious contender worthy of financial support of major party contributors. They could have an equally adverse affect, dismissing your effort as being regional or an attempt to secure the second spot on the ticket.[35]

Communications. The news media serve as a network to convey messages through a governmental system that is extremely decentralized and that has no consistently effective internal communications system. White House officials assume that since most top-level bureaucrats read the *New York Times* and the *Washington Post,* news items announcing a policy or describing a position that are prominently displayed there will receive attention faster than a memorandum sent through channels. Joseph Laitin, a former deputy press secretary who also served as press officer for several departments during both Democratic and Republican administrations, suggested, only partly in jest, that the fastest way to get the attention of official Washington is to leak a memorandum to the *Times* or the *Post.* Bureaucrats are more likely to be aware of the significance of an item when it appears in the media, he said, particularly if it appears to have been pried loose rather than officially communicated.[36]

In addition to the major daily newspapers, newsweeklies, and the television networks, less well-known specialist publications play an important role in carrying messages from the White House to the bureaucracy. These publications often inform government executives about the policies the White House intends to pursue vigorously or, conversely, send them a signal that the real intent of a White House statement was merely to appease an interest group.

One such specialist publication, the *National Journal,* with small circulation but great influence, was described by John Ehrlichman as playing a role as a "channel of communication to Congress and the bureaucracy" in the Nixon administration.[37]

Sometimes the administration uses the news media to communicate messages when direct contact with the intended recipient might lead to a conflict the White House could lose. James Reston has suggested that he and the *Times* were used in this manner by John Foster Dulles during the Lebanon crisis of 1958. Dulles told Reston that the administration would ask Congress for a resolution permitting it to intervene militarily in Lebanon. According to Reston, the publication of this story put the Senate leadership in a position whereby it had to go along with the administration or risk making the United States look weak. If the administration had gone directly to the Senate leadership with their request, Reston said, they might have been turned down.[38]

ORGANIZATIONAL ROUTINES

Organizational routines involve much more than the structure of organizations. They reach to the heart of the relationship between the White House and the media. Take, for example, one deeply entrenched organizational routine that reporters and officials claim they want to change, the daily briefing at which the press secretary stands before the White House press corps to make announcements and take questions. Despite widespread dissatisfaction and continuous complaints by both briefers and briefed, the format has not changed much since 1960, though the Nixon administration cut the number of briefings from two to one each day and moved them from the press secretary's office to a new briefing room. "There is clearly not something that is newsworthy every day," Jody Powell said, "and there is no particular reason there ought to be [a briefing]. To prepare yourself to answer a whole wide range of questions covering the whole federal government takes a good two to three hours out of the day on something that benefits neither the President nor the press nor the public and which seems to me to be a waste of time."[39]

Reporters interviewed at the White House during the Ford and Carter administrations also grumbled about participating in a time-consuming activity they seldom found productive. Reporters who covered the White House when James Hagerty was press secretary confirmed that then, as now, reading the notices and releases available in the press room or asking an assistance press secretary about current developments would produce as much information as that delivered at most briefings. For this reason a few White House reporters attend briefings infrequently. "I never did 'body watch' the White House, attending every briefing," said Martin Schram, who has covered the White House for *Newsday* and the *Washington Post* since the Nixon administration.[40]

The reason this "habit" has not been changed is that it serves important latent functions for both sides. The briefing provides reporters with an opportunity to find out what the White House "line" is, whether the line has changed, and what stories other reporters are chasing, as well as a chance to get information placed on the record from the Press Office. In the Carter administration, in which it is known that Jody Powell is close to the President, and in the Nixon administration, in which Ronald Ziegler was a particularly good indicator of President Nixon's moods, the briefing became a good place to "read the minds" of the White House or to try to get some feeling for the mood and character of the leadership.

White House officials described the benefits the briefing has for them. One can call the White House press corps the President's early warning system because what the staff learns from the briefing gives them a gauge to judge responses to their policies and proposals. Several reporters asserted that the most important benefit for the White House is that the briefing provides them with an opportunity to shape the media's agenda for that day. Dom Bonafede, White House correspondent of the *National Journal,* commented during the Ford administration that "every day when Nessen gets out there he determines, with his opening statement, what the news is going to be for that day. Whatever the White House decides is newsworthy, Nessen comes out and makes a statement on it. Sure, the reporter later on can ask him questions on other topics and other subjects, of course he can, but they are not going to ignore the original statement. That is going to be one of the big stories of the day."[41] Insofar as this may be a tactic to distract reporters from pursuing potentially embarrassing stories, it may work well with reporters for smaller news organizations, who are more likely to feel obligated to follow the agenda set before them at the briefing. James Naughton of the *New York Times* said that while the large organizations have the resources and the expertise to flush out information beyond what they are told at the briefing, "the smaller bureaus are almost compelled to work with the basic information that is given to them by the White House plus perhaps what they carry around in their heads."[42]

NEWS ORGANIZATIONS AT THE WHITE HOUSE

Generalizations about the behavior of media representatives, like those about the White House staff, indicate the increasingly bureaucratized manner in which its component organizations direct coverage of the news. In addition to performing the tasks involved in their traditional roles as correspondents, reporters assigned to cover the President who work for bureaus that have managerial and technical staff also cooperate with colleagues on stories that frequently are the product of directions from a central editorial office, if not the Washington bureau.

Unlike White House officials, who are aware of their need to understand the media, reporters tended to discount the importance of specialized education about the President in their preparation for a White House assignment. They indicated that before taking up their positions they did not receiv' briefings about White House operations from other reporters or from their editors. Edward Walsh of the *Washington Post,* who was assigned to the White House in late 1975, reported that his editors suggested that he read a number of books about the President by academics and reporters. He did not read them then, he said, nor did he intend to in the future. "The White House is a general assignment beat," he said, repeating a sentiment shared by many reporters. "It's just like covering City Hall."[43]

Reporters at the White House represent different forms of media, each of which has different needs and different ways of directing its staff. Among the reporters, technicians, and photographers who constitute "the White House regulars" are those who work for daily newspapers, newsweekly magazines, the wire services, newspaper chains, the television networks, the radio networks, "opinion" magazines, and the foreign press. In addition to the regulars, there are columnists, television commentators, and magazine writers who often cover stories with a White House connection. Different levels of news organizations also are involved. The President and White House officials are concerned with bureau chiefs, editors, and publishers with whom they meet to discuss both the manner and substance of coverage of the President.

News organizations require help from White House officials in order to cover the President. Press Office officials not only brief reporters; they accredit them so that they can get to White House activities; and, if they think it is necessary or useful to the President, they help reporters to obtain interviews with him or his advisers. Press Office officials also distribute copies of announcements, speeches, and schedules; make available facilities for writing and transmitting stories; provide electronic hook-ups, space, and information about how best to photograph, televise, or broadcast a presidential event; and provide other forms of assistance.

In general, editors, producers, and reporters have no quarrel with the agenda that the White House sets before them. They adopt reporting styles suited to their news organizations and their professional self-image that enable them to report what is happening and predict what is likely to happen. As reporters become familiar with Washington, they learn how a consensus forms for or against a president among influentials in Congress, the bureaucracy, the lobbyists, the law firms, and the elite journalists. They perceive events at the White House from the same cultural milieu as these other members of the Washington community. Most journalists give no indication that they are dissatisfied with this existing order. Antiestablishment commentary that occasionally appears is a vestige of the romantic notion that journalists are outsiders. There is not much evidence that the views of reporters, in contrast to those of a few columnists or commentators, are ruled by any articulated ideology.

Most of the struggles between reporters and White House officials are over organizational goals. Wire service and television reporters demand that presidential events be held in public at times and in places that are suitable to their style of "coverage" of this type of activity. Some reporters become angry if they don't receive "help" in the form of advance notice or special explanations of stories that are of particular interest to the region in which their paper is published or in which their editors or producers have an ongoing interest. Other conflicts may result from the arrogant demands of some reporters who are used to having their own way or from similar behavior by officials; still others stem from personality clashes and the desire of some individuals on both sides to display their toughness, as well as other forms of posturing. Some clashes are induced by the White House because of presidential pique at unfavorable stories and the desire, almost always self-defeating if acted upon, to get back at the tormentors.

Correspondents whose work brings them into the sphere of influence of the presidency do not set out deliberately to present a version of reality that differs significantly from what the White House wishes to present to the community of Washington influentials and the country at large. What their news organizations want most are interesting stories about what the President is going to do, preferably before they become common property. They want stories filled with illuminating details about individuals whose stars are rising and stories about those who are on the decline. Especially when the President's troubles are reflected in a decline in the polls or in defiant opposition from interest groups, Congress, the bureaucracy, and the private sector, correspondents seek to include embarrassing items about the kinds of deals White House officials have made or are about to make, blunders committed by the President and his staff in their relations with key people or groups, and contradictions between a president's words and his actions. When things are going well for the President, especially during the early months of his term or after a particular success, both correspondents and their organizations are less interested in such items. Because White House reporters for major publications and networks need continuing frank discussion with White House officials if they are to get important background information, they are less likely to produce stories that the White House finds offensive than are journalists who write signed columns of opinion and editorials or who participate in television-news talk shows. It is these White House regulars whose work is assessed in the next chapter.

THREE

MILTON'S ARMY: THE WHITE HOUSE REGULARS

They also serve who only stand and waite.
—Milton, *On His Blindness*

R EPORTING at the White House takes place at the tips of the media's tentacles. The tentacles extend from news organizations that represent publishing and broadcasting enterprises of diverse size, power, and interest. The needs of these organizations determine what appears as news. The reporters, photographers, and technicians assigned to cover the President and his activities on a regular basis must interpret these needs every time they decide how to get a story at the White House. Reporters, the most important group among these news gatherers, define news according to a mix of professional values, the demands of their organizations, the activities of other reporters, and their reaction to efforts by the President and his advisers to reach the public through them.

Unlike the tentacles, the regular White House reporters are quite visible. They show up at events scheduled for them such as briefings and news conferences and follow the President on his public and private travels. They are visible because of the large amount of time they spend waiting for something to happen—for the briefing to start, for the President to appear for a ceremony in the White House Rose Garden, for a visitor to arrive, for a statement or transcript to be released. A few correspondents wait because they know that eventually there will be an unscheduled announcement or event.

Reporters occupy their waiting time in different ways. Some sit or stand at the booths, desks, and phones that the White House assigns to them. If an event is delayed, they may join the technicians and photographers who, when they are not taking pictures, often lounge on couches and chairs provided throughout the press area. On the frequent occasions when the press secretary is late for the daily briefing, reporters waiting for him in the briefing room may be seen talking, reading, dozing, working crossword puzzles, or watching television. Others wander into the offices of one of the assistant press secretaries to check on some piece of information they need for a story or to inquire about the schedule of events, announcements, and appearances the

Press Office prepares for them. Still others gaze out the door of the press room to try to spy a newsworthy visitor to the West Wing of the White House. Collectively they resemble an army at rest—bored with waiting and easily diverted.

Before the 1960s this might have been an adequate description of almost all the activities of the White House regulars, according to the testimony of reporters and officials who were there at the time. Of course these same reporters were capable of great activity for long, sleepless hours after an important White House announcement or decision or when disaster, illness, or death struck the President. But until recently the typical routines of the great majority of correspondents involved watching, waiting, and pursuing their leisure. "It's better than working," Edward Folliard of the *Washington Post* told a visitor who looked in on a group of White House reporters enjoying the luxuries of spa living while covering one of President Eisenhower's numerous golfing vacations.[1] Former reporters and officials suggest that as late as the 1950s the White House press room maintained a well-stocked liquor cabinet that constantly required restocking. They talk about famous reporters who were so drunk at times that their stories had to be ghost-written for them.

During the Ford and Carter administrations more than forty reporters were asked what they thought of the quality of the work produced by the White House press corps. Several felt that many of their fellow correspondents, though not so flamboyantly nonprofessional as their colorful predecessors, remain quite happy with an assignment that provides them with stories that their editors are likely to use simply because of the White House dateline. These reporters suggested that White House stories often require little effort because they are based on handouts or on the statements of officials who are trotted out before them in the press room. "We're creatures of habit," said Peter Lisagor, one of the few Washington journalists not assigned to the beat who voluntarily spent a great deal of time at the White House. "We know that there's not that much to the job.'"[2]

It is possible that there are a number of reporters who are quite satisfied with the arrangements provided for the media at the White House. Because of turnover in personnel, there may have been as many as 120 reporters assigned by news organizations primarily to cover the White House during the years 1975 to 1979. More than half of this group participated in this study either through formal interviews or by answering questions and volunteering their observations in the informal setting of the briefing room. A major recurring theme of these discussions was their work routines as White House regulars. Their descriptions were consistent with our observations, namely, that physical or intellectual laziness, although present, is not prevalent among White House correspondents. Instead, the major factors limiting their activities seem to include the routines imposed on them by their organizations, their responses to what they see other reporters doing, and their own concepts of how they should cover the President. Not surprisingly, most reporters recognize the first of these reasons most clearly. Invariably they complain that the requirement that so much of their time be spent in forced inactivity makes the White House an unrewarding if prestigious assignment. Few expressed a sense of satisfaction with the job of reporting that they are able to do while standing and waiting for glimpses of White House activity orchestrated for them by White House officials.[3]

What the White House regulars define as news depends not only on the instructions and the routines of their organizations, but on the kind of medium they work for—print, television, or radio. Reporters may gather information for news services that transmit it to customers who have their own publishing or broadcasting outlets; to closed corporations that form a chain of newspapers, magazines, and stations; to a rewrite desk where it is integrated with other stories; or to an editor's desk where it is processed for presentation in the next news program or next edition. James Deakin of the *St. Louis Post-Dispatch,* a middle-sized afternoon newspaper with a circulation of approximately two hundred and sixty thousand, may follow different routines and look for different materials than Tom DeFrank of *Newsweek,* a nationally read weekly magazine with a circulation of almost three million. What DeFrank wants, and thus the way he behaves, is different still from Dom Bonafede of the *National Journal,* a small circulation magazine read principally by an elite audience of bureaucrats, lobbyists, and political cognoscenti.

Thus White House reporters follow a path constructed by presidential advisers that they hope will lead them to fulfill goals set by their news organizations. White House officials ration them facilities for work, access to newsworthy people, and reportable information in amounts that depend on the importance to the President of the type of media they work in, the status of their particular news organization, and the White House staff's respect for the influence and competence of a particular individual. In this context, several constraints that affect White House reporting are discussed here, namely, those placed on reporters by: their organizations; the way their type of media covers the White House; their relations with each other; and their concepts of what they are required to do. The framework for this discussion and analysis is a classification by type of media and news organizations that assign journalists to the White House.

Of the resulting six categories, the first three have the most structural and organizational influence and are given the most attention here. The special status, unique history, and influence of photographers at the White House require that they be treated separately. The seven categories are as follows.

Wires. The Associated Press and United Press International are national news networks that provide print and broadcast organizations with basic information and feature stories about the White House. Reuters News Agency, a smaller wire service, offers an interesting contrast to the two giants.

Television and radio. Reporters and crew representing the three commercial television networks work for the medium that most concerns White House officials. The radio news organizations considered here are three networks, National Public Radio, Mutual Broadcasting System, and Associated Press Radio.

Major national publications. Four daily newspapers and three weekly magazines not only are read regularly by influential people in Washington but also exert a large influence on the news that is published and broadcast by the other news organizations. They fall into three groups, presented here in order of their importance to the White House: the *Washington Post* and the *New York Times; Time* and *Newsweek;* the *Wall Street Journal,* the *Washington Star,* and *U.S. News and World Report.* Some of these news organizations are part of an interlocking directorate of media conglomerates. The *Times,* the *Post,* and *Time* have their own nationally syndicated news services; the *Post* owns *Newsweek; Time* owns the *Star;* Dow Jones, which owns the *Journal,* has a news as well as a financial ticker. Some also own broadcasting outlets, book publishing enterprises, and other newspapers.

Large circulation regional daily newspapers, chains, and affiliated news services. Many of the publications in this group are parts of corporations that own newspapers, magazines, and radio and television stations. The chains, groups of newspapers with a common ownership, such as Knight, Newhouse, Gannett, and Scripps-Howard, maintain Washington bureaus whose stories are available to each paper that is part of the organization. Some regional majors such as the *Los Angeles Times* and the old *Chicago Daily News,* influential daily papers in major media markets, also sell a news service to subscribers. The newspapers and services discussed in this chapter include most of those which provide regular White House coverage.

Although White House officials know that regionals and chains determine how they are regarded in Peoria and Los Angeles, even those with excellent Washington bureaus have less national impact than the major national publications because they are not read regularly in Washington. Their White House correspondents are affected by, first, the conflict between the values of Washington reporters and the local interests of their editors; second, the lower status they have because they are not read in Washington; and third, the reporting problems that result from the inclination of the White House to serve them only after the majors, wires, and the electronic media.

Elite and specialist publications. Publications with a specialized business, ethnic, or trade audience have Washington correspondents who spend a good deal of time at the White House. In most cases their general influence is limited unless their stories are reprinted in the *Congressional Record* or appear on the *Op Ed* page of the *Post*. Some publications, such as *Aviation Week,* have such excellent connections in government that they become sources for other reporters. Two small circulation magazines, the *National Journal* and the *New Republic,* which are widely read in the Washington community, maintain full-time White House correspondents.

Independents. The independents are reporters who represent several small regional organizations that pay for their services. These reporters often do not share the prevailing values of reporters for more prestigious organizations, nor are they protected by the status of such organizations from their colleagues' distaste for their idiosyncrasies. Consequently, although most independents are not outcasts, the pariahs of the White House press room are found in this group.

Photographers. News organizations send technicians and photographers as well as reporters to the White House. Both often are regarded as appendages of the reporters. In the case of technicians, who usually work as part of a television crew under the direction of a reporter, this view is generally correct. A technician's relations with White House officials reflects the relations established by the network and its correspondents. Photographers, however, have a relationship with White House officials that is governed by the latter's own set of rules. These are often more important in determining what information and images they convey to editors' desks than are the assignments they receive from their organizations.

Wires

Wire service reporters were the most visible members of the White House press corps before the advent of television news led to the emergence of "stars" like Dan Rather of CBS. The names of Merriman Smith, Marvin Arrowsmith, and Jack Bell, for example, once were among the best-known bylines in the country. By the 1970s, however, it seemed that only television could create journalistic celebrities. Even well-known writers such as Peter Lisagor of the *Chicago Daily News* and Helen Thomas of United Press International achieved public recognition as a result of their many appearances at televised press conferences and as participants in televised news discussion programs.

At the White House, however, reporters for the two major wire services still are the most visible. The Associated Press and United Press International have the most prominent booths in the small working area reserved for reporters that is located directly behind the larger briefing room. The Associated Press's staff of four is the largest reportorial group assigned to the White House by any news organization, while United Press International's three-person staff is equaled only by that of the television networks.

Until recently the wire services tended to retain the same White House correspondents from administration to administration. But during 1976 and 1977, although the chiefs stayed on, every other wire service reporter was replaced. Frank Cormier and Helen Thomas, the surviving correspondents for the AP and UPI respectively, both began their assignment at the White House during the Kennedy administration. Long service has added to their reputations. Each new administration recognizes that they are well-known veterans who have won the respect of both reporters and White House officials over the years. This status is useful to them because they represent organizations that need good working relations and assistance from the Press Office in order to fulfill their special obligations for coverage and information to subscriber news organizations.

The third wire service is Reuters, a British-founded news service. Their single White House correspondent, the veteran reporter Ralph Harris, has covered every American president since Eisenhower. Harris occupies a desk among the four rows provided for reporters behind the booths of AP and UPI. He maintains that as an independent news agency, Reuters should receive the same special assistance from Press Office officials as do the major services.[4] The other news agencies do not regard Reuters as their equal. On one occasion representatives of one of the major wire services complained to the Press Office that Reuters was getting more help than it deserved since the British government does not provide assistance to American news services.[5] White House officials did not take a firm position on this conflict. "I never really resolved what Ralph Harris's status was," Ronald Nessen commented after he left office. "I probably should have have paid more attention to it, but I didn't. I know that he felt that he was entitled to equal treatment but never got equal treatment."[6]

In practice, Reuters does not provide the kind of specialized coverage in response to the requests of its clients that AP and UPI do. Harris argued that this is not the central concern of wire services. "News agencies are organizations of historical record," he said. "The great bulk of their work evolves from the briefing and officially released information."[7] Harris is well respected for the way he does this job, and he is proud of the frequency with which his stories are used by American newspapers.

THEIR SPECIAL STATUS

Until the 1960s the wire services were the most important of the news organizations covering the White House. When Pierre Salinger first assessed the White House press corps as John Kennedy's press secretary, he found that

The sachems of the tribe were the senior correspondents for the wire services—Associated Press and United Press International. . . . A single reporter can rough you up in one city where his newspaper circulates but an unfavorable AP or UPI story can hurt you around the world. Because of their great influence, the wires demand and receive privileges that are denied to other news media at the White House. . . .

Like my predecessors, I would invite their senior correspondents into my office on the morning of a press conference and tell them whether the President would have a major announcement. They, in turn, would advise me of the probable line of questioning he could expect.[8]

After the struggle between the Johnson administration and the press over the accuracy of the information the government was providing about the war in Vietnam, such a cozy relationship between the Press Office and a major segment of the media could not be sustained. According to Ronald Ziegler, the press secretary's practice of exchanging information with wire service reporters on the day of press conferences no longer existed when he accepted the position in 1969.[9]

In the 1970s wire service reporters shared their former preeminence at the White House with correspondents representing network television and major national publications. In some ways, however, their status is still unique. Representatives of one of the two wire services open the questioning at presidential news conferences and close both the President's conference and the press secretary's daily briefings. AP and UPI reporters are placed on all White House pools, the small groups that accompany the President on occasions when it would be physically impossible to permit all correspondents to be with him. While other members of the pool must share their information with all White House reporters before they write their own articles, wire service reporters can file their stories right away. The fact that all news organizations may subscribe to one or both services is interpreted to mean that "when the wires are there, everyone's there."[10] Some of the stories they obtain on pools are extremely important to their status as reporters. For example, frequently the pool that flies on Air Force One will be visited by the President or another eminent traveler like the secretary of state, each of them looking to break the boredom of a long flight by talking to reporters. Even though their own reporters will get a pool report, this is one occasion when even prestigious newspapers will use a well-written and colorful story by the wire service reporter.

THE NEWS "BUDGET" AND THE "BODY WATCH"

If the wire services have lost their unique importance to the White House staff, it is because contemporary presidential assistants pay more attention to the immediate impact that television has on a mass audience and to the influence they think they derive from getting the President's message into news stories or columnists' articles in major national publications such as the *New York Times* or the *Washington Post*. Nevertheless, what wire services do is of vital importance to almost all other news organizations at the White House. The wire services' list of the major stories they expect to send during the day are read by editors throughout the country. What an editor reads usually is reflected in his own daily news "budget," the list of stories planned for the next publication or broadcast. The budget indicates the assignments editors give to their reporters as well as the space or time to be devoted to each story. The primary objective of news organizations is to avoid missing any important event at the White House, so the safest course for editors is to have their reporters cover the same stories as the wire services. The continued importance of wire service coverage of the White House, therefore, lies in the fact that what its reporters do gets to the heart of what most editors consider to be the basis of all White House reporting: "body watching." The "body watch" consists of observing and striving to make public all of the official and personal activities of the President. What may well be the opinion of most editors was summarized aptly by Mel Elfin, the Washington bureau chief of *Newsweek,* who said that "the worst thing in the world that could happen to you is for the President of the United States to choke on a piece of meat, and for you not to be there."[11]

In spite of the growing interest of many reporters in interpretive stories about politics or policies, the "body watch" of the President is what most editors expect and what the majority of White House reporters do most frequently during their working hours. No news organzation does the body watch as thoroughly as the wire services. Helen Thomas, the chief White House correspondent for United Press International, estimated that over 80 percent of her activity involves following the President or dealing with the Press Office to get information about him. It is an activity that is conducted under a great deal of pressure. Wire service reporters are working constantly to meet a rapidly approaching deadline, since one of their subscribers somewhere is preparing its next edition, broadcast, or telecast. Consequently, "We're always working on the story which occurred most recently," Thomas said. "We're not really typical of other reporters."[12] Furthermore, reporters from one service are under tremendous compulsion to file their stories before their rival. "If it's a hot story our office in New York will count who was ahead by minutes," Frank Cormier reported.[13]

Reporters from other news organizations often follow these same routines and face similar problems. The fact that a news organization receives stories from one or more wire services should in theory free its reporters to follow their own predilections as to what might become important news. It does not work that way. A reporter who is exploring the formation of policy at the National Security Council and thus misses an unannounced appearance by the President in the White House briefing room may receive a "rocket," a teletyped message from an editor demanding to know why the story was missed. Although reporters sometimes can convince their editors that the analytical or investigative story on which they are working is too important to be interrupted for routine White House activity, they frequently are ordered back to the body watch. "News organizations like the *New York Times* hate to use a wire service story on page one," Martin Tolchin, their White House correspondent, explained. Even though "it makes all the sense in the world to leave that kind of stuff [the body watch] to the wires, the White House is a place where you do not know what is going to happen next."[14] Most news organizations want to be certain that, whatever does happen, their reporter will be there to cover it.

RELATIONS WITH THE PRESS OFFICE

Wire service reporters and officials in the White House Press Office have developed close and cooperative working relationships based on the desire of all parties to facilitate coverage of the public activities of the President. The press secretary and his assistants know that most news reports about the activities of the President present him in a favorable light. Stories that involve formal and ceremonial actions by the President are considered likely to enhance his standing with the public. Consequently, Press Office officials usually do everything possible to help wire service reporters record that type of story. According to Ronald Nessen, he and his assistants in the Press Office during the Ford administration "would give the wire services some advance notice when there was going to be a very big story. We knew what their problems were and we tried to help them and give them guidance on [such stories as] weekend plans, travel plans, and big stories coming up."[15]

Although wire service reporters agreed that the Press Office is sensitive to their special needs, they also indicated that they felt the level of concern has declined. Frank Cormier complained that contemporary press secretaries don't always make certain that wire service reporters are present when they start talking to reporters about substantive matters in the briefing room. "Powell did it recently," he commented. "If they have something to say they should say it to the people who would get it across to the most people," he continued. "Salinger and Hagerty wouldn't say boo without making sure the wires were there."[16]

An adversary element creeps into this otherwise cooperative arrangement because press secretaries are concerned that if reporters get too near the President they might attempt to shift the focus of the story away from the event being presented to them. Reporters might question the President on subjects he would prefer to avoid. They might overhear and publicize statements he had meant to be private. They might see him stumble or bump his head and emphasize this accident instead of his dignified demeanor.

Wire service reporters are aware that the Press Office wants to keep them at the "right distance" from the event, where their view of it presumably will coincide with that of White House officials. In response they put forth aggressive demands for proximity to the President. Helen Thomas frequently used the briefing as a forum to make the press secretary explain why presidential activities would not be open to media coverage or why the President would not be available for questions. The nature of the event did not seem to matter. On one occasion she pursued vigorously an argument against the press's exclusion from a meeting between President Ford and midwestern publishers in which the President was going to discuss major themes of his administration;

on another she demanded with the same force that the press be allowed to accompany President Carter when he attended the opera.

Of course a major reason Thomas and other wire service reporters demand what is called "open coverage" of all presidential activities is that they work almost entirely from the public record. They do not have the opportunities to develop exclusive sources that other reporters who are not quite so burdened with the body watch may have. They are less able to produce analytical or investigative stories because the time they spend answering queries from member and subscriber organizations makes it difficult for them to work on one story for several days.

It may be that behind the demand for access is something other than the lofty notion of the people's right to know that Thomas asserts so eloquently at the daily briefings. A cynic's dictionary might translate *open coverage* to mean complete coverage by the wire services of all presidential activities, from political meetings to theater trips. Nevertheless, wire service reporters have been the chief public lobbyists for an open presidency. Any evaluation of the work of reporters at the White House must recognize that Helen Thomas, along with other wire service reporters and, to a lesser extent, reporters for radio and television, have been the strongest advocates for the press's right to see, hear, and question the President and his chief advisers.

Television and Radio

During the 1960s television became the battleground in what the public perceived as a war between the presidency and the news media. It was television news that carried the message to the American people that Lyndon Johnson's efforts in Vietnam were not going well. It was at television news that Spiro Agnew first aimed his attacks when the Nixon administration attempted to discredit its media critics.

On a daily basis the confrontation was and is less dramatic than what viewers saw during the Johnson and Nixon administrations. There is, however, a strong consensus among White House officials connected with media policy that it is their job to help the President dominate television. They believe that media dominance is essential for him if he is to be successful in building support for himself and his programs. In their official papers (now at presidential libraries) and in interviews with us, White House officials from the Johnson, Nixon, Ford, and Carter administrations have confirmed the comment made about them by Tom Brokaw of NBC, who said that they share "an inclination to think of television as an extension of the President."[17] Ronald Nessen could have been speaking for all of them when he expressed the view that for him "television is reality." Shortly before he left office as press secretary to President Ford, Nessen commented that "if it hasn't happened on television, it hasn't happened."[18]

Ronald Ziegler provided a singular exception in this regard. He suggested that the half-life of a television image is quite short in contrast to the more permanent changes in public opinion that can result from timely articles, columns, and editorials in the print media.[19] Ziegler made this comment four years after he was press secretary. Yet during the period when he was in charge of relations with the media, as well as during all other recent presidencies, most White House officials built the President's schedule around efforts to get events of their choice on the evening news. The lure of the evening news for them was the size of the combined audience for the three network programs, estimated at between 40 and 50 million viewers by Barry Jagoda, President Carter's first television adviser. "A presidential appearance on television in the evening dominates our national life for that moment," Jagoda remarked. "It is a way of bringing the country together for explanation or elaboration."[20]

Many television journalists do not agree that television plays so important a role either in determining the President's success in projecting a positive image or in getting his policies adopted. They suggest that White House officials think that television is crucial because it appears to them to be a visual scorecard on which they can see evidence of their accomplishments in their relations with the public. "Clearly their attention is focused on what is said every night, and they believe it has an impact," George Watson, Washington bureau chief of ABC News, commented. Watson suggested that presidential advisers don't understand that White House stories get on television because the networks "are mirrors more than movers of national politics and society, because we as a people attach such importance to the presidency."[21]

THE PHYSICAL SETTING AND THE DIVISION OF LABOR

Reporters for the three national television networks may be found in three long but narrow booths, each of which has a rear compartment that may be shut off and used as a sound studio for radio broadcasts. The booths are located at the back of the area that the White House staff has set aside for reporters to work in. Each network maintains a staff of three White House reporters and a crew of technicians. One reporter for each network is supposed to be responsible for radio coverage, but only NBC News seemed to segregate its radio and television coverage in any consistent manner during the Ford and Carter administrations. Each of the CBS reporters broadcast radio "spots," which include reading the hourly news and presenting short feature stories about the White House.

All reporters for CBS and ABC and the two television reporters for NBC covered stories that ran on the evening or morning news. In theory, the network's chief White House correspondent is responsible for the story that is most likely to appear on the nightly news, the network's most important and widely viewed news program. The second person is assigned to work on the "overnight," a general feature story intended for the morning news. In practice, though, reporters' appearances on the evening or morning news depend on the newsworthiness of the stories on which they have been working. Frequently this means that a story originally designated as important is scrapped.

Each of the three networks brought to the Carter White House at least one reporter who was previously assigned to cover the Carter campaign. This arrangement allowed the networks to have at least one person who knew the new President and, perhaps as important, the staff members who had become important presidential assistants. However, no clear pattern has developed among the networks regarding their assignment of newcomers or veteran White House reporters when a new president takes office. CBS emphasizes continuity, although that may be because its news operations have been more stable than those of the two other networks. In any event, two senior CBS correspondents remained at the White House after the transition from the Ford to the Carter administration, while only one junior ABC correspondent remained on the job and NBC underwent a complete turnover.

REPORTERS, TECHNICIANS, AND THE IMPACT OF TECHNOLOGY

Like the wire services, but unlike most other news organizations, the networks keep a reporter in the press room throughout the day when the President is at the White House. The mechanics of television news require that a crew of technicians also be on hand at all times so that reporters can prepare live or videotape coverage. If the network's chief reporter believes it is necessary, he will request a second crew. The procedure then is for one crew to videotape the basic story while the other shoots the cutaways, the long shots, and the wide shots. If there is enough time the videotape produced by the two crews can be combined into footage that will appear on the evening news.

Television reporters emphasized that a successful operation requires that the technicians assigned to the crew understand the types of videotape footage desired by the networks. Reporters also want technicians who have a sense of what constitutes news. In addition to such ad hoc on-the-job understandings, the relations between reporters and technicians involve arrangements born of the technicians' contract. The importance of this consideration is shown in the remarks of a reporter who asked not to be identified because of his concern that they might subject him to reprisals.

One of the good things about the mini-cams is that they are operated by a different union than the film cameras. The unions turned a lot of men into mechanics in New York. As a result you had a number of deadbeats running the news cameras. You could have World War III declared and these guys wouldn't have done anything if they were out to lunch. By changing unions the networks have been able to weed out the dead wood and keep the people they wanted. . . . As a result of bringing in this new blood I think we are in better shape on crew than we have ever been. You have to make sure these guys remain members of the team and don't become pieces of furniture. The correspondents must treat them like members of the team.[22]

An assumption often made by television's critics is that its technology influences its presentation of the news. It is vulnerable to manipulation, these critics say, because reporters know that while it is hard to get airtime for a complicated story that is difficult to show in pictures, it is easy to get on with stories that show the activities of an important and newsworthy person like the President. Television reporters did not agree that this is a serious problem. They maintained that the "Rose Garden strategy," often cited by print media journalists as an example of such manipulation, did not work. Thus although the White House staged ceremonial events for Presidents Ford and Carter in the Rose Garden during the 1976 and 1980 campaigns, television reporters were able to use narrative "voiceovers" to call attention to the fact that the President was avoiding the full exposure to the media that his opponent had to face. "We pointed out what they were doing in every story," said Bob Schieffer, senior White House correspondent for CBS News of the 1976 story. "I don't think Ford got anything out of it."[23]

In the opinion of these journalists, a more serious limitation on their performance as reporters is the prevailing view in their industry that their job is to present instant history. "I think we are a verbal and visual wire service, first and foremost," George Watson stated in response to a question about what his network hoped to get out of White House coverage. "We have to cover what is occurring first, and the perspective is secondary to that."[24]

RELATIONS WITH THE WHITE HOUSE PRESS OFFICE

Television reporters differ about the practical effects of the White House staff's perception that theirs is the most important medium. Have the special provisions for television coverage of the President imposed burdensome changes on other reporters? Are the relations between television reporters and the White House staff different in substance from the relationship other reporters have with the staff? Are television reporters compromised by their requests for special arrangements or facilities for television coverage?

Robert Pierpoint of CBS News, who has covered the White House since the Eisenhower administration, suggested that "simple irritation on the part of reporters who don't work for the broadcast media and who like to claim big changes in impact" was responsible for most of the complaints about television by print reporters.[25] Pierpoint agreed that the arrangements made for television have created problems. In making up the President's schedule, he said, modern White House officials want to time his appearances so that they can be shown on the evening news; formerly they would have been more sensitive to the noon deadlines of reporters for afternoon daily newspapers in the East and Midwest. In addition, he admitted that "minor problems" are created for reporters by television's equipment and lights. He maintained that these problems have little to do with the substantive manner in which the White House is covered. Pierpoint concluded that on the whole the advent of television has not changed life significantly for other reporters and that television reporters have not established relations different from theirs with the Press Office or other officials within the White House.[26]

Confirmation for Pierpoint's opinions was provided by John Carlson, deputy press secretary during the last year of the Ford administration. Carlson indicated that the Press Office tried to be sensitive to the needs of several national news organizations.

A lot of these guys like [Tom] Jarriel [of ABC News] and Brokaw are panicky about 4:30 or 5:00. A lot of times they'll call because they are confused about an announcement and want to make sure they have their facts right. I recognize their needs that way. If I get back to them at 6:30, they're lost.

The *Washington Post* has had a lot of problems because they are printing out of town. We try to give them stories on time so they can meet their editions. Magazines are the same way. *Time* and *Newsweek* publish on Saturday. If we know we are going to make a major announcement, we'll get it to them on Thursday so they can work the story and layout.[27]

Tom Brokaw of NBC News, on the other hand, found that White House officials were eager to exploit television. In his interviews with presidential aides, he said, it was clear that they relished the prospect of reaching his large audience.

Brokaw suggested that the Press Office's ability to invoke the "fairness doctrine" subjects television reporters to manipulation from Press Office officials who threaten to demand time to respond on the air to an "unfair" story. The "fairness doctrine" is the Federal Communications Commission regulation that requires the broadcast media to present a public issue fairly; it has been interpreted by the commission in specific cases to mean that proponents of all sides of a question must be heard. Brokaw said that the threat of invoking the fairness doctrine had been used by the Press Office to push a network into presenting an unsubstantiated administration "rebuttal" to the day's story.

The master at that was Ron Ziegler. During the final days of the Nixon administration, Ziegler made it a practice to call me at least every night about 6:20 [minutes before the nightly news was on the air], with some kind of rebuttal to the story we were working on that day. I know from my conversations with Dan Rather that he was called, too.

Whether their rebuttal had any basis in fact was not necessarily important to him. He was attempting to pump in the White House point of view to a story that may have been critical of the President. He correctly guessed that in most instances we would feel an obligation to include whatever it was he had to say about the story in our report. That was a deliberate misuse of media.[28]

At least one television reporter expressed concern that there are special relations between the White House and network executives that could compromise reporters. For example, the networks may ask a top White House official to appear at a "seminar" and brief them on administration policy. The networks also might request lengthy on-camera interviews with the President and other top officials. The reporter suggested that if these arrangements are made by a reporter, as they have been in some cases, then he would be obligated to the officials who provided the favor in a way that would make it difficult for him to report objectively on them. In fact, he suggested that this had happened to one network reporter whose toughness of reporting had declined. "The proper way to handle these matters is for the bureau chief to take charge of them," he asserted. "The reporter should be left to report."[29]

THE DILEMMAS OF RADIO

Radio reporters complain that they work for a medium whose importance often is overlooked by the White House. They are invisible to many officials because they possess neither the public recognition of their television counterparts nor the status and clout with Washington insiders of reporters for the *New York Times* and the *Washington Post*. Prior to the 1960s White House officials, Washington insiders, and the public at large all were aware of the importance of radio. Fifteen-minute news programs were broadcast on the four national radio networks every morning and evening. Well-known "commentators," radio's equivalent of the television anchorman, offered news analysis as well as the headlines. The White House maintained a radio adviser to the President.

Radio still captures an immense daily audience, estimated at over 92 million by an NBC survey.[30] In the 1970s, however, the nature of broadcasting changed significantly. Although today national news bureaus send out a few fifteen- or thirty-minute public affairs programs to their affiliate stations, most radio news programs run five minutes, including the commercials. White House radio reporters estimate that they usually have about forty-five seconds to present their news stories, the equivalent of a four- or five-paragraph newspaper article.[31]

Radio reporters have tried to improve their standing at the White House by reminding officials in the Press Office of the large audience that radio commands. They cite surveys that show that one-third of the American public gets most of its news from radio broadcasts and that an even larger percentage first learn of events on radio.[32] According to several White House radio correspondents, a major point they emphasize to the Press Office staff is that on weekends more people hear the news on radio than see it on television.

The clear point of what these reporters are telling White House officials is that if they provide better facilities, arrangements, and access for radio broadcasters, there will be a payoff for them in the form of a large audience. Walter Rodgers of AP Radio suggested that "both Ford and Carter have had to be educated as to what we do, how many people we serve, and how big our reach is. My biggest problem is, in this age of television, to convince Press Secretaries that I have a very broad impact. . . . We educated Nessen to listen to radio. But we have to reeducate every new administration. They are so mesmerized by television."[33]

Radio news reaches its large audience more frequently than any other form of media. Stations linked to the networks broadcast national news programs every hour, and independent stations may carry stories from the Washington bureaus of AP or UPI Radio even more frequently. This means that radio reporters at the White House are under constant pressure to meet a fixed and impending deadline. "If we can't get it on the next hour then it isn't news, it's history," remarked Russ Ward, NBC News's radio correspondent at the White House between 1974 and 1977.[34] Once it becomes history, of course, they go on to cover the next event. This means that radio reporters work on several different stories throughout the day. Walter Rodgers estimated that during the Carter administration's first year he reported five different stories each day.[35]

National Public Radio provides its White House correspondent with more time to prepare stories than the commercial radio representatives are allowed. This means that a reporter for public radio has the opportunity to use some of radio's technical capabilities effectively in the presentation of a story. The NPR reporter can combine recordings of live coverage, interview material, commentary by public figures, and his or her own analysis. NPR's evening news program, "All Things Considered," runs for ninety minutes and provides ample opportunities for the White House reporter to present news, features, and analysis of the presidency without the restrictions of a forty-five-second time limit. NPR White House correspondent Richard Holwill commented that these arrangements gave him an opportunity "to shape the tone of a story in a way that indicated the various levels of White House activity." Holwill contrasted his situation with that of other radio reporters, whose main responsibility is to relate "what has just happened."[36]

In 1977, an internal conflict at NPR allegedly resulted in a victory for those who wanted to emphasize human interest and feature stories and diminish coverage of public affairs. Holwill, who left NPR during this conflict, said that he and others in the losing faction felt that NPR's programming would become more oriented toward gossipy personal items. In any event, the conflict indicated that publicly supported radio is subject to the same pressures to please the largest possible audience as are the commercial stations.

Ultimately the dilemma of most radio reporters at the White House is that, however talented they may be, it is not likely that they will be given the opportunity to do more than cover the surface of an event. Although television reporters also are limited in the time they have to present a story on the evening news, they often have opportunities to present more detailed pictures of what they have seen on documentary or other "special" public affairs programs. A reporter for the print media may break into the inside pages of his newspaper or magazine with an interpretive article, even when the front page is reserved for "hard news." With few exceptions, radio news provides only the headlines and requires that listeners who want a deeper examination of events look and listen elsewhere.

Major National Publications

The news as it is perceived in the Washington community and disseminated throughout the country is shaped to a large extent by four daily newspapers and three weekly magazines. These seven publications play a national role in the United States, even though only the magazines and one of the newspapers are distributed throughout the country.

Among the "majors," as they are sometimes referred to collectively, there are three groups with differing amounts of influence in the White House-media relationship. The status of each group is determined by two factors: first, the importance of the publications in it to the White House, and, second, the group's influence on the manner in which other media throughout the country portray the President and his administration. The *New York Times* and the *Washington Post* score highest in this system and comprise the inner circle among the majors. The middle group includes *Time* and *Newsweek*. The outer group consists of three publications that only recently have become majors: the *Wall Street Journal,* the *Washington Star,* and *U.S. News and World Report.*

Prior to the 1960s there were fewer national publications in the United States. The country's vast internal distances reinforced regional differences to discourage the growth of a common audience for news. When this audience was created by television, publishing enterprises of national reach at last could be organized by managerial and journalistic entrepreneurs. But until well after World War II local interests determined what the public read in most media markets. Major regional newspapers, seldom influenced by national trends, dominated large circulation areas. Colonel Robert McCormick's *Chicago Tribune* and Norman Chandler's *Los Angeles Times,* both of which have been transformed since the deaths of these publishers, are two well-known examples of this type of publication. In the 1970s only a few such newspapers were in existence. The best-known of them is William Loeb's Manchester, New Hampshire, *Union Leader,* a personal vehicle for its owner, which comes to national attention every four years at the time of the New Hampshire presidential primary. National political reporters who flock to cover the primary describe the authority this paper seems to have over its readers. They point out that readers who rely upon it for information are virtually insulated from nationally formulated news.

Five qualities make the majors different from the rest of the media: (1) They reach the elite among policy influencers, including the President, who learn about the more important stories published about them immediately after they appear. (2) The information they provide about the Washington community becomes the common currency of the next highest level of influentials in the White House, Congress, the bureaucracy, the interest groups, research institutions, and the media. (3) Items that appear in them are accepted as authoritative by the rest of the media and are given national circulation by the wire services and the broadcast media. (4) They provide the most complete and continuing coverage of national affairs, and the only such coverage that consistently includes an insider's point of view. (5) They reach many citizens throughout the country directly, either because they have a national circulation or because local newspapers subscribe to their news services. Each major publication has at least four of these five qualities, and the first two are unique to them.

Only a handful of newspapers, such as the *Union Leader,* remain immune to the demands of their audiences for similar, if watered-down, versions of the national news presented by the majors. Some journalists and administration officials might quibble about our groupings or our assessment of the majors' collective influence, but most observers at least would agree that there is a group of major national publications that have an impact on the image and reputation of governmental and political leaders in Washington and the country all out of proportion to their circulation.

THE INNER CIRCLE: THE *WASHINGTON POST* AND THE *NEW YORK TIMES*

Memoirs and recollections of almost every recent administration indicate that even presidents who publicly appeared to be uninterested in what appeared in the press read the *Post* and the *Times* every day. For example, during the Eisenhower administration neither James Hagerty nor the President discouraged the widely circulated but apocryphal story that Eisenhower read nothing more serious than Western novels. Memoranda written at the time, now in the files of the Eisenhower Library at Abilene, indicate that on numerous occasions the White House geared-up activity because of the President's reaction to a news story he had just read. In 1978 Hagerty, who served as press secretary for the entire eight years, admitted that Eisenhower included both the *Post* and the *Times* among the several newspapers he examined every day.[37] President Nixon's aides circulated the story that he didn't have to read the disliked *Post* and *Times* because his staff provided him with a daily summary of important news stories. Yet Stephen Hess, an aide to Nixon, recalled that he once received a faster response from the President by writing a letter to the *Washington Post* than he would have if he had sent a message through official channels. Hess said he wrote the letter because he knew the President read the *Post*.[38] Presidents Kennedy, Johnson, and Ford did not hide their addiction to the *Post* and the *Times*. Their irritation at what they sometimes read in them usually was expressed in private conversations, but it sometimes became publicly known; as in the case of President Kennedy's attempt to get David Halberstam fired from the *New York Times*.

President Carter's newspaper habits are known from the list of newspapers he asks to have included in "The White House News Summary," an in-house publication summarizing major stories and commentary from newspapers, magazines, and television broadcasts. Claudia Townsend, who prepared these summaries for the President before she was made an assistant press secretary, remarked, "as far as I know he reads the *Times* and the *Post*. He usually looks at one of the Atlanta papers. He also looks at the *Wall Street Journal* and I imagine that he often looks at the *Washington Star*. For our purposes we feel that he reads the *Times* and the *Post* closely, and we don't include them in the summary."[39]

As for the key role played by the *Times* and the *Post* among the constituencies that are of great concern to the President, Leon V. Sigal in his outstanding 1973 study of the relations between reporters and officials in Washington noted: "In Washington, nearly everyone reads the *Post* and the *Times;* this applies to newsmen as well as to officials and the attentive public. . . . The two papers have considerable influence on the news that readers of other newspapers obtain . . . because they have an extensive audience in the journalism community. . . . Because of the size and quality of their staffs, the *Times* and *Post* enjoy a distinguished reputation in the field of journalism for their energetic and thorough coverage."[40]

ASSIGNMENTS

A reporter's assignment to or his removal from the White House beat provides an opportunity to chart the relationship between reporters and news organizations. New White House reporters, particularly those from the *New York Times,* were aware of their high visibility and felt a special obligation to perform well because of the tremendous national prestige of the newspaper. James Naughton, the *Times*'s White House correspondent during the Nixon and Ford administrations, commented that his job was affected by his feeling that he "worked for the best paper in the United States, if not the world." There is, he said, "a standard set for you to live up to, a pressure not to miss something because you represent the *New York Times*."[41]

The Washington Post. Both the *Times* and the *Post* have experienced considerable turnover in their White House reportorial staff since Richard Nixon became president in 1969. In the case of the *Post,* reporters have left for better jobs, other assignments, retirement, or release from what they considered to be a confining assignment. Yet from the Coolidge administration until the late 1960s, Edward Folliard and Carroll Kilpatrick were the only two reporters regularly assigned to the White House by the *Post.* Folliard, the first to arrive, and Kilpatrick were highly regarded for their acute accounts of the President's activities and the research they undertook for their White House stories. For Folliard an important part of the beat was catching and interviewing visitors who passed by the press room on their way to the West Wing offices of the President and his chief White House assistants.[42]

In many respects Folliard and Kilpatrick prove excellent examples of the ideal White House reporter of pre-Vietnam days as fondly remembered by both presidential assistants and other journalists. Their stories occasionally annoyed the White House because they contained comparisons of the President's past promises with his present policies, but the two reporters were regarded as sensitive to the problems of the Chief Executive. For example, although Folliard knew about the rift between Truman and Secretary of State Byrnes in 1945, and about Truman's decision to fire General MacArthur in 1951, he did not write a story about either event until after the President announced his decisions. Folliard also said that reporters should accept White House claims that national security interests are reason enough to withhold a story in situations involving the nation's adversaries. He cited his decision not to write a story even though he realized that a White House Press Office announcement on President Kennedy's cancellation of his schedule because of illness was a cover for the President's activities in planning and directing the showdown with the Soviet Union in the Cuban missile crisis.

Kilpatrick's role as a White House correspondent was similar to Folliard's. His assignment began during the Kennedy administration and lasted through-out the Nixon administration. There are no indications that Kilpatrick either volunteered or was considered to be a likely prospect to assist the *Post*'s editors and reporters as they attempted to track down the Watergate story. In *The Great Coverup* Barry Sussman, who coordinated the *Post*'s early Water-gate coverage, mentioned Kilpatrick's help only once, for his identification of burglar James McCord as a staff person for the Committee to Reelect the President.[43] In *All The President's Men* Bob Woodward and Carl Bernstein expressed their gratitude to Kilpatrick for remaining cordial to them even though he was extremely dubious of their stories about Watergate until rela-tively late. They also were grateful to Kilpatrick because he suffered a loss of his sources at the White House when the *Post* began its stories.[44]

Folliard expressed doubts about the approaches now commonly used by reporters to get stories. He had little use for investigative reporting because he believed that reporters should concentrate on public decisions rather than covert wrongdoing. "I wouldn't hire a reporter who said his main job was to uncover corruption and malfeasance," he said. "A reporter should cover major legislation—that's where the big stories are."[45]

Most of the comments made about Folliard and Kilpatrick by younger reporters emphasized the differences between old school and contemporary reporters. The younger generation made it clear that they would not withhold a major story until the President could announce it, or give the administration the benefit of the doubt quite so easily when officials invoked national secu-rity. "My sense of Kilpatrick is that he is a kind of older generation reporter, a much more traditional reporter," one of them commented. Of Folliard he said, "He was a very nice, good guy. Everybody liked him. He was very charming, and he never made a ripple."[46]

After Folliard retired in the late 1960s, Donald Oberdorfer and Kenneth Clawson were sent to join Kilpatrick at the White House. According to Ed-ward Walsh, a *Post* White House correspondent, Kilpatrick was to continue as the "inside man," covering the activities of the President, while Ober-dorfer and Clawson were to develop stories on their own, based on their perceptions of the policies and decisions the White House was making. These plans fell apart, however, when Oberdorfer was sent by the *Post* to Japan and Clawson quit the newspaper to become a White House aide in the Nixon administration. Lou Cannon, a veteran political writer, was sent to the White House next, and he was joined by Walsh in January, 1976, shortly after Kilpatrick retired. Walsh said that his assignment duplicated about 80 to 90 percent of the things that Kilpatrick had covered, which meant that he was expected to attend the daily briefings and follow the agenda established by the White House.[47]

In the fall of 1978 the *Post* announced the appointment of Martin Schram, who had been the Washington bureau chief for *Newsday,* as their "presidency" reporter. Schram produced stories describing and analyzing the White House decision-making process. The nature of these stories, which told who said what in private White House meetings and described the feelings of participants at different stages of an event, obviously required extensive and confidential contacts with highly placed White House officials. Schram's stories were "exclusives" in that they included details that only appeared in other publications or broadcasts after his stories were published, if at all. Schram's ability to maintain excellent contacts with important White House officials through the first months of 1979 gave the *Post* an edge in the Washington community over its chief rivals, and in particular over the *Times.* In the meantime Walsh and other reporters continue to cover the main activities of the President.

The New York Times. At the *Times,* control over White House assignments was one of the issues in the long war between the New York management of the newspaper and the Washington bureau. The conflict, described by Gay Talese in *The Kingdom and the Power,* an analysis of politics within the *Times* during the 1960s, ended with total victory for New York in the 1970s.[48] A reporter who was assigned to Washington at the time of the New York takeover said that the New York editors regarded the Washington bureau as an independent sphere that was a thorn in their sides:[49] "They were determined to bring it under their control, and they have done so. . . . The New York view was that the old regime in Washington tended to have diplomats rather than reporters. There was far too much socializing. A lot of the people came from highly social backgrounds. They presented their credentials rather than pressed for stories."[50] The appointment of the White House correspondent and of all other major national correspondents is made in New York by A. M. Rosenthal, the *Times*'s managing editor. The fact that such important decisions have been taken out of the hands of the Washington bureau chief certainly minimizes his power. One member of the bureau described the chief's position in extremely blunt language: "Rick [Hedrick] Smith is a wholly owned subsidiary of New York," he said.[51] In 1979 the position of bureau chief was abolished, a recognition of direct rule by New York.

In the spring of 1978 James Wooten and Charles Mohr, who had been sent by the *Times* to cover the Carter administration, were replaced by Terence

Smith and Martin Tolchin. Wooten and Mohr had asked to leave, but the paper's New York and Washington managers were not sorry to see them go. One observer felt that the root of the problem was that Wooten and Mohr had been hard on the Carter administration. The *Times* management, he implied, does not want its reporters in an adversary position with the President of the United States: "My sense is the *Times* was unhappy with the Mohr-Wooten team. They thought that it was a little too abrasive. There was no doubt, I think, that New York, Rosenthal, felt that they were being a little too abrasive. They were also being abrasive not just to Carter, but also the *New York Times* management, which is an even greater sin. The kind of person who is prickly with the President is usually also prickly with his editors. You almost always have a Peck's bad boy syndrome."[52]

COOPERATION AND THE ROUTINES

When James Naughton was assigned as the *New York Times*'s second man at the White House in 1969 for what turned out to be the first of two tours of duty there, he discovered that he was expected to follow a set routine. First the *Times* reporters covered the press secretary's daily briefing, and then they returned to the Washington bureau office to report on what had happened. The news editors there would consult with New York as to who would write what story, based on what seemed to be happening that day. Naughton was in the habit of typing out a memo to other *Times* people who needed the information he had learned at the briefing and from talking to other reporters. He discovered that he received an immense amount of help in return from these specialists in the Washington bureau:

I was surprised at the extent to which all these high-priced reporters and names and bylines that I had read for years were quite willing and eager to share information and in effect in some cases to give you a major story.... If I were writing a story in an area that required specialized knowledge, I would go to an Eileen Shanahan or an Ed Dale and be very pleased at their willingness to provide background or put some perspective on how important things were, or whether what the White House was saying was credible. I was able to get these things into the third or fourth paragraph of the story with a perspective I would not have had.[53]

The *Times*'s decision to assign two reporters of similar professional status to the White House during the Nixon, Ford, and early Carter administrations created tensions over the division of responsibilities between them. The *Times* attempted to divide the beat by assigning one reporter to cover the daily activities of the President, thus freeing the other to develop stories that do not have such neat beginnings and endings. The result was "unfair to the body watcher," James Naughton said, reflecting on the experiment with this division between R. W. (Johnny) Apple and John Herbers at the beginning of Nixon's second term. "It's just not humanly possible to divvy it up that way."[54] The three pairs of *Times* reporters at the White House during the period of this study divided assignments on an ad hoc basis rather than on any division of labor. As a result, both reporters frequently attended the daily briefing, presidential news conferences, and routine trips of the President. The need to satisfy the professional self-esteem of reporters took precedence over the organizational goal of providing coverage that would include some of the less accessible institutions and less tangible functions of the White House.

The *Washington Post* may have stumbled upon a solution to the *Times*'s problem. The division of responsibilities between the two *Post* reporters did not appear to create any problems during the period when the assignment was shared by Lou Cannon and Edward Walsh, perhaps because Walsh, who was Cannon's junior, accepted the role of second man. Cannon, a well-known political reporter, covered major policy stories with political and electoral implications. Walsh, who recently had been promoted from the local staff of the *Post,* covered the daily activities scheduled by the White House. In 1976, a few months after he began the assignment, Walsh said that he was free to cover whatever stories he chose within this sphere after consulting with Edwin Goodpaster, then the *Post'*s day assignment editor for national news. Walsh also said, both before and two years after his assignment, that he felt a national paper of record such as the *Washington Post* had a primary obligation to present the major activities of the President.[55]

Shortly after the 1976 presidential nominating conventions, *Post* editors and reporters held a luncheon meeting to plan coverage of the election campaign. In addition to Cannon and Walsh, Goodpaster and another national editor, Lawrence Fox, attended, as did the *Post*'s two top political writers, David Broder and Jules Witcover. The group decided that since neither Cannon nor Walsh had covered Carter, each would take a few weeks leave from their White House assignment to follow his campaign. After Carter's election Cannon moved to California as the *Post*'s West Coast reporter. Walsh, who now had some knowledge of Carter and was acquainted with several of his principal advisers, became the *Post*'s main White House correspondent, a position he occupied until the creation of Schram's "presidency" beat.

By 1978 Walsh's stories were reflecting his greater self-confidence as a reporter as well as the increased interest of the new national editor, Lawrence Stern, and other editors in institutional stories about the White House. The changes in Walsh's reporting were noticed by other correspondents. "Ed Walsh wrote my kind of story recently," commented John Osborne of the *New Republic,* the acknowledged authority on insider reporting about the White House.[56] Osborne was referring to the August 27, 1978, *Post* article by Walsh about the activities and influence of Carter's media adviser, Gerald Rafshoon, in which Walsh described and analyzed the media program that Rafshoon had introduced. The story included nothing that would fall under the traditional headings of hard news.

WORKING CONDITIONS AND STATUS

Two *Washington Post* reporters included in this study, Edward Folliard and David Broder, had enough status to be able to select and carry out their assignments as they chose. In fact, Broder was so well situated with White House staff that, unlike Kilpatrick, he even was able to maintain his access to important presidential assistants during the height of the *Post*'s conflict with the Nixon administration over its Watergate coverage. Both Broder and Folliard indicated that there were no important conflicts over coverage between them and their editors at the *Post*.

Walsh gave no indication that he felt any important constraints in his relations with his editors, either. In January, 1976, when Walsh first appeared in the White House briefing room, Press Secretary Nessen announced his arrival. Similar announcements were not made at the arrival of other reporters during the same period. Walsh said that he found that working for the *Post* gave him greater status with other reporters than might have been expected by a relatively junior reporter. "Reporters for other papers are concerned with what appears in the *Post* and the *Times,* " he said. "Because everyone reads them, they know what you've done and want to find out what you're going to do."[57]

When Martin Tolchin and Terence Smith arrived at the White House in 1978, they were given an even more auspicious greeting. According to Tolchin, Powell said, " 'The President wants to see you,' and we went in. I thought it would just be for presentation of credentials, but he was really quite interested in us. We sat down and had a twenty-minute meeting. He wanted to know our backgrounds, our interests, where we had been stationed, and what we had been covering, as well as what we thought about life in general. Then we got to talking about the Mid-East."[58]

These efforts by Carter indicate the importance to the White House of establishing good relations with *Times* reporters. In the past, administrations evidently thought it was more important to arrange meetings between the President and the chief officers of a publication rather than its reporters. In a memorandum dated August 20, 1965, now in the files at the Johnson Library, W. Averell Harriman suggested to President Johnson that he flatter the seventy-four-year-old chairman of the board of the *New York Times,* Arthur Hays Sulzberger, by playing up the important position that the *Times* occupied in national political life. Harriman wrote to Johnson, "The President might also wish to ask Sulzberger's advice on how to get more balanced reporting out of Vietnam, suggesting that perhaps this will be something Scotty Reston will be able to advise on when he gets back. I have known Arthur Sulzberger over the years and he responds to flattery of himself and the *Times.*"[59]

MANIPULATION

Times reporters face a special situation at the White House. They are so important to officials who want to transmit information that they frequently obtain a major interview with an official or have information "leaked" to them before anyone else. This can lead to a bargaining situation, as Martin

Tolchin indicated in response to a question about whether the White House had used him to try to send out messages:

> Tolchin: They did. There was a hiring that they definitely wanted in the *New York Times*. I was happy with that, it was an absolutely legitimate story.... They wanted to run it, for a very strategic reason of their own, on a certain day. It was very difficult to get it into the paper. I have no problem with that [kind of arrangement].
> Q. Do they pay you back for doing that?
> Tolchin: I am sure that they will.
> Q. They will give you something first, before someone else?
> Tolchin: They have in the past and they will in the future.[60]

Times reporters are expected by their readers to get inside information before it becomes generally available. John Herbers, deputy chief of the Washington bureau and White House correspondent during Nixon's Watergate years, was asked why the *Times* spent so much time and effort attempting to find out who Carter would appoint to major positions in his administration when the difference between a "scoop" of this sort and the public announcement was often a matter of only days or even hours. Herbers responded, "There are many payoffs. It shows that the *New York Times* is a paper that people have such confidence and trust in that they would confide in them with exclusive breaking stories. The *New York Times*'s reputation was built on our having some insights on things first. Our readers are in specialty groups and having information first is important to these people. It gives them the idea that we are an aggressive newspaper whose reporters don't sit idly by waiting for announcements to be made."[61] Getting this kind of story immediately enhances the *Times*'s reputation with many people who might not actually see the story, Herbers continued. "Any time we have a major story like that it is immediately sent across the country by the television networks and the wire services."[62]

A problem for *Times* reporters is that they are targets for White House officials who want to get their own views into the paper even when they do not accurately reflect the President's. For example, in January, 1976, some White House aides told Philip Shabecoff that President Ford would be introducing programs to expand medicare and spur jobs when he made his State of the Union Address.[63] Shabecoff wrote a story based on what these informants told him, but when the speech was released, it contained no new proposals.[64] Shabecoff was used by officials who thought that the President might be convinced to support such programs, or who hoped that a portion of the *Times*'s readership would remember the story about the programs and forget about the speech.

OVERCOVERAGE OF THE PRESIDENT

Reporters for both the *Post* and the *Times* agreed that their newspapers make too much of the President. "I suspect that we print too much about politics for many of our readers," Edward Walsh commented. Martin Tolchin expressed the same point in more colorful language. "I have had stories on page one just because the President burped," he said. "I don't think they belonged there at all."[65]

In the waning days of Gerald Ford's administration, John Herbers reflected on the tendency of the *Post* and *Times* to inflate stories about the presidency. "It's been difficult for me as an editor on my own paper to discourage the prominent display of White House stories which were not important," he said. Herbers went on to suggest that these stories were the result of "deeply ingrained habits" among reporters and editors who write and print what he regards as "nonstories" simply because they come from the President: "For example, the *Washington Post* on Sunday [January 11, 1977] had an interview with Ford which was exclusive in which he really said nothing, and I couldn't find anything in the story that we didn't already know. Yet it was prominently displayed high up on the front page of the *Post*."[66]

On January 12, 1977, the *New York Times* had its own exclusive interview with President Ford, and on January 13 the paper ran a front page report. The *Times*'s story offered no more news than the *Post* story Herbers had criticized. The stories, which described Mr. Ford's mood during his last days in office, did not differ much from each other, but the headlines did. "No Rancor or Regret" was the *Post*'s description of the story, while the *Times* opted for "Regret and Relief."

THE EMPIRE OF THE NEWSWEEKLIES: *TIME* AND *NEWSWEEK*

Time and *Newsweek,* the two major national newsweeklies, provide their audience with larger-than-life-sized pictures of the President and other important officials in the White House. For its first three decades, *Time,* the pioneer publication of this genre, presented serious news in melodramatic form, with major news figures portrayed as heroes or villains passing across a stage. *Time*'s cofounder, Henry Luce, aimed to change his readers' concept of their leaders by relating issues to personalities. There is some debate regarding his success in that regard, but *Time,* together with *Life* and Luce's other publications, clearly exerted a tremendous influence in transforming the presentation of news to the public.

Time's major competitor, *Newsweek,* started out as a more conservative version during the first two decades of its existence. In the 1960s, after Luce died and *Newsweek* was acquired by the *Washington Post,* differences between the two publications diminished. Today both present national news in a form that is dramatic and personal, but not flamboyant, and their combined influence is considerable. Consequently, Washington officialdom regards the appearance each Monday of *Time* and *Newsweek* on newsstands and government desks as an important event. Leading figures in the administration or the opposition are frequently on their covers. The impression given by their stories weighs heavily upon the reputation of the administration and its opponents.

Time and *Newsweek* have national influence. Before the national hook-ups for the television networks were completed in the 1950s, they were the only mass circulation publications bringing national news to the entire country. They are still the only print publications that approximate television news's connection to the American public. Presidential assistants may call the *Post* and *Times* when their object is primarily to inform the Washington community, but when their objective is to resonate the message of the President's accomplishments throughout the land, they are more likely to go to the newsweeklies.

Like the *Post* and the *Times,* newsweeklies influence a great many of their nonreaders. Frequently an exclusive story or interview in the newsweeklies will become a lead item in Monday newspapers or Sunday telecasts, which are "thin" on hard news about official policies because most government offices are closed over the weekend. As the week progresses more than 7 million copies of the two magazines arrive on the newsstands and at the households of that well-off, well-educated stratum of the population that the promotion departments of newspapers and magazines like to describe as the "opinion-makers."

REPUTATION AND STATUS AT THE WHITE HOUSE

The newsweeklies' high status at the White House changed when their position as the only national news publications was challenged by television news. Until the 1960s editors, bureau chiefs, and publishers of newsweeklies were given access to the White House of a sort that is received today by network moguls and anchorpersons. Hugh Sidey, a former *Time* Washington bureau chief and White House correspondent, recalled that when he first was assigned to work in Washington during Eisenhower's second term, "*Time* Incorporated was the only national press." Presidents and presidential candidates were pleased to receive coverage in *Time* and thus granted them access greater than that offered to the rest of the media. Even Eisenhower, who did not like interviews, met with Henry Luce, who then reported his discussions to *Time* editors and reporters. Sidey recalled that Lyndon Johnson told him that he would rather get "a paragraph in *Time* magazine or the *New York Times* than all the articles in all the other stuff around the country."[67] He quoted John Kennedy as saying "They read that goddamned magazine, that's what I'm concerned about. Wherever I go they quote to me what was said in *Time* magazine. It seems that that is where the world gets its news."[68]

In the 1970s the newsweeklies, like other forms of media, had to stand in line behind television at the White House when the President's chief objective was to send his message to the widest possible audience. Tom DeFrank, *Newsweek*'s White House correspondent during the Ford and Carter administrations, said that he did not get as much assistance from White House aides as usual when they saw an opportunity to get their story onto the evening news.

They [the Press Office] generally try to be flexible with us. If they know that I am working on a story and they know that something is going to happen in that area on

Monday [the day *Newsweek* comes out], they try to give me some guidance. Sometimes they don't. For instance when we were doing a story on abortion as a political issue [in the 1976 campaign], I knew that the President was going to make his position public in an interview early the following week. I tried to get some help, some guidance on that. I couldn't get any. It was a clear decision not to be helpful. They wanted to save it for TV, for an interview with Cronkite. . . . They have a bias towards the networks because it is the biggest audience, the biggest exposure. I would say they treat the news magazine a little friendlier than the daily. There are a few daily reporters they treat very well.[69]

STRUGGLES OVER THE COVER

In Washington, where the newsweeklies are not as closely read as the *Times* and the *Post,* a newsweekly presidential cover story is considered a coveted prize for the administration because of its national impact. Even Richard Nixon, who kept his personal contacts with the press to a minimum, was willing to make a deal in exchange for a cover. Nixon agreed to grant an interview to Hugh Sidey, for whom he had little personal use, according to John Ehrlichman, in exchange for his appearance on *Time's* cover.[70] Sidey said that that was the only time he got to see Nixon privately during the entire five and one-half years of his administration. "It was a straight trade off," he commented. "Nixon was going to Europe, and for having the cover, he gave an interview."[71]

A favorable cover story is a valuable prize for the White House because of the "poster effect" created by the President's picture appearing on magazine racks at stores and news stalls as well as on the coffee tables of subscribers. The cover story also has a large impact in official Washington, where word gets around quickly about its contents and whether it has boosted the President. "The lead story in a news magazine is always called the violin," said Mel Elfin of *Newsweek,* "because this is where you are supposed to unleash the cosmic music."[72] Of course a cover can have unfavorable effects on the administration. A cartoon of the President beset by woes he is unable to master is greeted with distaste by White House aides, who believe, probably rightly, that the circulation of such a drawing cannot help the administration. Perhaps even worse from the White House perspective is the prospect that a cover story may build up a rival to the President at a time when the country is hungering for a different face. Lyndon Johnson is alleged to have been affected by the appearance of Senator Robert Kennedy on the covers of *Time* and *Newsweek.*

The arrangements for a cover story on the President are usually worked out in negotiations between the Press Office and the Washington bureau of the newsweekly. Usually both sides are flexible about the actual interview with the President. The news magazine sends its White House correspondent and a photographer to the interview and negotiates for others to attend on a "need to know" basis. Since all stories for news magazines are written by the New York office, not by the correspondents who report the story, the writer from

New York attends the interview in order to get a sense of the person he is writing about. Frequently the bureau chiefs themselves attend. According to Mel Elfin, the White House generally has been helpful, except for a short period during 1969 when President Nixon ordered a "freeze out," meaning no more interviews for *Newsweek*. Usually, Elfin said, arrangements are made smoothly: "We go to the Press Office, or the chief of staff or a combination of the two. You just try and open up the doors. Access is a very big problem with reporters. You can't embark on a major cover story unless you are assured of access. . . . The lifeblood of any reporter is someone returning his calls. Smaller organizations don't expect to get call backs from the chief of staff. *Newsweek* and *Time* do. Kissinger once told his assistants, 'You will return the calls of *Newsweek, Time,* the networks, the *Post, Times,* and that's it.' "[73]

GETTING WHITE HOUSE NEWS INTO THE MAGAZINE

"Group journalism is different from classical journalism," Tom DeFrank said in describing how stories are prepared for *Newsweek*. "All the finished writing is done in New York," he said. "That is a very different process from a writer sitting down and doing his own story."[74] The reporting assignments on which the stories are based are a result of the discussions and bargaining that go on between the bureau chiefs in Washington and editors in New York. "I am on the phone to New York twenty times a day," Mel Elfin said. "It is give and take."[75] DeFrank said that every Monday the *Newsweek* bureau chief sends New York a list of proposed stories that the bureau believes should be covered during the following week. His ideas are usually incorporated in the chief's list, which is discussed in the Tuesday story conference. Hugh Sidey described a similar process for selecting story assignments at *Time*.

Reporters and bureau chiefs did not agree about the role reporters play in determining their assignments. Sidey said that he ran *Time*'s bureau with " 'hands off' as much as possible." The reporters "come up with ideas for stories that we then send to New York," he told us. "The less I have to do with them the better. I have been around this town a long time and I make suggestions."[76] Mel Elfin described *Newsweek* as "more a reporter's magazine than an editor's magazine." Reporters constantly come to him with story suggestions, he said. "My job is to smooth the reporter's way with New York and to plan and coordinate with New York."[77] DeFrank's opinion was that "basically it is the other way around. They set the assignments with my comments or recommendations considered."[78]

At both newsweeklies, correspondents on different beats have an opportunity to get together to trade information. Some reporters and bureau chiefs thought that this exchange made it possible for them to present a more complete picture of the activities of the President and his assistants. On the other hand, there is a strong sense that the need to entertain may block out stories that are less sensational but possibly more important. DeFrank concluded,

"Part of our problem is we are a mass circulation magazine and we tailor ourself to a mass audience, and sometimes more deserving stories go down the tube for that reason. I agree with [Walter] Lippmann that you can't afford to be boring, but some of the most boring stories are the best stories. That is a problem. . . . The stories with most news value are cabinet changes or scandal. The best stories are frequently without conflict or controversy."[79]

THE OUTER CIRCLE: THE *WALL STREET JOURNAL,* THE *WASHINGTON STAR, U.S. NEWS AND WORLD REPORT*

Although the three publications in this group do not influence the Washington community as deeply as do the *Post,* the *Times, Time,* or *Newsweek,* they are regarded as national publications, clearly distinguishable from even the most influential regional publications such as the *Los Angeles Times.* And because they are easily available and widely distributed in Washington, each of them serves as a conduit for important and significant White House stories.

The Wall Street Journal. The influence of the *Wall Street Journal* stems from the tremendous respect journalists and government officials have for the quality of its national reporting. The *Journal,* the only weekday newspaper available throughout the country, also has the largest circulation. Its audience in Washington consists of political and bureaucratic managers, especially those in the area of economic policy; in the nation, it is read by the corporate elite. It is a well-clipped paper; important articles are cut out, duplicated, and included in the reading files of prominent officials and executives. Stories published in the *Journal* frequently become the subjects of articles by syndicated columnists, are reprinted in other newspapers, and are cited on radio and television news broadcasts.

When a number of Washington reporters and government officials were asked to discuss publications and programs that consistently provide stories that are important to them, the *Journal* appeared on most lists, for the reason that it provides detailed, accurate analyses of White House and other Washington stories. Several reporters suggested that the high quality of stories came about because *Journal* editors gave their reporters the time, encouragement, and freedom to develop their own stories instead of making them wait for appearances or handouts from government officials. Unlike the other majors, the *Journal* makes no effort to provide a detailed account of the daily or routine events of public life. It supplies business and economic information to a national readership attracted by the thorough, specialized reporting in these fields. According to Dennis Farney, who served as White House correspondent during portions of the Ford and Carter administrations, it was difficult for him to get anything into the paper about a particular event other than a brief item in the two-column news summary the paper runs each day. He was expected to produce a major story every two weeks or so that did not cover the same ground as the daily or weekly media. Alone among reporters for major publications, he did not feel compelled to participate in the body watch or to produce a story on deadline that summarized continuing events. "We assume our readers have read the *New York Times,*" Farney commented. "The *Times* and the *Post* present single issue stories. I'm different from James Naughton in that I would not do a story about a daily campaign event except insofar as it fit into a detailed story about campaign strategy. I'm interested in writing about what will happen."[80]

What the *Journal* expects its White House reporter to observe are the underlying trends and forces in an administration, the President's role as a leader, relations between the staff and some group whose support the President needs, and issues the White House will have to face. Of course, similar stories appear in other publications, but reporters there complain that they seldom are given the freedom to work exclusively on them.

The manner in which the *Journal* works may be seen in the way a reporter puts together an "ice box story." Editors want to have a story stored "in the ice box" on any event that is likely to occur and would be of importance if it did. Farney cited the example of a story he wrote while Nelson Rockefeller was vice president in which he described what Rockefeller would have been like as president. The facts of that story were based on Rockefeller's record; the thread connecting that record to a projected Rockefeller administration was Farney's observation that his record showed that Rockefeller believed every problem has a solution.

The media and the White House people who talked about the *Journal* said Farney was a well-informed reporter who developed important stories about White House activities that they would not have seen. Farney suggested that the status he gained because he worked for the *Journal* helped him to gain entrance to some offices. It would have been more difficult for him to prepare his kind of stories if he didn't have the *Journal* behind him. On the other hand, his request for an interview with President Ford was turned down, he suspected, because the *Journal* had been critical of his administration. In spite of the newspaper's politically conservative reputation, Farney suggested, it had more entree with Democratic than with Republican administrations because Democrats are defensive about their reputation as antibusiness and hope that a story in the *Wall Street Journal* will give them a channel to the corporate elite, which would otherwise not hear them.

The Washington Star. The importance of the *Washington Star* in the nation's capital highlights the benefits a news organization derives from having a Washington audience. Although the *Star*'s national correspondents are respected, the Washington bureaus of the *Los Angeles Times,* the *Baltimore Sun,* and the *St. Louis Post-Dispatch* have several reporters with more visibility, because of their appearance on television interview and news analysis programs, as well as higher status in the Washington community. But because the *Star* is published in Washington, the same officials whose doors open wide for Jack Nelson of the *Los Angeles Times*, Richard Dudman of the *St. Louis Post-Dispatch*, or Charles Corddry of the *Baltimore Sun* are more likely to read about themselves in the *Star* than in those papers.

For many years the *Star* was the newspaper of choice of Washington's conservative congressional and business leadership and of the executive branch when the President was a Republican. Until the *Washington Post* merged with the *Washington Times-Herald* in the 1950s, the *Star* had the largest metropolitan circulation; it remained the wealthiest newspaper in the city for another decade. Like many afternoon papers, the *Star* has suffered a competitive circulation disadvantage against television's instant news. Managerial changes culminating in shifting ownership also added to the paper's problems.

By the middle of the 1970s the *Star* was changing its conservative image. Its new owners, Time, Inc., provided assurance that bankruptcy was not imminent. Well-regarded political correspondents such as Jules Witcover and Jack Germond joined a staff that already included a number of strong reporters. The *Star* attracted reporters, columnists, and features away from its rivals. In June, 1979, it even snatched away the comic strip "Doonesbury" from the *Post*. In July *Star* publishers declared war on the *Post* when they added a morning edition.

The White House correspondent of the *Star* for many years was Garnett (Jack) Horner, who was also president of the White House Correspondents Association for several terms. Critics suggest that during his tenure he was influential in keeping the association's business ceremonial, and thus prevented it from becoming an organization that reporters could use to present their collective grievances in disputes with the White House over issues such as the lack of press conferences, the timing of briefings, or the alleged abuse of White House authority on matters like pool assignments. Other White House reporters remembered Horner as an individual who got exclusive interviews because he was ingratiating to presidents. Perhaps his most celebrated exclusive was a 1972 interview in which President Nixon outlined his analysis of American society and his plans for the future. At that time some reporters alleged that Nixon gave Horner the interview to repay him and the *Star* for favorable treatment and to punish the *Washington Post* for its Watergate coverage. Earlier, Horner had a reputation for being willing to ask President Eisenhower questions at his press conferences that had been planted with him by White House officials. The transcript of one Eisenhower press conference shows that when the President began a response with the remark, "Mr. Horner, I'm glad you asked that question," he was interrupted by laughter.[81]

Horner's successor was Fred Barnes, a young reporter who attracted considerable attention and some semiquizzical comments from other reporters because he obtained a number of exclusive stories during the Ford administration. "Fred Barnes does a good job," Peter Lisagor commented in response to a question about which White House beat reporters he thought did well: "Fred seems to be the recipient of a lot of White House stuff they want out. Fred is available to them. Now how much he initiates and how much they call him in and say, 'Look Fred, this is the way it is,' I don't know. Particularly about the preparation of the State of the Union message, they'll do that frequently with him."[82] Barnes strongly denied the implication that the stories he obtained were the result of any special favoritism on the part of the White House. But he added that getting information from officials does involve recognizing that he is playing in their ball park: "Officials have the advantage in their relations with reporters because they have the poop." Because it takes a long time to develop sources in the White House, unfavorable facts about the sources sometimes are left out of stories if they are less important than the information the sources provide. Reporters need a great deal of detailed information about what's going on, he said, because "every little background arrangement is important to an understanding of the power struggle." At the same time, what they tell you has to be discounted because "at the White House, the selling of the President is institutionalized."[83]

U.S. News and World Report. Like the *Star, U.S. News* once was regarded as a publication aimed at the traditional conservative. Its founder was David Lawrence, a nationally syndicated columnist who spoke for the conservative wings of both political parties. While he was its editor, the magazine presented itself as the national newsweekly for the business community. Unlike *Time* and *Newsweek, U.S. News* always presented news in a low-key manner. Although the magazine has attempted to throw off the stodgy image some editors considered it to have, its format has changed less than those of either of its major competitors. Only a few correspondents said they read the magazine regularly; the others maintained that they received photocopies of stories of interest to them from someone in their bureau who kept track of what appeared.

In the latter part of the 1970s the reputation of *U.S. News* at the White House among both reporters and officials was that it provided solid but not innovative coverage. It was said that its reporters enjoy good access, that its reporters deal less in personalities than do those of the other newsweeklies, and that it publishes stories that differ from those of other papers or magazines—namely, long interviews in their entirety and analysis stories complete with extensive graphic and statistical materials. A less complimentary observation was made by Timothy Crouse in his 1973 book on political reporters in the 1972 presidential campaign, *The Boys on the Bus.* Crouse wrote that *U.S. News* had "minimal needs" from the Nixon White House: "Being almost a house organ for the Administration," he states, "[it] did not demand much investigative reporting."[84]

When John Mashek became its White House correspondent during the middle 1970s, other reporters were interested to find out what stories he was working on, which is a sure sign of respect among correspondents. The opinion among reporters and officials was less harsh than the one expressed by Crouse. They considered *U.S. News* to be reliable and accurate. "They do a good job," a Carter White House press aide said, "although I guess if it was known that we said it, it would hurt them.'"[85] In 1977 a number of government information officers indicated that they thought *U.S. News* was the best and "most objective" of the newsweeklies. To some extent, however, this opinion might have been based on the unstated premise that *U.S. News* was less likely to be sharply critical, and even if it were critical, it would be unable to damage their reputations in the way that *Time* and *Newsweek* can.

Large Circulation Regional Daily Newspapers, Chains, and Affiliated News Services

The regional press consists of all newspapers published throughout the country that are not regularly read in Washington. Regional publications are edited and produced for an audience that has a limited attention span for national news, especially when it consists of stories that require readers to be familiar with issues that don't affect them directly and personalities that have little dramatic appeal away from their Potomac setting. As members of the Washington community, however, correspondents for these newspapers' Washington bureaus share the values of national rather than local media, and they acquire the same status in Washington as national reporters for the *Post* or *Times*.

White House correspondents for the regional press feel conflict between their own ambitions and values, on the one hand, and their actual status and the demands of their home offices, on the other. Reporters for regional papers ordinarily receive less attention at the White House than do correspondents for the three commercial television networks, the seven major national publications, and the two major wire services. Editors in their home offices want their Washington bureaus to produce stories that have a local slant; bureau chiefs ask their reporters to produce stories that are important in Washington. For some reporters the White House assignment provides them with a status in the city that compensates for their lack of a Washington audience, which would give them immediate feedback on their stories and a sense of their status with their peers.

THE PROBLEM OF CLOUT

Reporters who write for newspapers published in Atlanta, Chicago, or Houston—in fact in any city whose circulation area does not extend to Washington—can expect that their initial reception at the White House will be based on the President's opinion of their paper, his need at a particular time to communicate a message to their readers, and the staff's perception of the correspondent's professional reputation. A reporter who recently has been assigned to cover the White House is helped if the President is a friend of his publisher or regularly reads and likes his paper; if he is working on a story the staff hopes will convey a message to members of Congress or other political influentials among his readers; most of all, if the White House knows that what he says and thinks affects what other reporters write. "A guy like Lisagor was the herd bull," David Halberstam suggested. "Nobody in Washington read the *Chicago Daily News*. What Peter Lisagor thought about a given President was very important because he had such awesome peer respect."[86]

The managements of some regional news organizations try to enhance their status by selecting as White House correspondents and Washington bureau chiefs reporters whose professional standing commands official respect. For example, the *Baltimore Sun* appointed Carl Leubsdorf as its White House correspondent in 1977, when he was a professionally visible writer known for his political coverage at the Associated Press. Leubsdorf joined the well-regarded bureau of a newspaper whose circulation area extends to within thirty miles of the nation's capital. When the *Los Angeles Times* appointed Jack Nelson as its bureau chief, that newspaper acquired as its most visible representative a Pulitzer Prize–winning reporter who was respected by Washington journalists, whose news analysis was seen in Washington on television interview and news discussion programs, and who increased the bureau's Washington status after the 1976 election because President Carter regarded him as one of the most important members of the press.

Only a few journalistic stars from regional papers attain a Washington reputation among both media and political influentials that converts into the kind of status expected by a reporter for a paper such as the *Washington Post*. "Regional reporters have to remind people they are covering who they are and what they want," complained Jerald terHorst, a political reporter and syndicated columnist for the *Detroit News* who once spent a month on the other side, as Gerald Ford's press secretary.[87] Even their best-known reporters complain that the White House does not perceive the importance of their local audience. "Sometimes I think those White House people don't know there's a place out there called Chicago," Peter Lisagor reflected.[88] Reporters who are not as high as Lisagor was in the White House pecking order, including those who are correspondents for newspapers owned by media corporate conglomerates and published in large readership markets, bring a much lower level of organizational clout to their relations with White House insiders. "If the *New York Times* wants someone to call them back, they get it," said Pat Sloyan of *Newsday*, a Long Island newspaper with a large suburban circulation. "If I want to see some of the same people, I have to stand on their doorstep."[89]

The White House staff provides the Washington bureau reporters for the regional media with less access and fewer exclusives because they have found that the national media has more influence in getting the President's messages to his audiences. Officials use specialty magazines and national publications to send messages through the political labyrinths of the capital. They use the national media to communicate with their constituents throughout the country because they have found that, with the exception of a media giant such as the *Los Angeles Times,* daily coverage of Washington in the regional press has a local rather than a national impact. An adviser to President Ford suggested that his contacts with the entire regional press were worth only 10 percent of the value of his contacts with the national media because what most local newspapers publish reflects what the national media produce. ''There is no such thing as regional press,'' he reflected as the Ford administration prepared to leave the White House in 1977:

What is the *San Francisco Chronicle?* The *San Francisco Chronicle* hasn't had an original thought in twenty years. The *San Francisco Chronicle* is AP, UPI, the *Washington Post,* and the *New York Times* service. That is the *San Francisco Chronicle* as far as national news is concerned. That means you are right back dealing with Phil Shabecoff, Ed Walsh, Frank Cormier, and Helen Thomas. No matter how you cut it and how you slice it you come right back to that. I have gone out to the *Chronicle* to meet with editorial boards on energy policy, and given interviews. Yes, that gets in. But day in and day out, what are they getting? They are getting AP, UPI, *Washington Post* service, *New York Times* service, the networks. That is what the people of San Francisco are getting.[90]

These comments about the *Chronicle* also apply to several more prestigious regional newspapers. When the front pages of the *Chicago Tribune,* the *Atlanta Constitution,* the *Los Angeles Times,* and the *Baltimore Sun* were compared with those of the *Washington Post* and the *New York Times* on ten randomly selected days between November 1, 1978, and January 31, 1979, those of the national papers included significantly more national political stories. The *Post* and *Times* each printed a total of twenty-eight such stories, while the *Chicago Tribune* placed twelve; the *Atlanta Constitution,* fifteen; the *Los Angeles Times,* twenty; and the *Baltimore Sun,* twenty-one. Over 40 percent of the front-page stories in the regional newspapers were from syndicated news services, while 4 percent of the front-page stories in the majors were from news services. During the ten days of this sample, official contacts produced more than one and one-half times as many front-page stories in the *Post* and *Times* as they did in the *Constitution,* the *Sun,* the *Tribune,* and the *Los Angeles Times.* Official contact with the two major publications and the wire services also resulted in more than 40 percent of the front-page stories in the regional press.

REPORTERS, BUREAUS, AND HOME OFFICES

There is no consensus as to how many reporters a newspaper must have in its Washington bureau in order to put an individual stamp on its coverage of national political life. Washington bureaus of regional newspapers range in size from a one- or two-person office that keeps an eye on the congressional delegation and hometown issues to the twenty-one reporters at the *Los Angeles Times* bureau who cover every major news beat in the city. Most large city dailies were represented by their own or their chain's bureaus with between five and thirteen reporters. Newspapers that assign reporters to the traditional Washington beats of the White House, the Pentagon, the State Department, Congress, the courts, and politics require at least six reporters.

Small bureaus. The *Houston Chronicle* and the *Kansas City Star* provide contrasting examples of small-bureau coverage of the President. The *Chronicle* sends one of its four reporters to the White House when its story has a White House angle, when a Texas issue such as domestic oil production requires a White House comment, or when a Texas personality such as John Connally or George Bush is in the news. According to Judy Wiessler of the bureau, the staff decided to leave the body watch of the President to the wires so its reporters could cover a beat such as energy or social issues across the lines of bureaucracy, Congress, and the White House. They assigned a full-time White House correspondent during the 1972 and 1976 campaigns, she reported, in order to provide local angles not covered by the wires.[91]

Joseph Lastelic, the bureau chief of the *Kansas City Star,* reported that, unlike *Chronicle* reporters, he called or visited the White House almost every day. Lastelic, who has covered assignments connected with the presidency since the Truman administration, said that he found that the White House provided useful information for his paper since almost every issue had a local angle. For example, he traveled with President Ford to Europe because Fort Riley near Kansas City is an embarkation depot for troops sent to Europe. He was interested in Vladivostok and Soviet relations because Kansas produced a great deal of the wheat that was sold to the Soviet Union.[92]

Washington bureaus of chains and news services. Many bureaus are appendages of media enterprises whose tangled corporate structure often involves multiple ownership of print, broadcast, and television outlets. Among the typical bureaus serving the regional media are newspaper chains such as Knight, Cox, Newhouse, and Scripps-Howard, whose correspondents prepare national news for all the newspapers in the group; news services, provided by Knight and Scripps-Howard, Hearst, and the *Los Angeles Times,* which provide information and feature stories to subscribers; and syndicates, which own several publications whose bureaus cooperate although they do not share facilities.

During the 1970s the Knight and Cox newspaper groups restructured their

Washington offices to form unified bureaus that would provide a level of news and analysis that individual bureaus with staffs of one or two could not provide. Both Robert Boyd of Knight and Andrew Glass of Cox stated that one of the central purposes of their reorganizations was to provide members with coverage of the White House that did not repeat wire service stories. Prominent political reporters were hired to cover the White House.

The Knight chain, which has sixteen members, also provides a news service to sixty subscribers who are not part of the group. According to Boyd, the bureau's primary audience is the editors of newspapers in Philadelphia, Detroit, Miami, Akron, and Charlotte. The ten reporters on the staff included four who were on the bureau's payroll and six who worked for member newspapers. Boyd maintained that because the bureau's size permitted specialization, it was able to produce investigative stories that could not have been obtained in a small bureau whose staff has to respond to daily demands: "We sent two reporters to Atlanta just after Carter's nomination who spent the whole of August going through the archives of the Carter administration. [They] spent three weeks reporting and one week writing three long stories about the way Jimmy Carter handled power as governor."[93] On the whole, however, investigative reporting was not common in the bureau, particularly in connection with the presidency. Boyd said that James McCartney, the veteran political reporter hired to cover the White House as Knight's first full-time correspondent in 1977, would prepare "analysis pieces, interpretive pieces, and background explainers." Because its readers are not interested in "insiders" Washington, Knight has not "gone in for the backstage stuff." The member papers tell the bureau that what they want are stories about issues that affect their readers directly, such as whether the President favors a tax cut.

The member papers and subscribers to the news services are pushing for more hard news coverage. "Their argument was that we could write it for them on their time and their length in a way that they could discuss it with us and shape it to their needs," Boyd said. "The wires were sending it on blanket and the *New York Times* and *Washington Post* services came in too late and too long, AP and UPI came in jumbled and higgledy-piggledy." He also suggested that there would not be real differences in their hard news coverage of the President and what the wires provided. "Frankly, I think that whatever increment we add is really very small."[94]

Andrew Glass described similar changes in the Washington bureau of the Cox Newspapers during the 1970s. In 1974 the chain established a Washington bureau that would carry the identity of the group instead of individual newspapers. The thirteen members are four newspapers in Texas, four in Ohio, three in Florida, and two in Georgia. Six of the bureau's twelve correspondents work for member papers and six work for the bureau. According to Glass, Cox enlarged its coverage of the White House at the beginning of the Carter administration to provide one of the most complete reports on the presidency available. Three reporters assigned as full-time correspondents were assisted by two reporters who would work with them on major stories. The staff collaborated in the production of three types of stories: a daily file, including stories on the briefing, press conference, and other activities of the President; short-term projects, which require several days of reporting; and big projects involving reporting on major policy developments such as energy, which would require reporters' attention over a longer period. Like Boyd, Glass suggested that the member papers were more concerned with having their own correspondent produce the hard news or personality feature stories than they were in supplemental stories based on investigative reporting. He added that because two papers in the chain are published in Atlanta, they wanted daily coverage of Carter, at least during the early days of the term. He felt that he had unusually good access to the Carter White House for a reporter who appears in the regional press because he had covered Carter during the campaign, but also because Carter and other members of the staff read his stories when they appear in the Atlanta newspapers.[95]

Washington bureaus for large city dailies. The owners, editors, and publishers of newspapers that serve major cities such as Detroit, Boston, Chicago, St. Louis, Baltimore, and Los Angeles believe that their publications are of national significance. During the years since 1960 they have increased the size of their Washington bureaus, hired reporters of high professional standing to staff them, and taken other steps to promote their status in the country as serious newspapers that present their readers with a solid picture of national political life. In particular, they want their White House correspondent to be able to prepare a bylined story on the major public events of an administration's history, and they expect that he or she will bring prestige to the newspaper by virtue of proximity to the President. Beyond this, editors in the home office want a local slant on a story. "Editors at home look at Washington through a narrower set of lenses than we do," Jerald terHorst remarked. "For example if automobile executives from Detroit visit the White House, our editors will want a story even if they only repeat what they always say." Reporters in the bureau have other goals. Because many are hired from other reporting jobs in Washington or are sent to the bureau as a reward for their superior coverage of state politics, they want to cover the major political events of the Washington community. "For a member of a bureau, Washington is your whole life," terHorst continued. "There is continuous conflict over what is the best story. Reporters feel that they should cover the most important stories in Washington; editors may accept your story, but then give it less play."[96]

There is a sense that the conflict between bureau staffs and editors is based on more than the different perspective on events as seen in Washington and elsewhere in the country: it involves the definition of news. One bureau chief suggested that the pressure on newspapers to become even more profitable enterprises had widened the gap:

In the economic crunch, papers have gotten increasingly into the hands of readership survey groups whom I view as the equivalent of people who came into television and told them to have funny news. These reader survey guys are going out and they're coming back with findings that people generally are not interested in international news and very little interested in national news. They're highly interested in gossip, scandal, entertainment. To the degree that publishers perceive their function as giving the readers what they want rather than educating them, the product is being depreciated. . . . In our case and I suspect other bureaus, there is an increasing pressure over the last year or two to produce what I view as unserious news.[97]

An editor who worked in his paper's home office suggested that differences in perspective in Washington and trans-Potomac America explain the different views of what is news. "After a while these guys forget about who they're writing for. They sit and talk to each other and try to prove how smart they are. They forget that we all don't have our own columns in the *New York Times.*"[98]

Elite and Specialist Publications

Reporters representing ethnic and trade publications usually cover the White House as part of a beat that includes several important centers of Washington news. A reporter for a business publication, for example, would follow a story from lobbyists' offices and think tanks to Congress, departments, and the White House; he would spend time at briefings, committee meetings, or interviews as the story develops. Sometimes publications such as *Business Week, Fortune,* or *Barron's* have excellent analysis of the development of policy in the White House. In the case of ethnic publications, the editors may assign a reporter to cover the President if they believe that his activities will be of particular importance to that group. As at almost all news organizations, the editors and publishers of ethnic and trade publications regard having a White House correspondent as a sign of being considered a serious publication. More journalists representing these organizations appear at each new administration.

The journalists who represent ethnic publications regard themselves as and are regarded by others as representatives and advocates of the groups that sponsor the publications. At the briefing black reporters for black publications ask the press secretary questions about employment, economic stimulation, federal jobs programs, and the appointments of blacks to political office. There is an increase in the number of blacks who attend the daily briefing when the President is visited by a black congressional caucus or a prominent black. President Carter frequently called on the reporter for Johnson publications at his press conferences in order to make certain that the black press would receive some recognition.

Joseph Polakoff of the Jewish Telegraphic Agency acted as an advocate for Israel and other Jewish causes at the briefing. As is the case with reporters from other ethnic media, Polakoff used the public forum of the briefing to attract mainstream journalists to stories he believes are important. In particular, in the early part of the Carter administration, he tried to attract their attention to what his questions implied were failures of the American government to hold the Soviets to their agreement to allow Jews to emigrate from the Soviet Union; to the status of Soviet dissidents, many of whom are Jews; and most important of all, to what he sees as lapses in the United States's willingness to assist Israel or what he sees as a willingness on the part of the United States to assist Israel's enemies.

A second purpose of ethnic reporters like Polakoff in attending the briefing is to use the press secretary as a contact through whom to exert pressure on the administration. Raising an issue at the briefing could alert friends on the White House staff of the causes he advocates and indicates to them that his group considers a particular issue important. This sometimes results in an abrasive exchange. For example, on February 13, 1978, Polakoff asked Powell, "Why is the United States sticking its finger in Israel's eye?"[99] Although such questions may result in new stories, the primary involvement of ethnic press reporters is to act as guardians of the causes they believe are central to their group.

Specialty magazines include small circulation, elite-audience publications on government and politics, such as *Congressional Quarterly* and *National Journal,* as well as magazines with a somewhat wider concern with social and literary issues, such as *National Review* and *New Republic.* The elite audience of journalists, government officials, lobbyists, and lawyers seeks and receives a deeper level of inside reporting and analysis from these journals than it receives in general circulation magazines. The *National Journal*'s Dom Bonafede and the *New Republic*'s John Osborne are extremely influential White House reporters because what they report becomes the basis of the way many other reporters understand layers of White House activity that they don't see as they pursue hard news stories and the body watch of the President. "We do very little of that [institutional] reporting," said Robert Boyd of the Knight chain. "I would have to get that from secondary sources such as Osborne. . . . The Bonafede stuff has been useful."[100]

Independents

Although most White House regulars are affiliated with major national, regional, or specialized news organizations, approximately ten accredited correspondents provide coverage for small daily and weekly newspapers, newsletters, and radio stations. Some represent several small media operations whose executives buy their services in order to get the prestige of a report from a special correspondent at the White House. Others spend time in the West Wing Press Office because it is their principal point of access to feature stories about the family life of the President they obtain in the East Wing offices of the First Lady. Most of them play a small role in the formal interchanges between president and press, although occasionally an article for a large circulation magazine such as *McCall's*, the *Ladies' Home Journal,* or *Reader's Digest* is beneficial to the President's image.

Several reporters in this group, however, play a conspicuous role as the pariahs of the press room. Their status as outcasts stems from what both reporters and White House officials describe as their outlandish and disruptive style of questioning at the daily briefing. Some journalists regard them as responsible for the lack of civility that pervades during many briefings. "What can we do about [Lester] Kinsolving?" a bureau chief asked, referring to the correspondent widely regarded as the most notorious desecrator of decorum of the daily briefing during the late 1970s. "He's making it impossible for other reporters to ask sensible questions."[101] Kinsolving, sometimes referred to by reporters as the "Mad Monk," is an Episcopal priest who irritated reporters because he wore his clerical collar to briefings during his first years at the White House. He had been a commentator for a local Washington, D.C., radio station before becoming a reporter and columnist for *Panax Newspapers,* a chain of conservative papers. The Press Office and other reporters felt he tried to monopolize the briefing with questions on such subjects as personal immorality by officials, terrorism by Marxist-led groups, and the President's failure to defend American interests.

Another independent reporter often regarded as an irritating producer of red herrings at the White House is Sarah McClendon, the proprietor and chief reporter for a news service that contributes Washington stories to a string of small newspapers and radio stations. McClendon has some public visibility because of her role at televised press conferences as antagonist to presidents from Eisenhower to Carter. Her questions about bureaucratic malfeasance and its coverup are usually turned aside at press conferences or debunked with withering sarcasm by the press secretary. Although at one time she appeared on the lists of almost all Press Office staff members and reporters as a person whose conduct put her beyond the pale, many have mellowed toward her, especially after she was vindicated on several occasions. She is more likely than Kinsolving to be defended by her colleagues against counter harassment by the Press Office. Most of them make a distinction in her favor between the two of them.

Kinsolving and McClendon are attacked by other reporters as loud, argumentative, self-promoting individuals whose questions provoke fights rather than elicit information, a description that is accurate but that ignores the fact that similar behavior by more prominent reporters is not unknown. Sam Donaldson of ABC News frequently interrupted the briefing official with rude questions and wisecracks, mixing clowning with antagonism. Another reporter asked Press Secretary Nessen complicated economic questions that were beyond his ability because, he said, he "liked to bring him to the level of his incompetence." Other reporters made comments that scolded the press secretary when they did not like his answers; they asked questions that were attacks ending with a question mark. These reporters are accepted in spite of this behavior, and are sometimes encouraged. Their colleagues believe that they are serious reporters, in part because they work for news organizations with clout in the industry.

As a consequence of their status as pariahs, other reporters do not follow up on issues raised by McClendon and Kinsolving, or the press secretary does not provide hard answers to questions that later turn out to be important. For example, during the winter of 1976, Kinsolving pursued Press Secretary Nessen at the daily briefing with questions about President Ford's positions on the proposed Panama Canal Treaty and abortion. Because no prominent Washington politician emphasized these issues at that time, Nessen was able to brush the questions aside as unworthy of serious considerations. The other reporters in the briefing room seemed to agree with Nessen in this instance. After the 1976 presidential election, however, Nessen claimed that he knew the Panama Canal and abortion issues were crucial to conservatives, who could support Ronald Reagan in Republican primaries if President Ford took the wrong stand. By allowing Kinsolving to carry the issue, Nessen created a delay before other reporters would force him and the President to make public statements that would run the risk of alienation of portions of the conservative constituency.[102]

Photographers

Photographers who cover the President are even more dependent than reporters on the arrangements provided by the Press Office. A "photo opportunity" is a setting created by the White House at which photographers may take pictures; usually Press Office officials make arrangements for pictures to be shot from angles they regard as favorable. Because President Johnson felt his left profile was his best, the staff arranged cameramen's positions so that they would film him from that side.

Molding photographers' routines to make it more likely that they provide good pictures of the President was a central concern of Stephen Early's during the Roosevelt administration. In those pretelevision days Early recognized the importance of still photographs to project the President's image, particularly those that would project confidence in the President's physical strength. On one occasion Early provided his assistant, William Hassett, with specific instructions on how the President should be filmed during a weekend rest at his Hyde Park home:

The *AP* and some of the other photo news syndicates are asking for a pictorial layout of the President at home. I hope the President will give the still photographers an opportunity to get some informal, intimate, home pictures, and the permission to make pictures of the home itself from the roadway; the fields; through the trees; scenes from the home; of the river; pictures of his new cottage on the hill; of the road that he built up to the new cottage; the President with any of the pets around the place; the dogs, Jack and Jill, I believe, are up there. If the President will get in his car and go out to the stables, have them lead a riding horse or two up to him so that he can be petting them while he is photographed; pictures of the President's little cubby-hole office; picture of the President with any of the children that may be there; with his mother; with Mrs. Roosevelt; around the fireplace; on the porch; out in the yard.

And then, for your information, of course, they will want more than this—the photographers will. They will want interior pictures of the President's bedroom; of the kitchen; of the servants. Those pictures I have definitely *turned down.*[103]

Unwritten rules govern photographer behavior at the White House. For example, although when they film a meeting they are often close enough to the participants to overhear their conversations, the code tells them not to repeat what they have overheard. Institutional pressures within their own organizations sometimes come into play. "Photographers are a tight-lipped, trustworthy group," said David Kennerly, who had been a prize-winning news photographer before he became photographer for the Ford White House. "We base our ability to get stuff reporters don't, on not talking. When I was at *Time,* I would be grilled by *Time* correspondents about Kissinger when I got into meetings."[104] Not all photographers refuse to cooperate with their own organizations. A United Press International photographer overheard President Eisenhower talking with his aide Bernard Shanley after a press conference in which he was asked about his candidacy for 1956: "You'll never know how close I came to saying 'no,' " said Eisenhower. The photographer told UPI White House correspondent Merriman Smith, who then used it in his "Back Stairs" column.[105]

When the President is out of the Oval Office, the media advance unit provides facilities for photographers to set up their cameras to take pictures of his meetings, his speeches, or his participation in ceremonies. On other occasions, such as when the President is with his family or playing golf, the Press Office must approve photographers' requests to take pictures. In the Ford administration David Kennerly decided when to allow cameramen from news organizations to take pictures and when the White House staff would provide them. Similar practices existed in other administrations. On some occasions, such as the Camp David summit meeting in 1978, only official White House photographs were available. But White House photographers still have unparalleled access, and therefore they have opportunities to capture historic moments. "We never release photographs unless we are asked to," Kennerly said. "But CBS, ABC, and UPI ask for the photos."[106] When Kennerly was the only photographer present, for instance, when the decision surrounding the Mayaguez incident was made, there was a great deal of interest in those photographs on the part of news organizations.

FOUR

THE WHITE HOUSE BUBBLE MACHINE

Leadership and Publicity

T HE WHITE HOUSE is a vast political communications center that sends messages to Congress, foreign governments, interest groups, bureaucrats, and the American public. Although White House advisers want to publicize most of these messages, they know that even those directed to specific groups or small segments of the public ultimately will be picked up by the mass media. Efforts to keep the contents of the messages private usually fail in a cauldron-like setting in which most items eventually boil to the surface. "They call this place the bubble machine," a Ford administration official reflected. "You see it that way, it literally is that."[1] Staff members may succeed in fine-tuning the reports spread by news organizations about the President, but they find it difficult to keep information secret when it has a high street value.

The prevailing view of insiders during the last several administrations has been that the White House is a place from which everything resonates. "Almost everything here is either a megaphone or a support mechanism for a megaphone," a former official suggested.[2] What becomes public affects the success of efforts to strengthen the President's capacity to govern. As Richard Neustadt demonstrated in his study *Presidential Power*, a president's professional reputation and public prestige have an impact on those in the political system whose activities can add to or erode his ability to implement his decisions.[3]

Publicity operations are the central White House activity that link the President's direct appeals for support with his staff's efforts to assist him by lobbying interest groups, Congress, and the bureaucracy. White House officials know that the same news organizations that amplify the President's messages also provide their audiences with information and images harmful to the administration. By influencing what appears as news, the staff hopes to win the media's listeners, readers, and viewers for the President. "Along this line, the President is going to want your creative and sustained thinking about the overall problem of communicating with the American people," Bill

Moyers wrote to Robert Kintner of NBC News shortly before the latter came to work at the White House. "Some call it the problem of 'the President's image,' " Moyers continued. "It goes beyond that to the ultimate question of how does the President shape the issues and interpret them to people—how, in fact, does he lead."[4]

In order to maintain the President's reputation in the Washington community and his prestige with influential molders of public opinion throughout the nation, White House publicity offices must be well-organized, staffed with knowledgeable personnel, and involved in coordinated operations planned and directed by advisers close to the Chief Executive. This chapter surveys the offices that carry out the President's three major publicity activities: direct press operations, which take place primarily in the office of the press secretary; planning and coordinating communications operations, a function of the senior advisers and offices such as that of the assistant for communications; and promotional operations that focus on particular programs, policies, or individuals and that are carried out by the President's speechwriters, advance teams, media advisers, photo unit, and Office of Public Liaison. This chapter also describes the importance of units that do not have a direct publicity function and of support services for media-related political communications.

The Nature of the Apparatus

White House officials command resources that provide important public relations services for the President. Highly visible operations, such as those carried on by the press secretary and his staff, are coordinated with less well-known activities that also play important roles in the formation and execution of White House media policies, such as scheduling, an activity that involves most of the President's senior advisers as well as the twelve persons listed in the White House telephone directory as working for the appointment and scheduling offices. One of President Ford's principal advisers stated that his central consideration in arranging the President's schedule had been the White House's desire to attract, or occasionally to avoid, media coverage.[5] Another high-level aide in that administration called scheduling a "propaganda machine."[6]

The organizational structure of prominent White House offices directly or indirectly involved with media strategies has expanded enormously since Herbert Hoover gave one of his three assistants the responsibility of handling press relations. The names given to offices are changed frequently (especially those that acquired a bad odor during the Nixon administration), but their functions remain the same and their evolutionary development continues. In the third year of Carter's presidency the Press Office included the Office of the Press Secretary, which was responsible for daily relations with the media covering the President; the Media Liaison operation, which maintained contacts between the White House and media influentials, including those from the ethnic and trade media; the White House News Summary, an internal communications mechanism maintained because the President and his advisers needed some feedback on the success of the operation; and the Photo Office, which prepared the pictorial record of the administration. The Office of the Assistant to the President for Communications, which had overall responsibility for coordinating communications activities, employed assistants for special projects and task forces as well as a television coordinator who negotiated arrangements between the White House and the networks. Major divisions of the office included the speechwriters, who prepared special speeches and messages; and media advance, which made arrangements for coverage of the President when he left Washington. Other White House publicity operations also attempted to affect what appeared in the media, even though they were less involved in direct press operations. Among them were those headed by an assistant who handled lobbying for the White House, a function that once was housed in the Office of Public Liaison; the President's chief political adviser, who established White House task forces to publicize the President's programs; and the Office of the Appointments Secretary to the President, which prepared and promoted the President's schedule and travel arrangements.

Several White House offices maintained media operations that were not central to their own functions but were still important to the President's efforts to send political communications through the media. Among them were the Office of the First Lady's Staff, which included a speechwriter and a press secretary; the Office of the Vice President, which also included speechwriting and media staff; the National Security Council, which maintained an associate press secretary for national security affairs; and the Congressional Liaison operation, which frequently used the media to try to influence Congress when a more direct approach failed.

In addition to the resources provided for general publicity operations by established political and support offices, there are informal coalitions of staff members presidents can call upon to deal with particular publicity programs. Because publicity is recognized as an important function by almost all White House officials, most of the staff, including those only temporarily involved, usually bring some knowledge or experience in the campaigns they are expected to manage. Both prominent advisers and lower echelon staff work in all types of publicity projects.

It is difficult to determine exactly what portion of the White House staff is engaged regularly in activities that involve media strategies. A high-ranking official in the Ford administration estimated that more than 60 percent of the political staff in the White House were used in promoting and publicizing the President.[7] A congressional staff assistant who has evaluated White House organizations in the postwar period estimates that 85 percent of those working in the White House, including those in policy-making and service roles, are involved directly in public relations activities.[8]

Perhaps as accurate an estimate as any of the level of staff participation in media policy may be obtained by examining a list of White House assistants who were making more than $40,000 a year at the beginning of the Carter administration.[9] Of a staff of forty-nine with salaries at that level or above in 1977, fifteen persons, or slightly more than 30 percent, were assigned positions that clearly involved media relations and policy. They were: the press secretary, two deputy press secretaries, two associate press secretaries, the press secretary to the First Lady, the chief speechwriter, the special assistant for media and public affairs, the director of White House projects, three staff members involved in public liaison, and three staff members who dealt with appointments and scheduling. Since 1977 several new high-level positions have been created, including that of the director and deputy of the Office of the Assistant to the President for Communications. Other positions have been upgraded. Thus the estimate of 30 percent of high-level staff is probably a low figure.

Although incumbent White House officials usually are reluctant to admit the full extent of the resources they commit to publicity programs, there is no question that throughout the 1960s and 1970s more of them performed a growing number of media-related communications functions on a regular basis. They created offices and hired personnel to further the three central publicity functions—direct press operations, planning and coordinating communications operations, and promotional operations—that make possible the continuation of effective White House political communication.

Direct Press Operations

During the summer of 1976, when the presidential campaign was well underway, the staff assistant in charge of appointments with Jimmy Carter denied a request for an interview with the candidate on the grounds that he had to give priority to reporters for news organizations. Once Carter was elected, he suggested, the press would no longer be given this priority: "We won't need the AP so much anymore."[10]

After the election, the staff recognized the naiveté of downgrading their relations with reporters. Shaping public opinion through the media is a matter of particular concern for an administration during its early days in office, when the press is allowing itself to be used as a clear channel for the President's ideas and image. "Trying to put your spin on the ball starts from the beginning," a Ford administration official suggested. "The press swallows it for a period of time, and then tactics change."[11]

The Press Office is the funnel through which most major items of information pass to the media. By deciding how information will be released and, to whom it will be given, the staff influences what news appears. It provides the stages from which news is announced, decides who will be in the audience, and chooses who will present information and answer questions. In this chapter the Press Office is considered as one part of the overall publicity efforts of the White House. Chapter 5 presents a more detailed analysis of the activities of the press secretary and his administration of the Press Office.

THE WEST WING PRESS OFFICE

The West Wing Press Office, which handles most regular contact with reporters, performs the functions that generate the stories and pictures that appear in the media. The staff posts schedules and announcements about White House activities that will be available for coverage by all reporters or by a pool, when briefings will be held, and what press releases or other documents will be available. The press secretary or one of his assistants answers reporters' questions throughout the day. When a correspondent cannot reach a member of the White House staff, Press Office aides often are able to convince the official to speak with the reporter.

Reporters and other media people are admitted to White House press facilities after they are approved by the Press Office and the Secret Service. In order to receive a White House press pass, the hallmark of the White House regulars, a journalist must: (1) work for a news organization with a Washington bureau; (2) be certified by the organization's news executives as a regular correspondent, photographer, or a member of a television crew; (3) demonstrate the need to be at the White House on a daily basis; (4) live in the Washington area; and (5) be a member of the congressional press gallery. Until 1976 the Secret Service could deny access to the White House without stating reasons. The courts held in the case of *Sherrill v. Knight*, however, that this arbitrary power was improper. The Secret Service still checks the backgrounds of applicants for possible security problems, but it must present reasons if it denies issuance of a pass.

In practice many journalists have press credentials even though they do not meet the five standards. On occasion Press Office officials have tried to limit the number of reporters who desire entry by enforcing the standards strictly. In practice they invariably cave in to press pressure, especially if it comes from an important individual or news organization.

The West Wing Press Office is reached by passing through the West White House gate on Pennsylvania Avenue, which is next to the Executive Office Building. White House guards press an electronic release to let in regulars after they show their credentials. Visitors to the office must stop at the gate and have their right to enter verified by the guards, a process that usually takes several minutes. Guards expect the visitor who enters to pass, without stopping along the driveway, to a low building that connects the West Wing with the main part of the White House. In the central portion of this building is the briefing room; reporters' phones and cubicles are in the section closest to the main building; some Press Office staff offices are in the area closest to the West Wing; the press secretary, his deputies, and several assistants are in the West Wing proper. Reporters with White House credentials may pass freely throughout this entire area, including the passage to the press secretary's office in the West Wing. All others are restricted to the lower-level areas.

Three assistant press secretaries, a press aide, and several secretaries occupy the lower-level enclosure, which is partitioned into three tiny offices and a somewhat larger secretarial room. These offices have the distinction of being the only section of the White House a passerby may enter without being observed by a guard or accompanied by an employee. Because lower West Wing Press Office staff ordinarily deal with routine information concerning the activities of the President, others in the White House refer to their activities as "the care and feeding of the White House press corps." Their actual responsibilities include serving as administration spokespersons, however, as they often are asked to give the White House view of a particular event by reporters who cannot get to the press secretary. Furthermore, since they possess bits and pieces of information that form segments of larger stories, some White House reporters find it valuable to cultivate them as sources. John Osborne, author of the widely read "White House Watch" column in the *New Republic*, has often plumbed these and other inconspicuous members of the staff for the remarkable depth of detail he uses in his stories explaining what's going on in the administration.

The press secretary, his deputies, and other staff are located in offices in the upper level of the West Wing perhaps five yards from the Oval Office. The press secretary has been one of the most important presidential assistants in several recent administrations, and the position is always significant—even when the occupant is not influential. Until the 1960s most publicity operations were managed by him and his staff of less than a dozen people. Even though he now shares responsibility for publicity with several presidential advisers, he still plays the central role in managing the White House's relations with reporters.

Although the status and position of the press secretary varies from administration to administration depending on the incumbent's relations with the President, there are three types of responsibilities that the office always is expected to meet: first, the Press Office is the clearinghouse of information from the White House to news organizations with representatives in Washington; second, it provides services necessary to news organizations that cover the President; third, it transmits information from the media to the President and his main assistants.

The Press Office as clearinghouse. The press secretary, together with the President, other senior staff members, and his own deputies and assistants, decides what information will be released and what forums are suitable to its release. Their main stage is the daily briefing, which, as the locale for the public airing of grievances, disputes, and bad feelings, is a source of tension between reporters and the White House. The briefing "produces misinformation," said Ronald Nessen of the Ford administration. "It produces stories where there is no news.''[12] To deal with this problem, argued George Christian of the Johnson administration, the Press Office should ''constantly try to develop more information'' and thus transform the briefing into a ''reportorial session where you legitimately give them as much as you possibly can.''[13] Information, or facts about an event, is not the cause of briefing conflicts; rather, they involve activities of the President that the White House does not want to explain to reporters' satisfaction.

The press secretary sometimes brings members of the White House staff to the daily briefings to answer questions on a particular policy that is announced that day. On other occasions the Press Office arranges special briefings at which senior staff persons explain wide-ranging issues and major policy developments. In the Johnson administration Press Secretary George Christian regularly had Walt Rostow of the National Security Council brief the press on Vietnam, while Joseph Califano answered questions on the ''Great Society's'' domestic programs and plans. Special briefings are held at regular intervals. At the beginning of the year, when the budget is to be released, the White House holds a briefing at which economic specialists from the White House staff and the Office of Management and Budget explain budget items and answer questions. The State of the Union address usually is preceded by a briefing where White House specialists answer questions about the President's legislative program. Frequently these special briefings are more satisfying than the daily briefing, both to the White House and to reporters, because they focus on questions whose answers provide benefits for both sides, such as what the budget includes for housing or defense. At the daily briefing the press secretary may be asked if the President knows about a particular housing problem, how he intends to solve it, and if he will punish the responsible parties.

The press secretary and his deputies make recommendations on who should speak to reporters at these briefings and which staff members should attend. The Press Office also arranges special briefings for reporters from television, major national publications, or news organizations whose interests in the story mesh with the purposes the White House hopes to serve by offering them information and explanations from prominent officials.

The Press Office as service operation for the press. The Press Office facilitates coverage of the President by offering facilities for reporters, photographers, and crew, through its sensitivity to the deadlines of news organizations, and, most important, by providing factual and interpretive background information to reporters. Press officers arrange for regular contacts between the President and the press at press conferences, at ceremonies, and in the briefing room or Oval Office, where the President makes statements. When the President travels outside of Washington, they make arrangements for both coverage and quick communications with news offices. If only a few reporters can accompany the President, they establish a pool.

The Press Office's primary service function is to provide a daily flow of information to reporters. George Reedy described why this is important in a memorandum to Lyndon Johnson, a president who often was insensitive to the routines of reporters and their news organizations.

1. The only thing that is really important about a press operation is that it be believable. When the press is satisfied that it is getting straight answers, even if it does not like the answers, everything has been accomplished that can be accomplished by the press office.
2. Believability is achieved primarily by attention to a number of relatively trivial details. Fundamentally, these divided into two elements:
   A. A straightforward recital of facts by the press office with no *apparent* effort to highlight those which are favorable and to mute those which are unpleasant.
   B. The establishment of a reasonable routine in regard to briefings, travel and press conferences. (Newspapermen are much more conservative in their personal habits than they will admit even to themselves. Therefore, variations in routine and unexpected happenings give them the impression of trickery and creates an attitude of disbelief.) [14]

The Press Office as transmitter of press information. The Press Office gathers intelligence for the President and his staff. White House officials want to find out what reporters know and what they are going to want to know. Staff members read the transcript of the press secretary's briefing, Richard Cheney of the Ford administration said, because it gave them "a feel for what is on the minds of the press."[15] President Johnson requested reports from his aides and the cabinet on their contacts with reporters, according to George Christian, because he needed to know "what the press was asking the staff."[16]

The questions reporters ask serve as an early warning system of potential troubles for the White House and thus may indicate the need to change a decision. This is because after publication or broadcast of an item new groups become aware of its importance to them and thus demand to be heard. By listening to reporters' questions, for example, the Carter administration could have learned in late 1977 that if David Marston, a U.S. attorney who was investigating two Democratic congressmen, was fired, the news would be widely broadcast and have important political consequences. Forecasts obtained early in the development of a story make it possible to maintain options that later might be lost. The press "affected what you did," George Christian commented. "Decisions were made because of it and you didn't do things because of it."[17]

Direct exchanges between reporters and the Press Office provide stories for reporters and intelligence for the White House. Officials try to mine a reporter's knowledge of Washington personalities and institutions so they can learn of political and policy possibilities that the White House had not previously considered. Press Office staff may give a reporter advance notice of a story in exchange for information about important activities not clearly visible to

White House officials. "We just sit there and talk; it's interesting," commented John Carlson of the Ford administration Press Office. "These people are pros who have been in politics for twenty years, and it's interesting feedback."[18]

OFFICE OF MEDIA LIAISON

Media Liaison had been known as the Office of Communications from 1969, the time of its creation by the Nixon administration, until 1977, when the Carter administration adopted the present name. The office's establishment demonstrated the White House's recognition of the importance to the President of the non-Washington-based media, including regional, ethnic, and other specialized publications or broadcasting outlets. In contrast to the West Wing Press Office, which ordinarily deals with individual correspondents who need information and access on a regular basis, Media Liaison usually works with editors, publishers, producers, network executives, and journalists in their capacity as representatives of news organizations.

Because it is so young and because it had no formal predecessors, the office's direction at any given time has varied according to the status and authority its heads have had in the White House hierarchy. During the Nixon and Ford administrations the office exercised important communications coordination functions. These later were placed under the jurisdiction of the new assistant for communications, a position created by President Carter in 1978 for his public relations adviser, Gerald Rafshoon. The main tasks of the office, however, involve direct press operations that serve to build ties from the White House to local news organizations.

The origins of the office. Even before they considered establishing such an office, White House officials knew the benefits a president derives from making himself available to news organizations that usually do not have access to him. During the Eisenhower, Kennedy, and Johnson administrations presidents and other officials often noted the contrast between regional and national media stories. Bill Moyers summarized the advantages in a memorandum to President Johnson: "When the President chooses a locale outside of Washington to talk about world affairs or domestic issues, the regional newspapers give it extra play. The President has favored them by making his pronouncements in their area, and whatever he says is bound to be accepted much more favorably."[19] Moyers recommended that the President leave Washington each month for at least two speaking engagements. Presumably the local media would cover what the President said instead of picking up the story from the national media. "This," he wrote, "would be an especially useful device in explaining our Vietnam policy."[20]

Because he felt that reporters for the national media were unsympathetic to him on Vietnam and most other issues, Richard Nixon created an office to maintain continuous contact with editors, publishers, and other news executives who he believed would be less biased. Nixon appointed as director his longtime press adviser, Herbert Klein, a former director of the American Society of Newspaper Editors. "Nixon knew how to maximize relations with the press," commented David Gergen, a Nixon speechwriter and director of the Office of Communications under Ford. He wanted "other outlets—editors and publishers outside of Washington were more favorable."[21]

Klein spent a great deal of his time explaining the administration's positions to editors and publishers in speeches and private meetings in their home communities. He found that most news organizations responded to attention from the White House by providing generous coverage of his remarks, by using some of the story ideas that he suggested, and, in some cases, by printing or broadcasting editorials and comments prepared by the Office of Communications. Sometimes these materials were presented without any indication that they had been prepared by administration staff.

Although Nixon's motives may have been personal and partisan, the need for a mechanism to maintain relations with the nonnational media has been apparent to subsequent administrations. Officials in the Ford and Carter administrations told us that direct efforts to work with executives and non-Washington-based reporters are necessary to get the President's message into the regional and specialty media. Reporters in Washington bureaus tend to have a Washington point of view, as was indicated in the last chapter. Once they have heard and reported on the reasons for a new presidential program, they are more interested in the politics of support and opposition to that program than they are in resummarizing the President's arguments. Yet it takes repetition to get a point across, especially if it is to reach the vast majority of people whose interest and attention span is often short when it comes to Washington events that do not have an immediate effect on their lives. According to James Connor of the Ford administration:

When a President goes to local papers, it is a great big thing to them and it is new. One of the things we learned is that the White House press corps gets tired of conveying the message. Repetition is necessary if the nation is going to understand it. But the White House press is sick and tired of it because they think they have heard nothing but it for weeks. The temptation is to think that they have conveyed a message to the nation because, by God, we reported a speech on this and an interview, and boy we really handled that one. Then we in the White House look at an opinion poll and find that two percent of the population has heard about the damn thing. But in the environment of the White House you have heard nothing else but this, and if you hear it one more time you are going to scream.[22]

Conferences and meetings. All three administrations have used Media Liaison to arrange special conferences and meetings for invited representatives of news organizations. The White House press is either excluded or limited to observing. The guests frequently begin their day with the staff from Media Liaison, which occupies a suite of rooms on the street level of the

Executive Office Building. The spacious office of the director includes a conference table at which visiting media executives may be briefed or entertained prior to being taken to a meeting with the President or another high government official.

During the Nixon and Ford administrations meetings and conferences were scheduled intermittently. Carter promised to meet twenty times a year at biweekly intervals with groups invited by Media Liaison. Television and radio representatives may attend these meetings but not record them. Peter Jay, a columnist for the *Baltimore Sun*, described a schedule of meetings for approximately thirty "regional correspondents" that was held near the end of October, 1977.[23] The day began with a one-hour session on foreign policy with Zbigniew Brzezinski and the deputy director of the National Security Council, David Aaron. This was followed by a forty-five-minute session with the assistant attorney general for civil rights, forty-five minutes with a State Department officer on the Panama Canal Treaty, lunch with a staff member in the White House Office of the Assistant to the President for Congressional Liaison, a forty-minute conference with the President in the cabinet room, and an hour with an official of the Department of Energy. Jay described the questions as "serious and intelligent." The President, he suggested, "was responsive, friendly, and characteristically well-informed, but said nothing that would come as a surprise to any moderately thorough reader of [the *Sun*] or any other major newspaper." Jay concluded that "the session was clearly well intentioned and had to be at least marginally useful both to the Carter Administration and [to] the invited journalists."[24]

Media mailings. The Nixon, Ford, and Carter administrations have used Media Liaison to prepare or reproduce articles of current interest for mailings to news organizations and interest groups throughout the country. During the Nixon administration the mailings were often of an extremely partisan nature, defending the administration against its critics and celebrating the President's triumphs. The office both bought mailing lists commercially and acquired them free through public sources. "There are 150,000 legal ways of getting a mailing list," William Rhatican noted.[25] Rhatican, an assistant to Charles Colson during the Nixon administration and deputy director of the Office of Communications for Ford, described the mailings as an elaborate, well-organized operation. Ultimately, Director Herbert Klein asked that the Republican National Committee rather than the White House pay for the mailings because, as he later explained to Patricia Bario of the Carter administration, the partisan nature of the mailings could have created trouble for them.[26]

During the Ford and Carter administrations the mailings continued at a slightly slower pace and contained materials that were less overtly partisan. "With the new campaign laws, you didn't have access to the large contributions which you need to do this kind of mailing," Rhatican commented.[27] Patricia Bario of the Carter administration said that they did not consider the materials they sent out to be partisan at all, although she admitted that the White House position on an issue would be fully presented in any document.

A White House memorandum to Bario dated September 20, 1978, summarized the 21 items that had been sent from the White House during the previous month. Five items appeared to be "backgrounders," explaining issues such as inflation, aviation policy, and hospital cost containment. These were sent to the entire mailing list, which consisted of 6,500 news organizations, interest groups, and individuals. Three items were sent to a list of 525, which included columnists and large dailies, newspapers with a circulation of more than 100,000. Six items, including transcripts of briefings and photographs, were sent to 110 Jewish media outlets (September, 1978, was the month of the Camp David meetings that President Carter had with Egyptian President Anwar Sadat and Israeli Prime Minister Menachem Begin). Three were sent to a black media list of 260, 2 to a Hispanic media list of 350, and 1 to a Greek media list of 15. Altogether 36,120 pieces were sent out during the month, 260 of them photos and 700 of them in Spanish. This total was slightly above the June through September monthly average of 35,551 items.[28]

Planning and Coordinating Communications Operations

Presidents and their advisers prefer to run assertive programs to sell themselves and their policies rather than spend their time responding to the events of the day. James Hagerty noted in his diary that Eisenhower "hoped I could get freer so that I could start fires rather than have to put them out all the time."[29] The obstacle for Hagerty, however, as for any press secretary, was that his time was taken up by the daily requirements of media relations. Consequently, even a well-ordered staff system such as the Eisenhower administration's was not equal to the task. Although concerned with problems of publicity and media relations, the Democratic administrations that followed Eisenhower were neither management oriented nor schooled in public relations approaches.

Kennedy and Johnson and their staffs developed a large number of ad hoc White House arrangements to deal with the media, but they never succeeded in successfully integrating these arrangements with the general policy objectives of their administrations. Officials with a media responsibility often did not become involved in publicity operations that were not part of their routine activities. For example, Pierre Salinger played only a small role in the Kennedy administration's publicity campaign to mobilize support for the Trade Expansion Act of 1962; in fact, President Kennedy chose the campaign's coordinator from outside the White House.[30] Lyndon Johnson discovered that his successful efforts to control political communications as Senate Majority Leader during the 1950s could not be transplanted to the White House.

Effective and continuous planning and coordination of publicity operations did not become possible until the White House interest in public relations was joined to a similar interest in the development of White House institutions to perform them. After Richard Nixon was inaugurated in 1969 he established the institutional structure that made it possible to centralize authority over most important publicity campaigns in the White House. Half a dozen aides, reporting directly to the President, could supervise most operations. Their ability to apply technical skills in routine publicity programs as well as in important national efforts gained support for them and made their opponents' task more difficult. In particular, the coordination of all offices that had a communications function enabled them to rally support for the President's goals. The President's senior advisers, along with the Press Office, speechwriters, Congressional Liaison, liaison with editors and publishers, and interest group liaison, worked with each other and directed activities that were conducted outside the White House by party committees, the cabinet, department information officers, and the public relations counsels and lobbyists for interest groups. The President's aides directed groups to concentrate on specific tasks and selected the role each would play in a publicity campaign, thus obtaining a high level of effort from them.

The Nixon White House developed a variety of media plans to deal with most of the major events and issues the administration confronted, from the campaign to sell the President's "Vietnamization" plan during the first term to "Cocktails with Clawson," an effort to distract the media from the Watergate scandal in the weeks before the President resigned. Even though it did not succeed militarily, Vietnamization was a publicity success, contributing to the favorable approval rating for foreign policy the President received as expressed in the polls and in his large electoral victory of 1972. "Cocktails with Clawson" and other publicity campaigns to combat Watergate failed because they could not overcome the relentless outpouring of unfavorable news from the special prosecutor's office, the courts, and the House Judiciary Committee. Still, in addition to Vietnamization, the administration scored a number of impressive policy victories in important areas in part because of their publicity programs. Coordination of White House publicity resources contributed greatly to these programs.

In contrast to the staff that worked for Democratic administrations from Roosevelt through Johnson, high-ranking advisers in the Nixon administration had a strong orientation toward management techniques, including public relations, as an approach to solving problems. Nixon's chief of operations, H. R. Haldeman, the former West Coast manager of the J. Walter Thompson advertising firm, kept the staff aware of publicity plans. In one of his frequent memoranda, Haldeman indicated some of the concerns that were important to the White House in planning publicity programs: "One point that's missing in our general planning for the week's attack, etc., is a projection for the coming week as to what we anticipate will be the major opposition attacks, so that we can plan our statements and activities with those in mind."[31]

The Carter staff was more management oriented than its Democratic predecessors, perhaps sharing the engineering and business outlook of the President. It reorganized some operations, eliminated others, and changed some names—neither the Office of Communications nor the Editorial Department could be found in the White House directory in 1977, although most of their former functions were performed elsewhere. Most important from a managerial point of view, Carter established the Office of the Assistant to the President for Communications to coordinate White House publicity activities.

THE PRESIDENT'S SENIOR POLITICAL ADVISERS

The President's senior advisers are a group of high-level assistants whose loyalty and interests belong to the President. The power and status of each individual lies less in his title than in his personal relationship with the Chief Executive. Those who have regular access to the President and are in the top salary range of White House assistants, such as the heads of the Press Office, and Congressional Liaison, are usually in this group. The heads of the National Security Council, Domestic Policy, and the White House counsel and the secretary to the cabinet are called upon to participate in decisions that involve their areas. The senior advisers are important in part because they bring to the President's attention the publicity consequences of his decisions.

These advisers play three central roles in planning and coordinating communications operations. They approve the plans for publicity programs after consulting with the President; they establish the priorities for such programs based on how likely it is that a particular campaign will get the President's message to its intended audience without excessive cost; and they decide how much time and effort the President must devote for the program to be successful. Presidents are involved in the most fundamental of these decisions, such as the creation of the position of assistant for communications by President Carter in 1978. They also may veto suggestions that they find unpalatable, as did President Nixon, who rejected staff suggestions that he meet more frequently with reporters.[32] Usually, however, the extent of his participation depends on his interest in the operation. Nixon was always interested and frequently participated in the details of planning; Ford was kept well informed; Carter apparently did not participate on his own initiative. "I'm not sure the President knows what I do with my time," Jody Powell told interviewers. "I'd be interested in finding out if he does."[33]

The Nixon-Ford staffs. Nixon's senior advisers brought to the coordination of publicity operations the same high level of efficiency and discipline that they brought to all staff operations. The President himself made it clear how the staff was to operate. In a series of eight memoranda the President wrote to H. R. Haldeman in September, 1969, he discussed the role each individual on the staff was to play in public relations, explained the tactics he wanted them to use, and demanded reports in which he would "be informed as to what action has been taken and, if action is not taken, why the decision has been made not to take it.'"[34]

A group of senior advisers and their surrogates met on Monday, Wednesday, and Friday to map out publicity plans for the days and weeks ahead. This planning group included Ronald Ziegler, the press secretary; Herbert Klein, the director of the Office of Communications; Patrick Buchanan of the Editorial Department; Charles Colson, who was in charge of special projects; and other senior staff advisers whose areas were likely to be subjects of discussion. Some of the other regular participants were: Dwight Chapin, who was involved with the President's schedule, John Ehrlichman or Ken Cole from the Domestic Council, and William Safire, a speechwriter. "The purpose of the group was to plan the public activities of the President," said William Safire, "and to see that Administration figures were lined up to make news in an orderly fashion—that is, no two major stories purposely broken on the same day, or if a bad story was due, to try and smother it with other news.'"[35] The group was instructed to plan long-range publicity efforts. "I know this is a subject that troubles all of us," the President wrote, "but I do not want to continue to slide along with what I fear is an inadequate response, and an amateurish response to what will be an enormous challenge in the next two or three months.'"[36] It was this group that was responsible for the plans for many of the major campaigns engineered by the Nixon White House. One of the most successful was the effort to gain support for legislation to sponsor development of an anti-ballistic missile. This project, coordinated and administered by Charles Colson, is described in detail later in this chapter.

Approximately one-third of the Ford administration's daily morning meeting of the President's senior advisers was spent on publicity matters.[37] One of the functions of this group was to coordinate White House statements for the press, especially the press secretary's answers to questions at the daily briefing. On other occasions it was decided that high-level officials would meet the press and answer its questions. Such meetings with reporters required senior advisers to formulate and coordinate the answers that would be given to the public. In one three-day period, three such sessions were held. On January 18, 1976, after the President issued an order reorganizing the intelligence operations of the Executive Branch, the senior staff held a press briefing at which Attorney General Edward Levi; National Security Council Adviser Brent Scowcroft; White House Counsellor John Marsh; Director of the CIA George Bush; and White House aide Michael Raoul-Duval made statements and answered questions. The next day, prior to the State of the Union Address, another briefing was held at which the head of the Council of Economic Advisers, the budget director, and several White House staff members appeared for the same purposes. On January 20, President Ford appeared with his entire cabinet at a briefing on his budget.

The Carter staff. The publicity operations of President Carter's political staff advisers have been similar structurally to those of the Nixon and Ford administrations. Unlike the situation that prevailed in earlier Democratic administrations, relatively few of the President's closest aides are responsible for publicity matters and speak with unchallenged authority in that area. A publicity triumvirate consisting of Press Secretary Jody Powell, assistant for communications Gerald Rafshoon, and senior political adviser Hamilton Jordan has been with Carter since he became prominent in Georgia politics in the mid-1960s. Their long relationship with the President placed them on a different footing from other members of the staff, who ordinarily took part in publicity operations only when invited or when a matter central to their responsibilities arises. Since the power relationships were well established, there was not the jockeying to get into meetings or become involved in important activities that there was during the Nixon and Ford administrations. "All of us are secure in our relationship with Carter," observed Hamilton Jordan. "We don't have to compete for his time or attention. As a result, we are remarkably free from friction."[38]

Carter staffers shared a clear understanding of who was in charge of what. Powell, as press secretary, was responsible for handling reporters. Gerald Rafshoon dealt with long-range planning and coordination of publicity between the White House and external organizations such as the Democratic National Committee. Hamilton Jordan, however, had more loosely defined responsibilities. "I want to be involved in less things rather than more," he said. "I get involved when there is a problem." [39] Jordan was responsible for developing the line of approach the White House took in response to both short- and long-term problems he has identified. For example, he designed a series of task forces to marshal support and coordinate the public and political pressures in favor of the Panama Canal Treaty, the Strategic Arms Limitation Treaty, civil service reform, hospital cost containment, and the establishment of departments of natural resources and education. Each task force was directed by a White House assistant responsible to Jordan.

At the beginning of the administration five senior advisers met with the President each Monday. As more staff sought to attend, the meetings became so large and discussion so general that the original principals sent their deputies as surrogates. By the middle of the term the senior advisers were meeting twice a month on a less regular schedule. Still, according to Gerald Rafshoon, the publicity triumvirate usually met or spoke with each other every day.

Scheduling in three administrations. Scheduling has been a critical publicity activity for senior staff in the Nixon, Ford, and Carter administrations. When they recommend how the President should spend his time—where he will go, whom he will see, and what he will do—the message these activities will communicate through the media is uppermost in their minds. One official in

the Ford administration said that what the President "did and all the things
that he planned, all of these symbolic events, is the way the President communicates what he does."[40] When asked if he saw scheduling as critical to his
job of coordinating communications operations, Gerald Rafshoon replied,
"Oh God, yes."[41] Even before he took office, Jody Powell emphasized the
importance of scheduling to members of the staff. "If you aren't in on it, you
might as well go home," he said.[42] A list covering the next two weeks of the
President's activities is circulated to important advisers for comment, and a
regular meeting is held each Friday to plot his schedule. According to former
speechwriter James Fallows this meeting is attended by "someone from every
branch of the empire who has an interest in what is coming up."[43]

THE OFFICE OF THE ASSISTANT FOR COMMUNICATION

A President's desire to assign one trusted adviser the responsibility for
coordinating, administering, and participating in planning strategy for all
political communications often is frustrated by his own doubts or those of his
staff. Most presidents won't let go of publicity operations because they involve their reputation as a leader. Also, finding suitable candidates is difficult
because the job requires professional status and experience in handling major
public relations projects as well as personal loyalty. (For this reason, it is
easier to make substantive area appointments such as national security adviser
or director of the Office of Management and Budget.) Finally, other staff
members resist this kind of appointment. The Press Office staff in particular
does not want an outsider to tell it how to deal with the media. These obstacles
prevented creation of a position to coordinate public relations during the
Eisenhower, Kennedy, and Johnson administrations. James Hagerty protected
his turf by containing the authority of Howard Pyle, the former governor of
Arizona who was appointed to run publicity programs in the Eisenhower
White House. John Kennedy believed that his instinctive sense for public
relations and his knowledge of how the media worked made delegation of
these responsibilities undesirable. Although Lyndon Johnson wanted a public
relations "genius" to do for him what he assumed Pierre Salinger had done
for Kennedy, he was afraid that if he let subordinates such as Robert Kintner
get "too big," they would become a threat to him.[44]

Throughout his five and a half years as president, Richard Nixon tried to
find someone whose management of political communications would make it
possible to mobilize White House publicity resources. Nixon, who had the
best sense of the managerial aspects of political communications of any recent
president, established a number of offices to administer and coordinate publicity activities. He created the Office of Communication as an instrument for
long-range planning and linkage to the executives of news organizations.
Nixon created the Editorial Department to develop themes, targets, and the
ability to respond to criticism. In this office he had individuals who wrote
speeches, developed political response themes for White House mail, com-

piled a daily summary of what appeared in the media, and performed research activities such as investigating and publicizing some of the less popular activities of the President's political opponents.

In a memorandum to H. R. Haldeman, Nixon expressed both his desire to bring a high-level White House assistant to coordinate White House relations and his unhappiness that there didn't seem to be a logical candidate for the job. "I have reached the conclusion that we simply have to have that full-time PR Director," he wrote. This director should "have no other assignments except to bulldog these three or four major issues we may select each week or each month and follow through on directives that I give, but, more importantly, come up with ideas of his own.'"[45]

In the Ford administration staff rivalries made it difficult for it to work well together until the year before the election, when a group headed by Chief of Staff Richard Cheney took command. In the spring of 1976 he cut off Press Office influence over major publicity decisions. He persuaded President Ford to appoint David Gergen and William Rhatican as director and assistant director of the Office of Communications, which from that time until the election coordinated personal publicity about the President but not about substantive policy areas. The success of their efforts is not generally recognized because even though President Ford won a difficult renomination battle against a more popular opponent and cut candidate Carter's 30 percent lead in the polls down to 1 percent, he lost in the presidential election.

Jimmy Carter's appointment of an assistant for communications in July, 1978, suggests that he succeeded where other presidents failed. He gave overall authority over political communications to Gerald Rafshoon, who had worked with him since his first gubernatorial campaign in Georgia in 1966. Rafshoon's loyalty to Carter was not in doubt, and his talents and skills in public relations on the national level had been tested when he promoted and ran the political advertising for Carter's successful 1976 campaign. Whether his success in creating the position solved his communications problem was doubtful. Carter's personal inability to communicate the ideas and commitments of his presidency continued to plague him, in spite of Rafshoon's organizational abilities.

Rafshoon's standing with the President and with his closest White House political associates made it clear to others in the White House that they had to accept his authority. Jordan had urged that Rafshoon be brought to the staff, and Powell agreed that it might be useful. As long as he maintained support from these two advisers, Rafshoon would be safe from sniping by others on the staff. Together with Powell and Jordan, he formed the publicity triumvirate of the administration. Jordan, the "idea man," formulated political plans; Powell dealt with the ongoing relationship with the media; Rafshoon tried to put everything together.

Rafshoon's appointment was part of a shake-up implemented by the President after a staff meeting at Camp David during the spring of 1978 recommended important changes to improve the administration's flagging reputation with influentials in the Washington community and the public at large. Like its predecessors in other administrations, Carter's staff felt it had a communications problem. Even more than its predecessors, it was right in its belief that it had failed to communicate the essence of what the President intended to do and why he wanted to do it. Some reporters indicated that the administration was trying to convince itself that its real failures were public relations problems or matters of presidential style. "With Pavlovian redundancy, White House spokesmen report that Rafshoon was drafted to get the President's story across to the public and to accentuate the administration's positive achievements, instead of the negative aspects as portrayed by the news media," Dom Bonafede wrote in the *National Journal* a few weeks after the appointment.[46] Even after the President's foreign policy triumph at Camp David, Bonafede remained dubious. "The perception of Jimmy Carter and his White House has been etched in rock," he wrote, "and, even though he will predictably regain some points in the polls, it is unlikely that there will be a complete turnabout in public opinion."[47]

Getting the White House to speak with one voice. Presidents and their chief advisers believe that one reason the media often present dissonant and uncoordinated images of the administration is that officials give differing emphases to problems in interviews, speeches, and other public settings. Consequently the assistant for communications was expected to find ways to make the various voices support each other. Rafshoon described what he was trying to do:

We don't send out conflicting signals as much as we used to. We coordinate media appearances with cabinet members and members of the White House staff. The President is doing more one on one interviews, inviting news executives, columnists and others from the media to dinner. We develop the talking points that he can use on particular priority issues . . . . Where Jody has to worry about the day to day press operation, I have the luxury of going to the President and saying, "here is our plan for inflation. You are going to make a talk to businessmen today. Why don't we have columnist A in there to talk to you for a few minutes on background."[48]

Rafshoon took steps to get all who speak for the White House to give the same message to the media. He controlled the schedule of speeches so that if the President's theme at the time was energy, a speech on health would not steal headlines away. He also coordinated the timing of public appearances and statements so that they would bring the maximum impact, and he urged the staff and executive department officials to prevent superfluous matters from distracting the media from the main event.

However, Rafshoon could not control the President. At the beginning of a two-week period in June, 1979, for example, the President met with a congressional delegation to try to rally its support for an expected close vote on the implementation of the Panama Canal Treaty. The meeting was part of a well-coordinated effort by several White House offices. In the course of it, Carter told two congressmen that he would "whip his [Senator Kennedy's] ass" if the latter tried to run against him. This statement became the big story on the evening news. The next day the administration asked to postpone the vote on the treaty because it still lacked the needed votes. The day after that, while Panama was still up in the air, the President introduced his proposals for national health insurance. Before any campaign could be launched to back his legislation, the President left for Vienna to sign the SALT agreements. When he returned he addressed Congress and the nation on the subject of SALT, which he described as an essential step for peace and security. The President's next appearance on the news took place the following day, when he spoke at a ceremony after the completion of a solar panel for the White House hot water system. There he urged the nation to give its attention to this important alternative to oil. Three days later he left for a world economic conference.

Not every discordant item on this schedule can be blamed on the President's insensitivity to the requirements of effective political communication. There are so many demands on him to speak, appear, and attend meetings that it would be impossible to organize a completely integrated schedule. Furthermore, the White House did have extensive follow-up plans to gather support for SALT and Panama. Nevertheless, potential supporters as well as fence-sitters might be uncertain as to whether the President would strongly commit himself to any of these programs.

Coordination. The assistant for communications provides the links between the outlets the White House uses to supply information to the media and the offices that promote the President. Among the information outlets are press conferences, briefings, interviews, press releases, speeches by the President, and speeches by those who speak for the President, such as the vice president, the First Lady, the national security adviser, and the economic advisers. Among the groups that promote the President are the Press Office, the speechwriters, the advance units, and the several offices that try to influence interest groups. The purpose of coordination is to force the energies of the offices through the channels of the outlets.

Perhaps the most important type of coordination managed by the assistant for communications involved organizing ad hoc efforts to meet specific problems or lobby for particular policies. The mode of the Carter administration was to form task forces to work toward such goals as government reorganization, welfare reform, national health insurance, and tax reform. Although some task forces were formed to show responsiveness to interest groups that require stroking, many others are operational. The assistant for special projects sat with these task forces and provided information to Rafshoon on how the activities of a particular group fit in with the activities of all.

In addition to his role as coordinator, Rafshoon was television adviser to the

President, a function handled by a separate office known as Media and Public Affairs before he took office. His direct administrative responsibilities included the units of speechwriters and of media advance. These three activities are discussed in the section on promotional operations.

Strategy. Rafshoon also played an important role in advising the President on how his policies should be presented to the media, special groups, and the public, as well as on the steps the White House should take to gather support. After he joined the staff, Rafshoon convinced the President to entertain elite journalists such as bureau chiefs, anchorpersons, columnists, editors, and other managers at small, off-the-record White House dinners. He also put a lot of effort into special projects that he felt would enhance the administration's reputation. For example, a memorandum obtained by the *New York Times* showed that during the spring of 1979 Rafshoon "compiled a master list of prominent opinion makers inside and outside the Government who can be used to rebut editorial and public criticism of the President's policies." The *Times* quoted Rafshoon as describing the list as "a ready mechanism to respond to misleading and inaccurate reports of statements about Administration programs and actions."[49]

These kinds of efforts bore fruit during the fall of 1978 in a successful campaign, coordinated and directed in the White House, to mobilize support for President Carter's veto of a water projects bill. This is usually an undefeatable measure because members of Congress perceive it to be vital to their political survival. According to an account published in the *National Journal*, the White House Domestic Policy Staff, the Interior Department, and the Army Corps of Engineers compiled a thick factbook that information officers could use to explain why the President opposed each of the twenty-seven projects. Public Liaison staff urged environmental and business groups likely to oppose the projects on ecological or economic grounds to rally congressional support for the President's veto. The Media Liaison operation mailed information on the projects to 1,750 newspapers, 500 radio and television stations, and 200 columnists. It also arranged for videotaped interviews with the secretary and deputy undersecretary of the army and an assistant secretary of the interior to be sent to local stations throughout the country. In addition, the White House intergovernmental relations staff lobbied governors for the veto. The President was sustained by a fifty-three–vote margin.[50]

PRESS OFFICE COORDINATION

Since Franklin Roosevelt's administration the press secretary has tried to assert authority over the public information officers of cabinet departments in order to coordinate their publicity activities with those of the White House. Typically, the press secretary clears their initial appointments, keeps in touch with individual PIOs to find out what news is likely to come out of their departments, and meets with them as a group so that they will be aware of

White House policy. For example, if a cabinet officer is about to hold a press conference, the PIO is expected to brief the Press Office about what is likely to come out. If an issue such as health care or the economy becomes an important news item, one of the assistant press secretaries gets on the phone with the relevant department PIOs so that the same position is described at each briefing. During the Nixon and Ford administrations the assistant press secretary for national security affairs held routine daily conference calls with the PIOs from State and Defense both before and after the press secretary's briefing.

The endemic conflict between the Press Office and the PIOs parallels that between cabinet officials and the President. The press secretary or his deputy gets the message to the department PIO if the White House thinks that either he or the secretary has "wandered off the reservation." Gerald Rafshoon suggested that unless the press secretary takes preventive steps at the beginning of an administration, some of the cabinet-level PIOs inevitably will make trouble for the White House: "It just got to the point where you know they are going to outlast us. We had these PIO meetings and I got to the point where I knew they were going to go back to their departments and ignore everything. They have different priorities. They think survival. They are interested in survival in Washington. They don't always have the same priorities as the administration. If I had been here in the beginning, I would have formed the PIO's from our organization. To me there's only one name that's going to be on the ballot, Jimmy Carter."[51]

As the only official assured of daily meetings with the President, the press secretary is in the best position to know what the President thinks should be presented to the public. Prior to the appointment of an assistant for communications, the Press Office was responsible for coordinating information within the White House. The press secretary attended the planning meetings in the Nixon administration and of the senior staff in the Ford administration. Powell attended those meetings before Rafshoon's appointment and continued to do so when he felt it was necessary thereafter. Strong press secretaries such as Powell will continue to play a major role in coordinating political communications because their relationship with the media is more important than that of any other White House adviser. Powell has an important voice in planning coordination, but he has almost none in administering it.

THE WHITE HOUSE NEWS SUMMARY

The White House News Summary keeps the President informed about the coverage the media give to his administration, provides items for his agenda, gives the staff an additional means of legitimizing their activities, and allows readers of the summary to learn whether the President is aware of certain items. The five members of the News Summary staff want to give the President a picture of what is appearing about him in publications and broadcasts. The summary includes a sampling of important stories, editorials, columns, and comment from national, local, and specialized news organizations. Although the summary's format is designed with one reader in mind, its distribution to 175 individuals and offices in the White House and throughout the Executive Branch gives it greater significance.

Keeping the President informed. Both the organizational structure of the staff and the organizational format of the news summary have changed in each of the last three administrations in response to the President's notion of how he should be kept informed about what appears in the media. Patrick Buchanan, who originated the news summary for the Nixon administration, organized it as part of the Editorial Department, one of the major communications and public relations resources of the Nixon White House. According to an official familiar with its operation, the news summary "was all written in code [words] and was partisan, but that is what they wanted."[52] Both the Ford and Carter administrations strove to make the summary a neutral reflection of what actually appears in the media. This does not mean that White House officials believe that the media provide an accurate or adequate portrayal of what they are doing. "I think that a main purpose of the news summary is to see whether people are understanding what he [the President] is saying and doing," said Claudia Townsend, an assistant press secretary and the first director of the news summary in the Carter administration. "You can tell from a newspaper's editorial coverage if a newspaper knows what a program is all about. We are not as interested in counting up positive and negative reaction as much as we are interested in knowing what is perceived."[53]

The Ford administration organized the news summary by topics or by particular stories. For example, when Sara Jane Moore attempted to assassinate President Ford, the news summary presented excerpts from different stories about the event in the media. The Carter administration organized the summary by categories within the media so that the reader learns what appeared in the wire services, the networks, and the daily newspapers. A separate magazine summary came out once a week.

An agenda for action. Because the news summary provides information about how he is perceived by the media, it also gives the President ideas about where and how he might respond. "I am aware that [President Carter] has seen stories about things that he hasn't liked," Claudia Townsend commented, "and he has moved to do something about it. . . . I think [the news summary] can occasionally alert them to problems or things that they are going to have to deal with."[54] Nixon almost always used the news summary as an agenda for action. According to John Ehrlichman the President made marginal notes on his copy of the news summary indicating what he wished to do in response to what he had read. The copy was then photostated and sent to the top advisers on the staff, often controlling their agenda for the day. Ehrlichman gave as an example the note "Fire this man by 3:00 o'clock

today'' that the President wrote alongside a story about the commissioner of
education, who appeared to be criticizing the administration for its antibusing
stance.[55]

Legitimating news. An item becomes important when it is included in the
news summary because the President almost certainly will read it. Thus staff
members want to receive the summary so they will know what the President
knows. Some members of the staff also would like to use it to mold the
President's thinking by having items in the summary about themselves or their
projects. According to James Shuman of the Ford White House, members of
the staff sent news clippings from newspapers in areas where they had made
speeches. Shuman said that this occurred at least ten times while he was
running the summary, but he did not use them unless they were appropriate.[56]
Getting into the President's news summary became particularly important
during the Nixon administration, an aide recalled:

I suddenly realized from conversations that there was a game of getting placement in
the President's news summary. It wasn't whether it was first place in the *New York
Times*, or the *Washington Post*, or how many words the AP carried. Where was it in
the summary of the news presented to the President every morning? Whether there was
any hanky-panky as to what position you got, I don't know, but that is all you became
concerned with in the White House complex. How was that pet project of yours played
up in the President's news summary?[57]

Reporters also are concerned about the news summary. ''Network people
are interested in knowing how their stories were treated,'' Claudia Townsend
commented, while reporters from the print media ''want to know if their story
was in it.'' The news summary legitimizes officials' belief that the media
make problems rather than reflect them. According to Claudia Townsend,
''It's not so much that they are an early warning system'' for political problems, ''it's that the problem is them.'' [58]

Promotional Operations

Promoting the President means using the powers and resources of the White
House to get each audience that the President wants to reach to focus its
attention on the issue at hand. In the Carter administration promotion campaigns were planned by the senior political advisers, coordinated by the Office
of the Assistant to the President for Communications, administered by ad hoc
groups such as task forces, and supported by permanent operations such as the
speechwriters, the advance and media advance units, media advisers, the
Photo Office, and the offices that provide links between the White House and
special interest groups—the so-called public liaison function.

Promoting a major program for the President requires broad imagination about the use of offices and individuals within the White House, liaison with existing groups elsewhere in the government and the private sector, and the creation of new organizations. All of the elements of a successful program were present in the successful drive by the Nixon White House in support of the Anti-Ballistic Missile system.

PROMOTING THE ABM IN THE NIXON ADMINISTRATION

The Nixon administration ran sophisticated, aggressive, partisan, and successful promotional campaigns for a variety of domestic and foreign policy issues. That they combined these programs with dirty tricks and illegal activities reflected the extremist attitude of the President toward real or potential adversaries, but this should not detract from the very real abilities members of the staff demonstrated in putting together promotional campaigns. Both Ford and Carter administration staff tried to imitate their operations. Though they lacked the Nixonians' malevolence, they also lacked their technical expertise.

The Nixon administration's success with promotion may be attributed to the advertising background of many of the top White House staff members. Still, political programs require a somewhat different organization, as can be seen in an examination of the operation administered by Charles Colson. According to his assistant, William Rhatican, the Colson operation worked in the following manner:

He had a small group of us, there were about five who he would turn to when a particular issue would bubble to the surface. He would call me into the office, for example, and tell me, "Bill, this is the problem that we have," or "this is the issue that we want to solve. I want to see a press plan by close of business today." What he meant by this was a piece of paper, a memorandum from me saying the issue as I understand it is this, whatever it was. The resources available are these. By resources you meant people, departments, agencies, people on the Hill, senators, congressmen, governors, and then outside forces such as the VFW, or the American Legion, or the Jewish War Veterans, or the Catholic War Veterans, or the Chamber of Commerce, or the "National whatever.". . . And I would sit down and I would work up a press line. Chuck would normally tell us, "The President is going to make this announcement tomorrow, so you have got to have the press plan done by then."[59]

Colson and his staff coordinated the activities of White House offices, executive agencies, and interest groups. Once they decided which governmental organizations they wanted to involve in a particular publicity operation, they orchestrated the actions of all the actors. According to Rhatican, "The kinds of things that we would come up with would be [as follows]: 10:00 A.M., the President makes his announcement. 11:15 A.M., assistant secretary so-and-so briefs the press. (Whoever the particularly knowledgeable guy on the issue was.) 2:00 P.M., the cabinet officer for that department would hold a full-blown press conference at his department. That cabinet officer we would try and book on the Today show the next morning. Book an assistant on the same issue on the CBS Morning News."[60]

On important issues the strategies became more complex and their coordination involved the direction of many different groups and activities. One of the Colson group's most significant efforts involved the administration's successful campaign to win passage of legislation giving the Defense Department authority to establish an anti-ballistic missile system, the ABM program, as it was called at the time.

In April, 1970, Colson sent a memorandum marked "Secret" to White House Chief of Staff H. R. Haldeman that described an eight-part publicity program formulated by his group.[61] First, the White House would get allied groups such as the Veterans of Foreign Wars and the American Legion to "undertake a major mail campaign" that would result in 10,000 letters to senators from fourteen states. Second, Colson formed a coalition of organizations that supported the ABM program and met regularly with their representatives. Third, he created two new groups "consisting of very prominent citizens" who favored the program. Colson described the members of these committees as "primarily scientists and other foreign policy and strategic thinkers." Fourth, he acquired funds to sponsor newspaper advertisements: "I have arranged a bank account of $25,000 which can be used at our discretion for a variety of things including possible newspaper ads," he wrote. (In fact, they did spend money on a newspaper advertisement, and it brought compliments from the President. In a memorandum to Jeb Stuart Magruder, Haldeman wrote that "the President was especially pleased with the Safeguard ad in the *Star* tonight and wants to be sure you tell whoever wrote it that it was extremely well done."[62] Magruder replied that the advertisement had been prepared by Colson and White House photographer Ollie Atkins.)

Colson's fifth strategy, according to his memo to Haldeman, involved a prominent public figure, a large circulation magazine, and the Office of Communications. Colson wrote that Henry Cabot Lodge had agreed to write an article on the ABM program for the *Reader's Digest*. The *Digest*, he said, had agreed to supply the White House with reprints of the article that would be sent to targeted individuals and groups in "a massive national mailing which will come out about the first of June."

Colson's sixth strategy was to have National Security Adviser Henry Kissinger, who was persuasive in small groups, give briefings for "very key Senators, like Ed Brooke." Although Colson did not mention it in this memorandum, Kissinger was also an important part of the Nixon administration's direct media strategies because these same persuasive powers worked so well on many influential columnists, editors, and publishing and broadcasting executives.

The seventh tactic involved the employment of an expert consultant who would develop a core of statements and arguments on the ABM issue that Colson's contacts could use in debates, letters to the editor, and speeches. Colson wrote that he had arranged with the Scaife-Mellon Foundation to have the "full-time services" of a consultant.

Colson's final proposal to generate support for the ABM program was to get the contractors and subcontractors to join the lobbying effort. "We have a list of all major contractors and subcontractors," he wrote. "We will make a very discreet approach through an outside source to generate political support in these regions affected."

In sum, the administration's plan to build support for the ABM program involved sending political communications through the media, contacting congressmen, using the White House's own publicity facilities, coordinating the activities of existing interest groups, creating new organizations for the specific purpose of lobbying for the measure, and financing external publicity operations. As was so often the case in the Nixon administration, the plan did not call on the President to hold press conferences. The President preferred to avoid face-to-face confrontation with reporters. Instead, Colson suggested that the White House use other prominent administration figures and invite notables from outside the government to participate.

According to Rhatican, the ABM campaign was typical of the way his office handled publicity for major programs for which the President wanted to build support. In almost all cases, he said, part of their strategy was to limit the period of direct involvement by the White House:

So, from our standpoint, all we could do with our press plans would be to orchestrate them for a pattern. The longest I can ever recall our press plans being orchestrated was the revenue sharing bill. That went for thirty days. Everything else was no longer than a week, because you just couldn't sustain it. What would happen, as we would finish our orchestration [was] that the country would pick it up. Our orchestration was enough to generate interest, editorials around the country, and congressmen and senators would go on speaking beyond that week period, so that the issue continued to surface.[63]

SPEECHWRITERS

Speechwriters articulate the basic themes of the administration in forms ranging in importance from major policy addresses, such as the State of the Union Message, to the President's remarks at ceremonies in the White House Rose Garden on the occasion of an appointment or an award. There have been speechwriters at the White House since Judson Welliver joined the staff of Warren G. Harding.[64] Earlier, detailees on the payroll of executive branch offices wrote speeches on particular subjects. More recently, a separate unit of White House employees has composed the overwhelming majority of addresses.

The size of the speechwriting staff varied within the last three administrations, depending on the other units with which they were joined. More than fifty persons were employed in the Nixon administration's Editorial Department, which included speechwriters, the news summary, a correspondence unit, a message unit, and a research department. In the Carter administration, where the speechwriters were first part of the Press Office, there were approximately twelve people in the speechwriting unit. The White House telephone directory listed only five individuals with the title of *speechwriter* in the unit when it became part of the Office of the Assistant to the President for Communications in 1978.

The organization of the speechwriting unit varies according to which party controls the White House. Democrats prefer loose organization, while Republicans prefer structure. In the large Editorial Department of the Nixon administration speechwriters worked closely with other units to prepare statements that satisfied the President's desire to stay on the attack in presenting the themes of the administration. Speechwriting also was integrated with other ongoing promotional activities, including the task forces, White House lobbying of interest groups, preparation of articles, letters, and advertisements for the press, campaign organizations such as the Committee to Reelect the President, and the preparation of formal statements.

During the Johnson administration speechwriting was not a separate organizational unit. "Almost nobody worked for anybody," said Harry Middleton, one of LBJ's speechwriters. "We worked for the President."[65] The Carter administration has shown more concern for organizational form. During the first two years of Carter's term James Fallows, as chief speechwriter, met regularly with the assistant for communications, other senior staff, staff in the office whose area would be the subject of the President's remarks, and, on occasion, with the President himself. He tried to delegate assignments to his associates based on their particular interests and skills. One writer would work on national security, another on domestic issues, another specialized in light or humorous remarks.

The speechwriting unit produces three categories of addresses: major speeches, talking points, and written messages. Major speeches require the most time, including consultation with staff members who work in the substantive areas. "We usually spend time with the policy people, [Domestic Policy Chief] Eizenstat and [National Security Adviser] Brzezinski after getting instructions from the President," Fallows said.[66] Talking points are prepared for ceremonial meetings where the President will speak without a prepared text, as when he greets a visitor or responds to a toast. Although talking points seldom contain vital information, they have symbolic importance. Preparation is necessary because the President appears at many events about which he knows little. Preparation helps to prevent extemporaneous gaffes, like one made by President Carter when he tried to be amusing in response to a toast while visiting Mexico. (Carter remarked that on his last trip to Mexico as a tourist he suffered from "Montezuma's revenge," a severe form of diarrhea.)

Presidential messages are prepared either by the speechwriters or by a special unit. The presidential messages unit prepares ceremonial telegrams to foreign governments on the occasion of their national days, proclamations for domestic holidays like Thanksgiving, and greetings to citizens whose achievement is considered worthy of note. Speechwriters prepare major messages such as those sent to Congress along with the President's legislative proposals.

Fallows indicated that in the Carter administration speechwriters play a minimal role in policy. "I don't get into any arguments over policy as that is the area of others; on style we are important." After he left the White House in 1979, however, Fallows wrote that Carter had failed to make his priorities felt or his goals clear to the public.[67] In other words, the President had not recognized the importance of speechmaking to promote his administration's policies.

Speechwriters have had a significant impact on policy in other administrations. According to Bryce Harlow, who wrote for President Eisenhower, "the speechwriters in the White House can have a very, very substantial influence on policy, either by the methodology of presentation of the material, or by the inclusion or exclusion of ideas, and by the fact that he has to work so intimately with the President."[68] Speechwriting may also be significant for a President who wants to convey his points through style as well as through substantive messages. David Gergen, who wrote for President Nixon, argued that style and message were interlocked because it was as important to the President to convey the message that he was aggressive and tough as it was to deal with a substantive issue. Gergen observed that "Nixon valued good lines, quotable lines. There was a competition to see if you couldn't make the quote of the day in the *New York Times*. Safire and Buchanan and Price all had a knack for the good line. Safire had witticisms and alliteration. Pat [Buchanan] was hard hitting, especially with Vietnam. One of Nixon's criteria of success was if the *Times* fulminated. Ford hasn't been as quotable; he doesn't have the same instinct for the jugular. Haldeman and Nixon thought grey prose would not be remembered."[69]

ADVANCE AND MEDIA ADVANCE

The White House advance unit is a division of the Office of the Appointments Secretary to the President. Media advance is a small section of the Office of the Assistant to the President for Communications. Both promote the President when he travels; advance, by setting up the details of his trip, from meetings to motorcades to motels; media advance, by making arrangements for the press that will cover him.

The advance operation. Although the 1979 White House directory listed only six names in the advance unit and three in media advance, a typical team preparing a trip for the President might include a staff of between twenty-five and forty members. In addition to five or six people from the two advance units, there will be personnel from the Secret Service, which is responsible for security; the Travel and Telegraph Office, responsible for chartering planes and buses and making hotel arrangements; and the White House Communications Agency, responsible for setting up communications sytems and providing support for camera and sound crews. Before an important trip, people from the Press Office, the scheduling operation, the Photo Office, and the Public Liaison operation might join the advance group. "We look at where the event is supposed to take place and talk among ourselves," said Eric Rosenberger, chief of media advance for the Ford administration. "Then we propose a schedule for the President that includes some options."[70]

Preadvance. Before the Ford administration's advance team made final arrangements, a small group would leave Washington five days to two weeks before the scheduled arrival of the President. This preadvance delegation included representatives of media advance, advance, a doctor, a representative from the White House Communications Agency, a speechwriter, someone from the Air Force One crew, a military aide, and a representative of the Secret Service. A marine accompanied them if the President was to travel at any point. The preadvance team took charge of technical details. Rosenberger recalled that on a trip to Anchorage, Alaska, twenty minutes were needed between planes because the cold and hot air from jets affect the runway.[71] The preadvance team would file and send a report to all units that needed the information for their own participation in the advance trip.

Insofar as it could, the advance team's arrangements made it possible for the President to travel on schedule, meet the right people, and get the proper amount of coverage on network evening news programs and in the newspapers. Before President Carter traveled to Iowa for a four-hour and forty-minute visit in May, 1979, the advance team made a wide variety of detailed arrangements. In a *New York Times* story on the activities of the advance operation, Martin Tolchin quoted Ellis Woodward, who said that his work was "a combination of politics and logistics." Tolchin summarized what these activities were: "For the past five days they have negotiated with the local police and explored hotel passageways, selected sites and assured the presence of crowds, arranged motorcades and conferred with airport officials, contacted local politicians and arranged media coverage."[72] A similar summary would apply to the work done by an advance team in most urban areas in the United States and in many places abroad.

THE PRESIDENT'S MEDIA ADVISERS

Promoting the President means making him look good. In particular it means making him look good as he appears through the print media in photographs, on radio, and most important of all, on television. Photographs are the responsibility of the White House Photo Office, a unit of the Press Office. Technical advice on radio and television has been the responsibility of a number of individuals with different titles who served as media advisers.

Harry Truman appointed Leonard Reinsch as a special assistant for electronic media at a time when radio was the most important direct contact between the President and the public. Reinsch recalled going to Truman's office when a major speech was scheduled, briefly discussing what the President would say, then raising his major concern, which was whether the speech was of appropriate length for the allotted time: "We were not trying to make a great orator of the President. We were trying to let him express *himself* to the people because I was convinced that the genuine qualities of President Truman becoming evident to the American people would endear him as a President and that his power of leadership would be enhanced." [73]

By 1953, when Dwight Eisenhower was inaugurated, television had become the major avenue of presidential communications with the public. Robert Montgomery, a well-known actor and television personality who helped Eisenhower during the campaign, assisted the President as an unpaid adviser. A similar arrangement was made for media advisers during the Kennedy and Johnson administrations. These consultants assisted presidents with makeup, instructed them on the technical aspects of speaking to cameras, suggested what they should wear and where they should sit, and taught them how to pace their speech.

The President's media advisers were not paid until the Nixon administration, when William Carruthers, media consultant, was paid from the White House special projects funds. It was not until a former television news producer, Robert Mead, was appointed to assist President Ford that the media adviser was made a regular member of the White House staff and was listed on the White House roster.

When President Carter took office he appointed his campaign television adviser, Barry Jagoda, assistant for media and public affairs. Jagoda, who had worked as a television producer, performed most of the same functions as other media advisers. His most famous recommendation was to have President Carter deliver a "fireside chat" on energy dressed in a sweater to symbolize the need to save energy. In addition to giving the President technical advice on how to present himself, the media adviser negotiates with network officials on whether the President's press conferences or speeches will be televised live or filmed—or carried at all. Jagoda recommended that regular press conferences not be held during prime viewing time because the interruption in scheduled programs would annoy their followers. Because he also worried about the perils of overexposure, Jagoda urged that the President not give televised speeches frequently.[74]

Robert Mead recalled that he spent most of his time helping Ford become a better performer, though he also was involved in making arrangements with the networks for the President's appearances. When interviewed in January, 1976, Mead described how he was helping the President prepare for the State of the Union address, which he was to deliver in a few days: "We will practice the State of the Union over the weekend. He [President Ford] will call them [technical crew] in when he wants to practice and we will set up the podium and lights and TV video recorder. We will play it back and they will do it again."[75] When Jagoda was the media adviser, he also was active in such media matters as public broadcasting, appointments to the Federal Communications Commission, and the reorganization of the government's foreign informational and cultural programs.

Neither Mead nor Jagoda lasted a full term, an indication that whoever holds the position is vulnerable if the President feels he is not communicating well through the media. Mead left after a quarrel with Press Secretary Nessen, who accused him of giving the President bad advice. Jagoda, who left without fanfare shortly after Gerald Rafshoon joined the White House staff, clearly was not a White House insider. Rafshoon told interviewers that he would give technical advice to the President and negotiate with the networks about televising the President's activities.

THE WHITE HOUSE PHOTO OFFICE

White House officials long have recognized that because they can control most of the settings in which photographers operate, most of the pictures taken of the President will show him favorably. When Lyndon Johnson became president he increased the advantage considerably by bringing to the White House a government photographer whose main job was to photograph him. Government photographers had been used before, but they had not been part of the White House staff. Johnson brought Yoichi Okamoto to a permanent position on the White House staff in response to advice from Press Secretary Salinger, who wrote him: "I do not think we should consider Okamoto's photos as aimed at the daily press. We can aim them in that direction from time to time, but I feel we should concentrate (as we have) on the mass circulation magazines. In the next six weeks, Okamoto spreads will appear in *Look* and *Parade* (each with over 7,000,000 circulation). We have other such spreads in the works—not only in the United States but abroad."[76]

Johnson gave Okamoto a job within the Press Office and an office in the West Wing. But the administration was not willing to put Okamoto cn the White House payroll for fear that reporters would claim that Johnson was using government money to advertise himself. Reporters also felt that a White House photographer would have greater access than the media. What Johnson did in this case provides a good example of how the White House has been able to enlarge its staff without the authorization of Congress. Not only was Okamoto's salary paid by the Defense Department, but his processing was performed in the Georgetown laboratory of the White House Communications Agency, which, as part of the Army Signal Corps, is a unit of the Defense Department.[77]

The Photo Office reached prominence during the Ford administration, when David Kennerly headed the White House staff of photographers. Kennerly, a Pulitzer Prize–winning photographer, developed a special relationship with Ford, who granted him almost unlimited access. Because Kennerly was the only media person present on a number of important occasions, his pictures formed the only record of those events. When the President and Henry Kissinger decided to liberate the ship *Mayaguez* off the Cambodian coast in 1975, Kennerly was in the Oval Office while they waited for news. His pictures of the President, Kissinger, and others were widely used by newspapers and magazines. Prior to the inauguration of President Carter, Jody Powell stated that he intended to "deimperialize" the Photo Office and bring it back under the wing of the Press Office.[78] In 1979 three persons were listed in the White House directory as photographers for the Photo Office, four fewer than had been employed by the Ford administration.

THE PUBLIC LIAISON FUNCTION

When he was an "outsider" candidate running for president, Jimmy Carter criticized the size and number of White House staff offices. He promised to cut the size of one and eliminate some of the others. In particular, he suggested that promotional operations were unnecessary appendages to the "constitutional" cabinet government he envisaged.[79] By 1978 Carter had not only decided to keep the public liaison function, he had appointed a strong political aide, Anne Wexler, to coordinate expanded efforts to lobby the support of interest groups. The interest groups in return get a place where they can contact the White House about their problems.

The public liaison function takes two forms. In one case, the White House holds conferences on a subject like inflation or energy and invites delegations to come to Washington to hear what the government is doing about it. The second approach involves inviting a small number of people to discuss how a White House program affects their group. For example, the White House contact with black groups in the Carter administration, Louis Martin, met with black leaders in June, 1979, to try to get their support for SALT. At the same time Anne Wexler, the staff person who works with economic and social interest groups, was trying to mobilize support for congressional implementation of the Panama Canal Treaty. The first approach was more common in the Ford administration; the second in the Carter presidency.

The Baroody operation: the Office of Public Liaison. During the Nixon administration William Baroody, Jr., suggested to the President that he establish a White House office to route contacts with special interest groups. Nixon was favorably disposed, but he resigned before he could act. Gerald Ford also was impressed by the idea and, shortly after he took office, created the Office of Public Liaison with William Baroody, Jr. as its head.

During the two and one-half years of its existence, the Office of Public Liaison organized 350 meetings in the White House and 24 White House conferences. Baroody described three kinds of meetings.[80] The first, known as Wednesday meetings, were held about every two weeks with groups of as few as 10 or as many as 250 people. Trade associations, business and finance groups, and other invited organizations were asked to list in order the issues that concerned them most. Baroody arranged for 18 administration officials to meet with the groups throughout the day to discuss different aspects of these issues. When possible, the Office of Public Liaison arranged for the group to meet and ask questions of the President. The White House press corps sometimes was permitted to observe these meetings but not to participate in the question sessions.

The Tuesday meetings, which were scheduled almost weekly, considered more specific issues. For example, a meeting with representatives of the construction industry discussed the problems of architectural barriers to the handicapped. According to Baroody, as a result of that meeting, President Ford signed an executive order to eliminate these barriers from government buildings that also described how it was to be done.

The third kind of meeting was referred to by Baroody as an "organizational dialogue." These meetings were held in response to requests by specific groups that wanted to discuss particular issues. Baroody suggested that the purpose of all three types of meetings was to "secure the end of the isolation of the presidency." In order to end the distrust born of Watergate, he said, "We wanted something... dealing with the confidence question in government and in mediating structures in society—contributing to the reestablishment of confidence in the President and government." They wanted the media to know about these meetings, report on them, but not ask questions. "If you're going to do those kinds of things," he said, "you are going to do it through the media."[81] In general they were successful. The favorable publicity the White House received, especially when it held "road shows," led one journalist to say that the Office of Public Liaison was one of the "slickest operations in town." [82]

Public liaison in the Carter administration. As noted earlier, candidate Jimmy Carter had suggested that the public liaison function was an example of the type of self-serving White House activity that he would eliminate. After his election he appointed Midge Costanza to Public Liaison and instructed her to be available to people who ordinarily don't get into the White House. Costanza followed the President's advice too well: staff members were upset at possible adverse reactions to White House meetings with a homosexual rights group.

As late as May, 1978, President Carter still was repeating his strictures against the public liaison function. "I wouldn't bring anybody on board to take care of a particular constituency group," he said. "I don't think we ought to isolate a certain constituency group and have them be able to go or be constrained to a particular person in the White House.... I don't like to segment my staff to be responsible for old people or farmers or labor or business or women or blacks or Spanish-speaking people. I'd have such a fragmented administrative mechanism here that I couldn't deal with it."[83]

Shortly thereafter the White House was reorganized and Anne Wexler replaced Costanza as the assistant to the President in charge of the public liaison function. Later Carter appointed assistants to deal with blacks, Jews, and a number of other groups. Wexler quickly impressed the staff and lobbyists for interest groups with her ability to focus on areas of agreement with groups and thus get them to support specific presidential policies, even when they felt generally unhappy with the White House. In an interview published in *U. S. News* in June, 1979, Wexler described how Public Liaison now operated:

There's a lot more access now to key people in the White House than there was in the early days.

One of the most interesting contrasts was how we pulled together our original energy plan in 1977 compared to how we handled development of the recent policy on phased decontrol of oil. There was not much consultation on the energy plan in the first months of this administration. But on decontrol of oil, we had extensive consultations not only with Congress but also with the entire spectrum of outside groups: Everything from oil companies and the business community to consumer and environmental leaders.[84]

According to the 1979 White House directory, there was no Office of Public Liaison. At the same time, it was quite clear that the public liaison function remained an important aspect of promotional operations.

The White House Publicity Factory

Most White House employees work in offices where promoting and publicizing the President is secondary to other functions that assist him to lead and to govern, such as developing his programs, processing his administrative work, and providing material and technical assistance for his activities. If the President reorganized the White House by creating divisions structured according to functions performed, the publicity units described earlier in this chapter would show up on an organizational chart as one of five political divisions. The other four divisions would include offices that plan and develop policy, such as the National Security Council, Domestic Policy Staff, and the untitled West Wing offices of senior political advisers; offices to bridge the constitutionally created gaps of the separation of powers and federalism, such as Congressional Liaison; offices that process the internal operations and flow of decisions within the White House, such as the Office of the Counsel to the President, the Office of the Secretary to the Cabinet, and the Office of the Staff Secretary; and offices organized to suit the personal needs of a particular occupant, such as the Office of the First Lady's Staff and the Office of the Vice President. A sixth division would support the activities of the others through offices that facilitate travel or implement routine administrative functions, such as the Travel and Telegraph Office and the Office of Records.

Even though media relations do not form the core of their activities, many offices provide access and information to news organizations. Others build walls to keep the media out. Most reporters don't know what's going on in the majority of offices, especially those in the support division, because the technical nature of their work seems far removed from the major events of the day. Nevertheless, almost every office in the White House at some time plays an important role in getting favorable pictures and messages about the President through the media to his public. "When you think about the presidency and the press or the communications function, the fact is that most of the people that work in the White House are engaged in one form or another of that activity," James Connor reflected a month before his term as the Ford administration's secretary to the cabinet ended. "What [the President] is trying to do is shape opinion in different parts of town and throughout the country," he continued. "It is through these external communications that he does it, and you don't do it any other way."[85]

The following analysis of four offices in the political divisions of the White House indicates that they contribute to media policy in ways that range from simply supplying information to the publicity offices to participating in the design and implementation of White House press operations. A brief account of some of the functions of support services shows how vital their staff and their functions can be to publicity operations. Finally, a case study of a White House ceremony illustrates the importance of coordination between the political and operational divisions of the White House.

POLITICAL OPERATIONS AND PUBLICITY

No self-activating mechanism forces the staff of a White House office to assist publicity programs. Although the National Security Council, the Office of the Vice President, and the Office of the First Lady have press units and Domestic Policy and other offices designate staff to handle media relations, the Press Office and the President's senior advisers often suspect that these operations are unreliable or even harmful to the President. This was the case during the Ford administration, when Kissinger ran the NSC, Rockefeller was vice president, and Mrs. Ford was thought to talk too much. The President's closest political aides want strong direction of key White House offices, and they recognize that there are conflicts between the President's publicity goals and the continuation of relations established by an office with a group that might be the target of a publicity campaign, but they are concerned about the sensitivity shown to the President's communications needs. If the President attacks Congress, for example, the Congressional Liaison operation may have a hard time keeping some carefully cultivated support from dissolving.

Thus an office's publicity activities depend on who directs it, whether its staff appreciates the relationship between the success of White House publicity and its own substantive functions, and whether the President and his top advisers know how to coordinate their other activities with their publicity programs. What the White House establishment hopes to gain from these offices are supplementary publicity resources, information, assistance in planning, and symbolic benefits. The Office of the Assistant to the President for Congressional Liaison, a "constitutional" office, can use its network of contacts in Congress to support White House press strategies; the Office of the Vice President and the Office of the First Lady's Staff, both personal offices, use the symbolism of a high office to enhance the President's image; the Office of the Secretary to the Cabinet, a process office, monitors and understands the internal communications necessary for planning and coordinating publicity; the National Security Council, a policy office, provides important information about foreign policy and defense to the Press Office and the speechwriters.

Providing a supplementary resource. When successful publicity is generated by other members of the White House staff efforts by Congressional Liaison to build support for the President and his legislative programs on Capitol Hill are simplified. Sometimes the White House plays "hardball," an expression the Nixon administration used for tough tactics. Once during the fall of 1970, when rising congressional criticism of the administration's Southeast Asia policy led Senator Frank Church to comment that "the doves had won," Jeb Stuart Magruder of the Office of Communications asked Congressional Liaison to rally the administration's "Senate spokesmen" against Church and promised, "We will activate our letters-to-the-editors apparatus against the Senator."[86] That same year the White House arranged for advertisements signed by local influentials to appear in the home press of congressmen whose support the White House was trying to win for the proposed Anti-Ballistic Missile system. In a softer vein, Media Liaison's regular contacts with news organizations from his home district may influence a member of Congress. If the press backs the White House position and the congressman believes that what he reads reflects public support, he may be won over. "Members . . . are going to react to the views of their constituency," said Lawrence F. O'Brien, who directed Congressional Liaison for Presidents Kennedy and Johnson. "We can only hope the constituency view transmitted to them by letter and personal contact will be more often than not our view, and therefore become everyone's view."[87]

The biggest boost in attracting the attention of congressmen comes when the President tries to rally public support. According to O'Brien, because the President "commands massive audiences on television and radio, and public appearances," proposals dramatized in that manner receive "closer attention on the Hill" than those transmitted by Congressional Liaison.[88] Just as they use the electorate to try to influence Congress, the White House asks its friends in Congress to help them generate publicity that influences the public. Through coordination with other White House offices, the liaison office affects the timing of publicity on presidential issues. Since it knows who supports the President, it can stagger announcements of support on an issue to make it appear that the President is gaining momentum.

Members of Congress appear as surrogates for the administration in political campaigns, in speeches, and on television news programs such as "Meet the Press" or "Face the Nation." They are asked to hold hearings on matters the administration wants brought to media and public attention, and to kill those that it wants to bury. Congressional Liaison's staff of thirty serves as the primary intermediary in all these exchanges because it has built contacts with members of Congress, watching out for their interests by keeping them informed of government activities that will affect their districts.

The *Congressional Record* is an important publicity tool that Congressional Liaison has made available to the President. During the Johnson administration the staff sent its friends in Congress reprints of favorable newspaper articles about the President for insertion into the *Record*. Presidential aide Jack Valenti described how Johnson expected the operation to work in a 1964 memorandum to Bill Moyers and Horace Busby: "We need to do the following: (1) Each day insert in the *RECORD* every favorable story-column-editorial appearing in newspapers in this area and around the country. (2) We then need to affix to each favorable piece an introductory preface so that it can be inserted without any effort."[89] The prefatory remarks were written by White House speechwriters.

In 1965 Johnson reminded his aide Marvin Watson that he wanted favorable editorials inserted. In a return memorandum Watson cited 141 favorable editorials that had been inserted in eighteen issues of the *Congressional Record*.[90] These editorials, it was thought, might influence members of Congress and others in government who made up the *Record*'s elite Washington readership, as well as news organizations throughout the country, which might be more attentive to editorials that appeared in the *Record* than copies of editorials sent directly from the White House.

Symbolic contributions. Neither the First Lady nor the vice president has more than a fraction of the President's potential to exploit the public's latent regard for his office. Before Eleanor Roosevelt, most First Ladies confined themselves to Washington society. Vice presidents prior to Nixon did little to belie the musical comedy version of them as forgotten and forgettable Throttlebottoms. Mrs. Roosevelt and Vice President Nixon, two strong political figures, built offices tailored to their ambitions. Subsequently their offices were enlarged and further professionalized. Important staff divisions have been created for publicity matters such as press relations, speechwriting, scheduling, and advance. Both offices wed the managerial techniques of modern public relations to presidential symbols.

First ladies and White House publicity. Franklin Roosevelt's administration created the First Lady's office to provide support for Eleanor Roosevelt's enormous range of public concerns. In particular, her strong associations with labor and civil rights added to the President's luster with these groups, a tremendous benefit for him because he could not commit himself too personally to these groups without alienating other important elements that supported him. An incident with widespread symbolic repercussions occurred when the Daughters of the American Revolution refused to permit black opera singer Marian Anderson to sing at Constitution Hall. Mrs. Roosevelt provided the Lincoln Memorial for Anderson as an alternate stage. Both the concert and the incident were widely publicized and provided benefits to the President with black leaders and among liberal whites.

Although subsequent first ladies, with the exception of Rosalynn Carter, have not pursued such overtly political activities, they have remained before the public. With the possible exception of Bess Truman, who was an extremely private person, first ladies have appeared with increasing frequency at public ceremonies emphasizing charity, cultural affairs, and the improvement of the quality of life. For example, Jacqueline Kennedy hosted a televised tour of the White House in which she lectured on the building's antiques, art treasures, and restoration; Lady Bird Johnson sponsored beautification programs; Pat Nixon, charitable groups; Betty Ford, theater and dance groups; and Rosalynn Carter testified before a congressional committee on mental health. Of course, all first ladies are used to emphasize the traditional family man qualities of the President, a subject discussed more fully in a later chapter.

By 1980 the First Lady's office consisted of a staff of more than thirty employees in four divisions: scheduling and advance, press, projects and community liaison, and the social office. Only the last of these is concerned with the traditional diplomatic and social aspects of the position. Most activities of the First Lady bring her to public events where she reflects the prestige of her husband's high office. The complaint by her staff has been that the West Wing political offices, including the Press Office, have not been sensitive enough to the potential publicity benefits the President can derive from her activities. Sheila Rabb Weidenfeld, press secretary to Betty Ford, complained that she had a great deal of difficulty getting the President's political advisers to understand that the noncontroversial activities of the First Lady benefited the President, and that even the more controversial, but still nonpolitical, social comments Mrs. Ford made helped him with those who agreed with her. [91]

The vice president. When Richard Nixon became vice president in 1953, he made the office an important political operation. Throughout the Eisenhower years, Nixon was an important surrogate for the President in party activities. Although Eisenhower was a hard campaigner, Nixon substituted for him in political organizing and fund-raising activities. He was used by the Eisenhower administration both to appease the conservative wing of the party and to respond for the President to accusations from Senator McCarthy that he was too soft on communism. He also used the vice presidency to launch his own presidential ambitions. As a result of Nixon's activities—and also because of the traumatic successions to the presidency in 1963 and 1974—vice presidents are likely to run, at a future date, in a race for the office. In every election since 1960 at least one former vice president was a candidate.

The vice president's abilities to represent the President are enhanced by his own large entourage. His staff of more than seventy includes at least thirty who handle his press relations, write his speeches, prepare his schedules, and advance his trips. The role of hard-hitting campaigner adopted by Nixon has been continued by Lyndon Johnson, Spiro Agnew, Gerald Ford, and Walter Mondale. Between campaigns the vice president asserts strong positions from which the President can fall back if they are not well received. Spiro Agnew, with his 1970 attacks on the media, offers perhaps the most striking example of a vice president who performed both of these functions.

Still, the attempt to integrate the vice president fully into White House publicity activities has not been accomplished, for the same reasons that the vice president has not been brought into the inner circles in other matters. Vice presidents have separate political bases, reflected in their staffs as well as in their personalities. The Kennedy-Johnson staff rivalry was extremely strong; many members of Kennedy's staff had hoped that Johnson could be dropped from the ticket in 1964. Ford's staff succeeded in dropping Nelson Rockefeller in 1976. In Rockefeller's case, his status as a well-established political figure with his own extensive contacts in the media led him to pursue what some of Ford's staff members regarded as a rival publicity policy aimed at building up Nelson Rockefeller rather than Gerald Ford. The built-in tensions between presidents and vice presidents make it difficult for the White House to exploit fully the latter's political stature and to call upon the constituency loyal to him that the President and his advisers would like to tap.

Internal communications. Another important base for White House publicity activities is the process offices, which manage the flow of decision-making through the White House. These offices tend to be the least accessible to reporters of all the units in the political divisions of the White House. "Most of the time process tends to be secretive," an insider in the Nixon and Ford administrations commented. "How you arrive at a decision is not something you want to set out. . . . If somebody knows a process or how a decision is reached, they can change the system on you.'"[92] A coherent publicity program requires control over internal processes. The President's chief political advisers need to know the priorities that are being developed so they can plan how to use the President to publicize and persuade.

The four offices that play the most important process roles are the Office of the Appointments Secretary to the President, the Office of the Secretary to the

Cabinet, the Office of the Staff Secretary, and the Office of the White House Counsel. Of the three, the Office of the Secretary to the Cabinet is the most important. "The cabinet secretary runs the whole processing section," a former occupant of the job recalled. "That job has a lot to do with policy formation because how you handle moving a policy issue through the White House can delay it, kill it, speed it up, do a whole bunch of things."[93] He controls the process through a number of management functions such as the budget and personnel. He also keeps track of meetings and of the decisions the staff is to implement or send to the President.

The Democratic administrations of Kennedy and Johnson appear to have been less concerned about establishing control over process than were the Republican administrations of Eisenhower, Nixon, and Ford. In the Carter administration Jack Watson, who held the title of secretary to the cabinet and assistant to the President for intergovernmental affairs, was thought by many observers to have been put in that job because Hamilton Jordan had no interest or appreciation of process. It is difficult to assess the role of process while an administration is still in office since officials believe that they maximize their impact on the media by minimizing direct contact. "I deal with the press once removed," one said. "I very rarely have any direct relationship with them at all."[94]

When Lyndon Johnson was president he used Robert Kintner, the cabinet secretary, as his personal emissary to the elite press. Because Kintner had been news president of two networks, Johnson felt that he should be able to use his friendships with elite journalists to obtain a sympathetic ear for what his administration was trying to do. Johnson, who wanted to use the strong suits of particular individuals on his staff, showed little concern for integrating them into a cohesive whole. Certainly he had little hesitation in changing the usual duties of the cabinet secretary. This made Johnson more vulnerable to staff intrigue. "In the Johnson White House, what you would do to get your own way would be to try to hit the old man at the best time to get him to agree to something, without letting anyone else know about it."[95]

Cabinet Secretary Kintner used his control over the management process to expand the number of staff members working in publicity. Since he also served as the liaison officer between the White House and the Civil Service Commission, he was able to convince Commissioner John Macy that it would be appropriate for some White House staff members to remain on the payroll of agencies elsewhere in government.[96] This practice of detailing has been one of the principal ways the White House staff has expanded without congressional approval. During the Nixon administration Congress increased the authorized number of publicity positions for the staff but announced that the White House was expected to curtail the process of detailing. Nevertheless, because of his knowledge of the budget and personnel mechanisms, the cabinet secretary can add staff and money when needed for publicity activities.

Information channels. The fourth contribution that the White House staff provides to publicity operations is information. The two major policy staffs, the Domestic Policy Staff and the National Security Council, provide information to speechwriters and Press Office officials. In the case of Domestic Policy, the press secretary feels qualified to handle most questions himself; on occasion he brings in a member of the staff to answer questions. Most press secretaries have a rudimentary knowledge of all but the most technical domestic issues. On the other hand, no press secretary has had the background or training to serve as a spokesman on foreign policy without assistance. Furthermore, as Pierre Salinger told an interviewer, "You could never remember whether the paper you just saw was classified or not. You could give away classified information without knowing it."[97]

The national security advisers also have been an important source of direct information to the press and of publicity for the White House. Their press contacts have been mostly with the elite press, although they hold press briefings as well. Most information about foreign policy that the beat reporters at the White House use in their stories filters to them through the associate director for National Security Council press relations, an employee of the NSC rather than of the Press Office. One staff member who was familiar with the operation said that the job was to "backstop the White House Press Office on foreign policy issues. That part of the job reflects the fact that foreign policy was made in the White House in the Nixon administration. Given tight foreign policy control in the White House, part of the job was to make sure the State and Defense Department public information officers knew the policy line. It made sure that the administration spoke with one voice."[98]

Because the NSC established the liaison operation, the Press Office had little to do with gathering foreign policy information. Press secretaries such as Ronald Ziegler and Ronald Nessen "had zero internalized foreign policy information," one NSC staff person recalled. "When questions came out of the blue, they couldn't expand on what they had been given."[99] Because of his close relations with the President, Jody Powell conducts foreign policy briefings for reporters such as those at the Camp David summit between Presidents Carter and Sadat and Prime Minister Begin. There he would speak about the President's plans or the developments in negotiations, but when questions of interpretation of the policy were raised, he would turn to Jerrold Schecter.

The liaison operation pulls together information from the Departments of State and Defense and the White House. At a morning conference call the press officers try to prevent different information from emerging at any of the three briefings scheduled each day. In the Nixon and Ford administrations a meeting of top-level NSC staff members was held each morning at which the NSC advisers would discuss the information they wished the press to have. Margie Vanderhye, who served in the liaison post during the Ford administration, described the meeting: "The purpose of the meeting would be to determine what would be given to the Press Office or how to respond to a question we knew would come up. Sometimes at the White House there was already a fairly good idea of what one was going to say. When one had the facts and had the guidance developed, it was honed or refined by the secretary.''[100] The Press Office liaison is responsible for dealing with reporters individually as well as in groups. ''They will ask me whether they are taking the right tack in a story and I will try to substantiate their impressions,'' said Vanderhye.

The press liaison person speaks with the press but is not the official spokesperson. When a question involves the interpretation of policy and the direction it is taking, the NSC adviser provides the information to selected reporters, particularly elite columnists and television persons. Brzezinski followed Kissinger's pattern of the special briefing. When Brzezinski spoke to a group of television reporters about his expectations for the President's trip to Eastern Europe, a correspondent for a nontelevision news organization tried to participate. Although he was an accredited White House correspondent, he was told that the meeting was limited to television. Only public foreign policy forums, which present the facts but rarely deal with the nuances of policy, were open to him.

The orchestration by the NSC of information provided to the media was brought to concertmaster perfection under Henry Kissinger. Kissinger held three kinds of meetings with reporters: intimate meetings with important columnists or commentators who regarded themselves as knowledgeable about foreign policy; meetings with important reporters from television who admittedly knew little about policy but whom he had to deal with because they were influential; and callbacks or quick interviews with reporters from the major national publications. He also developed special relations with reporters who traveled with him. He made his abilities of persuasion a tremendous asset to both presidents he served. When he left government in 1977, he took on high-paying consultant jobs for television and publications.

THE OPERATIONAL UNITS

''One of the difficulties of a new administration is facing an empty room,'' recalled Dan Malachuk, deputy special assistant for administration–White House operations in the Carter administration.[101] The documents and files of the previous administration have been packed up and are in transit to their ultimate place of deposit in the former President's library. Nothing is left behind and no one knows how anything works except for the occasional individual who may have served a previous president. Bryce Harlow of the Eisenhower administration described the helplessness of an incoming staff that realizes it lacks the technical know-how to exercise power: ''You're face to face then with a very interesting set of problems as you move into the building. How, for example, mechanically do you issue an executive order? What precisely do you do, and where is it published? How do you get it published? Where is it written, and where does the President sign what, and what do you do with it after it is signed?''[102]

The new arrivals turn to the staff of support services, the one source of continuity and knowledge. These ''permanent'' employees stay on from administration to administration, know how programs have been run in the past, and can show the ropes to the political people arriving with a new administration.[103] Support services assist all divisions of the White House, but their role in publicity operations is especially important. They provide such basic ingredients as sound, light, platforms, and mobility. Among the units that provide important services for the Press Office, the assistant for communications, and others working on communications activities are the Travel and Telegraph Office, which arranges travel for officials and the media; the Presidential Correspondence Office, which answers and tabulates White House mail; the Press Release Office, which prepares and sends out routine announcements and keeps records of those that have been made; the White House Communications Agency, the part of the Defense Department that sets up audio communications equipment for the White House, including that used for the daily briefing; the Presidential Documents operation, which sends out the President's remarks every week; the White House Records Office, which prepares legislative and executive orders and provides background information on them to the Press Office; and the Personnel Office, which develops information on nominations and appointments that are released by the White House. Although there is some flexibility in the operating style of these support offices, most administrations have tended to use them in the same fashion. All have existed in function and most by title since the early 1960s.

Prominent publicity institutions such as the Office of the Assistant to the President for Communications and the Press Office form the front lines for an administration's public relations activities; support services such as correspondence, records, and press releases make it possible for them to function effectively. When the public relations expertise of presidential appointees in the political units is merged with the experience of the permanent staff in support services, a smooth publicity operation becomes possible. Only through cooperation and assistance from the career staff do presidential appointees acquire the technical ability to conduct effective political communications.

A LITTLE WHITE HOUSE CEREMONY

President Carter stood in the Rose Garden on a warm spring day in 1979 to address a group of small businessmen assembled to see him give an award to one of their number. Reporters, photographers, and camera crews looked on as he spoke. ''This is Gary McDaniel and his senior partner, Virginia, who ten years ago invested $23,000 of their own money into a new business to produce air filters,'' the President began. ''And now this originally tiny, new flower in the free enterprise garden of the United States has become a flourishing garden, and their air filters have not only brought profit and now fame to the McDaniels but has also helped us to have a cleaner environment and Americans to have a better life.''[104] An audience of two hundred guests listened to the President. Carter remarked on the diversity of the audience. There were representatives from almost every state and sizable contingents of women, blacks, and persons of Hispanic origin. White House photographers took pictures of the scene that would appear in local and trade publications and in the scrapbooks of those who attended.

The stage manager. The President stars in hundreds of similar events in the Rose Garden or the East Room of the White House. The decision to schedule routine appearances usually is made in West Wing political offices by a middle-level deputy, who submits his recommendation to the Appointments Secretary to the President Phil Wise. If the ceremony is part of high-level policy-making, such as the Israeli-Egyptian agreement of 1979, or if heads of state or other important personalities are to attend, the discussions about the ceremony include the President, his chief White House political and policy advisers, and appropriate cabinet officials. Although some presidents, such as Nixon, became involved in the minutiae of an event, insisting on choosing the music, dress, and timing, most have left the details to the planners.

The project director, a West Wing adviser, is to make certain each political office plays its proper role in assembling the audience and media and in preparing the President for his part. The support units arrange the mechanics of preparing for the ceremony. In selecting a project director the President's senior assistants look for someone who knows about the subject of the ceremony or who knows and is known by members of the group. In this case they selected Stephen Selig, a deputy assistant to political adviser Hamilton Jordan.

Although this particular ceremony was a ten-minute ripple in the President's schedule, the arrangements involved participation by eight units from the political divisions: Jordan's office, Domestic Policy Staff, the Press Office, the speechwriters, the appointments office, the photo unit, Congressional Liaison, and the Staff Secretary.[105] The Press Office included the ceremony on the schedule it posts for reporters, announced at the press secretary's briefing that it would take place and that any reporter could attend, and escorted the reporters into the Rose Garden. The speechwriting unit of the Office of the Assistant to the President for Communications, along with the Domestic Policy Staff, wrote the "talking points" from which the President spoke. The Appointments Staff arranged the appropriate time, taking into account the deadlines of the media and other public activities of the President scheduled close to the same time. The photographers of the Photo Office recorded the scene, while the Staff Secretary's office arranged for the President to sign the pictures. Congressional Liaison notified appropriate congressmen about the ceremony, particularly those from the state of the award's nominees. Jordan's office coordinated the event through a project director.

Support services for publicity operations. The support operations for this ceremony included the Presidential Correspondence Office, the White House Communications Agency, printing and duplicating, Records Management and Central Files, press release, and Presidential Documents. While all administrations rely on the technical expertise of the support staff, their full integration into the political divisions did not begin until the Carter administration. "This President as a manager is interested in the management process," Dan Malachuk observed. Traditionally, the chief executive clerk, a permanent official, directed the administration of the operating units. Carter created the position of special assistant to the President for administration to control the operating units. The first occupant was the President's nephew, Hugh Carter, Jr., a management specialist who brought five political appointees with him. "The people who serve in those units now are more closely linked to the rest of the White House," Malachuk said. "The idea is to fold them more into the operation, to take advantage of their skills, to increase their skills, and to make them exploit, if you will, the resources. . . . They become a service organization whose client right now happens to be the Carter administration."[106]

Presidential correspondence. The Presidential Correspondence Office wrote letters to all of the participants following the ceremony. It can also be a useful office when an event is being set up, as the unit maintains computer classifications of individuals the White House may want to contact. Such lists are essential for the Public Liaison operation in its efforts to build support for the President's programs among the many powerful organized groups around the country. Correspondence can program a special list or use a list already on tape to meet a special need. In the case of the small business ceremony, the computer could provide a list of business persons in different states with some indication of race, sex, and ethnic background.

Most of what is done in the Presidential Correspondence Office is in response to the approximately 30,000 letters the White House receives each week.[107] In addition to preparing answers to the letter writers, the unit sorts and analyzes the mail. The Press Office gives reporters a "count" on how the mail is going on a particular issue or event. The White House itself gets a continuous analysis. Because the correspondence unit is an important communications system, relaying information to the President and his staff about the issues that are rising to the surface and sending messages to the public about the President's positions and priorities, it plays an influential part in the communications process.

The White House Communications Agency. WHCA provided the amplification and recording system at the ceremony. The sound system was constructed for the guests; the recording system was constructed so the Presidential Documents staff could transcribe and publish the President's remarks. The same amplification system was used by reporters to listen to the ceremony and, if they wished, television sound crews could plug into it.

WHCA supplies the sound system for presidential speeches and press conferences, the press secretary's daily briefing, and other briefings held in the White House. When the President leaves the White House, WHCA enables him to be in communication with all his contacts around the world. For example, the "hot line" with the Soviet Union can be activated in the middle of a parade line if that is the President's wish.

In addition to these basic services, WHCA also assists White House personnel by making it easier for them to watch and analyze television news. All the network morning and evening news programs are taped and edited for rebroadcast on a special White House television system that WHCA sets up. The editing process cuts out the commercials and the portions of the news that are unimportant to the White House. The edited versions are shown at 9:30 A.M. and again at 12:30, permitting those who may have missed them to watch and allowing the staff to compare coverage. WHCA also tapes the network Sunday interview programs and weekend news analysis programs like "Agronsky and Company" and "Washington Week in Review." In addition to replaying these programs, the television system picks up the audio from the press secretary's daily briefing so that White House officials may listen in to the questions of the day.

Records Management and Central Files. All material relating to the development of the small business award ceremony was sent to Records Management and Central Files. Such material remains there until the end of the administration, when it is sent to the President's library. The Johnson Library, for example, contains 34 million pages from that administration's days in the White House. Because there is no room for extensive files in individual offices in the White House complex, the retrieval abilities of Records Management and Central Files are important. Frequently staff members need either their own records or files on particular events like the Small Business Administration award ceremony in order to find out what was done, who was there, and what was said. Chris Camp, an assistant in the Press Office, explained the importance of records and files to George Reedy when he became press secretary. "This section's support is essential for fast and speedy reference work," she wrote. "They file and store all of your correspondence."[108]

Press release. The press releases that described the small business awards ceremony included some of the President's statements. Along with other remarks he makes during his term, they are stored and indexed in a computer from which information can be retrieved by the Press Release Office. Carter's remarks at the Rose Garden ceremony might be filed under several headings relating to the subject of small business, as well as under the names of those involved in the ceremony. In the Hoover administration the need for such an information retrieval system would not have been great, since there were only about 800 releases in the whole administration. In recent decades, however, there have been that many in six months. In just over five years, President Johnson produced 4,723 press releases; Franklin Roosevelt had 3,268 in twelve years. Quick and easy retrieval is important if the Press Office or speechwriters need to know what the President has said on a subject.

Presidential documents. Since the unit was founded during the Johnson administration, its staff has prepared a publication known as *Presidential Documents* that includes most of the President's public statements, including his speeches, messages, and press conferences. The staff that prepares *The Weekly Compilation of Presidential Documents* works for the General Service Administration in the Executive Office Building; its weekly compilation is printed by the Government Printing Office. It listens to tapes of the President's speeches and makes final corrections in the President's remarks. This job had been attempted by the Press Office, but it was not able to keep up with the large volume of material.[109] Because it is relatively inexpensive, *Presidential Documents* has a large circulation list, including many news organizations. Though it provides useful and necessary information and thus is officially "nonpolitical," it promotes the President by making his every word seem memorable and worthy of publication.

Other support services. The SBA award ceremony did not involve all of the support services. The White House Records Office completes the technical work necessary before legislation or appointments may be sent to Congress or before an enacted bill can become law. All official actions first must be cleared through this office. It is important to the Press Office because it does "all legal, constitutional bookkeeping on presidential commissions, appointments, etc.," Chris Camp explained to George Reedy.[110] It provides the information the Press Office needs to be assured that its announcements on legal matters are correct.

Travel and telegraph. If the SBA award ceremony had taken place outside the White House, the Travel and Telegraph Office would have made the arrangements. It would have rented an airplane for the press, made hotel reservations, and arranged all local transportation. It also would have rented a room for press use, stocked it with paper, phones, and rented typewriters, and provided whatever else was necessary for reporters to send their stories to their organizations.

The office has a staff of seven full-time employees; in marked contrast, one Secret Service agent made arrangements during Franklin Roosevelt's administration, when the press contingent traveling with the President was smaller. When President Roosevelt traveled to Jasper, Alabama, for the funeral of

House Speaker William Bankhead, he was accompanied by seven newspaper reporters, two broadcasting network reporters, four newsreel people and photographers, and two telegraph people.[111] Today even a routine presidential trip involves more than one hundred reporters.

Over the years arrangements that news organizations once handled themselves have become the White House's responsibility. William Hopkins, chief executive clerk for over forty years, observed, "You can't cut back on it. It is the same with material handed out by the Press Office. As late as Harry Truman's time the press secretary would tell reporters to look up an appointee in *Who's Who*. Once you start doing something, such as giving detailed information on appointees, you seldom can cut back."[112] No administration has tried to cut back on what previous administrations have given to reporters, whether it be information or travel arrangements.

White House ceremonies need assistance from the appropriate agencies in the executive branch. For this particular ceremony the Small Business Administration helped develop the guest list, set the appropriate date, and choose the winner of the award. Its director, Vernon Weaver, played a prominent role in the ceremony. Less obvious were the roles played by the National Park Service, the Navy, the Secret Service, and the Executive Protection Service. The National Park Service provided the platforms on which the principals stood and roped off areas for the press and for guests attending the ceremony. Navy photographers took moving pictures of the event for the National Archives. The Secret Service guarded the President. The Executive Protection Service provided security for the White House grounds and checked the credentials of the guests when they came in the Northwest gate.

The production of publicity takes place in many departments, shops, and adjuncts of the White House. Publicity now involves some of the staff all of the time and almost all of the staff some of the time. The changes have come about in a fairly short time. Some of the persons interviewed for this study, such as Bascom Timmons and Richard Strout, began their careers at a time when the President had only one assistant for publicity. Despite all the changes, this assistant now known as the press secretary remains the single most important administration official who deals with the media on a continuing basis.

FIVE

THE MANAGER OF THE MESSAGE

The Press Secretary to the President of the United States

A PRESS SECRETARY manages White House efforts to get the President's messages out through the media. His relationship with the media is second only to that of the President in its importance in framing the public's perception of the Chief Executive. As the official White House spokesperson, the press secretary is required to transmit news and images from the President and the White House staff to news organizations. As the gatekeeper for the flow of information in and out of the White House, he operates at the point where pressures from White House officials to obtain publicity for themselves and their policies collide with pressures from representatives of the media, who are competing to secure advantages for themselves and their news organizations. "Always in the middle," Lyndon Johnson wrote on a photograph taken of him in the Oval Office with George Christian, the fourth and final press secretary to serve him during his five years in office.[1]

Occupants of the office are important presidential advisers in a White House milieu in which sending political communications and engaging in public relations for the administration has become important to presidents. Yet, as he lacks inherent powers in the office or reasonable certainty that influential White House associates will support him, a press secretary occupies a position of obvious vulnerability.

The press secretary acts as both manager of the message and messenger boy in what often is regarded as a theater of the absurd. At his daily White House briefing he is expected to speak authoritatively for the President to reporters who alternately attack his explanations of administration policies and demand that he respond promptly to their requests for routine items such as texts of statements, press releases, and travel arrangements. Although reporters often say that no one cares what the press secretary thinks, it is his name that they attach to White House pronouncements and reactions in their telecasts and dispatches. In fact, it is media practices rather than White House strategies that have made a celebrity of the press secretary. It is in response to demands from news organizations that he is available for appearances before television cameras and radio microphones. It is news organizations that photograph him, place him on the cover of magazines, and caricature his features in editorial cartoons.

Immediately after the inauguration of President Carter, for example, the *Washington Post,* the *New York Times,* the *Washington Star,* and the news weeklies ran stories about the way Jody Powell was conducting himself as press secretary and the responses of reporters to him. Although reporters may contribute to a press secretary's downfall by pressing complaints that he does not respond properly to their demands for access to the President or provide accurate information about the Chief Executive's activities and policies, they cannot help him if they think he is doing a good job.

When reporters, editors, and others concerned with covering the President do not trust them, press secretaries lose their usefulness to news organizations and thus to the President as well. In the aftermath of the Watergate crisis, Fred Barnes of the *Washington Star* asserted, "the Press Office is not very important to me as a White House reporter."[2] Mel Elfin, Washington bureau chief and senior editor of *Newsweek,* characterized the staff in the Press Office as "not as important [to his magazine] as the nonpress office people." He described the press secretary's daily briefing as "worthless as a place for imparting information" because it is a place where "reporters vie with each other to see who can ask the toughest questions and never let Watergate happen to us again, while the press secretary stonewalls to show what a tough guy he is."[3]

Presidents who "act as their own press secretaries" by trying to manage and implement all aspects of White House communications policy usually do not delegate authority to the person who holds the job title. "Lyndon Johnson thought a press secretary was somebody who was supposed to go out and get his name in the papers," George Reedy said, reflecting on his own disastrous experience in the office.[4] If the press secretary does not enjoy the confidence of the Chief Executive, as Reedy did not, it is difficult for him to function as a spokesperson for the administration.

Some White House officials indicated that they viewed the press secretary as a messenger with a small role in major public relations decisions. A Ford administration official said that Press Secretary Nessen did not participate in the broad discussions of the administration's policy on the relationship between the media and the intelligence community until it was time to settle on details such as who should participate in a press briefing and what room it should be held in. John Dean recalled that John Ehrlichman and other aides close to Richard Nixon who shared a similar view of Ronald Ziegler instructed him "to tell Ziegler nothing."[5] Such views might lead one to the conclusion that the celebrity status of press secretaries consists of their being well known; they are famous for being famous.

Thus several presidents, many White House advisers, and a large contingent of journalists have seen little value for themselves or the public in a press secretary who acts as coordinator and chief agent of White House efforts to communicate the administration's message. Although the President's press secretary has emerged as a key White House official during some administrations since the job was created by Herbert Hoover, other press secretaries have played a much less influential role in the formulation and execution of

White House publicity. If the press secretary did not enjoy the confidence of the Chief Executive, he could not function as a spokesman for the administration; if he was shut out of the inner circle of White House advisers by key members of the senior staff, he could not have much impact on policy decisions; if he was not trusted by the representatives of the news media concerned with covering the President, he became useless except as a conveyor of the most routine information about the White House.

Insofar as this view accurately describes the role of the press secretary during the Johnson, Nixon, and Ford administrations, it is because those Presidents were unable or unwilling to delegate power to him in the management of their communications policies. Clearly President Carter acted differently. Like Franklin Roosevelt, Dwight Eisenhower, and John Kennedy, he gave a major role to his press secretary, Jody Powell, who was regarded by both White House officials and reporters as one of Carter's most trusted confidants.

The judgment presented here is that the press secretary plays a critical role for both the White House and news organizations, even when this role is not recognized. The growing complexity and diversity of White House publicity activities have created the need for an intermediary who can hold the confidence of the President, other members of the White House staff (including those who are suspicious of press contacts), and journalists. The service requirements of news organizations call for a Press Office staffed with persons capable of performing a number of jobs.

This chapter begins with a comparison of the broad and diverse functions performed by Stephen Early for Franklin Roosevelt and the specialized management required of Ronald Nessen during the Ford administration. It continues with an analysis of the performance of a contemporary press secretary as a transmitter of information, participant in the White House policy process, administrator of his staff, and agent for the President. The final section attempts to evaluate performances in office. Several individuals have served as press secretary for periods of from a few days to a month; only eleven men since 1933 have held the title long enough for us to be able to judge them.[6]

Press Secretaries of Two Eras

The degree to which White House publicity operations have become institutionalized since 1933 can be seen by comparing the activities of Stephen Early at the beginning of the period with those of Ronald Nessen in the mid-1970s. Franklin Roosevelt made Early the first press secretary with authority to speak for the President and delegated to him much of the responsibility of handling his relations with reporters. Gerald Ford told Nessen that he would be in charge of press relations, but a comparison of Early's routines with Nessen's shows that Nessen's activities were more specialized, more administrative, and more likely to be based on instructions from the President's other advisers.

EARLY SHAPES HIS OFFICE

In the diary he kept while he worked in the White House, Early describes his involvement in such tasks as preparing the President's correspondence and public statements, conducting daily briefings for reporters, meeting daily with the President, answering reporters' requests for information, scheduling appointments for the President, reading articles on the President that reporters let him see prior to publication, editing the President's speeches, handling the liaison between the White House and the Democratic National Committee, advising the First Lady on press matters, arranging meetings between the President and reporters, and giving instructions on what to say to information officers for cabinet departments and other important bureaus and agencies. He sometimes performed social services for reporters and government officials. He wrote letters of introduction to ambassadors for reporters traveling overseas. He helped reporters and officials find new jobs for themselves and their friends and served a friend in court for them. For example, he intervened with the State Department to speed up the process of getting a passport for A. J. Liebling, a well-known writer of that period; served as a go-between for Ambassador Joseph Davies and a book publisher; and made contacts with publishers for Samuel Rosenman, who was in the process of releasing selected presidential documents for publication.[7]

Early met with Roosevelt every morning in the company of one other aide, usually Louis Howe or Marvin McIntyre. Afterwards he returned to his office where he held his daily press briefing with the reporters clustered around his desk. Even though reporters saw Roosevelt at his twice-weekly press conferences, they considered the briefing and their other contacts with Early to be an important source of information. They believed that what he told them was authoritative and accurate. In fact, many reporters found Early more credible than the President and less likely to mislead them, deliberately or otherwise. Although they always produced a story, Roosevelt's press conferences were not entirely satisfactory from the press's point of view. Reporters were crowded into the Oval Office, which meant difficulty in getting heard or recognized for those not in front. In addition, Roosevelt had no compunctions about badgering or hectoring reporters if he did not like their questions; the rules of the game at that time excluded that sort of conduct by the President from being reported in an ordinary news story. Finally, the rules that kept everything off the record without the President's specific authorization made it possible for Roosevelt to deny some of the statements he made before reporters. In contrast, Early's briefings were regarded as a forum where reporters would get information in both the appropriate form and with the speed required by their news organizations.

A sense of the atmosphere in Early's office when an important news story was released can be found in the diary of Eben Ayers, a State Department publicity official who later worked as Early's deputy in the Press Office. His entry for December 22, 1941, reads:

So it went until nearly 7 P.M. Then things broke rapidly. A girl came from Early's office and everyone rushed to the doorway. "Press," she said and they almost ran, tumbling into Early's office and pressing up to his desk. There was a photographer, who climbed a chair at Early's right.

Early was seated at his desk. At his left was his telephone and the receiver was off, the line open, the receiver lying near his left hand. His face was serious, almost strained.

After all the newsmen had crowded into the room and the door had been closed, Early addressed the group. He said he would have an announcement in a moment—as soon as he received a phone call, over the line at his elbow. He said something about the necessity of a check with London. Then he took up the phone, spoke a word or two, replaced the receiver and made the announcement—Prime Minister Winston Churchill was in the White House!

There were two mimeographed statements, both brief and Early had them on his desk. There was a wild dive by the newsmen. The photographer's flash lights flared above the light of the room. One reporter, grabbing for copies of the statements, sent the lamp on Early's desk tumbling and swaying. Then they broke for the door. A few took it more calmly. One man was obviously angered by the actions.

"Is this a sample of a White House press conference?!"[8]

On quieter days Early's afternoons usually were unstructured. There were no regularly scheduled meetings, with either the President or reporters. He noted in his diary for May 8, 1934, for example, that after the briefing the "remainder of the day [was] given over to routine—telephone inquiries, requests, interviews, newspaper, and mail correspondence."[9] While his workload and responsibilities were heavy, the rigorous adherence to a "workaholic's" schedule had not yet become the requirement for survival on the White House staff that it is today. The following excerpt from Early's diary was typical of many breaks in the schedule that would occur before World War II:

This morning was taken up with the usual routine duties—saw the President at the White House, then returned to my office to hold my morning press conference. Arranged for photographs to be made in the President's office when he presented the First National Prize of the Ninth Gorgas Essay Contest. Wrote a memorandum to McIntyre, passing along directions given me by the President for a trip he proposes to make to West Virginia, next Thursday a week, and from there to Hyde Park.

Left the office about noon and took Helen and the kids to the circus.[10]

NESSEN RULED BY ROUTINES

Press duties that the press secretary performed from time to time in the 1930s have become required routines in the 1980s. Because television is now regarded as the most important communicator of news, the press secretary has to be prepared to consider it in every event. In addition, newspapers, magazines, and radio assign more people to cover the President than they did in Early's time. The foreign media also assigns reporters to the White House, and the Press Office has to prepare for an influx of overseas reporters when a foreign dignitary visits.

Approximately sixty reporters attend the daily briefing today; around fifteen or twenty did so when Early was press secretary. The number increases to more than one hundred when an important announcement is expected. Telephone traffic has increased at a similar rate. In order to answer inquiries and provide information to reporters, the West Wing Press Office during the Ford administration employed a deputy, three assistant press secretaries, a press aide, and several secretaries. The entire Press Office was staffed by more than sixty persons. The staff had become so large by the 1970s that Press Secretary Nessen held scheduled meetings twice a day with the deputy and assistant press secretaries, in addition to several unscheduled daily conferences with other staff members.

An analysis of Ronald Nessen's telephone and appointment logs for twelve days in early 1976 indicates how he, much more than Early, adhered to fixed routines.[11] His entire morning was spent in meetings, beginning with a 7:30 staff meeting for Press Office personnel, an 8:00 meeting of the senior staff, and another meeting with the Press Office staff to tell them how decisions by the senior staff would affect their plans for the day. Then he spent some time preparing for his morning meetings with President Ford, the White House scheduling group, and any other meetings the President might be holding with reporters, editors, broadcasting executives, or other news people. At 11:30 Nessen was scheduled to hold his morning briefing, although the start invariably was delayed from between thirty minutes to an hour by the other meetings that Nessen had attended.

During this twelve-day period Nessen spent his afternoons attending meetings with members of the senior staff or department public information officers, and at special White House briefings for reporters that dealt with the budget and the Angola situation. He also was responsible for opening meetings at which the President would later appear, such as a White House session for the Radio-Television News Directors Association and another for the Inland Press Association. He left the White House to attend gatherings of the Republican Women of Capital Hill and the Harvard Republican Club. Nessen also was present at White House ceremonies and events such as the bill-signing for the Marianas Covenant, a Medal of Freedom Ceremony, a session at which the President taped a public message, and a ceremony with the President at the Jefferson Memorial. During the late afternoon and early evening he gave interviews to reporters, answered mail, wrote memos to his staff and other White House officials, took care of the administrative operations of his office, and returned the calls that had piled up during the day. He was so flooded with requests to speak at meetings and attend social events that much of his mail was handled by the White House correspondence office rather than the Press Office.[12]

In contrast to Early, Nessen often was unavailable when reporters needed immediate answers to their questions. Three levels of staff members stood between him and reporters: the deputy and assistant press secretaries, staff assistants and press aides, and secretaries. His main contact with most reporters was at his daily briefing. His logs show that he rarely saw or spoke to individual reporters before the late afternoon. Only the network correspondents and reporters for the major publications could be reasonably certain they could see him even then. One of the reasons the deputy press secretary was given equal status to the press secretary was to give reporters the sense that they would be able to discuss their stories with a major Press Office official.

Stephen Early dealt with the President and reporters, but Nessen had an additional constituency, the White House staff. His obligations to them, which involved him in meetings throughout the day, limited his time with both the President and reporters. Although he met with the President every day several members of the senior staff also were present. Thus had a more formal relationship replaced the frequent, informal, one-on-one meetings between Roosevelt and Early. Jody Powell, whose service to Carter predated the period when he was a serious presidential contender, established a relationship with the President that was more like Early's with Roosevelt was than like Nessen's with Ford was. It is doubtful, however, that this kind of relationship could be established if someone who was not a political intimate held the job. In today's White House, where a number of high officials share the responsibility of communicating the President's messages, an outsider appointed as press secretary would find his relations and routines more like Nessen's than Early's.

The White House Publicist

A press secretary today is expected to be able to communicate the President's message through a media constantly undergoing, technical and organizational changes, oversee the performance of his own large staff, function as part of a large and sometimes imperfectly integrated White House staff, and provide services to journalists. In contrast to the era of Stephen Early, when there were few constraints on the job of press secretary, there is more a sense today of being "locked in." Shortly before he became press secretary, Jody Powell remarked that he could not do much to change the way his office is run, given the expectations of the media. Several months later one of his aides said that staff members found themselves constrained by the "institutional baggage" left behind by their predecessors.

One way of analyzing these activities is to examine four kinds of roles played by contemporary press secretaries: conduit, staff, policy, and agent. Conduit roles involve channeling information to the media from the White House and from reporters back to the President and his advisers. Staff roles include the press secretary's functions as administrator of the Press Office staff, and coordinator of other staffs with media-related functions. Policy roles involve the press secretary in planning and implementing the administration's media strategy. Agent roles include the function of explaining the needs and concerns of news organizations to the White House staff. Press secretaries have performed somewhat differently in each role, but the distinctions were more of style and function among press secretaries with varied backgrounds working for each administration.

CONDUIT ROLES

The most important and time-consuming role of the press secretary is that of conductor of news that ultimately reaches the public. The essential part of the conduit role is to deliver the President's message to reporters on a routine basis so that they in turn will transmit it to their publics. A great deal of this information is itself routine. In the daily briefing the press secretary provides the following: information about appointments and resignations, most of which are for positions not important enough to merit a ceremony with the President; information on presidential actions and policies, including the announcement of bills that have or have not been signed, accompanied by an explanation of the President's action; schedule information, including a list of the day's vistors to the President, the President's plans for travel (for example, whether he will spend the weekend at Camp David), a list of his meetings for the day, and an idea of whether there will be an opportunity for reporters and photographers to see him; and presidential reaction to—or prepared statements on—occasions such as the death of a distinguished citizen.

Some observers and Press Office employees regard the press secretary as a conductor of information in the most literal sense, with no more independence of action than a puppet on a string. Such a view was held by George Christian:

The press officer really is nothing more than a funnel, whether he's a State Department press officer or a White House officer. He's a funnel for information that the administration wants to get out, or he's in a position to field a lot of questions and take the brunt of a lot of inquiries. On something sensitive . . . [he] never says anything that isn't cleared ahead of time and is [not] completely administration policy. . . . I was told several times . . . by the President, "If you get questions on this subject, stonewall it. You cannot say one thing about it."[13]

Although all press secretaries at times have been given explicit instructions as to what they can say on a particular matter, their orders are not ordinarily so clear. In fact, what makes a press secretary valuable to an administration is his ability to go before reporters and articulate the administration's position without being instructed on what to say as well as his ability to provide the right emphasis on information the White House wishes reporters to present to their audiences. The range of questions he may be asked is considerable. For example, on February 7, 1977, Jody Powell was asked questions on the following subjects: the qualifications of the man picked to be CIA director; the Soviet arms buildup; the activities of the head of the General Services Administration; the natural gas shortage; the President's reaction to the slaying of missionaries in Rhodesia; the morning cabinet meeting; the nuclear breeder reactor; the possibility of Carter meeting with Soviet dissident Vladimir Bukovsky; whether the U.S. was sending concussion bombs to Israel; why Carter went to the Kennedy Center without telling the press; and the President's position on the investigation by the House of Representatives of the Kennedy and King assassinations.

In his role as a conductor of information to news organizations and to the President, the press secretary uses both formal and informal settings. The formal settings where messages are sent to the media are the briefing, usually conducted by the press secretary or his deputy, and the President's press conference, in which the press secretary plays a less direct role.

Formal settings: briefings and conferences. Until the Nixon administration, the press secretary held briefings twice daily in his office. A morning briefing was held to meet the deadlines of the afternoon papers and an afternoon briefing was held for the morning papers. The Nixon administration made two major changes: (1) it constructed a press area that included a ''briefing room'' in the West Wing of the White House by filling in the swimming pool; and (2) it reduced the number of briefings to one. The result of both changes has been to transform the briefings in ways that might not have been anticipated by President Nixon and his advisers.[14]

The briefing room creates a structured setting and a formal tone, even though some reporters sit on the floor and the air is filled with wisecracks and schoolboy whispers. The press secretary stands at a podium at the front, with his notes before him. A microphone sends his voice through the briefing room and into other White House offices that are connected to the system. A stenographer sits near the press secretary and prepares a transcript. This is kept on file in the lower West Wing Press Office, but it may have broader circulation.

The formal setting undoubtedly contributes to the expectation that the briefing ought to provide significant statements of White House positions. A comparison of the transcripts of briefings during the Roosevelt, Truman, Eisenhower, Kennedy, and Johnson administrations indicates that the briefings then were more concerned with transmitting routine information. According to Pierre Salinger, whenever the questioning got serious, he was able to change the subject with a joke.[15] Some reporters have suggested that the tensions of the daily briefing might be reduced if ''they filled in that bathtub'' and went back to the more casual atmosphere where reporters stood around the press secretary's desk.

Other explanations as to why the briefing has changed must be considered. First, announced press conferences virtually disappeared during the Nixon and Ford administrations, and although President Carter holds them more regularly, they often are announced only one day in advance.[16] The absence of an opportunity to question the President was the reason given for hard questioning in the briefing. For a number of years it was the only public forum where reporters could learn the White House position. Also, since reporters believe they were misled by White House officials during the Johnson and Nixon administrations, their adversative attitude at briefings is a way of assuring officials and each other that self-justifying explanations by White House officials will not end their investigations. James Deakin of the *St. Louis Post-Dispatch* said that what he and some other reporters known for sharp questioning at briefings were doing was to make the press secretary "explain and justify and defend what [the administration] is doing on the spot, and not in some prepared and staged fireside chat which is one-way communication. That's where the tensions come in. We're trying to get more information than what they're giving and trying to get them to justify what they're doing."[17]

Preparation for the briefing requires much activity on the part of many people. "It takes three or four hours out of the day and is not worth the time," Jody Powell commented.[18] According to an account of a typical day provided by former Deputy Press Secretary William Greener, Jr., during the Ford administration the preparations began with a meeting at 7:30 A.M., attended by all the professional staff in the Press Office, at which they discussed what they had seen on television news, in the newspapers, and in the news summary.[19] Next, either the press secretary or his deputy went to the daily meeting of the senior staff. The Press Office person usually would speak last, after the policy people had discussed their activities. He would ask other senior staff members to provide a fact sheet or background paper on a subject that he thought might come up at the briefing. He also might inform the senior staff that a newspaper or magazine has a deadline on a story and that they should be prepared to receive calls and answer questions. At the meetings he often would urge that information be produced supporting one of the President's programs, for example, "We've got a real problem in letting the momentum get out of the energy program. Now we've got to get some facts out."[20]

Later the Press Office staff would meet again to go over what had been discussed by the senior staff. Then, while the press secretary or his deputy attended the scheduling meetings in which they participated in the planning of future appearances by the President, the rest of the staff would go back to their offices to prepare answers to questions they anticipated would come up as a result of the first three meetings. Then the press secretary would check with the National Security Adviser while the deputy would "check out the press room, in particular the wire service reporters, find out what's hot, what's bothering them, the three networks. Get the answers and then get to Ron [Nessen] and find out what the President knows about this."[21]

At 10:15 the press secretary, his deputy, and four members of the senior staff would discuss with the President the questions for which they needed answers. Whoever was doing the briefing would sit to the President's left at the edge of his desk, looking at him. "It was our meeting. We'd say, 'Mr. President we have this story about so and so, and of course the question arises . . . was the President aware of that?' ''[22] At 10:45 they would return to the press secretary's office to smooth out their responses to questions they anticipated would be asked at the 11:30 briefing.

What they accomplished in this long session can be observed at the briefing. First, both Nessen and Powell were prepared with answers that state the administration's position on almost all major questions that reporters brought up. In Nessen's case he could take out a briefing paper or get one quickly from one of his aides if he was unfamiliar with the subject.[23] Powell, like Carter, appears to carry information in his head. On all important matters in both administrations a clear statement had been worked out from which the press secretary never budged. The administration line is ready. Second, in the prepared announcements with which the briefing usually begins, the press secretary has an opportunity to set the agenda for the media for that day. Although it is difficult to distract reporters from an obvious headline story, when there is none, the press secretary's management of the President's message often finds its way to a leading position in newspapers and on telecasts.

The press secretary's role as conductor of information is taken up by the President himself at press conferences. Nevertheless, the press secretary or one of his aides still plays an important part. Pierre Salinger conducted rehearsals for President Kennedy's news conferences, and in the succeeding administrations the press secretary or other Press Office aides have either done the same thing or prepared a "briefing book" for the President. Another way the press secretary helps the President get his message across at press conferences is by planting questions. The advantage to the President, of course, is that when he knows what's coming he can better calculate the effects of his answer.

Planting questions was common practice in the Eisenhower administration. In his diary, James Hagerty noted not only the many instances in which he planted questions, but also the instances in which reporters told him what questions they intended to ask at the press conference. A comparison of the entries in Hagerty's diary with the transcripts of the press conference shows that these reporters were called on by the President, that they asked the question they said they would, and that the President was well prepared to answer fully. For example, in his diary entry for June 30, 1954, he reported, "Roberts of the Washington Post told me that he was going to ask the President the same question he had asked Churchill. Namely, what are the possibilities for peaceful co-existence between Soviet Russia and Communist China on the one hand and non-Communist nations on the other?" [24] The transcript of the press conference shows that Roberts asked the question, just as he told Hagerty he would.

Informal conduits. Press secretaries often meet informally with reporters. Ronald Nessen's logs indicate that he spent time in the late afternoon talking to reporters in his office and on the telephone. All press secretaries meet with reporters in their office, where they can speak on a background basis; Jody Powell, for example, held "private briefings" several times a week. These meetings or "briefings" in the press secretary's office virtually replaced Powell's public briefings in late 1979 and 1980. Reporters who attended suggest that these types of sessions were productive for both sides.

Although these "briefings" are not public, something like the private meetings would take place in the press room after the briefing, and thus observers had the opportunity to overhear some conferences and conversations. If what took place at these meetings is similar to what occurs in the press secretary's office, the contrast with the official briefing is striking. The reporters and the press secretary seemed more at ease and friendly; the press secretary was considerably more articulate and forthright.

One incident that occurred during the 1976 primary campaign provides a particularly dramatic example of the difference in the relationship in formal and informal settings. At the morning briefing Press Secretary Nessen refused to move from the official White House position that neither President Ford nor his advisers were concerned about Governor Reagan's primary victories or planned any new strategies to cope with them. The briefing ended because President Ford appeared in the Rose Garden for a ten-minute unannounced press conference at which he answered reporters' questions on the same subject with the same answers. After the conference the reporters filed back into the briefing room and gathered around Nessen, who proceeded to describe the kinds of steps the administration was taking to meet the Reagan challenge, who the strategists were, whom the President hoped to win over, and how they assessed their chances in the primaries that were yet to come. Reporters who had seemed bored and frustrated during the briefing became alert and friendly. A meeting that was obviously productive for both sides was taking place.

We were so surprised to see this relationship replace the ill-willed baiting by both sides that seemed typical during our year's observation of the briefing that we turned to a Press Office aide for an explanation. We were told that what we were seeing was typical of small meetings in the press secretary's office, where no transcript is kept. Even if the conversation is on the record, the press secretary does not have to be so concerned that his use of a phrase or word might be distorted. He can speak candidly in this setting because his audience is limited to people he has invited and who understand what he is trying to say. In the more public meeting after the briefing that had occurred that day, the aide continued, the situation of the private meeting was duplicated because the reporters were more sympathetic to President Ford than to Governor Reagan. Although Jody Powell did not appear in the briefing room to talk to reporters informally the way Ron Nessen sometimes did, reporters indicated that in his private sessions Powell provided more authoritative and convincing explanations of the President's activities than he did at the briefings.

Conducting information back to the President. Another aspect of the press secretary's role as conduit is the expectation that he will keep the President and the White House staff informed about what is going on in the press. Press Office personnel, including the press secretary, often pick up information privately from reporters, who trade it to them in exchange for news tips or leaks.

The most systematic way the Press Office gets information back to the President is through the news summary. The informal mechanisms are equally important. Presidents ask their press secretaries to report to them on how reporters are responding to particular programs or to the President personally, and most of them read the briefing transcript. Lyndon Johnson allegedly had an amplifier that was plugged in to the press secretary's office so he could overhear the briefing. Even Richard Nixon, who maintained in public that he was not affected by what reporters were saying about him, would ask Ron Ziegler for a report on what happened at the briefing.[25]

STAFF ROLES

The growth of the White House staff since the early 1950s has had two consequences for the press secretary's conduct. First, there are now a large number of senior-and middle-level staff members whose desire to promote themselves or the policies they favor has led them to develop independent media strategies. Since one of these strategies is to leak information to the press, the press secretary often has been assigned by the President to trace the source of a story. A more important need of the President, but one that is not always recognized by him, is for White House officials and others in the administration to work together to present the same version of the President's message. James Hagerty required White House aides to channel their press contacts through him, a successful device that drew little press criticism since it placed all reporters in an equal position of dependency. Other presidents have not followed this policy, although both Kennedy and Johnson asked their aides to send them reports on their press contacts.[26] Pierre Salinger was given the job of coordinating information policy throughout the executive branch. He served as a personnel officer for the major jobs in public affairs, a function also undertaken by Jody Powell. Powell assigned his deputy, Walter Wurfel, the responsibility of meeting regularly with departmental public information officers for the purpose of coordinating administration communications policy.

The second consequence for the press secretary of the growth in the White House staff has been the creation of offices with publicity functions, including direct media contacts. The functions performed by these offices generally were controlled by Hagerty and Salinger in the Eisenhower and Kennedy administrations and by Lyndon Johnson personally. During the Nixon administration these functions were established in independent offices: the Office of Communications, the President's news summary operation, the separate unit of speechwriters, special units that were assigned a particular public relations function such as the office for Drug Abuse Prevention, and so on. Ronald Ziegler, Nixon's press secretary, had little to say about their operations. In the Ford administration these offices or their functions ultimately were placed under the control of the President's chief of staff, Richard Cheney, who coordinated these functions with David Gergen and William Rhatican, assistants brought in to centralize his authority. In the Carter administration they are the responsibility of the assistant for communication.

During the Eisenhower administration James Hagerty had formal control only over a small staff in the West Wing. At the beginning of the Carter administration the Press Office functioned in seven major subdivisions with a professional staff of twenty-four and an administrative backup of twenty or more.[27] These included:

1. The Upper West Wing office where Powell and two deputies plan and coordinate the major operations of the Press Office, where direct contact with the President is made, where coordination with the senior staff takes place, and where the Press Office itself is administered.
2. The Lower West Wing office, which has two associate press secretaries and which provides the basic point of contact for the White House press corps, services the immediate informational needs, of the press corps, and prepares the material for the daily briefing.
3. The Office of the Assistant for Media and Public Affairs (subsequently absorbed by the communications assistant), with three professionals who dealt with special media projects such as the fireside chats, the phone-ins, and town meetings; made physical arrangements for the President's television appearances; and made policy recommendations on such matters as the organization of the Corporation for Public Broadcasting and the creation of the United States Agency for Communications and Cultural Exchange.
4. Media Liaison, whose three professional staff members serve as the press office for the non-Washington-based media (including the specialty, economic, and ethnic media) by arranging Washington briefings for regional editors and sending mailings of background material on White House and presidential positions to the 110 American newspapers with circulations of more than 100,000, as well as to radio and television stations.
5. The White House News Summary, which has five professionals who provide the President with summaries of major stories from 35 daily newspapers, the three television networks, and, in a separate publication, fifty magazines.

6. The five professional speechwriters.

7. The Photo Office, which had a staff of seven.

In addition to supervising these major divisions of his office, the press secretary was formerly in charge of the press advance operation and the presidential messages unit. His office was aided by support services that provide communications equipment, produce and distribute presidential documents, and write press releases. The White House telephone operators and the correspondence operation also perform important support services for the Press Office.

In 1978, when President Carter appointed Gerald Rafshoon as his assistant for Communications, the administrative responsibilities of the press secretary were divided. Powell remained in charge of the West Wing Press Office, Media Liaison, the White House News Summary, and the White House photographers. Rafshoon directed media advance, the speechwriters, the TV coordinator, and a "projects" office that oversees White House task forces. In reality, most administrative duties remained the responsibility of Walter Wurfel, the deputy press secretary. Powell displayed few talents as an administrator. Although his opinion weighed heavily in all decisions made in the Press Office, he exercised little organizational supervision. Thus, part of the decision to reassign responsibilities that had been part of the Press Office stemmed from a realistic assessment by Powell and others of the nature of his abilities. But the decision also reflected the tremendous workload that daily press operations entail. Apparently a press secretary can deal either with reporters or with his own White House responsibilities, but not both.

POLICY ROLES

The status that the press secretary or any other member of the White House staff brings to the job is determined initially by the role that is bestowed on them as a policy adviser by the President. Presidents Eisenhower, Kennedy, and Carter delegated the major advisory responsibility for media strategy to their press secretaries. Presidents Johnson and Nixon tried to keep direct control of as many of these functions as possible by maintaining personal supervisory authority over them; Nixon also tried to reach this goal by delegating responsibility separately to different individuals, each of whom was directly responsible to him. In both of their administrations the importance of the press secretary was reduced. Because of the expansion of the media-related responsibilities, by the mid-1970s no one person could dominate day-to-day operations, coordination, and promotion. President Ford, who was as much the creature of his staff as any modern President, allowed his chief aides to organize and centralize communications policy, which they did, competently and effectively. Responsibility in the Carter administration is shared among Press Secretary Powell, Gerald Rafshoon, and political adviser Hamilton Jordan.

Basic policy roles. The basic policy role of the press secretary is to advise the President on when information should be released, by whom, in what form, and to what audience. The press secretary's advice influences substantive policy because the fate of an administration's programs depends in part on how information about them is presented. The Carter administration's proposals on energy and inflation, for example, faltered in part from the lack of a coordinated publicity campaign designed to build support for the President's programs.

The press secretary also advises the President on his image and how he can use it to his political advantage. He is concerned with how the President is projecting as a person because the personal view the public has of its President affects his political capital. A popular President has an easier time getting reelected, even when his program is faltering. It is not clear, however, that personal popularity can be translated into effectiveness with Congress and the bureaucracy. Presidents Eisenhower and Kennedy had reason to doubt it could.

Substantive policy. With few exceptions, press secretaries have not become involved in substantive policy decisions. James Connor, the secretary of the cabinet in the Ford administration, explained that even if the press secretary wanted to have a role in substantive policy, it was unlikely that he would have much influence: "Nessen's workload means that he can't be involved early on in the process. The press secretary or anyone else who comes late to the process is at a remarkable disadvantage. They don't know the state of play and by the time they have learned it, the decision has been made."[28]

In general, press secretaries have been most successful in a policy role when they limited their efforts to exercising influence over media and communications policy. It is important, however, that they have a concept of the significance of this role. Managing the President's relations with the news media involves more than answering questions at briefings, recommending when to hold conferences, and deciding the timing of other events. In the contemporary White House, where almost every activity has a public relations impact, it means that the press secretary has to be the best-informed person there: he needs to know what is going on, where it is taking place, and how it will affect the President's efforts to communicate with the media.

AGENT ROLES

The press secretary serves as an agent for his three constituents—the President, the White House staff, and representatives of news organizations—representing the interests of each to the others. He often needs to represent the press, explaining to the President or the White House staff why the press request is reasonable and should be granted. All of Johnson's press secretaries sought to persuade Johnson that he should give advance information on his travel plans. When he refused, his later press secretaries gave the information to the press, and then had it expunged from the briefing transcript so that the President would not know.[29] The press secretary also serves as a socialization agent, informing the White House staff what the press needs and what the rules of the game are. If the press has trouble contacting a White House aide, the press secretary often intervenes to explain to the staff person why the President's interests would be served by his talking with the reporter.

The press secretary also occasionally serves as an agent for the President, representing him in direct political dealings or at public functions. This role has become more common since the press secretary became a visible and important White House official. Pierre Salinger, who was a popular figure, frequently was sent by the Kennedy administration to give speeches.

The need to provide services for the media. Another aspect of the agent role is the service function that the Press Office is called upon to perform for the press. For a trip President Ford took through New York and New Jersey the Press Office made hotel reservations for reporters, chartered their airplanes, published a minute-by-minute account of where and with whom the President would be, set up platforms for photographers and camera crews and informed them about distance and light, secured telephones, typewriters, and telex machines for reporters at each site where the President spoke, and provided fact sheets in response to general requests for information. The press secretary, as on all trips, formed the press pool to accompany the President, duplicated its report, and provided transcripts of all remarks made by the President and some made by other high-ranking officials.

Because the executive branch is the focal point for national news coverage, it is important for the White House to be able to satisfy the requirements of news organizations for information about the President. The accelerating demand for news and gossip about the President and his associates made necessary a Press Office that could assist the White House spokesman. In addition, the technological changes in the media that presented new opportunities for manipulation of the media also made it more important that White House assistants possess the skills to service adequately the technical needs of news organizations.

Reporters' appetites for access to White House notables grew as presidents made themselves available in frequent press conferences and aides talked to reporters in briefings or interviews. In response to the increased availability of Franklin Roosevelt and his successors, as well as to organizational and technological changes in the media, more news organizations requiring more complex types of service from the White House sent representatives to Washington. Both Early and Hagerty were successes in their jobs because of the skill with which they met the various deadlines of news organizations with photo-taking opportunities, broadcast and telecast facilities, press releases, schedules, speeches, and much more.

The consequences of failure. Charles G. Ross, Harry Truman's press secretary, provided these services poorly, which created problems for the administration's press relations. Ross, a boyhood friend of Truman, had good access to the President and was able to keep reporters well informed about the President's thinking. Although correspondents liked the former reporter for the *St. Louis Post-Dispatch,* they were constantly irritated by his inability to understand and respond to their requests that he provide a continuous flow of information. Jack Bell of the Associated Press commented, "Charlie hadn't written a news story in years, he was an editorial writer. Charlie had Truman's confidence, but Charlie just didn't know the operation, the modernized operation. He had operated in the days when you had a Washington correspondent, and he wrote a story a week for the paper, and this wasn't exactly what we wanted. Everybody loved Charlie, but he wasn't worth a damn in the practical aspects of the job."[30]

Ross had been press secretary for two months when complaints began to pile up from both the White House staff and reporters. Ross's assistant, Eben Ayers, recorded in his diary that Truman's appointments secretary, Matthew Connelly, told him, "Ross finds it difficult to adjust himself to the compulsion of having to deal with many different matters at the same time,"[31] and he noted reporters' complaints about "the disturbing feeling on their part concerning the way in which Charlie Ross is carrying out the work of Press Secretary."[32]

After Ross died he was succeeded by Joseph Short, one of two active White House correspondents to be appointed press secretary. Short and his two assistants, Roger Tubby and Irving Perlmeter, were more satisfactory from the press's point of view. According to a contemporary comment, "They amount . . . to three press secretaries because each is capable of sitting in a closed meeting and relaying a portion of it to the press."[33] It remained for Dwight D. Eisenhower and Press Secretary James Hagerty, however, to bring media relations to the degree of White House attention they have enjoyed ever since. Each new administration since Eisenhower has recognized that the quality of the services it provides to the media matters very much to journalists, and so affects the way in which they communicate the President's image and message, and thus ultimately is important to presidential leadership.

Taken together, these roles—conduit, staff, policy, agent—give the press secretary a great deal of potential power. He begins his tenure with a large number of responsibilities, but unless he is able to satisfy his constituents, he gradually will find that his formal power does not insure influence. In the history of the office of the press secretary, there has been much variation in the ways in which individuals have performed these roles and in the abilities they have shown to preserve the delicate balance between their constituents.

The Press Secretary and His Constituents

The press secretary is expected to fulfill the needs of his three constituents: (1) the President, who expects the press secretary to reflect his views; (2) the White House staff, whose members sometimes try to influence events—and the President—by employing their own press strategies and at other times want to avoid reporters; and (3) the representatives of news organizations— reporters, photographers, technicians, columnists, bureau chiefs, and editors—who expect the press secretary to provide them with information, access, and services.

The problem for the press secretary is that he is expected to satisfy the needs of three constituents although ultimately he is responsible to only one, the President. Jody Powell indicated he knew well which master he served in an interview shortly before he moved into the White House: "I see it as a very serious mistake for the press secretary and the press to think for one minute that the press secretary works for the press. You have a service function for the press, to provide them with information, for providing facilities when you travel, and a whole range of things. You do them not because you work for them, but because you work for the President."[34] But in order to be effective for his chief, the press secretary must organize the President's relationship with the press. This means he must attempt to minimize conflict among his constituents.

Conflict between members of the White House staff and reporters is well known and well reported. A President's desire to get his message to the public in unobstructed form leads him to want to control when, where, and how much information is released to the media. For their part, reporters seek to get information about White House activities on their own terms. Often they look for information about divisions, discrepancies, and conflicts in the administration. In contrast, the President's advisers want to cast a mood of consistency and order. What often results are confrontations at the daily briefing or in the press secretary's office. Many of these clashes find their way into the media, particularly if colorful language is used and if they occur in the absence of major White House announcements. Press Office officials are aware that their activities will be reported. "Don't Screw Up on a Slow News Day" was the motto that Assistant Press Secretary William Roberts of the Ford administration displayed in his office.

Less well known are the tensions that arise because individual aides use the media for their own personal and policy advantages, regardless of the needs of the President. Staff members risk presidential wrath if they are discovered trying to take advantage of relationships they have formed with reporters. Yet they continue to try to use the media because for some of them it is the best way to get the President's attention, particularly in administrations where a few powerful aides limit access to him. White House officials on one side of a dispute may use the press to try to sandbag the President into committing himself to their policies. They also may try to use the media as a weapon in intrastaff warfare. In the Ford administration, for example, Robert Hartmann and Richard Cheney often attacked each other anonymously in the press. Hartmann represented Ford's old congressional staff, while Cheney was the chief of the advisers who became important after Nixon resigned. Some Ford advisers regularly leaked word of their low opinion of Ronald Nessen to reporters because they hoped it would force the President to select someone they believed would make a more effective press secretary. None of these actions were condoned by the President, but in spite of general admonitions to stop them, they continued.

Lyndon Johnson became so annoyed at what he felt was independent use of the media for personal goals that Marvin Watson, a member of the senior staff, was asked to keep a record of which staff persons talked to which reporters and for how long. Records in the LBJ Library indicate that there were periods when Johnson received daily reports from Watson relating to staff contacts with reporters. Press Secretary George Christian explained Johnson's action: "What he resented was other people on the staff dealing with a whole lot of press people. He did not like for a fellow who wasn't the press secretary to be saying much to the press—saying anything to the press for that matter—unless the press secretary asked him to do it. He preferred they stay out of that limelight. He took it for granted that he ought to have one spokesman, and that he didn't have to fiddle around trying to tell ten people what to say, that if he dealt with one man, he was just on a lot more secure ground than dealing with ten."[35]

PROFESSIONALISM

A press secretary who is to be respected by each of his constituents needs several kinds of skills and resources: (1) he must be well informed about what the President is thinking and doing, and he must be successful in articulating it; (2) he must provide the President and the White House staff with appropriate advice and see that advice taken, while as an administrator, he must satisfy the service needs of the press and the information needs of all three of his constituents; and (3) he must bring to the job an appropriate level of training and experience.

Reflecting the words and moods of the President. The largest part of the press secretary's job is to inform the press about what the President is doing, and what his goals are and how the administration plans to reach them. Press secretaries need to know how to convey the President's messages in a manner that increases the likelihood that the media will portray them the way the White House intended. As a professional, he must know the appropriate wording for statements so he can predict how his words will be interpreted. In order to maintain the credibility of the White House, the press secretary must provide a complete account that will not be challenged by seemingly contradictory information that leaks out later. Since presidents and leading advisers often believe that it is best to tell the public less than everything, a press secretary often has to convince them that they would be best served by ''going the hangout route'' (a Watergate expression meaning that it is better to give out bad news yourself because it will look worse if it appears to have been concealed).

While he is talking to reporters, the press secretary needs to be able to reflect the words and mood of the President. James Hagerty was particularly accurate in telling reporters what the President had said. Strangely, however, many reporters thought that Hagerty was acting on his own, perhaps because they had little personal contact with the President. Hagerty indicates they were wrong: ''Many of the times, the notes or the sentences were written in the personal handwriting of the President, and he said, 'say this.' And I'd get up, and say that. There wasn't any answer that I made when I *thought* I was reflecting the President's viewpoint. The only answers I made were when I *knew* I was reflecting the President's viewpoint.''[36]

An interesting example of Hagerty's accurate portrayal of the President occurred when Eisenhower continuously failed to include Senator Joseph McCarthy among congressmen invited to the White House for events attended by most members of the House and Senate. Hagerty was aware that he would be questioned on the matter at his briefing. He recorded, ''I told him [Eisenhower] that I had two choices—either just say I had no comment or say that McCarthy had not been invited. After thinking for a few minutes, the President said, 'why don't you just say that you never check on the guests the President and Mrs. Eisenhower invite to the White House and let it go at that.' ''[37] At his briefing the next afternoon, he said what Eisenhower had told him to: ''I do not check on the President and Mrs. Eisenhower's guests.''[38]

Advising and administering. The successful press secretary is regarded by his President and the White House staff as a professional whose advice is worth taking because he knows more than they do about publicity matters. Yet most successful politicians regard themselves as public relations experts. The most prominent example of a conflict over this role of the press secretary occurred between Lyndon Johnson and George Reedy. Reedy later said, ''The President unfortunately always regarded the press secretary and the Press Office as a public relations office. And I think most of the major problems I had arose from the fact that I tried to disillusion him and that couldn't be done . . . he was thinking of the Press Office as a place that produces stories for the press. I thought of the Press Office as a point of contact between the press and the White House.''[39]

The principal administrative duty of the press secretary is seeing that the Press Office gets information to reporters in a form they can use in time to meet their deadlines. If he does not meet these needs, news organizations will complain about his handling of the job, as they did with Charles Ross.

The impact of background and training. The experience of some press secretaries has had a strong bearing on their ability to satisfy the President, their fellow staff members, and reporters. George Christian, a Texan, worked in public relations, served as press secretary to Governor John Connally, was a political ally of Lyndon Johnson, and shared Johnson's distrust of those he felt looked down on Texans. Stephen Early, James Hagerty, and Pierre Salinger also had experience in political public relations. In addition, each had worked for the media and thus understood the kinds of problems faced by news organizations and their representatives. Early was a reporter when he met Franklin Roosevelt at the Democratic Convention of 1912, twenty-one years before he became press secretary. He kept up the acquaintance in the intervening years while holding a variety of media jobs. Though Hagerty did not know Dwight Eisenhower well before 1953, he had handled press relations for Governor Thomas E. Dewey of New York and so had learned how to arrange executive publicity while responding to the needs of the press. During Dewey's presidential campaigns in 1944 and 1948, Hagerty met many journalists who still were covering the White House in 1953. Pierre Salinger worked as press secretary for Senator John Kennedy for several years, served as campaign press secretary in 1960, and then moved into the West Wing office in 1961. The advantage that these background experiences gave to all four secretaries was summed up in the remark William Theis of the Hearst Newspapers made about Hagerty: "so, he didn't have to start running," Theis said. "He had been on the track for a long time."[40]

ACCESS, CREDIBILITY, AND STATUS

To a large extent, reporters and White House officials measure the press secretary's status with the President according to the nature and amount of access he has to the Oval Office. This often determines whether his words are accepted as authentically representing the President. All three factors—access, credibility, and status—affect the degree to which the press secretary is believed and accepted by all his constituents.

Access. A press secretary who does not have constant access to the President cannot serve either the President or reporters. Without access, the press secretary cannot be well informed about what is happening with the President, nor can he get the answers. The evidence from the logs of presidents and press secretaries at presidential libraries indicates that most press secretaries were able to see the President at least once a day. Obviously, the best-informed press secretaries had more than proximity: "Jody's in and out of that office twenty times a day," an assistant for media liaison said. "The White House regulars know that [he's] one of the better conduits."[41]

Stephen Early had a daily morning meeting with the President. When he needed to talk with Roosevelt, even if it was during his daily briefing, he called him. In one of his regular meetings with the press, a question was

raised about the validity of a morning *New York Times* story indicating
Roosevelt's approval of a piece of legislation relating to Guam. Early, not
aware of the law, called Roosevelt while the newsmen were there and was told
by the President that he had never seen the bill.[42]

Lyndon Johnson saw George Christian alone every morning in his bedroom
and in short meetings throughout the day. Christian recalled, "I told him that I
desired to have as complete access as possible, that I could not work as press
secretary without access. He said I would have no problems there at all, that I
could come into his office any time I wanted to, that I could come into his
bedroom any time I wanted to. He said that if there were more than two people
in his office and I was curious about what was going on, to walk in; and if he
didn't want me there, he would throw me out, that I ought to have the right to
go in."[43] Christian confirmed that he received the access he asked for.

Without such access, newsmen find their queries unanswered and soon
question the authority with which the press secretary gives his daily briefing.
Reporters often complained during the Ford administration that while Nessen
met each morning with the President, he was only one of several White House
officials in the meeting, and that there seemed not to be a close relationship
between them. Reporters sought information from others in the White House
whom they considered to be better informed on administration activities.

George Reedy said that he spoke to Johnson only once a day, for about five
minutes, on the telephone right before the briefing.[44] Reedy suggested that his
different interpretation of his responsibilities kept him away from Johnson,
although he maintained that he could always get through when necessary.
Reporters were aware that Reedy did not have good relations with the President. "Reedy aroused the worst instincts in Johnson," one reporter recalled.[45]

Credibility. The doubts that reporters had about the value of Ronald Nessen's access to President Ford influenced the credibility he brought to his
relations with the media. The *Wall Street Journal*'s White House correspondent, Dennis Farney, contrasted Jody Powell with Nessen by emphasizing the importance of Powell's confidential relationship with President Carter.
"When he talks, you lend credence to what he says, you assume he speaks for
the President. You never knew with Ron Nessen."[46]

A credible press secretary must also give his constituents a clear sense that
he is absolutely loyal to the President. President Johnson doubted Bill Moyers's
loyalty. (In the case of Ronald Nessen, the White House staff did not question
his loyalty to the President as much as they doubted his ability to serve him.)
A correspondent who covered the White House during the Johnson administration suggested that it was not clear to him whether Bill Moyers spoke for
the President or himself: "I never fully trusted Bill Moyers; he was interested
in promoting himself and his programs. He ingratiated himself with the press
corps. He was serving two masters and I distrust anyone who tries that."[47]

Status. Press secretaries who are among the President's closest advisers have the most status. They know what is going on at the top levels of the White House, they are asked for advice, and they often initiate discussions, as well. Stephen Early had such status. He was one of only three secretaries to Franklin Roosevelt and thus he was involved in much of the business that passed through the President's office. When Roosevelt was out of town, Early often became the focal point in the White House for political leaders as well as reporters. He observed in his diary, "Throughout the day was kept busy on the telephones, as I am the only secretary here to talk with Governors, Senators, and Cabinet officers, etc."[48] James Hagerty also was regarded as a senior adviser. His authority was particularly great during Eisenhower's trips.

PERSONAL RELATIONS

The quality of the personal relations the press secretary establishes with his three constituents is the third ingredient affecting his performance. This is a factor because the roles that the President, the staff, and the press play at the White House are likely to .ignite the elements of discord that are never far beneath the surface. The press secretary can soften conflict through the establishment of personal relations based on mutual respect and trust.

The most important of his relationships is the one he has with the President, because it sets the tone for his relationships with the staff and the press. George Reedy's personal relationship with his president strongly affected his credibility with the press and with the White House staff. "Johnson kept him on a short leash," said Frank Cormier, who, like other reporters interviewed for this study, was sympathetic to Reedy and felt that he had been badly used by the President: "Reedy was just a fellow who lumbered around here and held briefings. He was constantly answering the presidential phone in the middle of the briefing to get the word on what he was to say. [Johnson] was always telling us that 'poor old Reedy can't do anything that he likes, he can't chase the women, he can't eat, he can't drink. All he can do is go up there and have you people picking at him twice a day.' "[49] Although an exceptionally able person, Reedy could not establish useful personal relations with reporters because they did not believe Johnson respected him.

In contrast, the close personal relations established by Stephen Early and James Hagerty with Roosevelt and Eisenhower were well known to the press. Early was regarded by reporters as a bellwether of Roosevelt's moods; Hagerty, they knew, was fully informed on Eisenhower's thinking. Hagerty said of his relationship with the President: "For eight years I knew everything he did, and if I wasn't in his office when he made a decision, even including the secretary of state, he'd tell John Foster Dulles, 'stop in at Jim's office as you go out and tell him what we decided.' "[50]

Because the White House staff has grown in size and function in the last decades, the establishment of good relations between the press secretary and other senior-level aides is almost as important as his relations with the President. Although both Ronald Ziegler and Ronald Nessen established good personal relations with the President, neither was well regarded by the senior staff. Consequently, reporters felt that they were not reliable as sources of information about major decisions. "I never knew whether Ziegler was lying or whether the others thought he was too stupid to be told anything," a reporter commented.[51] White House staff during the Ford administration suggested that Nessen was too busy to be close to the policy process. In contrast, both White House aides and reporters acknowledged that Jody Powell not only had the respect of the senior staff, he was one of the most important members of that staff.

The press secretary's success in establishing close relations with reporters may make it possible for him to merge the interests of the President with those of newsmen. If reporters trust a press secretary, they will accept his judgment about whether a significant story is likely to develop, and they may even accept his suggestions about what would make a good story. Before press conferences they may go further and accept his suggestions about questions to ask the President.

Personal relations affect the formal relationship at a time of crisis. The antagonism between Ronald Ziegler and reporters during Watergate finally led to Ziegler's replacement at the daily briefing by his deputy, Gerald Warren. Warren, who had maintained a good personal relationship with the press during the Nixon administration, was able to deal with reporters without rancor, even though the information communicated by him represented the same administration line that Ziegler had presented. Reporters simply believed that Warren would not deliberately mislead them. Similarly, George Christian managed to maintain good personal relations with all three of his constituents during the Vietnam War crisis, even as reporters were describing the Johnson administration's "credibility gap." Still, neither Christian nor Warren could salvage the relations that Johnson and Nixon had with the press because the crises of the two administrations were political in origin and not, as the Presidents chose to believe, "public relations problems."

Perhaps the most visible effect of personal relations can be seen in the change that occurred in the atmosphere in the briefing room when Carter replaced Ford and Powell replaced Nessen. During the presidential campaign, Powell developed good personal relationships with many of the reporters who later were assigned to the White House. They knew, of course, about his close ties to the President and his status among the staff. In addition, they appreciated his self-effacing sense of humor and charm. When he came to the podium in the briefing room during his first months, the sense of contest that had prevailed during the Nessen period was replaced with an air of conviviality. The substance of the briefings, however, remained the same. Powell gave no more information in his briefings than had Nessen, but the atmosphere was different. The residue of good will he had acquired ran out after the administration's fortunes began to slump in 1977, but it did provide benefits to him for several months and may even have softened the impact on the White House of particular crises.

The Influence of the Press Secretary

Even a well-placed press secretary is limited in his ability to influence the critical relationship between the White House and the news media because of the structural factors—the permanent needs of the presidency and the news media—on which it is based. The deeper a particular factor is embedded in the relationship, the less likely it is that the press secretary will be able to alter it. Yet both White House officials and the representatives of news organizations have a great deal at stake in the survival and even the prosperity of the other. From the White House perspective, it is essential that the news media appear independent; to the extent that the media is thought to be controlled by government, its message is less likely to be believed. For their part, news organizations have strongly identified their own prestige as carriers of the message with that of the power and authority of the White House. It was for that reason that major stories about the Watergate crisis were developed by outsiders such as Woodward and Bernstein, who were not even part of the *Washington Post*'s national staff. Similarly, stories relating to the failure of the war in Vietnam were not carried by many "respectable" news organizations until several years after the same material had been published by the antiwar press.

Although the adversary elements in the relationship during the Johnson and Nixon years reached open warfare at times, there has been a subsequent return to an altered but still recognizable relationship in which the destinies of the White House and the news media are tied together. In this context, it does make a difference who the press secretary is. In particular, press secretaries who establish trust and respect for themselves during the early days of a new administration can use their influence to reduce the strain during the periods that inevitably follow, when the interests of the two sides begin to diverge.

If press secretaries are to be successful White House publicists, they must have a conscious understanding of or an instinctive feel for the roles they must play and the skills, positions, and relations they must acquire. The question that may be raised about the prospects for success under present conditions is whether the demands placed upon press secretaries are too great. Even traditional functions like providing services for the press have become immensely complicated because of the tremendous growth in the number and the increase in the diversity of representatives of news organizations whose demands can conflict with each other. For example, television network reporters demanded that they be allowed to set up their equipment to cover a luncheon in New Hampshire during the 1976 primary. After a short argument, permission was given, whereupon the remainder of the press corps straggled over in pursuit of the cameras and complained to John Carlson, a deputy press secretary in the Ford administration, that the White House was staging another media event.[52]

Of course the job of the press secretary is much harder if he works for a President who does not understand that in order to get his message to the public he is going to have to be accessible to White House reporters and allow his aides to get out information about his administration. Press secretaries who work in administrations where staff rivalries create a maelstrom of rising and falling among the power-seekers are also not likely to function well in their jobs. Since problems of press dissatisfaction, presidential incomprehension, and staff cut-throating have been endemic during the last several administrations, it may be that the roles of the press secretary can be performed only adequately, at best.

An informal survey among past and present White House reporters and officials asked who they regarded as successful press secretaries. Only the names of Stephen Early and James Hagerty were mentioned with any degree of frequency. Since both Hagerty and Early have been gone from the scene for a considerable time, it is likely that nostalgia has clouded the memories about them, blocking out the conflicts and outbursts of bygone days. But it is also true that their jobs involved fewer demands than those of their successors. They could concentrate on such matters as the fulfillment of the press's technical needs. Perhaps even these giants of the past today would greet the end of their tenure in office with a sigh of relief and a sense that all of their scrambling was not quite worth the effort.

III

TAKING ADVANTAGE OF POSITION

T HE INFORMATION most reporters want concerns the heart, mind, and intentions of the President. This kind of information usually can be obtained from individuals speaking privately rather than in public forums. This gives the President and other White House officials who serve as reporters' sources tremendous advantages. The careers of nine White House correspondents illustrate some of the different patterns of adaption that reporters may employ and the kinds of success they may achieve in the White House milieu. Elite journalists—publishers, bureau chiefs, leading columnists, and network executives—are so powerful they are treated as diplomatic representatives rather than as mere reporters. White House officials try to exploit the President's advantages by using the media to project his personal qualities, his leadership ability, and his policy goals. One of the President's chief public platforms for exploiting his advantages is the press conference.

SIX

THE SOURCE

S OURCES are people located near information reporters think they might want. White House correspondents want information about the President's plans and relationships. He is the person they concentrate their efforts on both because whatever he says about people or policy is newsworthy and because the majority of White House stories received by news organizations are inspired, instigated, or sent at his behest. Much of what reporters learn about him and his policies is transmitted through covert and unofficial channels. The people who provide this information are well-known public figures whose names, faces, and statements often appear in the media. Other sources, known as "moles" because they are buried from public view, are discovered only after diligent digging by reporters. In all cases, however, the identities of sources are concealed or at least clouded.

The sources discussed in this chapter either work at the White House or are part of the President's inner circle. With few exceptions the stories they give to reporters are supportive of the administration. Most of what they "leak" is meant to encourage news organizations to publish or broadcast stories that serve the goals of the President. Consequently, their development of relations with reporters usually is encouraged, or at least not discouraged, by the White House leadership.

Reporters who wish to seek news sources outside the President's staff can ferret a great deal of information about the White House from congressional leaders, high-level administrators in the departments, heads of interest groups, and others whose continuing access to the Chief Executive and his assistants provides them with excellent intelligence. Since some sources of this type have little or no stake in the administration's success, they are often quite willing to give reporters information that the White House does not want them to have. With the exception of wire service correspondents and others assigned to cover the routines of the White House, most reporters maintain that what they learn from their sources is more important than what they learn from official pronouncements, releases, and briefings.

Reporters draw from an arcane vocabulary to describe the authenticity of their information when they cannot reveal the identity of the person who gave it to them. If the person is speaking officially for the White House, he or she usually is labeled a *spokesman*. This means that White House officials will take responsibility for what is said, although they do not want the identity of the person who actually said it revealed. Reporters use the term *source* for persons who permit their words to be quoted or paraphrased but who cannot or will not claim that the White House will stand behind them.

According to usage that is general but not universal in Washington, the term *high-level source* or *high-level spokesman* refers to someone at the senior staff level at the White House or at the assistant secretary level or above in one of the departments. Beyond this, usage differs according to the rules of news organizations and the desires of individual sources or spokesmen to cloak their identities. Reporters try to use a designating label like *White House sources* or a descriptive statement such as ''it was learned at the White House'' so that the reader or viewer knows something about the origins of the story. In most cases reporters are expected to follow the wishes of their informant if they want the information. For example, reporters were told by Jody Powell at a background briefing in Jerusalem prior to the conclusion of President Carter's diplomatic mission there in March, 1979, that they could only refer to him as a *source*. As so often happens when a highly visible individual such as the press secretary or the secretary of state holds background briefings on important subjects, however, his identity was revealed, in this case by United Press International.

With a little detective work a close observer of public affairs usually can identify the high-level spokesman who holds background meetings with small groups of reporters. A background briefing is a session at which an official whose identity cannot be revealed explains a policy and answers some of the reporters' questions. A background meeting, which is less formal, may take place on Air Force One when the President or the secretary of state or other top aide decides to talk to reporters in the media pool, or it may occur in a meeting with an official that had been requested by a few reporters, The same rules that governed the background briefing apply to the meetings. Although a reporter's story may not indicate whether the spokesman provided information at a briefing or in one of the more informal settings, readers and viewers who want to find out usually will be able to gather clues from the various references that appear in several news stories.

White House officials cite reasons of diplomacy as justification for their use of the *spokesman* label. For example, during the Nixon and Ford administrations Kissinger insisted that he be identified as a spokesman rather than by name. The practice was defended on the grounds that even though foreign officials knew who the ''spokesman'' was, a public, on-the-record statement by a high official such as Kissinger could force them to respond publicly in a way that could precipitate a crisis. Thus, for example, if ''a spokesman'' warns the Russians not to do something, they may construe it as a message; if the secretary of state warns them, it could be taken as a threat.

Because some reporters dislike the spokesman label, they have found ways to let officials' identities slip out. They may tell reporters who did not attend the background session—and who therefore did not agree to its ground rules—who the spokesman was. Then, after the information appears elsewhere, they too are free to reveal the identity. A less furtive method is to ask the press secretary at the next briefing if the White House stands behind what the spokesman said. Since what a spokesman says is official, the press secretary at least will permit reporters to state that "the White House did not deny" the matter.

Sources are not quite as easy to identify as spokesmen. First, reporters have a vested interest in keeping their identities confidential, especially if the information they receive gives them a competitive advantage against other reporters. Second, because the message that sources are trying to get out usually does not represent a White House position that has been ratified by the President and his top assistants, reporters are more careful to cover their trail to protect both the source and themselves. Nevertheless, most Washington insiders can identify the high-level sources in a continuing story. For example, during the Iranian crisis of the winter of 1978 and 1979, Joseph Kraft rattled off to us the names of government officials in the National Security Council and State Department whom he labeled as the sources for stories that were appearing in the *New York Times*, the *Washington Post,* and several syndicated columns. Although Kraft did not reveal his own informants, it would not have been difficult to use this same information to determine the identity of the sources he used in the stories that he prepared at the same time.[1]

Sources and the Information Flow

Reporters develop sources because the official information and explanations they receive often provide a superficial and bloodless view of events and policy. Furthermore, the use of well-informed sources who provide information on an exclusive or at least on a limited basis add to reporters' prestige and usually help their professional advancement. Reporters believe they benefit from the willingness of many officials to be forthcoming in private with those they trust will not misunderstand or distort what they are told. In such situations officials may offer background information, describe the relationship between different aspects of administration activities, give a sense of the color and mood of meetings, and provide the personal responses of those who attend them. At times, of course, sources provide reporters with information that they could not obtain elsewhere.

The President and his chief advisers often prefer to speak to reporters on a background basis for many of the same reasons that reporters prefer this rule. Officials who dance around politically sensitive questions at on-the-record sessions may feel free to reveal their assessments of policies, politics, and programs at background interviews where the rules of the game protect them—or at least provide an opportunity for a later retreat from embarrassing positions. The development of strong and confidential relations with a reporter makes officials better able to form the story the reporter ultimately prepares. Some staff members have been recruited as White House aides for this reason. The President believes they will be able to use their contacts with reporters, editors, or other officials of news organizations to get the White House picture into the media. This was one of the reasons the Johnson administration wanted Robert Kintner to work for it, as indicated in a letter from Press Secretary Bill Moyers to Kintner, then the president of NBC: "The President was impressed by your letter mentioning your contacts within the world of journalism," Moyers wrote. "Once your feet are solidly on the ground here, quiet and discrete cultivation of these contacts can be most useful."[2]

In most administrations the common and central purpose of those who become sources is to further the reputation of the President. In this respect the White House is different from major departments such as defense, where career officials have bureaucratic commitments to their branch of service as well as policy positions that, if stated, could bring them into conflict with the political appointees who are their superiors. Virtually everyone who works at the White House advances according to whether he or she is furthering the President's goals. Although every recent president has been concerned that members of his staff have passed on harmful, self-serving information to reporters, what he regards as harmful leaks usually originate elsewhere.

Further, private rivalries ordinarily are more subdued than elsewhere in government, although there have been noteworthy exceptions. In the Nixon and Ford administrations many senior and middle-level staff members deeply resented Henry Kissinger's autonomous position and tried to undermine his reputation with reporters.[3] During the Ford administration officials sometimes used the media to attack each other because the peculiar manner in which Ford became president left him with members of four different staffs: the Nixon holdovers, Ford's vice presidential and congressional staff, his campaign staff, and those Ford appointed after he became president. Other examples are discussed later in this chapter. Nevertheless, the loyalty of most of those who work in the White House belongs to the President.

Although White House sources reinforce the administration's position, they have no compunctions about attacking rivals in the departments or in Congress. Harry Truman's White House staff leaked stories to reporters that contributed to the removal of Secretary of Commerce Henry Wallace because they believed Wallace was not helping the President. Similar incidents involving cabinet officers or other high presidential appointees whom the White House marked as antagonists of the President's programs occurred in subsequent administrations. Unfavorable material about these officials often led to their early departure or reduced their power within the administration.

From a reporter's perspective, the best sources are staff members who do not have prominent positions or official publicity functions. Visible staff, such as the chief political adviser, the head of domestic policy, or the White

House counsel, appear in interviews on the television networks' morning news programs, on the Sunday interview programs such as "Meet the Press" or "Face the Nation," and at on-the-record breakfast meetings with reporters such as those held by the Sperling group. Such top-level officials seldom provide reporters with better information privately than they do on the record. Consequently, although reporters like to interview them because of their proximity to the throne, they get more substantive information from officials at the second or middle level. "What Cheney [Richard Cheney, Ford's chief of staff] tells you in his office today, you'll get from Nessen in his briefing tomorrow," Aldo Beckman of the *Chicago Tribune* suggested.[4]

From the White House perspective, however, it is important that its highest officials develop relationships with prominent reporters, if only to prevent them from misinterpreting an isolated piece of information they may pick up lower down the line. Only the senior staff has a sense of how everything is put together at the White House. Some of the staff members, of course, may have no talent for dealing with reporters, and others may not be knowledgeable. Nevertheless, they play a vital role in keeping erroneous stories out of major publications. In addition, several prominent officials in every administration usually are able to convince reporters that they are worth cultivating; masters like Henry Kissinger are able to pick and choose between public and private channels to get their message into the media.[5]

There have been notable exceptions to the rule that officials with a publicity function are not good sources. Press secretaries who are well informed are asked by reporters to provide background guidance. Jody Powell's closeness to President Carter led reporters to seek him out as a source. Even the President sometimes provides tidbits of information that are useful to reporters with whom he has established a long relationship, as was the case with President Eisenhower and Roscoe Drummond, President Johnson and William White, and President Kennedy with Benjamin Bradlee, Rowland Evans, and many others.[6]

Specifically, there are five reasons why the President and his associates become sources for reporters. First, in small, private meetings, officials are able to have more influence over the tone, content, and placement of stories than they often are in press conferences, briefings, or on-the-record interviews. Second, the President and his staff use private encounters with representatives of the media to build media support for the administration and its policies, and for themselves. Third, they use private sessions to force the decision-making process. Fourth, they use the media to build political capital. Finally, officials provide access to reporters because they believe that media power is so strong they cannot avoid such contacts.

Fine-Tuning Stories

White House officials use private interviews with selected reporters to influence when and where stories will appear and what they will say. Their influence may affect a story that appears in the aftermath of an interview or, over a longer period, may shape the reporters' views of the President and the administration.

President Kennedy used intimate luncheons with editors of small-town and weekly newspapers to build support for himself and his policies from publications that were hostile. The tactic was successful. "President's Personality, Charm Permeates Luncheon," declared the headline of the *Maryville-Alcoa Times* after President Kennedy met with a group of Tennessee editors and publishers over lunch in the White House.[7] Other Tennessee newspapers featured equally favorable headlines: "Kennedy is Very Sharp"; "President Was Courteous, Delightful Host to Newsmen"; "Kennedy Rolled Out Red Carpet for 26 Tennessee Newsmen."[8] On the whole, favorable stories resulted from off-the-record meetings that President Kennedy held with state editors and publishers starting in October, 1961.

The ground rules limiting what these editors could publish helped determine the kind of coverage the President received. Although the editors and publishers were allowed to ask the President questions on any subject, they were not permitted to report his answers. This left them with two subjects to write about: their impressions of the President as a person, and the setting and circumstances of the luncheon itself. On both counts the articles were almost unanimously favorable. Press Secretary Salinger kept a file on the Tennessee editors' luncheon, including newspaper accounts of it; most papers carried front-page stories accompanied by a picture of the group seated around the table with the President. All of the writers noted the President's charm and commented on the depth of his knowledge. Some editors indicated that they disagreed with him on individual issues, but there was not a single unfavorable line about Kennedy as a person or leader. All the writers were impressed with the White House. One correspondent included pictures of his invitation and place card with his article.

Obviously, national publications and sophisticated local reporters today are not as easily swayed by an invitation to a White House luncheon as a group of country editors were in the early 1960s. Nevertheless, wooing publishers and editors bears fruit. Robert Kintner described the payoff from the visits that President Johnson was having with newspeople:

I have no doubt that the President's informative, interesting and warm conversation with Cowles, a Republican, has favorably affected Cowles' attitude toward the President. Since Mike Cowles maintains a strong operating control of *Look, Family Circle* and a group of smaller newspapers in the Southeast and since he has a substantial say on the policy of the *Des Moines Register, The Minneapolis Tribune* and the Cowles Newspaper Syndication and radio and television stations, I believe the effect of the visit will be felt for some time in the policy of these media.

Specifically, comprehensive treatment by the *Des Moines Register* of the President's visit and the friendly editorial in the *Des Moines Register* unquestionably came from Mike Cowles.[9]

When the White House undertakes a major publicity campaign on behalf of the President and his programs, officials provide a variety of opportunities for reporters to "learn the facts," including background briefings for selected reporters. During the Johnson administration, for example, the President often briefed a group of correspondents invited by the Press Office in an effort to establish the context for their stories on his trip, proposal, or announcement. When George Christian was appointed press secretary, he received some advice from his predecessor, Bill Moyers, on how to set up this type of briefing: "I would have Walter Cronkite, Chet Huntley and David Brinkley down along with their corresponding White House people," Moyers wrote, "in order for the President to give them a proper slant on the trip."[10] Moyers also recommended that Christian set up sessions for the President with representatives of the three news magazines, a group of foreign correspondents, and Washington bureau chiefs of newspapers such as the *New York Times* and the *Baltimore Sun*.

News people do not expect to get hard news from private meetings with the President. If the President does release important information to one or two reporters, he incurs the wrath of correspondents throughout the country. Thus the White House uses presidential interviews to show reporters how the President operates rather than to have him tell them his plans. Paul Martin of the Gannett News Service explained the value of these interviews to reporters as well as to the President in a letter he wrote to Jack Valenti of the Johnson administration:

The void in my estimation lies in this area: periodic access to the President's thinking by interpretive-writing, opinion-shaping bureau chiefs and top correspondents in Washington for major newspapers, newspaper groups, periodicals and radio-TV networks. I'm sure you do this on an isolated and individual basis from time to time. I think it should be done more often on a group basis.

News analysts and commentators as a rule tend to be skeptical and critical. Yet it is axiomatic that if you have something constructive to think about, then you are more apt to report constructively.[11]

While the President generally is most successful at using background meetings to obtain favorable coverage, other officials in the White House use similar techniques. High on the list of those who are given special treatment for this purpose are reporters for major publications, columnists, and television commentators. During the Johnson administration Robert Kintner lunched frequently with Walter Lippmann, James Reston, and television executives in order to provide them with a sympathetic, insider's view of what was going on in the administration. Speechwriter Peter Benchley, who later became a popular novelist, noted that Kintner "was his media man and Kintner had control—it's a weird kind of control—but he had so many contacts in the networks, having been the president of two of them, that he could call anybody in television or since he came from New York anybody in the stage or movies or anything else and get advice and could tell him what to do and listen to them."[12] Johnson raised the estimation of his administration in the broadcasting area through his appointment of Kintner, and among foreign policy reporters and influential publishers with his choice of Averell Harriman. These men knew the habits and behavior of media influentials Johnson wanted to reach.

Harriman knew the executives of several important publications, and thus was able to give Johnson advice on how to act and what to say when the President met with them. Prior to a meeting with Arthur Hays Sulzberger of the *New York Times,* Harriman gave Johnson the following advice: "The President may also want to comment pleasantly about the important role Scotty Reston plays in Washington, that he is glad he has gone out to Viet-Nam, and refer favorably to his articles from Saigon. . . . He might add that he looks forward to getting his reactions when he returns."[13]

Every administration has one or two individuals like Harriman who are able to play this role. It is the Kissingers, the Bundys, and the Strausses who have the prestige required to command press attention and who can influence what appears in the media about the administration. During the Nixon and Ford administrations Henry Kissinger became almost presidential in his ability to mold the view of American foreign policy of reporters at all status levels. In the Johnson, Kennedy, and Carter administrations, only the President could play this role.

Generating Support for the White House Position

The President and those around him use their contacts with reporters to build support for administration programs and for themselves. Developing support requires getting reporters information at the right time and in a form they will use. Most political appointees in the White House are involved in the process at some point, though only a few see reporters frequently.

THE IMPORTANCE OF THE PRESIDENT'S PERSONAL ROLE

Most administration leaders believe that the President needs media support in order to get his programs approved and implemented. Consequently, officials use background dinners, intimate gatherings, and interviews to win press approval for specific programs and to win support among those who control news organizations. President Eisenhower had black tie dinners with publishers, while President Carter has small White House suppers with publishers, editors, and leading reporters. Deputy Press Secretary Tom Johnson of Lyndon Johnson's administration recommended that this approach include other public opinion leaders: "If the format of this backgrounder could be repeated for key groups of public opinion makers," he wrote, "the President would significantly strengthen nationwide support for his policies. . . . I am confident that increased broad-based support would flow from such briefings."[14] His specific advice was for the President to meet with 200 leaders drawn from labor, business, the clergy, city and county governments, and newspapers. The President also was advised to follow John Kennedy's lead and meet informally with influential media people, including those who opposed him. According to a memorandum to Johnson prepared by a White House group that was "developing items for columnists," "The idea was that you are the most effective person with these people; whether they are friendly or not, you can have a tremendous effect on them if the interviews are spaced and are relatively short."[15]

If a president does not engage in personal diplomacy with the press, pressures from reporters for access to other top-level officials increase. The White House responds by providing them with surrogates from the cabinet and the senior White House staff such as the director of the National Security Council or the President's political adviser. President Eisenhower seldom met with the press on a background or off-the-record basis, but his secretary of state, John Foster Dulles, got together with reporters regularly at the homes of correspondents such as Richard Harkness.[16] The tactics he used at these meetings with reporters enabled him to influence their stories so that what appeared was often more supportive of administration policy than the reporter may have intended. Chalmers Roberts of the *Washington Post* described the dilemma in which he and other reporters found themselves:

In all of these things, he always was trying to put over his point of view, which is a perfectly proper function for a secretary of state. And it became something of a game, for the reporter to be sure he wasn't just buying a pig in a poke and becoming just a transmission belt for the administration, a problem which is still unresolved and probably never will be resolved because of the internal conflict that's built in between the press and the government. . . . Somehow or other, he had an intuitive feeling that you had to feed the lions, so he always had some tidbits for us in the form of hard news. . . . And that always provided a news peg on which to hang whatever his views were on the current topic. It was a sort of device to be sure that this got into the paper and into the radio and TV, and got a good display, one way or the other.[17]

Horace Busby of the Johnson White House explained the value of regular contacts between senior officials and correspondents who have influential readers and viewers in Washington and around the country:

What is important for the newspaper men [is] to have an occasional visit and general discussion which gives them the feeling that the White House is on top of every situation, competent, informed, and optimistic. The soft sell approach, such as this, causes the newspaper men to give the President the benefit of the doubt on "close calls"—and the knowledge that they have friends at the White House who will talk with them, becomes the kind of bargaining power or leverage which is the fundamental or successful press relations.[18]

The most common forum of presidential discussion with reporters on a background basis is the background briefing. A president discusses with reporters the reasons for a policy's development and what the policy has accomplished or what he hopes it will accomplish. Apparently the substance of the policy is seldom discussed. Frequently background briefings are used to scotch rumors of rifts among officials. President Carter invited Hedrick Smith and Jack Nelson, bureau chiefs of the *New York Times* and the *Los Angeles Times,* to his office to deny the widely circulated story that Vice President Walter Mondale had been excluded from the inner circle of advisers and had assumed the traditional vice-presidential role as outsider.

The files at presidential libraries reveal the kinds of advantages these briefings have for both the White House and reporters. The substance of policy does not appear to be a major concern, as indicated in the following excerpt from a memorandum George Christian wrote to President Johnson prior to a background meeting with reporters. Christian made the following comments and recommendations:

1. All of the speculation about a rift is being fed by some who want to discredit the administration, the war, the President and McNamara.
2. Despite all the speculative stories, there has been no serious rift between the President and any of his advisers; and no lack of cooperation between McNamara and the Joint Chiefs. . . .
7. This should be the occasion to praise McNamara as the best Secretary of Defense this country ever had; the man who firmly established civilian control over the Pentagon; a trusted adviser in every field of government; a man who deserves anything his government and his President can help him achieve. I think it is highly important to emphasize the President's admiration for McNamara, your confidence, etc. Any hint of anything else at this time would be magnified out of proportion.[19]

The principal value of this type of background session is that it controls speculation about what the President plans to do. Carroll Kilpatrick, the White House correspondent for the *Washington Post* who attended this briefing, told a press aide, Loyd Hackler, that this was one reason the background session with President Johnson had been valuable to him. Hackler reported to Christian that Kilpatrick

was very impressed with the session which he and others had with the President on Wednesday. He said he understands many things now that weren't clear before. . . . He said the deep backgrounding and good fill-in on issues were very useful, and he thinks would head off some of our problems. For instance he said, if reporters had been given real substantive information following the meetings in Germany such as the President gave them Wednesday, then the speculative stories based on the brief public statements would have been less damaging.[20]

THE ROLE OF MIDDLE-LEVEL STAFF

When the President and his chief advisers discuss policy with reporters, as they occasionally do, most of their discussions are intended to prod the media into portraying the administration as competent and on the right track. With few exceptions, White House needs mesh nicely with those of reporters, since correspondents usually are more interested in what the President is going to do and how his actions will affect his overall position than they are in the substance of policy. For example, reporters, especially the White House regulars and the elite journalists who cover the presidency, ordinarily care about policy proposals such as energy or welfare reform more in terms of how the President's success or failure will affect his overall standing than in terms of specific provisions.

Of course, some reporters are concerned with the policies themselves. They turn to or are sent by the senior staff to middle-level officials. Unlike senior-level staff members, who are concerned with the place of individual policies in the President's program, those at the middle level tend to be officials whose job requires them to be involved with specific policies. Middle-level staff members are thus more likely than their chiefs to serve as advocates of particular programs. Although they are loyal to the President, unless they are the deputies of one of the chief advisers, they are not likely to know how hard the administration will push for the programs they are developing. Consequently, on occasion they will use their contacts with reporters to try to win presidential approval for their ideas or to halt proposals advanced by others.

It generally is believed at the White House that the manner in which a policy is presented to the press is as important as its substance in determining how the public will ultimately view what the President is trying to do. Officials believe that staff at the middle level are the best conduits to the media through both official and unofficial channels. The authorized sessions take the form of on-the-record briefings where middle-level officials appear as specialists. At these sessions the policy is presented in detail to reporters who are free to ask questions of both the briefer and the specialist. Senior staff officials suggest that it is better for both the President and reporters if a dozen interested correspondents are invited to a background briefing than if a large number come to an open session. A particular policy can be explained there in more detail than it could be before a large group of press people concerned with many different issues. The small session also gives the White House an opportunity to pinpoint the audience. Barry Jagoda, a middle-level official who served as President Carter's assistant for media liaison, stated that when he released information on the President's plans for legislation affecting the Corporation for Public Broadcasting, he used private briefings limited to reporters for the *New York Times* and the *Washington Post*. He did not use the regular White House briefing to announce the developments because, he explained, the press secretary's daily "briefing is not a good format for explaining a subtle story."[21]

Presidents often work directly with middle-level staff in specific policy stories on which they have a lot at stake. Lyndon Johnson had officials who were close to these policies talk with reporters. He asked officials from the National Security Council to meet with the press on Vietnam. The deputy director of the National Security Council, Robert Komer, who had recently returned from Vietnam, was regarded by the press as a credible source. After Komer made the rounds of the Washington press corps, he told Johnson he had succeeded in affecting the attitudes of reporters and thus the stories they prepared. Komer wrote:

Warring with the Press. I took on all twelve (count 'em) of the *NY Times* Washington Bureau at lunch yesterday. My wounds are still bloody, but one direct result was Reston's 22 November column on "Why Westmoreland and Bunker are Optimistic." I'm proud of myself. . . .

I gave *Don Oberdorfer* of Knight papers a 15 minute quick fill-in on a series about the VC he plans to do in Saigon. *Spencer Davis* of AP sat still for an hour on pacification (mostly on the record). Maybe a story, maybe not. Took 2 hours to beat up Rowland Evans and Stewart Alsop on the theme "I told you so." They (and most of the two dozen or so press types I've backgrounded) have been hit hard by the new documented case that we're at long last on the upgrade in Vietnam.[22]

BUILDING SUPPORT FOR PERSONAL INTERESTS

From the perspective of several Presidents, when staff members talk to reporters without official approval, they are doing so for their own advantage. Former President Lyndon Johnson remarked: "I had a test one time. I said, 'whenever you see a man in the State Department or Defense Department's picture, one-column picture, in a certain newspaper, that is usually his pay-off. That's his little bribe. It's not money, but it's really a bribe for his accessibility and his willing [*sic*] to give them guidance from time to time, which is another way of saying that we give you this information.' "[23] There are people in every administration who are frustrated by their lack of visibility and who thus, when they have an opportunity to talk with reporters, do give away more than their superiors would like. John Osborne commented that he has found information in extremely unlikely places because "some of the moles love to be noticed."[24]

A President and his chief advisers may exhibit some tolerance for a cabinet official, bureaucrat, or general who talks to reporters in exchange for personal publicity, but no such easygoing attitude applies to a member of the staff who is too much in the public eye. In both the Nixon and Ford administrations most high-ranking White House advisers were unhappy about the lavish publicity (and praise) received by Henry Kissinger. There is evidence that neither Nixon nor Ford was any happier and that only Kissinger's extreme skill at playing the bureaucratic game prevented them from getting rid of him. Other aides who once glowed in media praise have not escaped as easily.

Bill Moyers, once a close adviser and press secretary to Lyndon Johnson, earned a reputation with both Johnson and many reporters for seeking the limelight at the expense of the President. According to columnist William S. White, "My opinion was that Moyers did the President infinite harm in the Washington press, because it was commonplace to see articles making note of the wise, compassionate attitude of Mr. Moyers and the difficulty of dealing with this terrible man Johnson.''[25] The favorable publicity Moyers received ultimately hurt his credibility with reporters as well as administration officials. Newsman Robert S. Allen expressed in strong terms a view that most newsmen, friends of Johnson, and staff members held in a more moderate form: "Moyers was just a schemer and a climber. He used Johnson; worked his way into Johnson's good graces and then maneuvered and connived and always pushing Moyers and not the President. Moyers—he was disliked and distrusted by the working newsmen.''[26] After Moyers left the White House Johnson "used to rip him up and down verbally," according to *Washington Post* reporter Chalmers Roberts.[27]

Staff members and other administration officials who try to play one role with reporters and another with their colleagues in the administration are big losers when their duplicity is discovered. During World War II the ambassador to England, Joseph Kennedy, sent letters to the State Department expressing approval of President Roosevelt's position of American support for Great Britain. At the same time Kennedy wrote Arthur Krock, his friend and a columnist for the *New York Times,* that he opposed American intervention. Unfortunately for Kennedy, Krock turned over his letter to administration officials, who decided to force him out. What happened next was described by Walter Trohan, White House correspondent and later bureau chief for the *Chicago Tribune,* a newspaper that was strongly anti–New Deal and anti-Roosevelt. According to Trohan, Press Secretary Steve Early approached him and said:

"Would you write a nasty story about Joe Kennedy?" I said, "Anytime I can write a nasty piece about a New Dealer I would be happy to do it."

And he showed me a file of letters that Kennedy had written to Mr. Welles at the State Department which were sent to the White House. Then he showed me letters that Kennedy had written Arthur Krock which were a 180° the other way. Krock in his innocence sent them over to the White House saying, "Here's some letters from Mr. Kennedy I thought you'd be interested in."

To me Steve said, "The guy's running for President."[28]

Shortly after Trohan's story appeared Kennedy was forced to leave the government. He never held a high office again.

The Moyers and Kennedy cases exemplify the perils of favorable publicity. Thus what most staff members seek is a good relationship with reporters rather than favorable publicity in the media. A good relationship may protect them when the going gets rough. James Fallows, chief speechwriter for President Carter, was asked why he talked to John Osborne of the *New Republic;* he responded, "He is kind to sources, which makes him worthwhile to talk to."[29]

Some reporters know why officials cultivate them. Robert Novak, syndicated columnist, described this motive bluntly: "Some people think they are buying protection, that in a difficult situation we won't be critical of them. . . . For example, Al Haig was a good source for us as a junior person. He felt that we would treat him softly once he became a major actor. We couldn't do that and now he is angry at us. We may protect a regular source, but only if it's a small point. ''[30] Some reporters protect their White House friends from exposure as long as the relationship produces news. However, when a series of bad decisions or personal problems becomes a story, the implied protection is dissolved. The source of the *Washington Post* story claiming that White House drug adviser Peter Bourne used illegal drugs was a reporter for the *Post* who claimed to have been present at a party where he saw Bourne use them. The reporter (or his editors) protected Bourne, a useful informant for many reporters, as long as his use of drugs was not a news item. When a news story broke that Bourne wrote an illegal prescription for a White House staff member, the *Post* reporter no longer had a reason to withhold the information about the earlier incident.

Forcing a Decision

White House sources often leak information in order to speed the process by which decisions are made. Sometimes a president will authorize others to release information because he thinks its appearance in the media will make the decision-making process move his way. On other occasions the President is the person a member of the staff wants to force a decision upon. The media frequently are used to get an official to resign and to test public response to a possible decision.

The release of information can force a reluctant official to resign by letting him know his superiors want him to. Merriman Smith, longtime White House correspondent for United Press International, recalled that he was used as the carrier of this message when President Eisenhower and other officials wanted Chief of Staff Sherman Adams to resign. Adams was under fire before a House investigating committee for allegedly accepting a complimentary vicuña coat and hotel accommodations in exchange for contacting a regulatory agency for the donor. While these developments were in the news, Smith received a telephone call from Homer Gruenther, a middle-level staff person in Eisenhower's White House. Gruenther told Smith, "If I were speculating —Lord knows, I don't know anything—but I'd sort of—you'd get a lot of readers with a story saying he'd [Adams] never even come back, except possibly to clean out his desk.''[31]

It was clear to both Smith and Lyle Wilson, the bureau chief, that Gruenther's story must have been authorized at a high level in the White House. Smith recalled that he said to Gruenther: "Homer, I know you're not on this policy level.'' Gruenther's response was to remark that ''. . . it would make a fascinating story.'' Wilson told Smith that he was willing to go along with the story even though Gruenther did not occupy an important position because "Homer's just doing an errand for somebody. They really have canned him when they get Homer feeding you like that.'"[32] In this case Wilson and Smith felt they did not actually need to receive the information from a high-level source in order to use it because they felt the message had been sanctioned at the top.

Although the President was trying to force him out of office as quickly as possible, Adams did not respond. Consequently, the same reporter was used a second time. Smith was called by the President's appointments secretary, Tom Stephens, while he was working on a story in Charlottesville, Virginia. Stephens let Smith know that he should be in Washington "very early tomorrow morning." Smith correctly interpreted this comment as a signal that the White House had run out of patience, and he wrote a story saying that Adams finally would be fired the next morning.

As Smith later found out, Eisenhower himself was the high-level source behind his middle-level contacts: "I asked Eisenhower later about that. I said, 'You know old man Truman used to fire people this way.' I said, 'He let the AP fire Louis Johnson, and he let me fire Howard McGrath. Then the next time I'm allowed to fire Sherman Adams. Now why didn't you do it?' He said, 'The fellow wanted time, and I wasn't going to say, ok, get out, now. He said he would have all his business cleaned up—and it just dragged on, frankly.'"[33] Eisenhower followed the pattern set by his predecessors of using the press to hasten the implementation of a decision. Once the decision to remove Adams had been made, it was simply a question of when he would go. Merriman Smith was called in to make certain it would be sooner rather than later.

Press strategies are not reserved for cases in which the decision has been made and the only remaining question is its execution. Trial balloons are released to test public responses to proposed policies. In the Ford and Carter administrations some staff members implied to reporters that the administration planned to deal with the energy crisis by placing a large tax surcharge on gasoline. In each case hostile reaction led the administration to deny that any such decision ever was contemplated.

Staff members in several administrations have tried to insure that an appointment or other major decision would be made by releasing the information to the media before an official announcement. This technique was counterproductive in the Johnson administration. Johnson so rebelled at the idea of having his hand forced by others that invariably he would delay or nullify the appointment or proposal. Andrew Glass of the Cox Newspapers recalled that once when he called Hubert Humphrey to confirm a story that President Johnson was sending him to Vietnam to reassess American policy there, Humphrey replied, "If you print it, it's wrong." Cox printed the story and Johnson did not send Humphrey on the mission.[34] Johnson's ire at premature announcements of what he was going to do became so well known that some officials tried to kill appointments or decisions they opposed by leaking the information to reporters. They could assume that the appointment or decision never would be made.

Building Political Capital

The use of sources to communicate information on a background basis is particularly well suited to efforts by White House officials to use the media to build political capital for the President and his programs. It is in these situations that the White House's flexible approach to the media is most likely to cross the line that separates legitimate publicity from manipulation. The techniques the White House employs include "letting them through the line" or planted leaks, compiling derogatory information, and feinting.

"LETTING THEM THROUGH THE LINE."

Frequently the White House wants to get out more than one story on the same subject. Since reporters are suspicious of information that is just handed to them, White House officials employ a technique sometimes known as "letting them through the line" that involves permitting a reporter to "discover" a story through questioning.

The technique is not always employed in a subtle manner. In 1976, when Richard Nixon traveled to China as a private citizen, Press Secretary Nessen stated during his morning briefing that neither President Ford nor his advisers were concerned about the trip. According to a reporter who attended the briefing, Nessen "signaled" that this was not the whole story. The reporter knew that President Ford was trying to put distance between himself and Nixon as part of his own reelection strategy. Therefore, he was not suprised when Nessen suggested to him that he talk to a senior presidential adviser, who told him that there was considerable concern.[35] These interviews were arranged for reporters from major publications and networks if their reporters pressed Nessen for more information. For example, the *New York Times* followed a quotation from Nessen's remarks that Nixon's trip "is not expected to have any domestic consequences" with the reporter's point that "comments by White House staff officials indicated that the President was annoyed by the news of Mr. Nixon's planned journey to China for several reasons, one of which is that it comes in a delicate political period."[36]

A somewhat more subtle application of the technique occurred during the Carter administration after President Carter had delivered a tough, apparently anti-Soviet speech at Wake Forest University. Some of the President's advisers were concerned that the speech would upset some of Carter's peace constituencies. Consequently, one of the authors of the speech told a prominent Washington reporter who had requested an interview that the speech was meant to convince the public that Carter would be tough with the Soviets in forthcoming SALT discussions.[37]

COMPILING DEROGATORY INFORMATION

Some officials in almost every administration believe that they can build political capital for themselves by compiling and then releasing at opportune moments information that will be harmful to their opponents. Sometimes this takes the form of reminding reporters who are friendly to the administration or unfriendly to its rivals of possibly embarrassing statements or positions that one of those rivals has made in the past. Often, however, staff members cross the barrier between political hardball and dirty tricks. President Nixon's staff kept files filled with current political information detrimental to his opponents. Senator Edward Kennedy was a continuing target of information-gathering groups in the Nixon White House. Howard Hunt assembled information on the senator's accident at Chappaquiddick. Charles Colson gave Jeb Stuart Magruder, the deputy director of the Office of Communications, a picture of Kennedy in Rome with a beautiful woman who was not his wife and asked him to see if it could be placed in the media. Magruder gave the picture to the *National Enquirer,* where it was published; later it also was displayed in *Newsweek.*[38] As is often the case when derogatory information is leaked, the rule that was followed was that the more salacious the information to be given to the media, the lower on the staff hierarchy the person who releases it should be.

Especially since the Nixon administration, reporters have been sensitive to unsubtle efforts to plant derogatory information. Jody Powell discovered this in 1977 when he tried to show that Senator Charles Percy of Illinois, one of the chief legislative antagonists of Budget Director Bert Lance, had been guilty of using company aircraft and offices while a Senator. The efforts backfired when the *Chicago Sun-Times* revealed that Powell had been trying to spread the false story.

FEINTING

"Feinting," or deliberately planting a false or misleading story in the media, is a subtle technique that permits the White House to build up political capital by later withdrawing a decision the President never really intended to make. Lyndon Johnson did this at least once with considerable success. He told his aide, DeVier Pierson, to leak a story to the *Washington Post* that the administration was considering a cutback in the domestic rice production. When stories about the proposed cuts appeared, a predictable outcry was heard from congressmen from rice-producing states. Outraged, they requested a meeting with the President. Approximately one dozen congressmen came, Pierson recalled,

and spent about an hour telling the President all of the bad things that were going to happen if he cut back rice production. About mid-way during the meeting he called me over and whispered to me that when they finished that he wanted to have me make the strongest case I could make for cutting back production. So they finished, and he said "Well, I'm concerned about this." He said, "What do you think about it DeVier?"

And I did make the strongest case I could for cutting back and, you know, to the great loss of friendship of all the Congressmen and Senators in the room.[39]

The congressmen renewed their pleas that the President not cut the allotment, but Johnson would not make a decision. Instead he told them, as Pierson recalled, that "it was a terribly difficult decision to make, but he would think about it."

When President Johnson made his decision, he made it clear that he wanted something in return. Pierson described the events: "So after a couple of days he said, 'You call around to Ellender and the others and tell them that I have decided in view of their personal interest in this that I won't do it, but I'll be needing their help on some other matters.' This is chip-building in the classic sense, and he built some chips with some critical people by making them ask for something that I suspect he intended to do all the way along."[40] Johnson had used the press to create debts in Congress that otherwise would not have existed, thus improving the prospects of passage for programs that might have been marginal. Because he had someone on his staff who was not at a high level transmit the information to the papers, no one could pinpoint the source as the President. If something had gone wrong as the events were unfolding, Johnson could later claim that he had no connection with the story.

Responding to the Power of the Media

Perhaps the most important continuing pressure on White House officials to become sources comes from the media itself. The President and his staff respond to media requests, including those they would prefer to avoid, because they believe that they could be badly damaged and lose important channels to the public if they refused. They believe that they have no alternative to meeting with reporters. Their reasons are personal as well as institutional. For example, members of the White House staff often are asked to confirm or deny stories that reporters have uncovered. If they don't respond they fear they will damage their personal relations with the media. Since White House officials, like others in government, regard their relations with reporters as being important to their careers, most form new friendships with reporters after they take office and build on old ones. They regard reporters as part of the Washington establishment, a part that is as important to them as the legislative branch or the bureaucracy.

A person's perception of presidential power changes when he becomes president. From the outside the presidency appears to be an all-powerful position. Once a president takes office, however, he becomes more aware of the power of those outside the White House, especially those he perceives as his antagonists. The media form one of the powers surrounding and restraining the presidency, as incumbents see it.

Frequently the press secretary and others on the White House staff would prefer not to respond to reporters, yet they do so because they believe that avoiding them would harm their long-term relationship with the media. There is an unwritten White House rule that if a reporter has all of the facts about a story and asks the press secretary for confirmation, the press secretary will let him know if it is correct or if there is something wrong, even though the White House might prefer to make its own announcement. Ronald Nessen commented on the operation of this process during the period when he was press secretary:

I was perfectly willing, often did confirm stories that people had, they or their editor just wanted to be sure that they had it right. I would listen and I would say, "I am not going to stop you from running that one," or "I think that you are way off on that," or something like that. . . . I said that I would never lie and I never did, but what I did do sometimes was, that I didn't tell everything that I knew, when I knew it. This could be a matter of hours or days or weeks, the story eventually comes out, sometimes it is only the timing that you are inhibited on.[41]

As mentioned previously, White House officials respond to media power by forming friendships with reporters. Information is the chief commodity that passes between them, but protection of each other's interests is also part of the relationship. Reporters, especially those who are expected to do more than summarize White House announcements, need to make certain that their picture of what is going on in the White House is accurate. They need to be aware of developments in the West Wing as they occur. Officials, for their part, need to know that they are going to be given the benefit of the doubt when a potentially harmful story surfaces.

"CHINAMEN"

In order to protect their own status in the media, many high-level officials develop long-term confidential relations with a small group of reporters, and sometimes with only one. Many, such as Melvin Laird and Nelson Rockefeller, have their own political ambitions. Reporters refer to these officials as their "Chinamen."

Chinamen are usually individuals who are in a position to be well informed about what is going on and who trust that the reporter will not harm them. Frequently, but not always, the relationship antedates the official's White House appointment. This was apparently the case with Robert Woodward's Chinaman, "Deep Throat." The official knows that even if ground rules are not discussed at every meeting, the reporter will not use information that would reveal its source. The term *Chinamen* covers a whole range of officials and friends of the President who have access to the President and, usually, to the inner circle of the White House. They have a clear sense of what is going on even when they don't tell the reporter hard news. Kenneth Crawford provided an idea of the kinds of information that a reporter can obtain from a person close to or part of the inner circle of the President. In his case, George

Allen, a close friend and neighbor of President Eisenhower in Gettysburg, "was always a great source, not of any inside information because he was very careful about that, not to give anything away. But the general thinking of the administration George knew, and in that sense he was very helpful to me. I had the feeling that I knew always about what directions the administration was going in, and what its reasons for it were.''[42]

Although some Chinamen provide information about problems and conflicts in the administration that the President would prefer did not appear, they are usually supportive of the White House position. They justify their relations with reporters on the ground that they help the President. But a major consideration for them is that important friends in the media are necessary for their own advancement and protection.

LESSER SOURCES

Officials also use reporters as sources of information. Reporters know this and try to have something for them. One reporter described the process in the following manner: "Reporters in this town are cross-pollinators. They are the bees going from flower to flower picking up a bit of pollen here and there. When you go into somebody's office, if he is a heads-up guy and curious, he knows you know a lot of scuttlebutt so he will give you something and he will ask you questions, too. Sometimes you have to guard against that; you will end up giving more than they give you.''[43]

Officials believe that the personal relationship makes a difference in the way they are treated by the media. One senior Ford administration assistant explained, "the personal relationship has an impact in a subtle way. The number of breaks over a four-year period that they are going to give the guy. Everyone in that office makes mistakes and to the extent to which those mistakes are hyped up. . . . The extent to which reporters put a spotlight on it, and not just one or two, but a lot of them. To what extent it is used.''[44]

From the reporter's viewpoint, a low-level source whose mistakes are not of news interest is valuable because the reporter rarely is faced with the predicament of harming a trusted informant or losing him. "My favorite kind of source is one that is not a principal actor,'' Robert Novak commented. "That way you don't get the kind of conflict that one day the guy is giving you information and the next day you are knocking the hell out of him in the column.''[45]

Assessing the Source System

In the ideal system of open government proposed by (prepresidential) Woodrow Wilson and other Progressives, reporters would be able to receive all information that did not violate military security or that the government was not holding as a public trust, such as tax returns. Presumably all conversations between reporters and officials would be on the record. Sources and spokesmen, well placed or otherwise, would not exist.

Obviously these conditions do not exist. At the White House, as in other bureaucratic organizations, there is often a nagging tendency to withhold even trivial pieces of information. For example, we obtained a copy of the Ford administration's comprehensive White House telephone directory, after we had been told by administration officials that such a directory did not exist. This experience is multiplied many times for reporters who have to wheedle or beg for routine information.

Nevertheless, factual information is not at the heart of the development of the source system. George Reedy reflected:

Everybody has the incorrect picture that what the press is clamoring for are a series of facts, and that is not it. What they are clamoring for is what the President is going to do. Now you see this is information of a very peculiar category. It is locked in the mind of the President. Covering the White House is not like covering the Defense Department, where what you do is dig out facts, or like covering the Labor Department where you dig out facts. What you are trying to do is dig out the intentions of the President.[46]

Reporters want information about what the President might do, how he regards a particular policy, and what his attitude is toward particular individuals. They can try to get this information at briefings or press conferences, but it is more likely that they will obtain it (or parts of it) in confidential interviews with officials who want reporters to prepare stories that will convey White House messages to appropriate audiences.

There is nothing inherently wrong with the source system. The relationship between reporters and officials is not necessarily devious or manipulative on either side. Sources do provide a great deal of important and useful information to the public that might not be obtainable otherwise. Despite what some reporters think, many officials feel an obligation to keep the public informed by meeting with representatives of news organizations. These officials recognize that the Press Office and the press secretary cannot provide in public the thorough analysis of an ambiguous situation that they can provide in private. Thus the source device permits officials to speak with relative candor. It is more likely in this situation that an official will avoid the stonewalling and dickering over the nuances of language that have become a common feature of the press secretary's performance at the daily briefing.

A second point to be made in defense of the source system is that the President's right to get his message to the people cannot be exercised in public forums alone. The White House press corps and the national media usually do not have the attention span—or its managers assume that its viewers and readers do not have the attention span—to follow long and complicated stories, except for those like Watergate that are filled with drama and excitement. The source who deals with important reporters and columnists becomes involved in a dialogue with the attentive public, whose consent is an important part of democratic decision-making. The picture of administration developments presented at this level ultimately may filter down to the public at large.

The disadvantages of the source system are perhaps more frequently discussed than its advantages. It is a system that has so many built-in advantages for the White House that officials are tempted to abuse them, especially since they view themselves as responding to press distortions of their positions and activities. All administrations tend to want to control access and information under their jurisdiction. The source system frequently is abused by officials who first withhold information and then leak selected portions of it to reporters who are unable to verify or challenge what they are told.

A second disadvantage of the source system is that it places a premium on bargaining, bribery, "old boy" networks, social connections, and a protection racket. Most reporters and officials are aware of all of these pitfalls and try to avoid them. But even the most virtuous on both sides are pushed in the direction of providing or seeking information in circumstances in which the terms of the relationship itself become more important than the primary function of each party as reporter or official.

SEVEN

THE NATURE OF THE BEAT

T HE NEWS presented by White House correspondents is a product of rules of the game that apply to all reporters assigned to cover the President. These rules include requirements of the medium of communication in which they work, the expectations of their news organizations, and rules that stem from the professional values of journalists as well as from the personal values of the group assigned to the White House. Besides the rules, the White House milieu itself is often the most important determinant. The atmosphere there provides a life support system rich in the ingredients that enhance a journalist's status but thin in elements that encourage high-enterprise reporting. Editors and producers provide space or time for the prominent display of a reporter's stories about the public presidency. But in order to cover the Chief Executive's activities, correspondents allow officials to herd them to briefings, ceremonies, and conferences where they are fed a diet of statements, releases, and rehearsed answers. Those who try to get information independently must wait for an escort before they can visit West Wing offices. Reporters who are not satisfied with the sustenance provided at scheduled media events find that officials who dispense information privately usually dictate the terms for its use and consumption. "There is no place where a correspondent can be more easily led than at the White House," commented James Naughton of the *New York Times*. "It is the nature of the beat."[1]

Reporters congregate in the briefing room and the adjoining press areas at the center of the public White House, where they hope to get a sense of what is going on inside the private areas. What they get are echoes of their own thoughts rather than cross-currents of information flowing among White House officials. "The press room is hermetically sealed," remarked *National Journal* correspondent Dom Bonafede, who rarely mixed with other reporters there. "The mood in the White House press room is a mood the press itself creates."[2] Barriers limiting unscheduled and informal movements by reporters affect their ability to cover the President. "I might as well be in Silver Spring," Andrew Glass commented while standing at his desk—which was located only a few corridors away from where the President and most of the senior White House staff were sitting or standing at theirs. "You have no idea of what they're really doing. . . . The only time you see them on the job is in a situation stage-managed by them."[3]

Not surprisingly, reporters emphasize the frustrations rather than the benefits of their assignment. They suggest how difficult it is for them to get away
from the pack when their organizations require them to follow all the other
reporters attending the President. Another concern they share is that the range
of technical stories involved in White House coverage is too great for a
generalist reporter. Others complain that restrictions imposed by the staff
allow the White House to shape their stories. Most comments reflected these
negative concerns. "You can be manipulated so easily because you can't find
them," Curtis Wilkie of the *Boston Globe* said in explanation of why, despite
its prestige for a political reporter, he did not want the assignment.[4] "It is very
easy to get isolated here," Bob Schieffer of CBS News reflected. "I can see
how you can have an imperial presidency."[5]

Only a few reporters responded positively to the assignment. Dennis Farney
of the *Wall Street Journal* found satisfaction because "you were covering
something that was demonstrably important and significant." At the same
time Farney admitted that he felt "a pervasive anxiety, a fear that someone
has something that I should have had."[6] Reporters admitted that, despite their
knowledge that they were being used, they often produced the stories the
White House wanted. Peter Lisagor suggested that the White House can shape
the news because news organizations place pressures on reporters that leave
them vulnerable. "Anyone who says they're not being manipulated is lying to
you," he argued:

The competition and competitive pressure is such that guys have to get a story. If they
get something that someone else might not have—no matter how self-serving it may
seem and no matter how hard-nosed they may feel themselves to be—they may often
go with the story. They may hedge it as they go with it by stating that "this is the
White House account," or suggesting that the "reader should judge for himself which
of the versions he wants to believe," or adding that "other sources were saying
thus. . . ." But they'll still go with it, and they'll be manipulated to that extent.[7]

Reporters on the Beat

At the beginning of the 1980s the majority of White House regulars appeared to be between thirty-five and forty-five years old. A few reporters for
major news organizations were first assigned to the White House when they
were still in their late twenties or early thirties. James Naughton of the *New
York Times*, Fred Barnes of the *Washington Star*, and Edward Walsh of the
Washington Post were among this group. A small crowd of veteran correspondents were further into middle age, but John Osborne of the *New Republic* was the only regular who had passed seventy. Editors apparently realize
that the physical strains of the job—the toll that the long hours extract from a
reporter's energies—require the stamina and good health that usually accompany the earlier portions of life. "I certainly wouldn't hire someone as old as I

am," Osborne commented.[8] According to the *New York Times*'s Martin Tolchin, a man much younger than Osborne, "It is an extremely hard, demanding job. I fell asleep at 9:30 in my chair last week. I am exhausted. It is physically hard. I've increased my jogging just to stay in shape for those damn trips. It is a physically, intellectually, and socially demanding job."[9]

Perhaps because of the constant physical effort, only a few contemporary correspondents spend many years as White House reporters. In contrast, when Timothy Crouse observed the White House regulars for his book *The Boys on the Bus* in 1972, he found a crowd of veteran correspondents who treated the assignment as a "sinecure," "one more quiet men's club," and "a slow death."[10] By the middle of the 1970s, however, members of the prewar generation whose activities might have merited these caustic comments had passed from the scene. The senior White House correspondents in 1980 did not fit Crouse's description. Among them were well-regarded and vigorous correspondents such as Frank Cormier and Helen Thomas of the wire services, Robert Pierpoint of CBS News, James Deakin of the *St. Louis Post-Dispatch,* and Ted Knap of the Scripps-Howard chain.

Many younger reporters regard the job as a way station to higher professional positions and leave the White House assignment after two or three years. "The White House is a big ticket . . . an institutional ticket," David Halberstam commented. "The guy who goes to the White House goes on to some bigger job within the paper."[11] New York Times correspondents Tom Wicker and Max Frankel became *Times* editors, while James Naughton left to take a position as a national editor of the *Philadelphia Inquirer.* Hugh Sidey left the White House beat to become chief of *Time*'s Washington bureau. According to Dennis Farney of the *Wall Street Journal,* his paper views the White House "as a place where you bring in someone you want to test—you give it to a younger reporter. The most prestigious reporters are on the Hill."[12]

GENERALISTS AND EXPLAINERS

Although some reporters had covered specialized areas such as economics or defense before they were assigned to the White House, most were generalists with a broad background as political correspondents. With the notable exceptions of Dom Bonafede of the *National Journal* and John Osborne of the *New Republic,* reporters did not regard the presidency itself as an area about which it was necessary to acquire specialized knowledge and information. Even those with expertise in some specific areas—economic problems or urban affairs, for example—did not have a backgound in issues involving domestic policies, international relations, and defense. This has consequences. "A guy who really understands diplomatic affairs is usually an absolute dunce on domestic affairs and vice versa," Martin Tolchin suggested.[13] As a result, White House correspondents skim the substance of many issues to focus on politics or personalities. The organization's specialists report on technical issues, but they may neglect the White House angle because they are unfamiliar with the administration.

Some reporters maintain that generalists have the right preparation for the White House beat. "There is no great difference between covering the White House and covering the county courthouse, as far as I can see," John Osborne said. "I have done them all."[14] Other reporters claim that as explainers of the news, their job is to provide what Herbert Gans referred to in *Deciding What's News* as a "mirror image" of reality.[15] These correspondents believe that technical stories are not their responsibility. They are explainers. For them, reporting is a reflection of the thing reported. Bob Schieffer described himself as an explainer and maintained that his job as a network correspondent was to report "what it was that was said today and what does it mean." A correspondent should gather the facts, then try to present them in a context that makes sense to the viewer or reader. Thus, Schieffer said, when he arrived at the White House as Ford took over from Nixon, "there was the muffin story, and you do that kind of story because he [Ford] didn't do anything. Then he did something, he pardoned Nixon. There was an issue and you get a different kind of reporting there. It took a long time before Carter did anything at all. . . . When people turn on their TV at night, they want to know what happened. I try to tell them that and what it means to them."[16]

REPORTING AS A PRODUCT OF RULES AND ROUTINES

The rules of the game that govern the relations between reporters and White House officials and among reporters have become progressively more complex since reporters were first invited into the White House during the McKinley administration. At the beginning of the period the informal rules predominated. For example, if President McKinley walked through the room where reporters sat, the correspondents would not disturb him. If he stopped to talk to them, however, they were then free to ask him questions.[17]

The rule of access. As in the past decades, the first rule of the 1980s is that access to the President and the White House staff is controlled by the administration. At times this power is exercised firmly, as it was during the Eisenhower administration, when the Press Office was the only real source of information for most reporters; on other occasions, as in the Kennedy, Ford, and Carter administrations, officials usually were accessible. The fact that White House officials retain this control leads some reporters to describe themselves as prisoners. "This is why most people don't like the White House once they get there," James Naughton remarked. "They are a captive of the system."[18] Even in "open" administrations, correspondents cannot drop by an aide's office as they could if they were covering the House or Senate. As a result, reporters develop sources, whom they meet outside of the White House. Offering lunch in one of Washington's better restaurants is a technique used by reporters from news organizations with generous expense accounts.

Frank Cormier related that during the Kennedy administration the best way to get to presidential assistants was to take them to lunch: "They liked to eat, and it was relatively easy to lure them to a good restaurant."[19]

Because reporters don't have a convenient and informal entrée to officials they can question, they often wind up at deadline with only the officially released account of an event. Although experienced and well-situated reporters may suggest to their audience that the White House may not have been entirely forthcoming, they are reluctant to present contradictory interpretations on their own authority. Unlike the columnists of the *Op Ed* page, reporters are hard news and source oriented. John Dean, White House counsel in the Nixon administration, recalled that although correspondents were unhappy about the version of Watergate they were given by Press Secretary Ziegler during the fall of 1972, the hard questions they asked at briefings were not reflected in their stories. "I was amazed at how small a part of the hostility that Ziegler absorbed made it into print," Dean recalled.[20]

David Halberstam suggested that the tough questions White House reporters ask at the press secretary's briefing stem from the same kind of frustration he saw in Vietnam, where reporters who never left Saigon for the front spent their anger on officials who gave them information they could never verify for themselves: "The guys who went to the 'five o'clock follies'... were ferocious there. They would tear flesh off the briefer, and they would never get anything. There was a lot of combat and scratching of flesh and flaring of whatever. For all of it, they really got nothing.... Some of it, some of the anger they were taking out on the briefing officer was their own frustrations. They didn't know how to get a handle on the story."[21]

Although reporters have techniques for getting information out of the White House, an administration that is determined to "keep the lid on" can do so. Peter Lisagor maintained that it was the power of Congress, not the press, that broke the Watergate story: "When things got really kinky, we were shut out from going to original sources. The sources then became the FBI and whoever 'Deep Throat' was. If you look over the history of our recent experiences, you'll find that the really big stories were broken by congressional committees with subpoena power."[22]

The rule controlling release of information. A second rule of the relationship is that the White House can specify what reporters may or may not attribute to a particular official. Although most press conferences have been on the record for thirty years, background briefings and interviews are used extensively by the President and other officials. In particular, briefings given by the President's national security adviser continue to be closed. A National Security Council press official explained that this practice is used to exclude accredited correspondents from the Soviet Bloc, whom they regard as intelligence agents rather than reporters.[23]

When White House staff members give interviews, they usually want to talk "on background," meaning that they will not be named in the story. Officials want the protection from direct interrogation that background gives them, but they also fear that if their name appears too frequently in the media, the President, others on the staff, and reporters will think they seek publicity for themselves. This appears to have been what happened to Bill Moyers: "Moyers rarely knew if he was speaking for the President, and as it turned out he was often winging it on his own. He was telling you what Bill Moyers thought, not what Lyndon Johnson thought. . . . Moyers used to give answers off the top of his head. They were glib, sometimes charming, sometimes highly quotable, but they were not Lyndon Johnson's"[24]

Reporters support the custom that permits officials to determine the basis on which their comments will be made public. Several correspondents suggested that the press secretary's "private" sessions in his office were more fruitful to them than his on-the-record sessions at the daily briefing because the public sessions were interrupted by "clowns" and "show offs" who were not interested in information. "I'd rather go to ten briefings in Jody's office than one out here," Frank Cormier confided. "I don't care how many private sessions he has as long as we [AP] are invited."[25] Powell agreed with these reporters. He said that when he spoke on background it was unnecessary for him to use vague language to respond to reporters' questions. In his office, he said, he could speak freely before a group whom he could trust not to try to embarrass the administration by abusing and distorting his confidences. "Often you don't even have to tell them what can or can't be used," he reflected. "Those guys know."[26]

Routines of coverage. The routines involved in coverage of the public presidency make some reporters part of a conveyor belt system transmitting information from the White House to the media. Some correspondents complain that they are props in shows staged by the White House. They suggested that getting the daily story from the White House is a form of stenographic reporting in which correspondents transcribe what officials say. Another frequent complaint is that because the White House forces all reporters to follow similar routines, the result is "pack journalism"—a derogatory term implying that reporters present the same story in the same way because they think and act alike.

In addition to routines organized by the White House, reporters follow routines originating in the values of the profession. These also lead to similar behavior by many correspondents. For example, *news* means to look for what is new. "Our leads might all be the same because we are all looking for the new element," suggested James Deakin. "There isn't all that much that is new, so if there is only one new thing, then we will lead with it."[27] A second rule is "don't get scooped." This means a reporter can't afford to let a story get past him. A third rule is that conflicts and personalities make news. A fourth, that readers and viewers are interested in the politics of an issue rather than its technical aspects. Each of these routines leads reporters to trudge over the same ground that their colleagues are covering. It places most reporters in a defensive position and explains why there is so little investigative reporting at the White House. "The White House press corps is the last place the Watergate story would have broken," Peter Lisagor asserted. "Plainly from the way Woodward and Bernstein worked it, it was the last place. No one ever saw them around there. And yet a call from Bob Woodward to Al Haig would cause tremors in that building. But nothing would happen if Al Haig got a call from Helen Thomas."[28]

How Nine Reporters Cover the White House

The manner in which White House reporters respond to the constraints imposed on them by the beat depends on their personal characteristics and institutional constraints. Although a few organizations send individuals whose only talent is the ability to promote themselves, most reporters represent news enterprises that required them to display considerable imagination and flexibility before they got the assignments. Among them are a number of reporters who are among the best journalists in Washington. Many of them have or will have distinguished careers, although not always as White House correspondents.

The group of nine selected for close scrutiny here includes several types of reporters.[29] They were correspondents for radio, television, news services, weekly magazines of analysis and opinion, and daily newspapers between 1975 and 1979, when we were observers in the White House press room. In experience they ranged from veterans to short-timers. Their adaptation to the beat was more successful than that of the average reporter in that they were able to use their individual talents while exploiting their organizational clout. As might be expected from individuals with diverse backgrounds, there was a diversity of views among them about the objectives of White House reporters.

Five of the reporters had regular daily or even hourly deadlines: Frank Cormier of the AP and Walter Rodgers of AP Radio were expected to file stories several times a day. Bob Schieffer of CBS News ordinarily prepared one story, but he could be called upon at any time to cover a breaking story. James Naughton of the *New York Times* and James Deakin of the *St. Louis Post-Dispatch* prepared daily stories, but they also worked on longer "weekend" articles. The other four reporters had deadlines that were less constant or immediate. Dom Bonafede prepared a short article on the presidency on a weekly basis and a longer, in-depth study every four to six weeks. John Osborne prepared a weekly column. Peter Lisagor prepared a column and worked on stories that appeared twice a week. Dennis Farney's stories appeared when the *Journal* believed that his analysis presented materials that were not available in the daily press or on television.

The personal histories and professional histories of the nine match those of the group present at the White House: the young reporters who hope to use the White House assignment as a stepping-stone to other positions, and the older men who have made a career at the White House or who wish to remain there. By 1980 three of the four younger journalists had already moved from the White House to positions closer to their career goals: Dennis Farney had become a correspondent at the House of Representatives for the *Wall Street Journal,* a more prestigious assignment on that newspaper; James Naughton had been appointed city editor at the *Philadelphia Inquirer;* and Bob Schieffer became the anchorman for the CBS Morning News. Of the younger reporters, only Walter Rodgers remained at the White House. The senior reporters— Cormier, Deakin, Bonafede, and Osborne—stayed on the White House assignments. Peter Lisagor died in 1976. Lisagor and Deakin began their White House assignments during the Eisenhower administration, Cormier during the Kennedy administration, and Osborne when Nixon took office. The ages of the senior group ranged from the late forties to seventies, while the younger reporters were between thirty-five and forty.

The nine reporters were born or grew up in the central or eastern United States. Deakin, Farney, and Naughton came from the Midwest; Osborne and Schieffer from the South; and Cormier, Lisagor, Rodgers and Bonafede from the eastern states. Eight completed college. None went to an Ivy League college; six went to colleges in the Midwest. Farney, Rodgers, and Cormier have graduate degrees.

No one career pattern emerged by which they arrived at the White House press room. James Naughton was assigned to the White House barely three months after going to work at the *Times,* while Schieffer was with CBS for six years before going to the White House. Some switched media forms and news organizations before coming to the White House. Their routes: (1) shifted within same medium: James Naughton went from a small local paper to the *Cleveland Plain Dealer* before the *Times;* John Osborne went from *Time* to freelance journalism to the *New Republic;* Walter Rodgers worked at Metromedia Radio News before working for AP Radio; (2) remained at same publication: Peter Lisagor, *Chicago Daily News* (except for one or two years); James Deakin, *St. Louis Post-Dispatch;* Dennis Farney, *Wall Street Journal;* Frank Cormier, AP; (3) shifted between media: Dom Bonafede, United Press International, *New York Herald-Tribune, Washington Post, Newsweek, National Journal;* Bob Schieffer, *Fort Worth Star Telegram,* local Texas TV station, CBS.

Four were with the publication they first joined when going into journalism while another four switched no more than three times. Only Dom Bonafede changed five times. Only he and Schieffer switched from one medium to another; Bonafede went from wire to print and Schieffer from print to television. For those who stayed with the same publication, all served apprentice terms outside of Washington. Lisagor and Deakin worked at their papers' home bases, Chicago and St. Louis; Cormier worked in Chicago before coming to Washington; and Farney went from Dallas to New York to Washington.

THEIR STUFF

Unlike most other assignments, the White House beat has all reporters start off with the same basic information. "At the White House everyone has to deal with the same data," James Naughton commented. "Even on the Hill there is much more latitude." Routines are more carefully constructed and controlled by the White House staff than in other areas of media coverage, with the possible exception of the national security beat. What reporters do with the material given to them depends on such matters as the flexibility of their deadlines and whether they perceive their audience to be a general one waiting for the news or a coterie of experts who want to find out the inside story.

The five reporters with daily or hourly deadlines recognized the importance of their role as a conduit of information. They let the President get his words to the public through them. "The news is the President's message," James Deakin asserted. "The reporter doesn't come between the reader and the President." Beyond this, the reporters presented diverse views of their responsibilities. Deakin argued that beyond the conduit role, "The second function is the analytical function, the critical function. In news stories these days that is part of the news. You start off with the basic reporting of the news, . . . we complete the picture."

James Naughton maintained that *Times* reporters have special responsibilities because their newspaper is so widely distributed among political and governmental influentials. Thus he saw his first responsibility as presenting "a history of the important developments at the White House which is part of our tradition of being a newspaper of record." Once that is done, he wants to present "'some sense of what it all means, the feel of it, the flavor of it, whether it's relevant, if it's important, and who the people are who are involved." Bob Schieffer felt a responsibility as a television reporter because "we are the basic medium for news." What this means to him is, "I am aware every time I do a story that it is going to have some impact. It has made me a more accurate reporter, and makes me go that extra length to make sure it is right."

Walter Rodgers also discussed the special responsibility he felt toward his audience, which provided him with a sense of purpose in reporting:

I often feel a very personal constituency of listeners out there, very much greater than any member of the House of Representatives, in that I have an obligation to tell them what I see happening, about the institution in which they have a vested interest. If I see a president extolling the virtues of morality and personal ethics and living up to the code I try to report it. If on the other hand I see a president who talks one game and plays another, I feel it is incumbent on me to tell my rather vast radio audience or constituency, if you will, be they in cars on the way home, or at the breakfast table, what I see. In that sense I see my philosophy of journalism almost as one of another leg in the representative democracy.

Dom Bonafede and John Osborne viewed their job as covering the institution of the White House rather than the President. Osborne explained, "I've been interested all of my working life, which is over fifty years, in the mechanics of government." Another approach, emphasized by Lisagor and Farney, was to view the White House as a web of relationships. Lisagor said that his "own area is devoted primarily to trying to assess and make some sense of various relationships within the White House." Farney described his style as "an attempt to impose themes and threads on a jumble of events" and to do it in a "lively" way. Rather than an institutional approach, "It is a delicate balance between people within the institutions and the institutions themselves. . . . You can't trace a decision by the way the paper flowed; it could have taken place in a hallway where Jordan met Rafshoon and it would be immaterial where the paper went." Since he and other *Journal* reporters assume that their readers also read the *New York Times,* they do not have the same need to get the scoop as the reporters with daily deadlines.

STORY DEVELOPMENT

Even though they all begin with the same information, the nine reporters considered here use a wide range of techniques to add to it and transform it into their own story. Four distinct styles have developed: horizontal coverage, at the pleasure of the President's schedule, protective coverage, and anthropologists at the county courthouse. None of the nine reporters fits into one of the categories with absolute precision. There is always some spillover. The dominant portion of the work of each does fall into one of these categories, according to what they have said about their reporting.

Horizontal coverage. Publications that have chosen not to be responsible for up-to-the-minute coverage of the President have an opportunity to report on what is happening at the White House as part of a story about a substantive issue that may cut across several institutions. Peter Lisagor typified the correspondent who used reporting at the White House as one part of his attempt to report on governmental activities. The home office at Lisagor's paper, the *Chicago Daily News,* had different expectations from its Washington bureau than did news enterprises that expected its reporters to maintain the body watch of the President.

Where we [the Washington bureau] can bite into a story, we try to do it. As a small bureau we have to. We're a supplementary arm of a paper. They get all the wire services out of this town, so we try to develop a special story. . . . I'm not a beat man. We cover this town horizontally; we follow a story through. . . . I come upon stories that are buried, that are shirt-tailed into the tail end of a story in one of the major papers that I think we would be interested in. The town is so complicated and complex that often things that can be developed into meaningful stories are tossed away not only in other stories, but sometimes in columns. The Hill and many agencies are badly covered, so we get ideas out of a breaking story and we decide that we ought to find out more about it and develop it. I'll give you a case in point: This nuclear plant danger story has developed and we keep reading about charges and countercharges. No one has stopped long enough to satisfy me and find out, "Is there any truth?" "Where does the truth lie?" I have a man working on it. [This remark was made three years before the Three Mile Island accident.]

Lisagor's idea of horizontal coverage included stories he felt provided a new slant on an old situation or a problem in White House relationships. As an example of this type of story he described his attempt in March, 1976, to find out the status of Henry Kissinger after his removal from his joint positions as secretary of state and national security adviser to the President:

Some time has elapsed now. What is the situation now? How has it shaken down? I'm trying to find out both from his standpoint and the White House standpoint how he feels. Is he comfortable with it? Does he feel he has the same clout he did? Does he feel he is in trouble? In the course of this I came across today something I didn't know at all and that is that they say that President Ford's Campaign Committee is conducting an anti-Kissinger campaign. I've never heard that so I'm going to try to find out is it true and why it is. Have they decided that Kissinger is a political liability?

Because of his unique position as the *Daily News'*s best-known national correspondent, the author of a nationally syndicated column, and a member of two popular news-discussion television program panels, Lisagor was in a position to use horizontal coverage without fearing that he would be distracted by the more routine assignments of presidential reporting.

Other reporters used horizontal coverage as their major style when they had the time. James Deakin, who covered White House daily activities, also prepared stories that spanned a broader analytical terrain. He described how he operated and where he tried to fit in the analytical stories:

Morning starts at 9:00 and is occupied with phone calls more than anything else. Phone calls I'm making to get a story, and whatever reading I can get in. Then I go to the briefing. If there is a story I want to do out of the briefing then the afternoon is spent on phone calls and interviews that are necessary to put that story together, using the briefing as a starting point. Then late in the afternoon [I begin] writing a story for the next day. . . . If I don't have a story that has to go out, then I write for the next day, then I try and find a fresh lead and go heavy on the interpretation. Because it will appear on Tuesday after it has already been covered. The specialty story that is timeless such as the abortion story. Analytical, keyed to a continuing news issue, but are not themselves a straight news story. These aren't a straight White House story. These I write late in the afternoon.

Deakin would use the horizontal method to check out information, in contrast to Lisagor, who used it as a way of generating stories. When getting information from the White House, he said,

You will check it with someone who will know the situation and may be on the other side of it. As often as not the person I check information with is a senator or congressman because they are part of the picture. For example, Ford's proposal for an interest break for low- and middle-income housing. If there were such a proposal to come out, I would go to the Domestic Council or OMB, whoever was putting the legislation together, and see what the nuts and bolts of the legislation were. I would go to the people on the Hill who were concerned with housing and get the other side of the picture, to see if they thought it was a sincere proposal or not and put everything in the story. If I suspected it was a trial balloon I would include that.

At the pleasure of the President's schedule. Walter Rodgers and Frank Cormier lay at the opposite end of the flexibility spectrum from Lisagor. While Lisagor was able to look in at the press secretary's daily briefing before exploring stories elsewhere in Washington, Rodgers and Cormier had to spend their workday in their booths near the White House press room. Their schedules were determined by the President's. "Your life and your time are not your own," Rodgers commented. "You serve at his [the President's] pleasure and his schedule." On a typical day at the beginning of Jimmy Carter's term, the White House schedule announced that the President had fourteen appointments. Rodgers had to stay nearby even though reporters were excluded from some events. "If it's a closed meeting, the object is to talk to someone who is present at the meeting. Most of the time you have to grab them out in the driveway," he said, referring to the practice of stopping West Wing visitors who exit to their cars parked in the White House driveway. Rodgers and other reporters hope to elicit, coax, or merely record a statement from visitors on such occasions, and thus penetrate the meeting. They are often frustrated by uncooperative respondents or by visitors who sneak out a side entrance, where reporters cannot wait.

Rodgers spent much time waiting for the President to make a public appearance in the Rose Garden or for either the Chief Executive or his spokesman to make an announcement in the press room. During much of this waiting time, he received and tried to respond to questions from his organization. Sometimes their requests arrived at moments when he had to interject himself suddenly into ongoing proceedings. "One example was the Sakharov thing," he said, referring to a 1977 incident involving the Russian dissident. "There was a slight break in the briefing and I went down to my booth on another matter. My office asked if I heard about [the President's] letter to Sakharov. I hadn't, and I dashed back up to the briefing which was still in progress and interjected that query into the briefing."

Unlike print media reporters, who prepared their material for an editorial office where further additions and revisions could be made, Rodgers wrote and then broadcast his stories from his booth. On those occasions when broadcasting the President's remarks to a group at the White House was permitted, Rodgers would pick up the pool tape that was played through the multiple-feed system in the White House, which has outlets in the press room and in the radio and television booths. Rodgers recorded the White House tape, edited it, and then prepared his story. Overall, Rodgers estimated that he prepared five stories daily for broadcasts that lasted approximately forty-five seconds each.

As chief and senior correspondent for the AP's White House bureau, Frank Cormier's responsibility extended to a variety of stories that had to be sent over the wires almost continuously. He supervised coverage of public White House functions, attended press conferences and briefings, and relayed information of all sorts to his office as soon as he could get it. "I'm a major conduit," he said.

I can't skip a briefing. If we didn't cover all the rat-holes in a sense, we would have all the newspapers and radio stations upset with us. And we would lose them as customers. . . . Time puts constraints on you. Someone always has to be here to answer the phone for call-backs, and you can become a prisoner of the phone. . . . There is always a pile of questions on the desk every morning from papers all over the country. They don't always require a story, just answers. If it's a story, it goes across the wire. If it's a message, we have a message wire and just send it to the bureau in the state the paper is in, and maybe they then send or phone the message.

For the conduits, waiting is a major part of reporting. "I spend too much time waiting for briefings that don't happen on time," Cormier groused. Cormier, like the other wire service reporters, was particularly dependent on the Press Office to provide the information behind most stories: "Volumewise, you get more out of the Press Office than any other way. We go to all their briefings, we go to them in their offices with inquiries, we go through all their press releases. Qualitywise, it can go the other way. We get the most interesting stories from people who just work around the place and who have no connections with the Press Office."

Protective coverage. Although reporters for daily newspapers or network television do not have the continuous immediate pressures to get out stories that news service reporters for wires or radio broadcasts do, they do not have the flexibility of reporters who prepare one major story a week. Bob Schieffer of CBS and James Naughton of the *New York Times* regarded themselves as responsible for building the record of news for that particular day. Consequently, they spent a great deal of time following stories that would not be used or that would be absorbed into a story of more news value. "Most of the news we do is protective coverage," Schieffer suggested. "Most of the stories we do aren't ever going to go out. . . . That's our job, to go out there and protect, and make sure he doesn't make any news." His responsibility was to get the news fast and accurately. When he began his tour as CBS News's chief White House correspondent in 1974, the only instruction he got was "Don't get scooped."

Editors for the *New York Times* are even more concerned than editors for television news about not letting any information slip by its correspondents.

As the unofficial but publicly recognized journal of record, the *Times*'s primary concern, according to correspondents who worked there, is to get the complete story, and to get it accurately portrayed and assessed. According to Naughton,

The *Times* cares about proper grammar and getting middle initials right. This is an editor's paper. The *Times* cares about accuracy, cares not only about tone but about getting the right tone, cares about balance, and cares about fairness. . . . You know anybody can go over there and record what happens, but giving the feel and the intonation or the significance of what's going on at the White House to the reader. If anything, that's the more difficult part of the assignment.

What distinguishes protective coverage from reporting at the pleasure of the President's schedule is the addition of the correspondent's assessment of the story to what is presented to the readership or viewership. The reporter takes what the White House gives and is prepared to transmit it, but he adds elements to the story that go beyond the record. "The way you get the lead on most stories is to sit back in the booth and figure out the way it is," Bob Schieffer said. "Scheme it out in your mind, find out the way it is, and then call up and check." Undoubtedly the additional time available to a journalist who works on one daily story as opposed to five explains much of the difference between reporters who are conduits and those who provide protective coverage.

James Naughton agreed that protective coverage meant protecting himself from getting scooped. He added that it also meant protecting his audience from getting fooled, as they would if all they get is a straight report of what the administration is saying and doing. During an interview several weeks before the 1976 presidential election, he asserted that a reporter would seriously mislead the audience if his story was limited to White House statements:

What I am interested in these days is political, and there's a great deal of laying stuff on you, blowing smoke at you. For example, the argument of the Ford campaign that he [President Ford] will be able to carry the South. That is just bull. There is no way unless Jimmy Carter falls dead flat on his tail that that will happen. . . . Strategically, it is a move to throw Carter off. You take that kind of snowball, try to see what is inside of it—a little piece of ice that is useful to report.

The mixture between coverage of presidential routines and what might be called "non-event-oriented analysis" varies greatly among media forms and within the same medium. The similarities between protective coverage as provided by Schieffer and Naughton break down because of the different ways in which CBS News and the *New York Times* use time and space. Schieffer was confined in his White House stories by the two-minute format ordinarily provided for any one segment of a story on television news programs. Consequently, he had not spent his time on the "obvious news." In contrast, Naughton had the opportunity to prepare analytical stories, including some that were not related to a hard news happening. These stories, which did not appear on a regular schedule, were sometimes the product of his own ideas, but also were generated by editors in Washington and New York. Sometimes, he said,

something would occur to me because of something that came up at the briefing. I would suggest it to the desk and they would then accept or reject it. They might say we need a piece on Nixon's relationship with the Jews—or with blacks. . . . This required breaking away from the routine and doing some enterprise reporting. . . . The bottom line is that you are flexible enough and the bureau is large enough that they could adapt to the news and they could adapt to whatever talent they have out there in the news room. We didn't have to have *x* number of analytical pieces a week.

Anthropologists at the county courthouse. The three reporters who viewed the institution of the White House as their beat worked for publications that did not require on-the-spot coverage of breaking stories. Their editors expected in-depth background information and reflective articles on how the incumbent administration operates the machinery of power and how they have altered or adjusted that machinery. John Osborne's column appeared in most editions of the *New Republic,* a moderately liberal weekly that leans toward the Democrats. Osborne has specifically disassociated himself from the magazine's political tendencies, but otherwise seems at home with its format. Dom Bonafede worked for the *National Journal,* a small circulation, elite publication that allowed senior editors such as Bonafede the time to develop lengthy stories describing important operations in the White House. Dennis Farney reported for the *Wall Street Journal,* the unusual national daily described earlier in this book, where he also had the opportunity to develop analytical stories about institutional developments.

The difference between the three reporters in this group and the two who provided what we call "horizontal coverage" is that the reporters in this group focus on the institution rather than on issues. This also distinguishes them from the two who described themselves as serving "at the pleasure of the President's schedule" and the two correspondents who said that they provided "protective coverage." The anthropologists are far less interested in close-up observation of the President. For example, when John Osborne was asked how important it was for him to see and interview the President, he responded, "Fortunately it happens to be totally unimportant, so I never do. . . . The only president that interests me is the public president." During the Nixon and Carter administrations he neither saw the President nor requested interviews with him. He did, however, meet with President Ford, because he found it useful to get a feel of the man and what he did.

Osborne specialized in the people who work in the White House. Washington journalists regarded his column as the most authoritative source of information about those presidential assistants who hold key positions at all levels of staff appointment in the White House. He describes in detail their personal characteristics, quotes what they say about their job and their relations, and then provides his own account. The tremendous amount of detail makes his column difficult at times for noninsiders to follow, but much of what he writes turns out to be of more general significance. His detailed analysis of the Nixon White House, for example, holds up very well as a study of the men whose characters were revealed in subpoenaed papers at the time of the Watergate investigations.

Dom Bonafede specialized in operations. Although he wrote a weekly one-page column of commentary in the magazine, his major assignment involved monthly articles five or six pages in length. Most of his time was spent preparing these longer articles. For one major article on White House lobbying on Capitol Hill during the Ford administration, he interviewed more than fifty people:

I have to talk to everybody . . . over there in the White House office and between ten and twelve people on the Hill. . . . I talked with other people [besides those in the Congressional Relations office] in the White House who are involved in congressional relations, like John Marsh or the people in Cheney's office or Rumsfeld's before that, and then go up to the Hill and talk to Rockefeller's people, talk to members of Congress, particularly committee chairmen, talk to outside groups, lobbyists, trade association people.

Dennis Farney tried to focus on an aspect of a White House operation that would not be apparent in a story that focused on an issue, an event, people, or organizational structure. In 1978 he wanted to follow the advance team that prepared the way for a trip by President Carter through Venezuela. In particular, he was interested in checking out the widely held belief that "television dominated everything a President did," from both the President's and the network's side. "The purpose of the story was twofold," he said. "It was an interesting story in an anthropologist's way describing how the two institutions work, and on the other level it was a guerrilla operation to show White House schedulers and television people colluding to structure events." Farney arrived in Venezuela, where he was able to persuade the White House advance team to permit him to ride the bus with them. He interviewed White House staff and television producers, one of whom told him that if it were not for the presence of television, he doubted that the trip would have been made. In his story he built up a case that stated that a great deal of presidential travel is scheduled for reasons other than the substantive work accomplished among heads of state.

RELATIONS WITH THEIR AUDIENCE

A critical determinant of the shape of reporters' stories is their perceptions of their audiences. Their target audience influences the subjects they and their editors choose as well as the amount of detail they report. In the end, however, reporters have to look within themselves for their style of story. Their views of their audiences are shaped by their views of themselves. Dennis

Farney did not feel obliged to review the pertinent details of recent events for his readers: "I take it on faith that it is an educated person and would be interested in anything that I find interesting," he said. Bob Schieffer suggested that the audience that watches television news probably responds as he did—or would let him know that it did not by turning him off. Therefore, he said, "I report for myself, to satisfy my own curiosity. I figure things that will be of interest to me will be of interest to others."

James Naughton of the *Times* and James Deakin of the *St. Louis Post-Dispatch* described their perceptions of their audiences in terms of the expectations of their news organizations. While Naughton was conscious of the *Times* as an institution, Deakin felt that he had a great deal of independence as the correspondent for the Washington bureau of a newspaper that had always granted the bureau considerable independence. John Osborne felt that the audience of the *New Republic* had changed, that it now had a larger and less liberal readership. He also felt that he was expected by management to produce his own kind of story. Peter Lisagor found his audience through his appearances on television news discussion programs.

Dom Bonafede, more than any of the other nine reporters, felt he had a clear knowledge of who was in his audience and why they read him. The small—3,000 copies—circulation is segmented by profession:

The corporate people are interested in the flow of legislation, the prospects of proposed legislation, what is likely to happen. They are also interested in the actors in each governmental decision and development. . . . The academic people obviously are interested in process, the daily process, the decision-making process, the power struggle, the organizational changes. . . . The bureaucrats like to learn, and we get this from a lot of them, they want to learn about what's going on in their own shop, but then they also learn about what's going on in the other departments and agencies, what's going on in the White House, and in Congress, that they don't know.

Walter Rodgers said that he felt special ties to his listeners. Although he has a large audience (between 450 and 500 stations) at 6:00 P.M., eastern standard time, he regarded his relations to them as "Jeffersonian. I believe you can educate the people as to what is going on. It is a faith in the collective wisdom of people."

RELATIONS AMONG REPORTERS

Reporters influence each other in several ways. What respected correspondents write or broadcast may influence the slant others take in preparing their stories. Reporters are often sources of information for other reporters as they describe what is going on, what has been said, and what may develop. All of this adds up to a collective—and subtle but important—influence on even the most independent reporters on the beat. Even though operations among correspondents are normally competitive, circumstances exist where they rely on one another for information.

Competitive pressures. Competitive pressures among reporters manifest themselves in the briefing. A reporter's dilemma consists of getting information that no one else has in a setting where everyone is present. Reporters do not like to ask questions that might reveal aspects of what they had hoped would be an exclusive story. "I don't take part in the briefing [for that reason]," Bob Schieffer remarked. "As long as you have contacts that you can talk to privately, it's best if you have a story not to give it away." Reporters do listen carefully to what others ask. "If a reporter asks a question out of left field, I will try and figure out what he is working on," Frank Cormier said.

Cooperative pressures. There are a number of incentives for cooperation on the White House beat that modify the pressures toward competition that usually are so prominent among reporters. The first stems from the fact that the White House makes it difficult for all reporters to get the kind of information they want. Add to this the fact that stakes are high for all White House reporters, and it is not surprising that reporters there are more predisposed to cooperation than they otherwise would be. Reporters will try to obtain exclusive interviews and will guard information that has been leaked to them. On the other hand, especially for reporters who don't work for a network or a major publication, it may be more important to broadcast the gist if not all of the inside details of the story. In fact, a reporter who does not work for the high-status news organizations may be eager to share at least part of his story with a reporter who does because his editor may not regard it as legitimate unless it is carried in a respectable forum such as the CBS News or the *New York Times*.

At the President's news conferences, reporters rely on each other to get information they all will find of interest. Correspondents expect the senior Associated Press reporter to base his decision to bring a conference to an end on whether the important subjects have been raised. Cormier, not the President, ends the conference; he does so when he thinks all the major substantive questions have been asked. Cormier said, "With news conferences it depends on how frequently they occur. During Watergate they happened so infrequently that I let them go on for five or ten minutes over the normal half hour." Cormier was also responsible for ending the press secretary's daily briefing. He let them continue until reporters had clearly exhausted their need for information or the press secretary's willingness to give it to them.

Reporters are more generous in sharing information or in working as a team to prevent information from getting by them at the White House than they are on more open beats such as Congress. White House reporting is essentially defensive reporting. Correspondents know that each is in danger of getting caught between the activities of the staff and the demands of his organization. Sharing information is an insurance policy.

Reporters as a source of information. Some reporters find the press room a useful place for gathering information. James Naughton described how he picked up materials as part of his morning routine:

I would leave [the *Times* bureau] and walk over to the White House and check the postings to see if there is anything beyond the routine. Talk to colleagues over there, get the feel of what they may or may not have heard. . . . Sometimes a Nessen or Carlson or someone would have wandered back and said something useful. . . . They may have heard something you didn't; they may have read a story that you hadn't seen. There is always some kind of conversation going on oriented around Nixon or Nessen or Ziegler or what have you at the White House. And a sort of informal exchange of information through gossip.

Some reporters would join a group for lunch at Kay's Delicatessen or stop for a drink after work at The Class Reunion, where they might pick up useful tidbits or clues to stories. When they travel with the President on trips, particularly campaign trips, the buses and hotels become places for long conversations. Although some reporters shun the social aspects of these trips because they fear that their stories will be stolen or because they are concerned about contamination from the pack, it is clear that reporters are often valuable sources of information and interpretation for each other on these occasions. Dennis Farney explained how he saw this process work: "There is a lot of trading of opinions and hypotheses among reporters. In trading perceptions, there is a tendency to reach an agreed interpretation. The main reason that I don't like to test hypotheses is I want them to be my own and don't want reporters to burden me with doubts by arguing against it."

White House reporters spend a lot of time together, and it is hard for them not to socialize while waiting for briefings or ceremonies to take place. Frequently the conversation will turn to what one's lead is going to be. The senior wire reporters and the correspondents for the major publications find that reporters ask them what the thrust of their story will be. "Sometimes reporters want to know what the wires are leading with to protect themselves," Frank Cormier observed. James Naughton reported similar experiences: "This is frequently a tail-covering exercise, especially when you are on the road. . . . Sometimes they ask to insure that their story is going to be different, so that the news is not homogenized news across the country. . . . Mostly, as self-assurance or as reassurance to make sure that they are not too far off the mark."

Influences of reporters for elite organizations. Reporters for elite organizations legitimize news. What the *New York Times* reports may be broadcast on television more quickly than the same story prepared by the network's own correspondent would be. James Naughton commented:

We are the outlet for other opinion-makers to frame their references. The networks use these reporters as their reference. For example, after [one of the televised 1976 presidential] debates, "The Today Show" reported the debate as it had appeared in the *Times.* . . . What we cover, the networks find important. Network correspondents and news magazine correspondents have trouble from time to time getting things in their magazines or on the air that have not been covered by the *Times* and therefore certified as genuine, legitimate news.

Because the *Times* plays such an important role in the determination of what becomes news, a reporter whose organization failed to use a story may give it to the *Times* reporter. Naughton said he believed that when that happened, reporters gave him information "so they can gig their people, and get them interested in a subject.

RELATIONS WITHIN NEWS ORGANIZATIONS

With others on the beat. The leading newspapers, the networks, and the wires assign more than one person to the White House. Among the nine reporters, Cormier, Schieffer, and Naughton worked regularly with at least one other reporter; Lisagor and Deakin, occasionally; Farney, seldom; Bonafede and Osborne, almost never. Reporters tend to work out their relations informally, especially when one reporter is designated chief correspondent. "I tried very hard at the outset of my second assignment at the White House to be fair to Phil [Shabecoff], not to take all the big stories and leave Phil the drudge work," James Naughton recalled. "We tried to the extent that we were able to split up the better parts of the White House assignment."

With other reporters in their organizations. Reporters also share information with other reporters in their news organizations who are not on the same beat. They work closely with other reporters in their news rooms; they exchange information that often leads to major stories. All reporters testified to the cooperative atmosphere at their organizations, but seemed to believe their situations were unique. "There is very little pride of ownership of information or withholding information," James Deakin said of the Washington bureau of the *St. Louis Post-Dispatch.* "We have very few prima donnas in this place. There is practically none of the cutthroat ambition you find on other papers. We all know we are going to be on page one." Walter Rodgers described a similar situation among radio correspondents for AP in Washington. "If I have a tape of something they missed they come down and listen to it," he said. "If I pick up something they don't have, I give it to them. They are always giving me something. We have a very good working relationship."

Colleagues who share information do not always share sources. Especially among reporters with a high public and professional visibility, there is a tendency to think of sources as personal connections. Bob Schieffer described how he learned about this attitude early in his career at CBS. "One time I covered the State Department for a week when Marvin [Kalb] was going on vacation,'' Schieffer recalled. ''He gave me a basic mechanical rundown, not sources though. Sources are a very personal thing.''

Relations with editors and the high command. Relations between reporters and the managers of their organizations varied considerably among the nine correspondents in our group. Lisagor, Bonafede, and Osborne kept their editors informed of what they intended to do. They received requests to look into some matters, but rarely were instructed about the nature of the story. Cormier and Rodgers, at the other extreme, received instructions constantly. They put their own slant on a story, they were listened to when they told their chiefs what they thought a good story would be, but basically they responded. Deakin had considerable freedom, in part because his editors knew that he made himself responsible for what they would consider to be important stories. James Naughton, like other *New York Times* reporters, related that most stories on that paper are shaped either directly by editors in New York, indirectly through the reporter's consciousness of what he is expected to do, or with the approval of editors when he originates the idea.

Network reporters have the most complicated arrangements because they deal with different news programs, and each has its own organizational structure. Bob Schieffer described the nature of his relations with different editors and producers within this structure: ''I deal with the Washington producer of the evening news, the producer for the morning news, and the producer for the radio news. It is almost like working for a news bureau that services several news organizations, because each of the news programs is an entity unto itself. It is so complicated to put on a news program. If we ran things like the army where you leave everything to the chief of staff, you would never get the news on the air.'' In spite of all this consultation, Schieffer, like the other reporters, seldom was given direct instructions to stop what he wanted to do in favor of what the management wanted him to do. As Dennis Farney put it, describing his relations with the *Journal* management, ''I would have the sense not to waste my time on something they didn't want.''

Only a few reporters have sustained contact with the high command of their organizations. Publishers and news directors appear before the assembled correspondents to rally the troops before a big news event. From time to time there would be a kind of pep talk, a '' 'Let's go out and do very well,' '' James Naughton said, describing the role sometimes played by top management at the *Times.* ''There was a pep talk before the [1976 Democratic] convention in New York with various executives. We were encouraged to do our best, to outwrite, and outdo, anybody else covering that convention.''

Reporters do not like to be regarded as the agents of the management of their organizations, although they use its prestige. They want their relations with those White House aides who dispense information to be kept separate from any negative (and sometimes even positive) associations those aides may have about their organizations. Dennis Farney related an instance when following instructions of the high command created problems for him. Farney was given a question to ask Jody Powell during the transition period prior to Carter's inauguration. "I had been instructed by the New York high command to ask about wage and price controls. Carter had made statements during the campaign but they wanted me to ask it. Powell accused me and the *Wall Street Journal* of trying to paint Carter into a corner on this thing. . . . I never could convince Powell that I wasn't a running dog of Wall Street."

REPORTERS' RELATIONS WITH THEIR SOURCES

The nine correspondents we interviewed described four aspects of the relationship between reporters and sources: first, how reporters establish sources; second, at what level in the White House reporters find sources useful; third, why reporters think their sources talk to them; and fourth, whether reporters are "soft" on their sources. The views they expressed about their relationship are somewhat different from those presented in the previous chapter, where the source was considered from the more general perspective of political communications operations in the White House.

All reporters interviewed for this book agreed that the only way for a reporter to establish sources at the White House is to cast as broad a net as possible. "When I first came in I didn't know who to talk to, so I just started calling everybody," explained Bob Schieffer. "They want to talk to you. The sources need the reporters, just like the reporter needs the source." James Naughton also recommended trial and error as the best, and perhaps the only, procedure to locate useful sources. He suggested that over a period of time a reporter would develop a small group of reliable respondents he could call:

Perhaps eight of them for general atmosphere, clues as to what is going on, sounding boards for my interpretation—to add something to it or suggesting an alternative theme or thesis. Another four would be used when I want to be sure I am getting in a little closer. . . . [But] in the year and a half I've been there I've found only one individual who is both knowledgeable and articulate for my purposes, and he is very well positioned, generally knows in a broad spectrum what is going on, and has not mislead me.

Some source-reporter relations were established when both the official and the correspondent worked elsewhere in Washington. Reporters who covered the President when he was a candidate strike connections with aides who later become officials. Some relations are formed at dinners or other stations that are part of Washington's social scene, although these connections are more likely to be established by columnists, bureau chiefs, and other elite journalists than by the White House regulars. Reporters agreed that for those assigned to the beat, there is no substitute for a process of prying open doors and gradually establishing contact so that eventually telephone calls are answered and useful responses are forthcoming.

The level of the White House at which a reporter is most likely to establish a fruitful relationship depends on the correspondent's individual and organizational status. A high-level staff member may be slow in responding to a request for an interview from a reporter whose organization is not considered important. When he does give the interview, he may not deviate far from information and interpretations on the public record. That reporter might find more responsive contacts at a middle level, while a reporter for one of the important print or broadcast organizations would receive help from the high-level assistant.

John Osborne and Dom Bonafede said they tried to establish relations with the top people first, but each reporter gave a different reason. Osborne suggested that the top people knew more and could be more helpful than their subordinates. "Naturally you go to the center and see if you can get anything," he said. "I don't absolutely go only there. I wait for the way they toss the ball." Dom Bonafede talked to the chief of an office first because it gave him entrée to everyone else:

Unless you are in solid with the number one guy, you're not going to be solid with the number two or three. The lower level people are going to help you more once you talk to the number one guy. When I talk with the number one guy I always tell him that I am going to talk with his people—his undersecretary—and is it okay if I tell them you say it is all right to talk to them. He will always say "sure." Then I call the lower level guy and say, "I just talked with your boss and he said it's okay to talk with me." He feels almost compelled to talk to me. In a big office, like the Domestic Council [now Domestic Policy], that always comes in handy.

Dennis Farney agreed with Osborne that top-level people were the best sources. He felt that they should be used sparingly, however; because of their time constraints he did not want to overstay his welcome and thus lose an opportunity to see them at a crucial moment. "I tried not to see them in sit-down interview situations more than once every two weeks," he said. "I went to middle-level people instead."

Most reporters felt that middle-level aides were the best sources. The staff involved in the highest level of policy decisions protects the President in private interviews the same way they do in their public statements, by weighing each word carefully so that it could not reverberate to harm the administration. Consequently, most reporters used high-level sources only to confirm or deny a story. Even then, much of what is communicated is by indirection. "The senior staff communicate like the British upper class," James Deakin remarked. "They grunt and wiggle their eyebrows. Impressions can be confirmed without the person saying anything." Middle-level staff members are the best explainers of policy because they are free from the constraints of high visibility. Since what they know rather than who they are is of interest to reporters, what they say in explanation of the President's policies really is likely to be on a background basis.

The knowledge that officials talk to reporters for reasons other than their

concern for First Amendment freedoms does not surprise most correspondents. They recognize that their sources give them stories for a variety of
reasons, most of them involving advantage for the President, but some of
them involving their interorganizational quarrels. "You get stories because
they are on the other side of something they want to stop," Bob Schieffer
said. Other factors are the audience and the treatment the source wants to get
from his organization. John Osborne explained that this was true of his relatively good access in the Nixon administration, which was otherwise odd
because he worked for the liberal *New Republic:* "I am fairly sure that was
the case with the Nixon staff. I was nice to them in my magazine. They
thought that they could get a reasonably fair break out of me . . . some of them
had sense enough to see and conclude that the *New Republic,* limited though
the circulation, did have and does have, high impact. I know that had something to do with my news access."

Most senior reporters who have been on the beat for a large portion of a
president's term acquire a well-placed source whom they can consult on
particularly important stories when they need to check the accuracy of what
they have pieced together. Sometimes these sources, like McGeorge Bundy
and Nelson Rockefeller, have a public status. Some, such as Henry Kissinger
and Melvin Laird, appear to cultivate reporters and invite the relationship.
"What does he get out of it?" Dom Bonafede asked. "Oftentime he has an
axe to grind. He gets some reflection of his point of view. Maybe he just does
it to help the President. . . . Their overall purpose is public persuasion. To
manipulate the public to his leadership."

Another expectation of many officials is that there will be personal benefits
to them and their immediate operation in exchange for providing information
to reporters. Reporters know that officials hold many high cards. Because
they rely so heavily on interviews to gather information, they have to be
careful in their relations with their sources. "They can pretty well kill you, as
in the Nixon era when they didn't like you," noted Dennis Farney. He found
some of his sources would complain about his stories, but only once did it
result in his being cut off from further contact. Sometimes their complaints
can be quite direct. "One day when I was in Jordan's office," Farney recalled, "he picked up a Washington wire item from the *Wall Street Journal*
and said, 'That is just a lot of shit,' and then went on to elaborate how dumb it
was and how reporters were getting the wrong idea. . . . Powell would be
more sarcastic. He would lump me in with the Washington syndrome."

Because reporters are concerned that interviews granted in the White House
setting may elicit subtle White House demands that they repay officials, they
try to hold their meetings in less formal surroundings. In addition to their
concern that they may be soft on their sources in the White House, reporters
believe that officials are more likely to respond with their opinions rather than
the bureaucratic line when they leave their offices. James Deakin felt that the
constraints of time, schedule, and proximity to their work prevented many

officials from talking to reporters. Particularly for the vast majority of aides who are not trying to cover up anything, the opportunity to talk at length with a reporter is not spurned: "Trips are invaluable for contacts because they are free from that telephone. They are free for lunches and drinks and it is very informal. This is one of the circumstances where you develop sources. What I don't do is invite them to my house for dinner parties."

Dennis Farney took the opposite position. He felt that meeting with people in formal circumstances in their offices during the workday made it possible for him to keep the proper distance from his informants: "I maintained an arms-length relationship with the people. Since I would use anything that I found interesting in an interview in a story, I would want sources to realize that I was the kind of guy who would use anything. I didn't want them to assume that I was their friend. . . . But one is inclined to be a little kinder to someone you have to see all the time than a minor functionary you are never going to see again."

In the final analysis, the rules on dealing with sources are quite loose. They vary with the kind of relationship the reporter and the source have. Most reporters regard sources who provide them with factual information as more vulnerable than those who provide them with background tone. A lot "depends on the individual reporter," James Deakin noted. "The ethics of the profession are pretty ad hoc. . . . You have to decide for yourself what the ethics are."

EIGHT

DIPLOMATS AND NEGOTIATORS

Media Influentials and the Higher Circles at the White House

WASHINGTON, a government installation, responds to powerful office-holders and nongovernmental influentials. Included in this second category are an elite corps of journalists. Through their power in the media, they influence Washington reputations. In addition, they control channels to important segments of the public whom neither lobbyists nor officials can reach with the same impact. Their status, which opens the doors of influentials, provides them with access to information considered valuable among insiders. Because these influentials and insiders link information to power, elite journalists possess many commodities to trade in exchange for the continuing access they need for success in the media.

Most individuals among this elite group first acquired status because they worked for important news organizations. In this respect they are not very different from influentials who rise through their work on the staffs of leading members of Congress, powerful officials, influential lobbyists, or the White House itself. In order to reach the higher levels of status and prestige, however, they must have personal as well as organizational status. Members of the elite occupy important positions in the administration of their news enterprises, possess public visibility, or command respect because they are considered to be important people. Among them are syndicated columnists, reporters who command their own audiences, the anchors of the major network news programs, and bureau chiefs. The status of members of this elite is based on several factors. Bureau chiefs' reputations are based on the strength with which they represent their organizations. Columnists and elite reporters owe their eminence to the influence of their regular audience, the credibility derived from their past performances, and the fear they can evoke among Washington's strivers and power-seekers. Anchors are regarded highly in Washington because of their national prominence.

Only Hollywood gives an equivalent rank to the representatives of news organizations who cover the city's main industry. Only the nation's capital, however, pays so much attention to journalists' political clout. "In New York you [reporters] have your nose pressed against the window," Martin Tolchin said as he reflected on his changed status when he moved from the *Times*'s city hall beat to its national bureau. In New York, he surmised, those who run the city regard reporters as people who have not made anything of themselves. The contrast in Washington was made clear when he received invitations to social functions where he mixed with the prominent: "In Washington you are much closer; you're part of the whole social circle. . . . At our first dinner party my wife and I sat next to Abe Fortas. I was fascinated—just meeting him and talking to him. We didn't talk about anything relevant. It is fascinating to see these people close up."[1]

In Washington, those with important political positions seek contacts in the media as readily as journalists look for sources among officials, aides, and lobbyists. The fact that a new Washington correspondent was placed next to a former presidential adviser and Supreme Court Justice at a dinner party reflects the status of the *New York Times*. Elite journalists are even more eagerly sought after. Officials and lobbyists vie for places at dinner parties next to one of the leading reporters, editors, producers, or columnists.

White House officials regard the regular beat reporters as tradesmen who must enter through a special side door to conduct their business. They meet with the President at formal sessions such as press conferences held at times and places that the White House chooses. The regulars can count on access to Press Office assistants and expect responses from lower- or middle-level aides, but they wait in slowly moving lines for senior staff members to grant them interviews or return their calls. In contrast, the telephone calls of elite journalists are put through immediately to top assistants. The President and his advisers recognize the importance of those at the top of the media pyramid. They invite these select news people to small White House gatherings, where they chat with the President. Treated as no mere tradesmen, they are invited in the front door and asked to stay for dinner. White House officials recognize them as diplomats and negotiators who can carry the President's messages to the publics he must reach.

White House officials believe that elite journalists can adversely or positively affect the President's reputation. In 1978 President Carter's advisers convinced him to take new measures to persuade the public of his competence. One of the major recommendations resulted in the appointment of Gerald Rafshoon as the assistant for communications. After assessing polls that showed a year-long decline in public perception that Jimmy Carter could provide effective national leadership, Rafshoon urged the President to accept a longstanding staff recommendation that he meet informally with media influentials. Subsequently, eight dinners for news people were held between July 19 and September 26, 1978. According to Press Secretary Jody Powell, these dinners "were spent in fairly informal discussion of events and issues to give them an opportunity to be impressed with the President's broad command of the issues."[2]

Almost all of the major print and broadcast enterprises were represented at these dinners. Among the most prominent were *Time* Inc., the *Washington Star*, the National Broadcasting Company, the *Washington Post*, *Newsweek*, the *New York Times*, the American Broadcasting Company, the Columbia Broadcasting Company, the *Los Angeles Times*, and *U.S. News and World Report*. Both White House and news organizations' perceptions of who was important can be gleaned from a guest list the authors obtained from an official. The *Time*, Inc., representatives were its bureau chief, managing editor, and two corporate editors. The *Washington Post* sent its publisher, managing editor, the editor of the editorial page, and an assistant editor. According to the White House official, the President felt it was more important to meet with executives from these two organizations than their reporters and columnists. When other news organizations responded, their anchors or columnists attended along with the executives. James Reston of the *New York Times* was invited along with Tom Wicker, an associate editor; Max Frankel, editor of the editorial page; and Hedrick Smith, the Washington bureau chief. When NBC had its turn, anchors David Brinkley and John Chancellor were joined by Les Crystal, president of the news division, and Fred Silverman, president of the network. A third group included nationally syndicated columnists and the anchors of television news discussion programs. These journalists saw the President in meetings when no executives were present. The columnists—Jack Germond, Jules Witcover, Joseph Kraft, and Haynes Johnson—were writers whose influential audience included editors and leading reporters of most Washington-based news enterprises. The television guests included Robert MacNeil, Jim Lehrer, Martin Agronsky, and Paul Duke. Among them they anchored the three most influential news discussion programs: "The MacNeil-Lehrer Report," "Agronsky and Company," and "Washington Week in Review."

Other recent presidents cultivated elite journalists at important moments of decision-making or merely to keep ties between them and their administrations. Republican Presidents Eisenhower and Nixon invited executives because they felt they would get more sympathy at that level. John Kennedy, who mixed easily with both groups, encouraged his main advisers to do the same. Gerald Ford's staff set up White House meetings with key executives and reporters at crucial times during his short term, particularly as he campaigned for the nomination and election.

No president, however, outdid Lyndon Johnson in courting media influentials, as well as some news people of more marginal importance. Johnson's efforts at persuasion often became ludicrous and backfired. His offer to make "big men" out of well-known correspondents became a joke. But even those who laughed wanted continued access to the President. Proximity to Johnson was important to media influentials in the same sense that proximity to a president is always important. They know that perception of status is closely linked to status in Washington. If a president thinks a journalist is important and treats him or her accordingly, then that journalist becomes important.

Another aspect of Washington life reinforces the impact elite journalists have on the President's Washington reputation and his national prestige. Those in the top circles tend to watch each other closely while they are watched by other influentials in Washington. What is said at elite forums such as the Sperling breakfasts, the news discussion programs, or the news interview programs frequently becomes the focus of news stories and editorial comments, as well as becoming the opinion of those in Congress, the bureaucracy, and the lobbies—who are all in a position to help or hinder the administration. Thus not only do many journalists in this group receive diplomatic courtesies from the White House as representatives of important news organizations, they expect such treatment as representatives of their audiences.

The Diplomats: Columnists, Elite Reporters, and Anchorpersons

At the top of the reporting profession is a small group of syndicated columnists, elite reporters, and anchorpersons for network news and news discussion programs. Syndicated columnists do not dominate public opinion today as they did during the half-century from 1920 to 1970, the era of journalistic thunderers. Writers such as Arthur Krock, the Drummonds, the Alsops, Dorothy Thompson, Heywood Broun, and Walter Lippmann exerted considerable national influence. Their national position has declined because the personalization of the journalist's message on television has more impact on much of the audience for news than the written word. Columnists still occupy an important position in Washington because their audience there includes many influential leaders. All recent presidents personally courted columnists— with the one exception of Richard Nixon, who delegated this chore to John Ehrlichman and the very willing Henry Kissinger.

An elite reporter commands the attention of the White House because his or her byline on a news story or presence on a news broadcast is an assurance to an influential audience that what is said or written is authentic, accurate, and significant. Sometimes beat reporters acquire that status—Tom Wicker and Max Frankel of the *New York Times* did on the White House beat. Often they acquire a column, although they continue to write news stories—as was the case with David Broder, William Greider, and Peter Lisagor. Eventually elite reporters become editors or work fulltime on their columns, although David Broder, Jack Germond, and Jules Witcover produce and contribute to news stories almost as frequently as they write columns. Elite television reporters include interviewers for news specials such as Bill Moyers or Barbara Walters. Others, like Mike Wallace and Dan Rather, prepare documentaries. Some are simply well-regarded reporters without portfolio, like Roger Mudd and Bruce Morton.

COLUMNISTS AND ELITE REPORTERS

Columnists have achieved the goals expressed by many reporters when they discuss how they would like to operate. They are guaranteed space, they have no assigned topics, they are free from the pressure of breaking news stories at deadline, and they have the opportunity to introduce their own perspectives into their stories. A columnist does not suffer the public anonymity of an editor, and he or she can continue to write. In the 1970s the proliferation of news space at the wealthy newspapers and the vast increase in the number of magazines gave many reporters the opportunity to become columnists. Writers use their blocks of space to comment on life and styles as well as on politics; some writers move freely from one area to another.

Most outstanding reporters on national affairs eventually acquire columns of their own. At the *New York Times* reporters such as James Reston and Tom Wicker became both editors and columnists, while Anthony Lewis and Russell Baker settled for writing alone. Several other writers, such as David Halberstam and Richard Reeves, left the paper to write longer works, although Reeves has reappeared as a nationally syndicated columnist. Similar career patterns characterize the experience of many other correspondents who were outstanding reporters in the 1960s and shifted to columns, free-lance journalism, or the editorial side in the 1970s. At least two-well-known columnists, William Safire and Garry Wills, spent little or no time in daily journalism. Safire became a *Times* columnist to answer the charge that no authentic conservative voice appeared on the *Times*'s *Op Ed* page. Wills has been a successful free-lance magazine writer. In the 1980s some reporters have selected alternative avenues of advancement that are more lucrative than writing. James Wooten of the *Times* and Marilyn Berger of the *Washington Post* became television correspondents. In contrast, Elizabeth Drew, who had been an interviewer for the Public Broadcasting System, took the more unusual step of becoming a writer, in this case the reporter-columnist in Washington for the *New Yorker*.

COLUMNISTS AND THE PRESIDENCY

From the 1930s through the 1960s, a small group of columnists occupied a unique position in national political life. Although all recent presidents reacted to what they wrote, White House concern with the efforts of the columnists rose during the Johnson administration. Columnists were taken so seriously by Johnson that the White House staff was given responsibilities for contact with specific individuals. In a White House memorandum, Press Secretary George Reedy suggested that McGeorge Bundy be responsible for Joseph Alsop, Marquis Childs, Walter Lippmann, and James Reston.[3] The administration felt that these elite journalists were important because what they wrote had the authority to set the public perception of what the President was doing and underscore the themes and tones of the administration. In a memorandum to the President, Ben Wattenburg of the staff described an article that Hugh Sidey was in the process of preparing on the subject of Johnson's assistants. Wattenburg told the President of three points he wanted to give to Sidey. The President approved Wattenburg's plan and wrote across the memo "measure each word."[4] The President regarded people like Sidey as sufficiently important to the administration for him to want and at times demand that the staff tell him of a prospective meeting. If he objected, as he sometimes did, he would veto the meeting.

The Nixon administration also regarded columnists as important molders of opinion. In a memorandum to H. R. Haldeman the President wrote, "On the PR side, I think it might be well for you to see how Buchanan, Safire, et al., could have columnists—television commentators and others—prepare the way for the Lindsay victory in New York." The message the President wanted to get out was that he didn't "want it interpreted as a referendum on Vietnam. . . . It is vitally important that this be nailed prior to the election and, of course, be nailed immediately afterwards as strongly as possible."[5]

Some elite journalists have been concerned that columnists get too close to the White House. Peter Lisagor suggested:

Columnists are brought in the White House and officials explain their position. If the columnist feels it's reasonable, then they go on and propagate it. . . . A good columnist will also write that "although the White House says this, there are other people in town who say something completely different." Then he will attempt to make a judgment. But did you see the story that some major columnist in this town permitted the CIA to write his stories? I'm sure a good deal of that happens.[6]

On the other side, however, columnists try to influence the White House. In 1978, after Carter, Begin, and Sadat met at Camp David, Joseph Kraft was asked if he wasn't concerned that an unflattering portrait of Begin that appeared in his column might be regarded as offensive by Jews since some of the description approximated uncomplimentary stereotypes. Kraft suggested that his description of Begin was similar to the view of President Carter, who had made no secret of the low esteem he had for the Israeli Prime Minister: "I wanted to show the President that in spite of Begin's unattractive personality, he [the President] should look at what he had accomplished."[7] In this case at least, Kraft's column was directed at an audience of one.

Like other elite journalists, columnists have an entrée to the White House that the regulars do not. "Kennedy was a friend of mine and I could see him virtually when I wanted to," Hugh Sidey of *Time* reminisced. Other journalists of Sidey's status also report that they get in to see the people they want to see at the White House. If they establish a relationship with an aide or a deputy rather than a top official it is because they find them better sources. Of course the officials themselves decide the nature of their relations. For example, Robert Novak reports during the Johnson administration National Security Adviser McGeorge Bundy was not available to him but that the staff was accessible. On the other hand, during the Nixon and Ford terms, Kissinger welcomed him and his collaborator, Rowland Evans, but discouraged his assistants from talking to them.[8] Bundy later explained his response; he had found Evans and Novak hostile to the administration, not interested in reporting what he might explain, and therefore not worth the investment of time.[9]

Joseph Kraft, however, remembered that "Bundy was a marvelous source . . . the best kind of source I could get."[10]

What distinguishes the way in which these top journalists cover the President is that they are crosscutters who seek news and reactions to events from a variety of sources in Washington and elsewhere. Because they have better access and more flexible deadlines, they are able to focus on perspective and opinion rather than hard news. All of these elements are related. Because they have better entrée, they can get a more authoritative version of what is happening. Because they have more flexible deadlines, they can wait for the people they want to see to become available. Because they deal in opinion and perspective, they can use information that does not fit the needs of reporters seeking hard news. Because they are crosscutters, they can check information from independent sources. Thus they may get better information from White House sources when those sources know that their version of an event will have to measure up against what is being told elsewhere, Joseph Kraft suggested, "The columnist is . . . slightly higher on the pecking order. Thus you have—this was once very true—an independence of your own. You are not on the end of a string being pulled by Jody Powell. The other thing is that you are a crosscutter. You don't just cover the White House. . . . I always cover a crap game, and the four or five guys playing the game. The best kind of source I can ever get is the guy who manages the crap game."[11] The crap games Kraft referred to were economic policy, national security, and politics.

Perhaps because of the apparent proliferation of columnists and the ensuing cacophony of voices, columnists have lost some of the force of their punch. Among those who still are considered in Washington to be influential analysts of the presidency are David Broder, Joseph Kraft, and Robert Novak. Broder is the most respected writer on politics among other Washington journalists; Kraft has both an important elite audience in Washington and considerable importance as an opinion-molder in the many cities in which his column appears; Robert Novak, of the team of Evans and Novak, is regarded as an authoritative voice among top segments of Washington's defense establishment and among political conservatives nationally.

Broder. David Broder of the *Washington Post* is an example of the elite journalists who write signed columns of opinion and analysis that appear on the *Op Ed* page but who also report hard news stories on elections or interpretive news stories on campaigns. It may be that Broder's expertise in almost all aspects of the process of electoral competition lends itself to this sort of division. Jack Germond and Jules Witcover, who coauthor a political column ranked only slightly behind Broder's in prestige, also divide their time between their column and preparing news stories that appear throughout the newspaper.

Broder's essential influence on the political process is the legitimization of candidates and campaign organizations. His assessment of whether prospective presidential candidates have a clear idea of why they want to be President, whether they have struck responses with voters, and whether they know how to organize a campaign and use it to communicate themselves are all regarded almost as highly as the consultants' reports made by the Washington community. In particular, Broder is watched and respected by other journalists, many of whom mentioned that their own assessments of candidates and campaign organizations are checked against Broder's. "He is awfully good," Martin Tolchin of the *New York Times* commented. "When he has a story you can bank on it, you really can."[12] For example, on Sunday, March 1, 1980, a front page story in the *New York Times* stated that Gerald Ford was about to begin a drive to take the Republican nomination. The story was then disseminated through the media. On Wednesday, March 5, Broder's column analyzing the prospects of that candidacy appeared on the *Op Ed* page of the *Washington Post*. Broder's analysis of pros and cons created the framework by which Ford's prospects would be judged by most other political writers, by the strategists in the corps of other contenders, by the attentive public, and ultimately by Gerald Ford himself, whose withdrawal from the nominating contest was undoubtedly affected by this assessment.

The national political story is an assignment Broder can create because of his status at the *Post*. According to several *Post* reporters and editors, he shapes the direction the paper takes in its coverage of political stories. He doesn't give orders. He doesn't command from an editor's chair. He listens to others. But the scope of the *Post*'s coverage tends to be determined by what he thinks. The President and his White House staff become a major part of Broder's journalism as he perceives them as part of his political story. "There are the beat men who . . . handle the basic flow of news out of there," he said shortly before Carter's inauguration. "We attempt to supplement that by moving people in on particular stories. The transition struggle will take me in and out of the White House."[13]

Broder's triple-barreled influence is loaded with the authority he commands from having the story right, from his syndication as a columnist, and from the organizational abilities he commands as the *Washington Post*'s chief political writer. The combination is vital. For example, during the early months of the 1980 campaign, some of the best reporting and analysis was done by Fred Barnes, national political writer for the *Baltimore Sun*. Although Barnes was well regarded by his colleagues, his articles, published in one newspaper in Baltimore, could not have the impact of Broder's articles and columns published in Washington and syndicated nationally.

Broder has been criticized by some of his *Washington Post* colleagues for being too concerned with a smoothly operating political organization and not concerned enough with the substance of political problems. They suggested that in 1972 he focused on how well-run the Nixon reelection campaign was and therefore did not snuff out what they were up to.[14] By 1980 Broder changed his operation. He did become involved in the substance of politics; he showed a decidedly conservative bent in his evaluation both of electoral institutions and of policies. He used his position to point out that Jimmy Carter's smooth campaign during the winter of 1980 enabled him to avoid dealing with the hard issues, just as Nixon's had in 1972.

Kraft. Joseph Kraft, a nationally syndicated columnist, works under quite different circumstances from Broder's. He works alone (out of his house) and is not part of a news organization. While Broder writes for a large audience seeking news and perspective, Kraft interprets what is happening in Washington with the intention of providing for his readers a feeling of what is important.

Like most columnists concerned with national politics, he uses the White House as a central part of his subject matter. Contact with the President ordinarily is not important, he suggested, because he seldom reveals much. He would try to get one interview with the Chief Executive to assess how he is holding up under the strain of office, but he did not find that interviews with the President supplied the kinds of materials he needed for his column. On the other hand, he has had useful relations with advisers close to the President. His contacts with the Kennedy administration were particularly good, in part because he had worked as a speechwriter in the election campaign. From the perspective of some officials in the Nixon administration, his contacts with that administration were too good. They tapped his telephone as part of their efforts to track down disclosures of information.

Kraft felt that he was different from White House correspondents because of his interest in policy, and different from other columnists in that they seek the revealing piece of information whereas he is interested in information that provides a basis for analysis. In order to reach his objectives, Kraft said, he had to become a "specialist in specialists":

If an issue comes up I will call up people who work on it for their profession. I need people who can help me, I don't go after nuggets. I need people who can help me analyze things, and tell me what I ought to think in areas where I don't have the time to watch it. . . . The other thing is you really have to work like hell. . . . You get the perception of what is happening at the White House. . . . You have to be as knowledgeable about the Hill as the good Hill guys.[15]

In addition to his syndicated column, Kraft writes several longer articles each year for the *New Yorker,* often based on his extensive foreign travels. Unlike his column, which is punchy, opinionated, and controversial, his articles are detached, reflective, and universally esteemed. He is almost always welcomed by the leaders of any country he visits as an important person with whom it is useful to spend time. In 1978 and 1979, for example, he met with leaders of Iran, Ethiopia, Israel, and Mexico. It is not surprising to find that he is the only journalist we interviewed who thinks that fluency in several languages is an important ingredient for a reporter or columnist who included as topics foreign as well as domestic issues. Another element adding to Kraft's status in Washington is his frequent participation on television in news interview programs and news discussion broadcasts.

In preparation for his columns, articles, and public appearances, Kraft had found it useful to ask nongovernmental people for information that reveals more about the administration's policies. In particular, he appears to be the only major national writer who touches base regularly with academic experts on policy areas, including some located far from Washington. He found that some of his academic informants have good contacts, in some cases proving to be better than officials. Undoubtedly they would not have the same constraints or reticence as would officials who talked to Kraft:

I probably have better academic contacts than any other columnist.... Brookings people have their opposite numbers in Budget that they are constantly in touch with. The Harvard people have their opposites. If you really want to find out what Jack Watson is doing, a very good way to do it is to talk to Graham Allison, where he comes up with a lot of his ideas. If you want to know about China, to know what to ask Kissinger, talk to John Lewis or Alan Whiting.[16]

Novak. A White House official related that a joke during the Nixon administration was that Melvin Laird was so influential he had a private line to Evans and Novak. Novak agreed that the former secretary of defense and presidential adviser had been one of the best sources for the column that he and Rowland Evans produce. He suggested that defense establishment leaders' interest in their column was a reflection of his and Evans's own interests. "The place where we have our strongest point of view is in foreign policy and defense policy. We get more people at the Pentagon and the NSC than the White House."[17]

Novak and Evans write what they regard as a reporter's column of opinion. As with most columnists, their direct contact with government sources provides the basis of the materials they use for their column. Although high-level informants such as Laird provide useful background to and explanations of policy, the revealing details for which their column is well known are mined at the middle-staff levels in the executive and legislative branches. Documents such as the records of congressional hearings and other published government materials supplement what they learn through interviews. In contrast to Kraft, they do search for the nuggets of information they believe reveal mood, character, or the real direction policy is taking. Digging up new material is an important part of their operation. "It is a mixture of reporting and opinion," Novak said. "It is not a straight reporting column. . . . We try in each column to provide new information. The columns tend to have a point of view." In response to questions about their readership, he said, "We really don't think about that too much. I think about the people who read our column as being people who are fairly sophisticated, interested in politics, particularly the inner workings of the political, government, diplomatic structure. We try to write about what is current, of importance, and of interest. We try to write a readable column."[18]

Novak agreed that many Washington influentials would like to use their column to suit their own purposes. At times they would let themselves be the subject of a planted story because "the criteria is, is it accurate and valid . . . if it is just a phony we just won't write it. The motivation doesn't bother me." He denied that a large number of columns are the result of leaks. They have to work hard to get sources to talk to them. Frequently the information they are looking for appears in a clue form. Especially during the Nixon administration, their interviews were often conducted in a kind of code because aides did not want to be identified as the source of items in their column: "The Nixon White House was a good deal tougher, a good deal buttoned up, but we had good sources there. It was a lot of fun to report it and we came up with a lot of stories that broke a lot of inside stuff that was going on there. The rise of John Ehrlichman was first reported in our column."[19]

The Evans and Novak column has been the subject of much anger from the White House since its inception during the Kennedy administration. Lyndon Johnson referred to them as "errors and nofacts."[20] The accusation that a staff member had been the source of an unfavorable description of White House activities in their column was enough to send that aide to the Johnson White House's equivalent of Coventry. Novak reported that unhappy staff would accuse him of receiving his information from a particular aide whom they accused of inaccuracy as well as disloyalty to the President. Invariably they would mention someone from whom the pair had not received pertinent information. Officials assume that their material comes from some one White House insider. The reality, he suggested, is often quite different: "We often get very good leads as to what is happening at the White House through Capital Hill. The beat structure of newspapers is too segregated. The cross-fertilization we find very helpful in tips."[21]

Although they produce a partisan column that seldom gives serious attention to information that might contradict their conservative point of view, they are widely read across a broad spectrum of Washington opinion. They are the best reporters among the journalists whose only published newspaper appearance is in their syndicated column. They have excellent contacts among professional politicians, and they have the best news sources in the conservative defense establishment in Congress, the Defense Department, and the National Security Council. What one reads in their column constitutes required reading because their own influence makes it an amplification, and not merely a reflection, of the views of insiders.

Novak also appears on news discussion programs and news interview programs, and with Evans he has written several books on the presidency. The books differ from the columns in that they are more scholarly and detached. Perhaps because they are less partisan and less directed to problems of the moment, their books provide a more balanced account of a president's activities.

THE ANCHORS: IMPORTANT VOICES IN A COLOSSAL ENTERPRISE
In the 1960s and 1970s the Cronkites, Chancellors, and Brinkleys—news anchors who do not really have a message—took over the position columnists once occupied with the public. In the 1980s the format will change after the retirement of key figures such as Cronkite. Television news will move away from the presentation of stories by a central authority.

John Chancellor and Walter Cronkite, and two remaining anchors who "personified" the news at the onset of the 1980s, still play that role. They legitimize government announcements. Consequently, their presence at the White House has a different significance from that of even the most prestigious writers. In contrast to well-known columnists who sometimes may be seen in the White House press room waiting to be ushered by an aide to an inner office, Walter Cronkite was observed hurrying to an interview with President Ford after being waved past the gates by White House security forces who required no more identification than his famous face.

White House officials pay particular attention to the men who are the anchors of the network's nightly news programs. They know that they command a vast audience, hold the respect of the public, and occupy a position of considerable status with the television media and even among print journalists. The anchors acknowledge that there is considerable difference between their world and that of ordinary correspondents. "There is the reporter's world and there is the anchorman's world," suggested John Chancellor of NBC. "I try to live them both as much as I can. But if I'm honest with myself, I'd say I live in the anchorman's world. . . . I have an important voice in a colossal enterprise. Being a reporter is more fun, but anchoring the news is more important. And I couldn't be more pleased being where I am."[22]

The anchors rarely report the news, but when they do, they carry a particular authority with their message. If they take a political position, the effect upon the public is multiplied by the power of their medium beyond the impact of a similar position taken by an ordinary reporter or a columnist. When Walter Cronkite returned from Vietnam in 1968 shortly after the Tet offensive, he put together a special program on the war in which he presented the conclusion that the American effort in Vietnam was a failure. David Halberstam pointed out that Cronkite's conclusion had a tremendous impact on the President: "In Washington, Lyndon Johnson watched and told his press secretary, George Christian, that it was a turning point, that if he had lost Walter Cronkite he had lost Mr. Average Citizen. . . . He realized that he had lost the center, that Walter both was the center and reached the center, and thus his own consensus was in serious jeopardy."[23]

Lyndon Johnson's assessment of the credibility of a network anchor jibed with poll results that showed that the public viewed anchors as being more believable than most politicians. During the 1972 election campaign, the Oliver Quayle polling group asked the people in their sample to rate their trust of several prominent persons whose names appeared on a list. Frank McGee, then anchor for "The Today Show," ranked far ahead of all presidential and vice presidential nominees with this group. Other surveys have shown an equally high public standing for other anchors, a status reflected in their treatment by the White House. During a press briefing on December 19, 1977, Jody Powell was asked whether he had asked to have the anchors as the President's interrogators on a televised question and answer session. Powell replied that he had. When he was then asked why he hadn't asked for the White House correspondents, he replied: "It is nothing personal. We wanted their chief negotiators and diplomats to be involved in this thing."[24]

The contemporary White House prefers to save for the anchors the kind of important public announcements the President wants to give to one journalist. For example, during January, 1976, White House reporters repeatedly asked Press Secretary Ron Nessen about President Ford's position on abortion. Nessen sidestepped these questions with the response that the President was in the process of preparing his position. The Ford stance on the abortion question was finally made known to the reporters, but not until the President had first given it to Walter Cronkite in a filmed interview for the nightly news. Until the mid-1960s, important presidential positions would have been saved for one of the elite journalists or columnists. This practice changed when the anchors became national figures and after the network news programs became half-hour broadcasts that introduced the evening's television fare.

Television journalists tend to have a high regard for the anchors, while correspondents for the print media respect their clout without necessarily admiring them professionally. For television journalists the anchor positions of the various news programs represent the top of their profession. Not only do the anchors influence what appears on their news programs, they often obtain contractual agreements from the networks that permit them to prepare documentary and news analysis programs. Print journalists tend to look down on television news as more entertainment than information. Although many reporters for newspapers and magazines admitted that they rarely had the opportunity to watch television news, a typical comment of many was that the two-minute news story provides an inadequate basis for coverage that gets below the surface of a story. In addition, print correspondents complained that television news sensationalized and overdramatized the presidency. "I think there are some institutional problems ever since the White House front lawn has become a studio," Hugh Sidey commented. "The survival of the television reporters is to get on that evening news. If there isn't any news, they make it."[25]

These opinions of the professional level of television news coverage were shared by many White House aides. "You have one network [CBS] that covers the news, and two that are completely inadequate," a former Ford administration official commented.[26] Although some anchors were singled out for derogatory comments by print journalists—Howard K. Smith and Harry Reasoner were the chief targets—most print journalists focused on the medium rather than its messengers. One anchor who received a great deal of positive comment was John Chancellor. "Print reporters take Chancellor very seriously," David Halberstam commented. "They like the fact that he has a great awareness of the brute force of the instrument he uses and therefore is very subtle and cautious and just."[27]

OTHER ELITE VOICES AND LOCALES

An elite audience in Washington and an attentive public throughout the nation tune in on a number of news discussion programs and interview programs. Both of these formats provide a basis for the formation of opinions and assessments of the administration. In addition, there are a number of locales where officials are invited by reporters to explain what they think is important and to answer questions. Participation in these programs or an invitation to these locales is a recognition of a reporter's importance in Washington. Frequent participation, especially on the television programs, makes a reporter recognizably important.

The White House tries to use the programs and locales to develop specific kinds of messages for the participants and their audiences. Administration officials monitor them carefully. "We coordinate media appearances with cabinet members and members of the White House staff," Gerald Rafshoon said in reference to the tactics of the Carter administration. His office made arrangements with the networks for appearances on interview programs by cabinet secretaries and members of the White House staff. It tried to prepare officials who were invited to the meetings run by journalists with information supporting the President's positions. It looked for ways to get the administration's message onto the news discussion programs. By selecting the administration's representative, it tried to focus discussion on the President's issues as analyzed from the President's position. The administration, Rafshoon said, hopes to make certain that the people who become its spokesmen "do not send out conflicting signals."[28]

The talk shows. Two major news discussion programs, "Washington Week in Review" and "Agronsky and Company" are broadcast at the end of the week. The third, "The MacNeil-Lehrer Report," is broadcast every weeknight. While all are nationally syndicated by public television, their most important following is in Washington, among an audience that uses the programs to rate the President, his chief lieutenants, his allies, and his adversaries. "Washington Week in Review" provides analysis of the week's events, while "Agronsky and Company" emphasizes opinion. The format for "Washington Week" consists of a discussion of a series of issues presented by the moderator. The issue is addressed by a reporter who is the specialist in the area of politics or national defense that the moderator raised. The other panelists then ask questions or bring in relevant information from their own areas. "Agronsky and Company"'s format consists of a moderator who raises topics for four panelists, each of whom gives his opinion. "The

MacNeil-Lehrer Report'' format entails two moderators who bring in a panel of government or private sector experts to answer questions on a specific subject. The panelists analyze different aspects of one subject, although on some occasions there is one guest, such as a high White House official, who is asked questions on a variety of subjects. The panelists usually are invited to respond to one another's comments.

"Washington Week" and "Agronsky" have created journalistic stars. The regular participants on "Agronsky" have particularly high ratings, as does the program itself in Washington. "That show is special," Hugh Sidey commented. "It gets the highest public affairs rating, three to one over 'Meet the Press' and 'Face the Nation.' "[29] The five regulars, all established journalists for national publications, do not make special preparations. This gives the program an unstructured quality that its viewers like and that other elite journalists admire. "I'd like to have a show like 'Agronsky and Company,' " John Chancellor commented. "I watch it almost every week, because the people on there disagree with one another and are loose and easy."[30]

The regulars on "Washington Week" become part of the journalistic elite if they had not been so before. For those reporters without a regular Washington audience, the show is especially important. Jack Nelson, bureau chief of the *Los Angeles Times,* said that his appearances on "Washington Week in Review" were beneficial to him as a reporter and bureau chief because so few people in Washington read his newspaper: "I am better known for being on 'Washington Week in Review' than for being bureau chief of the *LA Times,* even in LA. . . . The fact is that it does give me an identity with people in opinion-making positions. I know it opens doors for me. If I call a top government official they will not have seen the *Los Angeles Times,* but they will have seen me on 'Washington Week in Review' and they are more inclined to give [my] call some priority."[31]

These three news discussion programs contribute to the consensus in Washington about which events and people are important. Their interpretations of what the news means affects what officials and journalists think. Their judgments, which reflect the opinions of Washington insiders, are closely followed by White House officials.

The Sunday interview programs. "Face the Nation," "Meet the Press," and "Issues and Answers" produce news. On a typical slow news Sunday, they may dominate that evenings' newscasts. Each of these programs is important to the White House when their guests support or criticize the administration. White House officials and cabinet officers appear frequently to present the President's line. Administration officials are carefully prepared for their appearances so that they can establish and defend the President's positions before the public. Even though their viewing audience is relatively small, the important aspects of their message will be rebroadcast or carried in publications.

The viewing audience of officials and reporters watch the interview programs to get a feel for the kinds of questions that may be raised about their actions and programs. The answers may be unintentionally revealing to a knowledgeable audience. In the days that follow, they may become the basis for inquiries that will lead reporters to new stories.

The Sperling breakfasts. In 1966 the establishment of the Sperling breakfast group provided a new forum for producing news and creating opinion. Godfrey Sperling of the *Christian Science Monitor* and a group limited to eighteen of his colleagues have met regularly since their first meeting. Sperling explained the group's origins: "Chuck Percy [Senator Charles Percy (R.-Ill.)] was coming to Washington and he didn't know anyone, so I called up Bob Novak and Alan Otten and Peter Lisagor and three or four other reporters, and before I knew it I had twelve people. And they came. It made a lot of ripples, so I had another. And another."[32]

The membership consists of columnists and bureau chiefs for major news organizations, which, for them, includes the news magazines and those newspapers with Washington bureaus regarded of regional importance, such as the *Los Angeles Times* and the *St. Louis Post-Dispatch*. The wire services and television journalists are excluded, as is the *Boston Globe,* the competitor of the *Christian Science Monitor*. Since Sperling's group was formed, several other groups with membership rosters have been founded. Most of them share Sperling's format: officials are invited to small meetings where reporters explore their thoughts and find out what they know. Originally the discussions were on background to permit freer conversation, but important stories were passed from someone who had attended to a reporter who had not and therefore was not bound by the rules. Both officials and reporters now insist that everything said be on the record.

Peter Lisagor, one of the original members of the Sperling group, suggested that the meetings provided immediate news but also gave him access to people and activities that were related to his interests but whom he did not ordinarily see. They provided the kind of background that enabled him to add perspective to his stories: "It has now become a morning press conference. It's useful to those of us who would not see these people in our normal course of business. It saves us a lot of steps and gives us a good feed on a lot of congressmen and senators."[33] Another point journalists who attend these meetings made is that they provide useful occasions for reporters and officials to size each other up. "I think it is valuable for journalists to get a close-up look at all these officials in a relatively informal atmosphere," Jack Nelson suggested, "and for them likewise to get to know some of the journalists."[34]

The regulars on "Washington Week" become part of the journalistic elite they are locales where the participants develop their sense of what is important, a sense that will filter through when, for example, a bureau chief discusses stories with the reportorial staff. Collective judgments are reached there that may be responsible for the formation of media "groupthink," a less desirable phenomenon. Jack Nelson explained the process: "I think there is a lot of independent journalism, but I think that when so many people are concentrating on one story there has to be a certain amount of sometimes reaching a collective judgment, even if you don't realize what you are doing. It happens around the *Christian Science Monitor* breakfasts where everybody listens to the same sort of questions and hears the same kind of cynicism being expressed.''[35]

Negotiators: The Bureau Chiefs

Bureau chiefs are the principal negotiators in complex relationships that determine how and by whom the President will be covered on different occasions. Consequently, the chief is the official in the organizational structure of news enterprises who most often deals with the White House. Negotiations are also a crucial part of the chief's relations with reporters in the bureau, with editors, producers, and publishers. Three major categories of negotiating duties include: negotiations within the organization; negotiations of network bureau chiefs involving the broadcasting of the President's speeches and press conferences; and negotiations with the White House involving access and special arrangements for their organizations.

NEGOTIATIONS WITHIN THE ORGANIZATION

The Washington bureau chief for a news magazine such as *Time* or *Newsweek* is involved in a great deal of negotiations because the stories his reporters gather in Washington are written for publication in New York. Mel Elfin described the complex process of bringing together reporters, writers, and editors: "There is a story conference every morning in New York at 10:00 A.M. I get plugged into it, and we will kick it around. . . . There is no way of putting a percentage on where the ideas come from. Reporters are constantly coming to you with story suggestions. The White House correspondent sits in on the morning conference.''[36]

A bureau chief for a large regional daily newspaper who played a less active role than Elfin did not get the same results. The chief, a distinguished reporter but a reluctant negotiator, found that he and the bureau were excluded from the decision-making process. "We have virtually no control over the play of the story" he complained, "except to the degree which we can educate them and persuade them the story is worth more than street crime.''[37]

At television networks there is a more complicated arrangement. Reporters may be working for several radio and television news programs, all of whom have their own staff and their own producers. Negotiations take place among the various reportorial, technical, and managerial staffs. George Watson, former ABC bureau chief in Washington, described the negotiating and decision-making process in television news:

I think the three networks are more similar than different. In the evening news, the executive producer in New York either makes the line-up himself or he makes it in consultation with his deputies. We have a meeting every morning that links the major domestic bureaus—New York, Washington, Atlanta, Chicago, Los Angeles. It is a conference call in which all of the bureau chiefs, the assignment managers, the producers, are talking together about what is on the menus, that is, what we are covering, what we anticipate happening, and what we are attempting to move along as a story. Using that call as a primary ingredient, you add in the wires, the newspapers, the day books, the whole input. I think by 12:00 P.M. you have a pretty good feel of what is going to happen and what the 6:00 P.M. news is going to look like. . . . I think that every day the White House is a fertile field for producing a piece of the evening news. It is the most productive beat in town. The White House correspondent is the most used correspondent at any of the networks.[38]

NEGOTIATIONS INVOLVING THE PRESIDENT'S ACCESS TO THE PUBLIC

The most important negotiations network bureau chiefs carry on with the White House involve the requests that are made for air time for the President and the arrangements that will be made for physical coverage of the event. The bureau chief also handles the network's request for special coverage of the President or for meetings between high White House officials and network executives, producers, and editors. The White House correspondent tries to stay clear of these arrangements. One correspondent explained why it was important that the bureau chief rather than a reporter handle these responsibilities:

I would never want to be the one to set up arrangements on news conferences and things like that, and feel like I have done a guy a favor and then I have to turn around and report on him. It's better to keep all those administrative details away from the reporter. Those guys [the bureau chiefs] have to put the con on somebody to speak at a seminar and the guy says "yea," then you're obligated to him. Maybe you don't want to be and maybe it won't affect your reporting, but I don't see how it wouldn't. In our case, special requests and things like that are handled by those people and we are free to go ahead.[39]

Network pools. The network pool, not to be confused with press pools, was created for radio coverage by Stephen Early during the Roosevelt administration. Although it now concerns television rather than radio coverage of the President's use of air time, the pool is organized in the same manner. The pool chairman is responsible for relaying requests from the networks to the press secretary and requests from the administration to the networks. The assignment rotates every three months among the bureau chiefs for the three networks.

Most of what the pool chairman does is not controversial, especially when presidential requests for air time are routinely approved. During the Ford administration, however, the networks balked at carrying a speech they believed would be political. The address, which involved the President's appearance before the Future Farmers of America, was the one in which he announced his program to combat inflation. Ron Nessen related his view of

how the dispute developed into a major conflict with both sides using pressure
tactics as well as negotiating skills. "The networks refused to carry it, osten-
sibly on the grounds that it contained no news," Nessen recalled:

I suspected the real reason was that the networks felt Nixon had misued TV coverage to
promote his political goals and they weren't going to let Ford get away with the same
thing. . . . On the morning of the speech, when I told the President the networks would
not carry his speech voluntarily, he directed, "Well, do what you have to do." That
meant "requesting" time from the networks, virtually commandeering the airwaves.
Traditionally such requests were never rejected. So the networks carried the speech on
TV, but under protest. Walter Cronkite cancelled an interview scheduled with Ford the
following weekend to demonstrate his displeasure. Arthur Taylor, then president of
CBS, wrote the President that "these kinds of tactics threatened the free, vigorous and
independent press of America."[40]

NEGOTIATIONS INVOLVING ACCESS TO THE WHITE HOUSE

Most arrangements a bureau chief makes with the White House involve
technical matters that arouse little political heat. For example, Lyndon
Johnson often requested air time with little warning; subsequently, the networks kept a television crew at the White House twenty-four hours a day so
that they could go on live when the President wanted to. The White House
theater was converted into a studio with a film crew always present. Johnson
then did not have to leave the White House for live coverage—as he did in
1964 when he drove across Washington to the local CBS studio when he
announced settlement of a national rail strike.

The bureau chief is the usual negotiator for reporters in his organization
who want a White House press pass. The bureau chief must make a formal
request stating that the individual regularly covers the White House for the
organization and needs the access that the pass allows.

White House correspondents make most of their own contacts with staff
sources, but the bureau chief is there to open some doors when the need
arises. "My philosophy is to let the White House correspondent carry the ball
and make his own contacts," Mel Elfin asserted. "If he needs the prestige of
the bureau chief or the contacts of the bureau chief to open a few doors I will
do it, but not until I am asked."[41]

Bureau chiefs are responsible for making sure that their reporters get their
turn on the pools traveling with the President. The pool assignments made by
the White House are usually fair. Most journalists want to keep the power in
the hands of the White House staff rather than create a committee of reporters.
Nevertheless, the existing situation has its share of conflicts. The White
House has used the denial of pool assignments as a punishment against recalcitrant reporters. One bureau chief recalled the dilemma that negotiating to
decide who would accompany the President on an important trip created for
him: "To ask to be put on pools is to open yourself to political pressure. . . . With the China trip, the Chinese said there could be ninety-five

reporters. We should have picked them out, but Nixon picked them out. There were some obvious people left out. I got on with only the most strenuous pressure.'"[42] He believed that as a result he and his organization were compromised in a relationship where an exchange of favors was expected.

Bureau chiefs are responsible for setting up meetings between the executives of their organizations and the President or officials at the highest levels of the administration. The purpose of these meetings, as Hugh Sidey described it, is for "the editors [to] get to see the man, look him in the eye, hear him. It's just a new dimension for them.'"[43] *Newsweek* holds a series of dinner meetings at which the magazine's executives meet the officials; *Time* organizes seminars. Both types of sessions are off the record. Mel Elfin explained how he set up the meetings and what he thought *Newsweek* got out of them. The examples he cited were from the transition period immediately before Carter's inauguration.

I just wrote a letter today to Cy Vance congratulating him on his appointment and recalling that in a way he was responsible for my debut in the social circuit. The first one I ever organized was for Cy as a stand-in for McNamara back in 1965.

Around ten people attend. There are three or four people from the Washington bureau and the same number from New York. The New York people would be the editor, the managing editor, the senior editor in charge of that department, and a writer. They look for a sense of the person. Was he sharp, was he smart, was he honest, was he candid, did he treat us like grown ups? Then you may get a sense of some of the politics. Spiro Agnew kept talking about all the money he could be making if he weren't vice president in December of '69. We should have known something right then and there. He said that in the past ten months he had a chance to look at the presidency and it didn't pay enough. It does give you an insight into the man.[44]

Sometimes close relationships between the President and bureau chiefs can produce benefits for the President. President Kennedy was able to use his friendship with a bureau chief to get the network to change a story he didn't like. Robert Pierpoint, one of CBS's White House correspondents, had a story that Khrushchev was going to Geneva for an international meeting to negotiate an arms agreement. As Pierpoint recalled what happened,

I then tried to find out if Kennedy was going to go. I found out that Kennedy was going to go only if Khrushchev was going, but that Kennedy did not want to go. I started to do a story. I put it on the radio at six o'clock. The wires picked it up and Kennedy got upset and tried to stop it. I was going to do the story for the evening news. Kennedy called my boss, who at that time was Blair Clark, an old friend of Kennedy's, and I got instructions from the loudspeaker while in the booth that I was to put a White House denial into the story. At first I strongly objected—this was only a matter of minutes until air time—and I was told that the orders were from Blair Clark to deny my own story, and I had to deny it on the air, which I found distasteful but nevertheless I was under orders to do so and I did so.[45]

NINE

SQUEEZING MORE JUICE
OUT OF THE ORANGE

White House Strategies for Portraying the President

T HE DESIRE of presidents to dominate the news in small ways as well as large has been so universal during recent decades that it has become an attribute of the job as well as of the job-holders. Reporters are well aware of the hot breath of the Chief Executive in numerous direct and indirect ways. Chalmers Roberts of the *Washington Post* recalled a Sunday when Lyndon Johnson called him about an article that had appeared that day. Johnson just wanted to add something, not complain, Roberts remembered. "He just wanted to squeeze more juice out of the orange, I gather."[1]

Newly elected presidents in the 1980s and thereafter will find they have to develop new techniques to continue to gather benefits from the build-in advantages of incumbency. The President and the White House staff today are faced with a press corps vastly more sophisticated than the one that existed before World War II, news media that actually produce stories about some of the ways in which the White House tries to manipulate them, and a large attentive public that is cynical about both the White House and the media.

A contemporary president uses his numerous advantages as occupant of the White House to obtain favorable coverage in the media. The large, well-organized and well-financed White House staff makes elaborate and extensive preparations for the President's appearances at press conferences, public addresses, and ceremonies. It sets the ground rules and picks the locations for appearances by him or other White House officials. Although administrations differ considerably in their attitudes toward news organizations, they use the advantages of incumbency in similar ways to project their version of the President's personal qualities, leadership skills, and policy preferences. Thus each administration attempts to develop a positive image of the President by focusing the attention of the media on the man and his family. Each presents the President as a vigorous and capable leader. Each emphasizes that the President is an advocate of policies and a political philosophy that reemphasize traditional values while directing the country toward a better future.

Officials regulate the activities of reporters in many other, less public, ways. Their control over the rules and regulations governing reporters' activities affects the way the media portray the President. Officials determine whether an event may be covered by all accredited reporters, by a small "pool" of reporters and photographers who represent the larger group, or by none, information in that case being disbursed by a government briefing officer. White House officials decide whether an interview is *on the record,* meaning that an aide's remarks are attributed to him by name; *on background,* meaning that a vague attribution such as a "White House source" must be used; *deep background,* in which no attribution is permissible; or *off the record,* meaning that the information the reporter is given may not be used in the story. Each group of White House officials exploits these advantages. "What we are trying to do is give them no choice on what they will use," a Ford White House official commented. "We are trying to make them use what we want them to use, not what they want. That is what we are trying to do, and it works often."[2]

News organizations play an active role in projecting the President's character and achievements to the public. They often collaborate by presenting a favorable image to the public, especially at the beginning of an administration when many journalists are fascinated by the President's personal habits and are willing to present an uncritical picture of his vision of how he will build the "good society." Before the explosion of media coverage of the President in the 1960s, the White House could anticipate that its techniques for projecting the President would succeed throughout his term. Today, although a president receives considerable benefits from media coverage, a larger and more diversified and sophisticated press corps also is anxious to show that he has warts.

This chapter describes some techniques White House officials use to project a positive image of the President. The first three sections deal with their efforts to secure a favorable portrayal of his personal qualities, his leadership ability, and his policies. The fourth segment discusses the argument that the news conference is more a controlled instrument of presidential publicity than a free forum of interchange between president and press. An important part of the analysis in all sections is the manner in which news organizations collaborate with or resist White House efforts to exploit the President's advantages.

Projecting Personal Qualities

During presidential election campaigns, almost every nonincumbent candidate permits reporters to get close to him because he expects to benefit from maximum public exposure. Thus even when the well-known Hubert Humphrey ran for president in 1968, he felt he had to make himself accessible to more reporters than he usually did and to answer almost every question they cared to ask. Prior to the Republican convention that same year, Richard Nixon, who usually exhibited reporterphobia, appeared on numerous interview programs and once was accompanied on a campaign tour by Hunter Thompson, the correspondent for *Rolling Stone*. Long-shot candidates are even more accessible to reporters. Before Jimmy Carter became a major contender for the Democratic presidential nomination in 1976, the seat next to him on buses and planes was almost always available to reporters. It was during this period that Carter gave the long interview published in *Playboy* in which he revealed his primal lusts as well as his political attitudes; this was also when he spoke on-camera to Bill Moyers of PBS about his religious, moral, and other personal commitments and beliefs.

An incumbent president also wants to project his personal qualities through the media, but once in office he controls the terms of a reporter's access. As candidate, he seeks to entice the interest of correspondents from all respectable news organizations, including some that have little influence. But as president, he can decide whom he will see among a large number of eager reporters, including the most influential columnists and anchorpersons. Those granted interviews usually do not ask probing questions, perhaps because of their respect for the office and their nervousness in the presence of an incumbent. A reporter is likely to raise questions that enable the President to show his more attractive traits so that he will be allowed to see the President again. Exclusive access to and information about the President raises the status of correspondents with their readers, viewers, and organizations, even if the information they obtain is trivial. The need to validate their credentials by showing that they have access to the Oval Office is felt as strongly by prominent journalists as it is by junior reporters. Among the letters requesting interviews with the President are many in which reporters virtually promise to produce favorable stories. "I can assure you that the portrait I have of him now is that [of] one of our greatest political leaders entering on an historic administration," Theodore White wrote to George Reedy in 1964, requesting an interview with President Johnson. "This will remain my portrait whatever his attitude is to me."[3]

For reporters who had easy access to the candidate during the campaign, the contrasting inaccessibility of the President is tremendous. "I had a real relationship with Carter during the campaign," Andrew Glass of the Cox Newspaper chain commented. "Now I have no first-hand way of knowing what the man is like."[4] White House aides often are able to determine when, where, and under what circumstances the President will be available to reporters. Of course news organizations can, and sometimes do, tell their reporters either to ignore events that are staged for their benefit or to label these events as theater rather than news, but on the whole, and in contrast to what some presidents and their aides may feel has been the case, correspondents and photographers still respond favorably to opportunities to get close to the President.

A MAN OF THE PEOPLE

The White House tries to project an image of the President as a man of the people, even though once in office he is a celebrity with a retinue of aides and attendants whose every activity is followed by the media. The President's aides make complicated arrangements and engage in a great deal of promotional activity in this effort to portray the President as an average citizen. In the Carter administration, for example, the President arranged to visit small towns such as Clinton, Massachusetts, and Salinas, California, where he stayed with local families before appearing at nationally televised town meetings. On television and in photos, the President was shown sitting at the breakfast table in casual conversation with his hosts. Later he was seen answering townspeople's questions in a setting that emphasized the participatory and homespun nature of the event.

The preparations for these visits, however, were anything but casual. The trip to Clinton, Massachusetts, involved advance work by White House staff personnel from the advance unit, Press Office, Travel and Telegraph Office, Media Liaison, Office of Special Projects, White House Communications Agency, and Secret Service. Other staff members were responsible for the President's schedule and for making the plans for his visit to be shown on television. By the time the President arrived the White House staff had made arrangements for a press contingent consisting of more than 90 persons who traveled with the President and another 450 local news media employees.[5]

THE FAMILY MAN

White House officials portray the President as a warm family man in order to soften his public image as a partisan political leader. Lyndon Johnson, a Washington veteran with a reputation as a fast operator, received a memorandum reflecting these concerns from Horace Busby of his White House staff:

A good, strong, happy family image is the best counterattack on political smears: i.e., to offset any image of you as "one of the boys in the back room." For this purpose, pictures are worth thousands of words. The following photographs are suggested, for image purposes.

1. President and Mrs. Johnson strolling *alone,* hand in hand, in White House gardens. *Secondary objective:* to convey President in repose, as antidote to press and public worries over President's non-relaxation.

2. President and daughter (but not Mrs. Johnson) bowling in Executive Office Building alleys. Suggest using photographs by Okie [the official White House photographer], released to all media, showing graceful in-motion Presidential form.[6]

Since the public expects an admirable model of family life, White House officials invariably present the President as the nation's ideal husband, parent, and grandparent. Warm family portraits taken by photographers on the White House staff are available to the media. Photographers who work for news organizations are given opportunities to film the President with his children, grandchildren, and parents. Animals, especially dogs, are also part of the Chief Executive's public domestic life. Theodore Roosevelt's menagerie even included a turkey.

Of course the White House takes risks when it exposes the President's personal life to reporters and photographers. The marital problems of the President's children have been covered, as have some of the less attractive exploits of presidential brothers. Howls of outrage were emitted by animal lovers when Lyndon Johnson was shown lifting his beagle by the ears. Usually, however, stories and pictures display the President and his family in the friendly settings selected by careful stage managers.

PROJECTING THE PRESIDENT THROUGH THE FIRST LADY

The President's wife plays an important role in projecting the image of the administration. Although some first ladies—Eleanor Roosevelt, for example—have followed independent agendas and acquired their own followings, in most cases there has been an attempt to find a symbolic connection between the First Lady's activities and those of her husband. "The West Wing is the head and we are the heart," said Sheila Rabb Weidenfeld, press secretary to Betty Ford. "We can help translate the policy. [We] take something social and make it a statement."[7]

Some first ladies become the President's alter ego for those segments of the public that sympathize with his politics but find his personality unattractive. Ford administration officials allowed Betty Ford to display her flair for life and express her tolerant social attitudes because her husband was widely viewed as stodgy and conservative. Before a national television audience, Mrs. Ford discussed the possibility that her children, like many other young people, might deviate from conventional premarital sexual morality. She also appeared with her former teacher, Martha Graham, a modern dance innovator, to demonstrate affinity for the arts and to remind Americans of her vitality. When her husband traveled to meet leaders of the People's Republic of China, she visited and danced with a Chinese ballet company. These and other activities were partially the results of efforts by Sheila Weidenfeld to use Mrs. Ford's personality to attract people who were turned off by her husband's.

The most typical role of the First Lady is representing the President at cultural, charitable, and fashionable events. On occasion a president tries to distract the media from his problems by emphasizing the First Lady's attractive qualities as she performs these activities. John Kennedy used his wife in this way in 1961 when his diplomatic meetings with European leaders failed to achieve either real or symbolic achievements. Although reporters had some indication that these private meetings were not going well, Jacqueline Kennedy's social and ceremonial doings provided an attractive diversion. White House Press Secretary Pierre Salinger seized this opportunity to satisfy the media's desire to cover her activities. By assisting reporters in covering her performance he shifted the focus of news organizations away from the President's problems. President Kennedy undoubtedly was quite happy to describe his role, as he did, as that of the "man who accompanied Jacqueline Kennedy to Paris."[8]

USING THE CHILDREN

The President's children, like his wife, often present a difficult target for his enemies to hit and an attractive subject for the media to present. Like the First Lady, the children thus are used as surrogates when it might be difficult or inconvenient for the President to appear. President Ford's son Jack stood in for his father on several occasions during the 1976 presidential campaign; on the final Sunday before the election, he appeared on "Meet the Press." President Carter made his son Chip part of the American delegation that tried to sell the Egyptian-Israeli peace agreement of 1979 to Arab governments in Jordan and Saudi Arabia. President Nixon's daughter Julie defended her father against charges stemming from the Watergate investigation.

News organizations are interested in the romantic activities of the young adults in the President's family and the play activities of his small children. The White House allows reporters and photographers to cover social scenes or childhood activities. The weddings of the daughters of Lyndon Johnson and Richard Nixon were given extensive media attention. Stories and photographs presented the nuptial services as important state occasions. During John Kennedy's term, his children were a continuing subject of newspaper and magazine stories. Even Amy Carter's tree house on the White House grounds was a subject for a photo opportunity.

MEDIA COLLABORATION

News organizations usually are willing partners in White House efforts to publicize the personal life of the President and members of his family. Because his personal qualities are easier to portray than the complex policy developments of his administration, editors have a larger appetite for family stories than for articles about governmental reorganization or natural gas deregulation. This is especially true of editors of publications that are not read by policy-makers in the capital. "It's a lot easier for me to get into several newspapers in the chain with a story about Amy than with a story about an important policy decision," Andrew Glass said. "If they use both, the Amy story is likely to get on page one, while the policy story will be buried on page twenty-nine."[9]

The desire of news organizations to obtain exclusive personal glimpses of the First Family leads to opportunities for considerable manipulation by the White House. According to George Reedy, one of Lyndon Johnson's press secretaries,

One of the reasons—probably the most important reason—the President has such an unusual ability to "manipulate" portions of the press is his monopoly over a certain type of news. Specifically, this means that stories about the President himself—his personality; his taste in food and drink; his lifestyle; his relationships with his family; his taste in pets—are just as important to the White House press corps as revelations of "hard news." . . . Many of the journalists themselves are unaware of the potency of this weapon because they come to take it for granted. Do not underrate it.[10]

Because some reporters know their editors or producers will reward them for exclusive stories and pictures featuring the President's personal life, they may exchange favorable coverage of the President in the policy area for access to him and his family.

Projecting Leadership Qualities

White House officials want the media to portray the President as a decisive commander who is well regarded by political chiefs in this and other nations. When they suggest how he should respond to a crisis, implement a decision, or engage in diplomatic meetings, they consider how a particular course of action will "play" in the media. Obviously other factors influence the President's decisions, especially since many crises present limited options and his fundamental character traits often determine how he chooses from them.[11] Nevertheless, on many occasions publicity benefits weigh heavily in the decision-making process. Former officials admit that publicity considerations are not neglected when a President decides to send in the marines, fire an unruly and unpopular subordinate, do something to demonstrate that he is an expert who is respected by the nation's intellectuals, or meet with other national leaders.

Although the media usually provides the President with publicity benefits by focusing the public's attention on activities that are designed to make him look like a leader, more thorough and intense coverage of the President by news organizations has led to a larger number of critical stories. In general, however, the balance is still in the President's favor. Officials in the Ford and Carter administrations recognized that some unfavorable stories are part of the price that must be paid for the favorable stories that outnumber them. Such moderate acceptance was not characteristic of the Johnson and Nixon administrations, perhaps because it seemed to them that Presidents Eisenhower and Kennedy had paid no price at all.

APPEARING DECISIVE: MILITARY LEADERSHIP

Military decision-making provides great opportunities for a president to win the respect of the media and the approval of large segments of the public. "The elements of a nation's strength are its tools for influencing events . . . for example, an aircraft carrier in the right place at the right time," columnist George Will wrote in the *Washington Post* in February, 1979, as part of a strong attack on President Carter for what Will thought to be an unwillingness to make effective use of the nation's power. Will's attack was typical of many media critics of Carter's "indecisiveness." Conversely, most recent presidents have benefited from the public perception that they were decisive military leaders: Roosevelt and Truman during World War II, Truman and Eisenhower in Korea, Eisenhower in Lebanon, Kennedy in Cuba,

Johnson and Nixon in Vietnam, and Ford in the Mayaguez incident with Cambodia after the Vietnam War. Perhaps because he really was a military leader, President Eisenhower did not have to intervene militarily in order to obtain this reputation. President Carter discovered during the first two years of his term that his policy of allowing local conflicts to unravel themselves in Africa, Iran, and Southeast Asia was a source of tremendous media criticism to the effect that he was permitting American power to slip away.

Presidents often recognize their need to be regarded as decisive by potential adversaries and military allies. The three presidents who served between 1965 and 1975, as well as their staffs and supporters, vowed that the United States would not be viewed as a helpless, pitiful giant during their terms. Their desire to be portrayed as decisive military leaders by media critics also played an important part in their decisions to use military force.

President Johnson's character was exhibited in his decisions to take decisive military actions against factions in Vietnam that he believed were out to destroy him personally. ''Ho Chi Minh wants to nail my carcass to the wall,''[12] he said to the columnist Joseph Kraft, who had just told him that his personal contacts with Vietnamese communists indicated there might be a basis for a nonmilitary solution. Johnson also desired publicity that showed him as a strong military leader, and he was sensitive to press criticism that he was not providing such leadership. According to David Halberstam's account in *The Best and the Brightest,* Johnson became angry when Joseph Alsop used his widely syndicated column to charge that the administration was unwilling to make tough decisions to resist the Viet Cong. Consequently, he looked for military opportunities that would show him taking direct positive action. Halberstam wrote that Alsop

knew intuitively that the thing Johnson feared most was that history would write that he had been weak when he should have been strong, that Lyndon Johnson had not stood up when it was time to be counted, that his manhood might be inadequate; and in late 1964 and early 1965 he played on that theme masterfully.... [Johnson] was very angry about the columns, but he was not unaffected by them. They posed the question as he knew it might be posed out in the hinterland, as he, Lyndon Johnson, might pose it himself against a political adversary.[13]

APPEARING DECISIVE: FIRING CONTRARY SUBORDINATES

A president hopes to appear strong and decisive when he fires a subordinate who challenges his authority. There have been cases where such decisions backfired, most notably the famous Saturday night massacre of 1973, when President Nixon's decision to fire Special Prosecutor Archibald Cox created an adverse public reaction. Regardless of the ultimate results, however, the decision to remove a subordinate is usually taken because the President and his advisers feel that it is necessary for the President to reaffirm his image as a strong leader. For example, President Ford told a news conference that his decisions to remove Henry Kissinger from his White House post and James

Schlesinger from the Defense Department were made because he desired to have his "team" in positions of authority.[14] Ford's statement was made after news of the impending move leaked to the media. After Kissinger and Schlesinger left office, however, several aides admitted that they hoped that the President's announcement would show that he and not the powerful Washington figures held over from the Nixon administration, was in charge.

Reporters recognize that a president's advisers urge him to get rid of a subordinate in order to make a show of strength, and they may refer to this motive in their stories. When President Carter fired Bella Abzug as co-chairperson of the National Advisory Committee on Women in 1979, the *New York Times*'s White House correspondent Terence Smith reported that the decision reflected "the urging of his advisers to project a decisive image in preparation for the re-election drive he is expected to mount in 1980." In a story labeled "news analysis," Smith wrote, "The dismissal fits in with the new tougher and more 'Presidential' posture that Mr. Carter's advisers have been urging him to adopt in his third year in office. At all costs, they want him to avoid giving the impression of vacillation and indecisiveness that many believe sometimes characterized his first year."[15]

BEING IN COMMAND: THE PRESIDENT AS EXPERT

A second element of leadership that the President and his advisers are anxious to communicate is competence. One way to do this is to appear knowledgeable about the problems of the government and the nation. President Kennedy's performances at presidential press conferences are acknowledged to have been prime exhibitions of this quality. Kennedy responded to reporters' questions with detailed information that he seemed to have at his fingertips. This expertise was well rehearsed. Kennedy, like his successors, had the assistance of a staff that was able to predict a majority of the questions and to provide him with the appropriate answers.

The White House creates special situations for the President to display his expertise. This was the case when President Ford answered reporters' questions at a special briefing on the budget in January, 1976. Since the budget is a vast, complicated document covering a large number of governmental activities, the President's ability to field a wide range of questions served to rebut the notion that he lacked intellectual capacity. This, in fact, was the intention of his advisers. According to a presidential adviser, "As the budget came through, somebody had the idea, let's have the President brief the budget. We went over there, and gave the budget briefing, and it took almost three hours, and it absolutely knocked their socks off, and it helped kill that competency question. If the guy knows this much about the budget and handled it as well as he did, he had been underestimated. That was an effort to communicate something about the President."[16]

BEING IN COMMAND: THE PRESIDENT AS EFFECTIVE INTELLECTUAL

Although presidents are advised to avoid forming too close an identification with the intelligentsia, most recent incumbents have recognized that their ability to mix well with intellectuals adds to their images as leaders who can cope with the major problems they must confront. Especially since the Soviet Union's success in launching the first space satellite, presidents and presidential candidates have emphasized their ability to cope with scientific problems. Presidents Eisenhower, Kennedy, and Johnson appointed science advisers to prominent positions on the White House staff and publicly met with members of the Science Advisory Board. In his 1976 campaign Jimmy Carter suggested that his work as a member of Hyman Rickover's nuclear projects qualified him to lead the world's foremost nuclear power.

Presidents have appointed economists, political scientists, historians, and sociologists to prominent positions in their administrations. Contacts with writers, philosophers, and artists also are thought to be important to show that the President is capable of the deep understanding of issues that these intellectuals regard as their special achievement. The President's advisers are also aware of the excellent access to the media that these intellectuals possess through their friendships with editors and producers. President Johnson was advised by Horace Busby to build ties to this group: *"If there is an important segment still withholding judgment on the President, it is the intellectual community—including the artistic community. A frontal assault on these groups would not be too successful. But the time is ripe for a varied, subtle exploitation of Presidential acquaintances and friendships."*[17]

BEING RECOGNIZED AS A LEADER: THE VALUE AND PROBLEMS OF FOREIGN TRAVEL

Meetings between the President and foreign leaders are excellent opportunities for White House officials to portray the President as the embodiment of the national interest. Since most of the meetings and ceremonies do not involve negotiations that might lead to an agreement, it is reasonable to assume that their public nature constitutes much of their importance to the President. This includes the desire to enhance the President's standing with Washington influentials as well as the electorate.

During trips abroad and receptions in Washington, the President participates in impressive ceremonies that are reported by the media, but the actual negotiating sessions are closed. Thus correspondents usually have to accept the version given to them by government briefing officers. In Washington, reporters may be able to get around the blackout because, with so many people in Congress or the bureaucracy informed, someone is likely to talk. In a foreign setting, however, it is difficult for reporters to verify officially released information by checking with independent sources. Stories obtained from "leaks" by members of the President's entourage are likely to be self-serving versions planted by the administration. Finally, the "results" of the meeting often consist of a communiqué that is difficult for reporters to assess on the spot.

Thus favorable publicity is a reward White House officials expect to obtain from their relations with reporters on presidential trips. Television is their primary target because it shows off the President in a glamorous or exotic setting. This appeared to be true of the preparations for a meeting in Iceland between President Nixon and Georges Pompidou in 1973. A foreign service officer who had been assigned to work with the President's aides described their activities: "All they cared about was how things would look on television. White House aides fussed about the lighting, about who would stand where, what the background would be, and the furniture. The entire time I was assigned to the detail, no one asked me a substantive question. I'm sure they didn't care. All they seemed to care about was television."[18]

Traditionally the media have provided bountiful and favorable coverage of presidential trips. A sample of stories in the *New York Times* and *Time* magazine about fifteen trips taken by presidents since 1953 showed that the coverage was overwhelmingly favorable. Whatever its diplomatic objectives, foreign travel has served to maintain or resurrect the positive image of a president's leadership qualities. President Kennedy, for example, found that foreign trips helped to overcome the widespread impression that he was too young and inexperienced to be an effective leader.

To no president was foreign travel more helpful than it was to President Nixon, whose low ratings in the polls soared after his trips to the People's Republic of China and the Soviet Union during 1972. Especially in the case of Nixon's China trip, the ceremonies themselves were diplomatic events. The impact of pictures of the President of the United States at the Great Wall or in the Great Hall of the People, after twenty-five years of little contact between the two nations, was not unlike that of pictures of the astronauts planting the American flag on the moon. The television networks were willing partners with White House officials in conveying the image of presidential success to the people. The networks' news services were extremely eager to portray every ceremonial detail of the China trip. According to Eric Rosenberger of the White House Media Advance Office, "They [the TV people] rented a TWA 707 with their equipment and went a week ahead of time. They built a TV station with mobile sets that had studios, offices, editing, mini cam gear. . . . There were ninety-six press corps and sixty-nine technicians from television and radio."[19]

It is not surprising that the increase in presidential travel corresponds to better television coverage of these events. However, the ever-larger press entourages that have followed presidents since Eisenhower's 1959 world swing—the first of the big media trips—have created problems for the White House. Foreign trips no longer provide the automatic favorable coverage a president once could expect. Except when their movements are limited—for instance, as it is when they travel to countries governed by dictators—reporters have been able to ask questions of people other than official spokesmen. Many organizations send specialists on the host countries in addition to the reporters who describe the ceremonial activities. These specialists often provide a perspective different from the official version.

For example, when President Ford met with other world leaders at Helsinki in 1975, his staff issued statements and held briefings in which they emphasized the friendly diplomatic interchanges between Ford and other leaders. Obviously they hoped that stories about these meetings would enhance the President's stature as a world statesman with the public. Although there were pictures and stories describing the friendly atmosphere of the meeting, about 25 percent of the stories about this trip in *Time, Newsweek,* the *New York Times,* the *Washington Post,* and the *Baltimore Sun* dealt with the lack of meaningful agreements on disarmament and other basic East-West issues.

Discussions of a president's domestic problems may be included by some reporters in their stories about his foreign excursions. When President Carter participated in an economic summit meeting in Bonn in July, 1978, he probably expected news stories supportive of his efforts on behalf of the dollar and American exports. Although some stories on these lines did appear, other stories suggested that the President had a weak negotiating position with the leaders of the other major noncommunist industrial powers because he had been unsuccessful in getting antiinflation and energy conservation programs through Congress. Thirty-four percent of these stories about the trip mentioned Carter's domestic problems.

The media's coverage of President Nixon's travels during June, 1974, provides a dramatic contrast to their coverage of trips taken by President Eisenhower. A survey of stories in *Time* and the *New York Times* during three Eisenhower trips uncovered no unfavorable news stories and few critical editorials and columns. Nixon received altogether different treatment. Instead of describing the cheers of the crowds in Egypt as a tribute to Nixon's successes as a diplomat in the Middle East or his meetings with Brezhnev as a symbol of his success in achieving detente with the Soviet Union, as administration leaders undoubtedly had hoped they would, many news stories described the enthusiasm that Nixon could generate abroad as a backdrop to his continuing problems with Watergate at home. *Time*'s issue of June 24, 1974, for example, put the trip on its cover with the headline "Seeking a Needed Lift." Approximately 50 percent of the stories about the trip in the five publications mentioned earlier dealt with Nixon's Watergate problems. In addition, the same publications ran separate stories about Watergate and impeachment proceedings along with the trip stories. Often the two types of stories shared the front page. Thus not only did the trip fail to distract the media from the President's problems, it served to emphasize them.

Nevertheless, foreign travel remains an excellent presidential vehicle for displaying his leadership qualities. Most of the stories that appear on television or in print are straightforward accounts of the planned events of the trip that reflect favorably on what the President is doing. Further, there are many legitimate opportunities for trips that fill a useful diplomatic purpose and also contribute to the President's standing in the polls. If a president obtains a popular objective such as a trade concession from a meeting abroad, he can expect general applause. From the White House perspective, however, the fact that foreign travel can result in unfavorable stories at all emphasizes the changes in the rules of their relations with news organizations.

Projecting Policy

"Aspirants to the White House invariably seek to project images of decisiveness, whether or not they have any idea what to be decisive about," observed the *New Republic*.[20] Recent history supports this comment. It is not clear that the desire to achieve domestic and international goals lies at the heart of presidential candidates' reasons for wanting the job. Many presidents enter office without concrete goals; their objectives are acquired later, in response to the demands of events and their constituencies. But even those presidents who clearly have had no specific objectives have believed that they should appear to be advocates of what the headline-writers describe as "bold new programs." This was even true of Calvin Coolidge, whose bromidic comments in response to serious problems are better remembered than his effective manipulation of his publicity advantages as president. According to Elmer Cornwell, "Coolidge made it clear that the growing leadership and opinion-forming potential of the office could be used as effectively by a President who sought only to reign as by one who also wanted to rule. The potential was there, the mass media saw to that—in an ever rising spiral. The presidency merely had to keep pace."[21]

Liberal, conservative, and "pragmatic" presidents all use similar formats and forums to project their programs to the public. Often the forum becomes more important than any particular message to be communicated through it. The President may address a joint session of Congress or the opening of the United Nations; he may speak to a meeting of one of the numerous associations that offer him standing invitations; he may address the nation on radio and television. In addition, the President uses the symbols and ceremonies of his office to associate himself with particular causes or programs. Presidents hold public bill-signing ceremonies; they welcome important domestic or foreign leaders associated with particular policies to the White House; they have their staff arrange conferences on subjects the administration wishes to sponsor; and they call for briefings and conferences at which the President or an aide attempts to enunciate policies. "You have lots of ways to communicate," said a White House aide in the Ford administration. "There can be symbolic ways as well as the more traditional ways, such as speeches. Symbolism with presentations, events. You have got to get into them—like dedicating a hospital. There are a whole series of things that you can do that are symbolic, that reach into different constituencies and communicate messages."[22]

ADDRESSES TO CONGRESS AND OTHER AUDIENCES

In 1918 Woodrow Wilson resurrected the practice of turning the President's constitutional obligation to "give to the Congress Information of the State of the Union'' into a full-dress, personally delivered exhortation to adopt his legislative programs. Subsequently, it has been expected that the State of the Union address will be an occasion for the President to lay major policy proposals before the public. The electronic media now permits the President to use addresses to Congress to reach three audiences: the Congress, the news organizations covering the speech, and the audience that hears or sees the speech as it is delivered or reported later on news programs. Calvin Coolidge delivered the first nationally broadcast State of the Union Address on December 6, 1923. The radio microphones present then have been followed by newsreel cameras and, finally, television equipment.

The President and his aides know that a public judgment of his commitments will be made on the basis on what he says in this address. During the Roosevelt administration the address served as a dramatic review of what remained to be done to end the depression and the war. Lyndon Johnson viewed the occasion as being significant enough to be scheduled for coverage on the television networks' prime time.

The White House staff wants the media to emphasize those portions of the speech concerning what the President believes to be the central concerns of his administration. In order to insure that they understand what the President means, reporters generally are given copies several hours before the address is delivered. Aides brief reporters and answer their questions on the substance and style of the speech. Ronald Nessen recalled that ''there was a lot of work done to make sure that there were favorable stories.''[23] He said that in 1975, at the time of his first address, Ford's image was that of a man who was moved by, rather than in control of, events. The President himself took charge of the preparations for the speech. He sent his major economic and domestic policy advisers, as well as his senior staff and speechwriters, to Williamsburg, Virginia, for three days to put together the speech. Ford instructed speechwriter Milton Friedman to go through Franklin Roosevelt's State of the Union messages for the years 1943 through 1945 to ''get a feeling of crisis.''[24] The preparations that Ford's staff made for this address were only slightly greater than was usual in the 1960s and 1970s. What may have been most significant was that although Ford did not have proposals for innovations in policy, he recognized that the public expectation that the President show himself as a policy leader had to be satisfied.

The President has other forums to present ideas and proposals to the public. He can ask to address a joint session of Congress. He can accept one of the numerous standing invitations he receives from major groups and associations. Usually the President selects a friendly group to announce the direction of his policies. Republican presidents might appear before the National Chamber of Commerce or the National Association of Manufacturers, Democrats before the AFL-CIO. There are even occasions when the President deliberately selects a hostile group. For example, President Carter announced his program for granting amnesty to Vietnam War draft evaders to the Veterans of Foreign Wars in 1977.

NATIONAL ADDRESSES CARRIED BY THE MEDIA

Calvin Coolidge was the first president to address the nation regularly on the radio.[25] His successors made more elaborate use of the medium through the 1930s and 1940s; in the 1950s television replaced radio as the primary instrument for presidential communications with the public. Television creates an opportunity for the President to capture a prime time audience of nearly 100 million viewers. But it also may display his weaknesses as a performer, engender resentment from viewers whose regular programs are interrupted, and ultimately result in overexposure. "The importance of television has grown with each year, but you risk overexposure," Pierre Salinger commented. "The less you see him, the better."[26] Consequently, presidents tend to limit their appearances to those occasions when they have an important announcement or are seeking to enlarge their traditional constituency.

Before a television address, great care is taken to prepare the President's appearance and to smooth his delivery. Since actor Robert Montgomery held the position for the Eisenhower administration, there has been a television adviser either on the White House staff or available to the President. When President Ford gave his first television addresses, he was coached by Robert Mead, a former television producer, in the use of the teleprompter.[27] Jimmy Carter's first television adviser, Barry Jagoda, advised him to wear a sweater when he appeared for a fireside chat on the nation's energy crises. The sweater became a symbol of the need to conserve fuel.[28] Even before the advent of television, the President had an electronic media adviser. President Truman called on J. Leonard Reinsch to advise on his radio speeches.

CEREMONIES

Presidents use ceremonies to demonstrate their policy commitments because they are usually telegenic, easy to stage at the White House, and invariably receive coverage on the evening news. Lyndon Johnson permitted live television coverage of his signing of the Civil Rights Act of 1964, in order to show his support for integration. Johnson and his successors also used the White House Rose Garden, a lovely and easy-to-photograph spot near the Oval Office, as a stage for ceremonies of greeting and award. Occasionally reporters ask a question of ceremony participants, but by and large they cover the event as the White House puts it before them. Reporters, photographers, and cameramen stay in a roped-off area while the President and his invited guests mingle.

When Jimmy Carter wanted to demonstrate to the Senate and the nation the importance of the ratification of the Panama Canal Treaty to good relations with Latin-American leaders, he held a public ceremony. He held a public signing of the treaty to which he invited the leaders of the nations of the Organization of American States. Carter's aides told reporters that because the speech Carter delivered was so important, the American negotiators for the treaty, Sol Linowitz and Ellsworth Bunker, prepared it along with James

Fallows, the President's chief speechwriter. The ceremony was carried live on network television during prime viewing time.

The News Conference

Admirers of the news conference regard it as an important democratic institution, the American equivalent of the question period in the English Parliament. On the surface, it does appear that the conferences allow representatives of the media to invoke a president's unrehearsed response to questions, probe the justifications a president offers for his policies, inquire about his activities, and try to get him to reveal his character spontaneously. "The value of the press conference, as we saw it," said *Washington Post* correspondent Edward Folliard, "was that by asking questions and getting answers from the President, we found out how the President felt about, oh, the issues of the day; found out what his hopes were; what his worries were; had a chance to, oh, size him up, so to speak."[29]

While reporters do reap these benefits, the news conference is most important to news organizations because it is an event in which they are important public actors. A presidential appearance almost always is a source of news, but it does not necessarily provide information. Although conferences have been held in many different settings and have been governed by varying ground rules, control seldom has passed out of the hands of the White House. Reporters usually receive the information the White House plans to give them.

Throughout the twentieth century presidents and their aides have molded the shape of the news conference to their needs. The roots of the conference can be traced to the presidency of Theodore Roosevelt, who saw the advantages of projecting his ideas and personality to a group of reporters. Since then presidents have adapted the conference to their own styles, whether they were activists like Woodrow Wilson or passive like Calvin Coolidge. It is Franklin Roosevelt, the creator of the modern news conference, who can be credited with creating a forum that works to the advantage of both the media and the presidency. A closer look indicates news conferences always have favored the President.

THE MYTH OF FRANKLIN ROOSEVELT'S FRIENDLY NEWS CONFERENCES

Although presidents held—or were scheduled to hold—semiweekly meetings with reporters during the 1920s, it was during the administration of Franklin Roosevelt that news conferences became central to White House media policy. Roosevelt's conferences have been described as informal events at which the President and reporters exchanged important information and good-natured banter. According to a sentimental version of the history of relations between presidents and reporters, this permissive and fruitful atmosphere soured when everything the President said was placed on the record, and ended with the introduction of the live television news conference.

It is true that Roosevelt promised to keep reporters fully informed of all the events and appointments of the activist administration he was leading to combat the depression. Reporters found the press conferences useful at first, according to Leo Rosten, the great chronicler and analyst of the Washington press corps of the 1930s. They quickly learned, however, that the President was not trying to help them get stories, but rather to get them to frame stories in ways that were favorable to him.[30] The rules did not favor free discussion as much as they restricted reporting opportunities. Roosevelt's extensive restrictions forbidding quotation or attribution to him of much of what he told reporters meant they could not include in their stories materials that the President wished to exclude.

A less sentimental picture of Roosevelt's news conferences emerges from a contemporary account in the diary of Eben Ayers, a White House aide in the Roosevelt and Truman administrations: "As usual at press conferences, only those in the front row nearest the desk, are able to see anything that goes on. Likewise, they hear best. Otherwise the best place in the room from which to hear is the extreme rear. The shape of the room and ceiling affects the acoustics in such manner that it is more difficult to hear at other points."[31] The Oval Office setting of Roosevelt's conferences, though often remembered as intimate in contrast to today's large auditoriums, was not ever congenial for many reporters. It became impossible for them as the size of the crowd increased. Truman had to move the location of the conferences when 348 reporters spilled out of the Oval Office, into the Cabinet Room, and onto the terrace.

Joseph A. Fox of the *Washington Star* recalled that the informal setting made it possible for Roosevelt to browbeat and humiliate reporters, an ability later Presidents lost in the glare of television lights. Fox once asked Roosevelt about a story that had appeared that day in the *New York Times*. Roosevelt replied, "Joe, I don't have time to answer damn fool questions." Fox pursued the matter. He said, "Mr. President, this wasn't intended as a damn fool question, I was just trying to check on the story of the *Times*." Roosevelt responded, "... it's still a damn fool question."[32] Eben Ayers noted in his diary that once, in the summer of 1944, when the President was asked if he had picked a running mate for the election campaign, Roosevelt "flared up somewhat at the question and snapped back that that sounded like an unfriendly question and he would not answer it."[33]

After Roosevelt died, Truman changed the format and setting of the conference to create a more formal and structured relationship. Truman stood before reporters in an Executive Office Building auditorium like a professor in a large lecture hall. Reporters sat and took notes. In this setting, Truman and his successors tended to respond to questions with official pronouncements on policy rather than with informal remarks. When the Eisenhower administration permitted television cameras to film them and the Kennedy administration allowed live broadcasts of them, the conferences took on the trappings of a media event.

THE TELEVISED CONFERENCE

The introduction of television completed the transformation of the press conference into a news event in which the President's performance is graded by observers in the media and the public. The decision to allow in the cameras reflected White House concern that reporters might be filtering the message the President was trying to get to the public. James Hagerty described in his diary one incident in which television was used to overcome what he thought was press bias: "Pres [Eisenhower] upset at press reaction . . . straight New Deal in thinking and in writing. . . . Real reaction will be favorable. That's why I'm glad we released tape of statement to radio, TV and news reels . . . we'll go directly to the people."[34]

The televised press conference created a theater in which the President calls upon reporters to play their supporting roles to enhance his starring performance. "It is important that the President appear vulnerable," said Barry Jagoda, President Carter's television adviser.[35] In truth, the President risks little. The format puts more pressure on the reporters, who are often nervous, than on the President, who is used to this public role. Raymond P. Brandt, veteran Washington correspondent for the *St. Louis Post-Dispatch* told James Deakin that even after forty years as a national reporter he felt nervous whenever the President called on him for a question.[36]

Most of the features of the contemporary press conference were formed during the Eisenhower administration. From that time to the present, reporters have been free to use all the information that they learn at the conference. The White House staff began releasing a transcript of the conference to the press. Television cameras were permitted to film the conference, and the networks were allowed to broadcast it after a White-House review. This requirement was lifted by the Kennedy administration, which permitted live coverage. Kennedy's three successors did not continue his practice of holding frequent, regularly scheduled conferences, and some commentators wondered if the traditional conference had been abolished. But President Carter returned to the general practices that prevailed between 1921 and 1963. He held regular conferences throughout the first two years of his term, although his commitment to meet with reporters twice a month was somewhat less strenuous than the twice-a-week schedules of the 1920s and 1930s. The Carter administration also regards it as the President's prerogative to withhold from reporters the date of a conference until one or two days before, even though it appears in the President's schedule several weeks in advance.

THE NATURE OF THE CONTEMPORARY CONFERENCE

The contemporary press conference often is viewed as an open forum where reporters raise questions that concern the interests of the public. Reporters are not limited by constraints like the requirement that existed from 1921 to 1933 that they submit questions in advance. They are not restricted in the use of information that the President declares to be on background, off the record, or subject to review, as was the case before 1961. The press conference serves useful functions for reporters, most of whom strongly advocate that they be scheduled frequently and that the rules permit them to ask questions without restriction. The absence of the constraints of early periods, however, has not prevented presidents from maintaining control. The President decides when to hold a conference, how much notice reporters will be given, who will ask the questions, and what the answers will be.

Thus the ad hoc character of the conference is an illusion. The President has a number of ways to set its tone and control what happens. He may begin the conference with an opening statement in which he announces a decision, appointment, or proposal that may become the basis for a number of reporters' questions. "President Kennedy used these statements to get across his foreign policy goals," McGeorge Bundy, his national security adviser, commented.[37] Although this technique does not always sidetrack reporters, there are few questions asked at a press conference that the President's staff has not anticipated and that he is not prepared to answer. Those few questions that come as a surprise usually reflect the parochial interest of a particular correspondent. These questions seldom threaten the President, and in fact may be what correspondent Martin Schram referred to as "Wichita questions," using a label that may have reflected his own cosmopolitan biases. Schram, the *Washington Post*'s "presidency reporter," suggested that a reporter who asked President Ford during his November 26, 1975, news conference what the President and the nation had to be thankful for that particular Thanksgiving provided a perfect example of a question that had little bearing on important presidential actions or attitudes.[38]

Frequency and settings of news conferences. Presidents schedule or avoid news conferences according to their perceptions of such matters as publicity benefits, the fuss reporters will make if they go too long without holding them, and their desire to avoid questions. In general, presidents hold news conferences at regular intervals when things are going well; they find reasons not to hold them or to tinker with their formats during periods of trouble. Although conferences were scheduled twice a week by presidents during the 1920s and 1930s, President Hoover cancelled many of them in 1931 and 1932 when his efforts to combat the depression proved to be ineffective. The frequency of Franklin Roosevelt's news conferences dropped off considerably during World War II, when the President's interest in "guiding" reporters was less than it had been when he was pushing for New Deal programs.

Lyndon Johnson, who went for many months without holding a news conference, responded to press criticism by citing his high monthly average of conferences, a figure with little bearing. Johnson held an average of more than two conferences each month, but during 40 percent of his months in office he held only one conference, or none at all. Between August 29 and December 6, 1965, he did not hold a single conference. At times Johnson's three successors also have avoided conferences, changed their settings, and altered their

Table 1. Monthly Average of Presidential News Conferences, Roosevelt through Carter (first 28 months)

	Average per month	Total number of press conferences	Number of months in office	Percentage of months in which at least two press conferences were held
Roosevelt	6.9	998	145	99
Truman	3.4	334	94	86
Eisenhower	2.0	193	96	64
Kennedy	1.9	64	34	62
Johnson	2.2	135	62	60
Nixon	0.5	37	66	6
Ford	1.3	39	30	43
Carter	1.8	50	28	75

formats. Richard Nixon suggested that news conferences were not important because he had alternate ways of communicating with the American public. Gerald Ford counted meetings with reporters at campaign stops in his list of conferences. Jimmy Carter announced that he would substitute town meetings and regional conferences for some Washington news conferences in response to media and congressional criticism of his July, 1979, purge of top cabinet officials.

Table 1 shows both the number and the frequency of conferences held by presidents from Franklin Roosevelt to Jimmy Carter. Since what presidents count as a news conference varies considerably, this chart includes sessions with rather different formats and settings. The lists for Presidents Eisenhower, Kennedy, Nixon, and Carter are limited to meetings for which the press was given advance notice, that were open to any accredited reporter rather than to an audience invited by the White House, and that were held in formal settings such as the auditoriums of the Executive Office Building or the State Department. Presidents Johnson and Ford, however, allowed themselves more latitude.

President Johnson counted conferences called without notice on Saturday morning, sessions at which he responded to reporters while walking rapidly around the grounds of the White House, and one session at which he took no questions. These shifting settings and formats suited his purposes. For example, on one occasion he held a conference without notice at 5:00 P.M. that only reporters who happened to be in the press room attended. The press secretary suggested to one reporter that he might ask Johnson a question about ''how things are going up on the Hill.'' He did, and Johnson responded by discussing proposed civil rights legislation; he then briefly commented on his relations with Bobby Baker, the former Secretary of the Senate and Johnson protégé who was accused of abuses of power and of corruption. Johnson then left the room without answering any more questions. At a subsequent "full dress" announced press conference on January 25, 1964, Johnson turned aside a question about Baker with the comment that at an earlier conference "I spoke fully" on the Baker issue. On March 12, 1966, Johnson held three of the conferences he included in his total. He answered four questions at the first, nine in the third, and none in the second.[39]

President Ford included meetings with reporters outside Washington in his total. Of the thirty-nine conferences he held, only fourteen met the definition used in the Eisenhower and Kennedy years. On the other hand, President Carter met twice a month with non-Washington journalists, but he did not include these conferences in his total. President Nixon also met with reporters in the Oval Office for questions on two occasions—March 21 and July 20, 1970—but he did not count them in his total of news conferences.

The avoiders. Perhaps because they feared they would suffer by comparison with John Kennedy, Presidents Johnson, Nixon, and Ford tried to avoid the formal televised press conference. As discussed earlier, Johnson in particular played games with reporters by calling conferences with no notice, by holding them on Saturdays when some reporters would be off duty, and by holding them away from the cameras in unusual settings such as the White House lawn, where he could make reporters feel the full force of his personality and his office. In 1966, for example, Johnson's staff tabulated forty news conferences. Of these, twenty were "impromptu," that is, reporters were told that the President would meet with them in his office or on the White House grounds immediately. The White House gave reporters between thirty minutes' and five hours' notice before six other conferences; one day's for nine others; and for five conferences they gave notice of a day and a half or more. Because many of his conferences were not televised, it was possible for Johnson to badger reporters as effectively in the "open" 1960s as Franklin Roosevelt had in the 1930s, when he told one to wear a dunce cap and awarded another the German iron cross. Once, recalled James Deakin, he asked a question that implied criticism of Johnson's Vietnam policies. "Johnson put that big head of his next to me and said, 'Mr. Deakin, why do you always sell your country short?' "[40]

President Nixon also avoided the formal news conference. Unlike Johnson, however, he saw no need to make himself available to reporters in less formal circumstances to compensate for the dearth of formal conferences. He seldom gave interviews or permitted questions when he appeared at public ceremonies. His failure to provide the press with alternative opportunities to meet with him may have been responsible for some of the harshly phrased questions that reporters asked him when he did hold conferences. But this too helped the President. The public response was that it was inappropriate for reporters to behave with such incivility toward Nixon. Although reporters were angry because their questions went unasked for long periods, it appeared to the public that Nixon was correct in his claim that the press was not sufficiently respectful of the presidency.

President Ford also seemed to prefer more controlled and structured meetings with reporters to formal televised news conferences. He held impromptu question and answer sessions with reporters in the White House Rose Garden that were announced minutes before he appeared. At these conferences Press Secretary Nessen decided when questioning should stop and whether certain subjects were inappropriate. President Ford also held conferences for the non-Washington press corps at which White House reporters were permitted to observe but not question. Although White House officials justified these conferences on the grounds that non-Washington reporters ought to have an opportunity to ask questions of the President, White House reporters regard these conferences as an opportunity for the President to respond to "Wichita questions."

Since presidents usually control their news conferences, the fact that they avoid them seems curious. One explanation is that they regard them as a favor to the media that they can deny in response to press attacks. The White House response to why they are avoided even though the President makes a favorable impression in televised conferences, is that the amount of preparation and anxiety that precedes each session decreases the value of the publicity. Lyndon Johnson often met with his entire cabinet in order to prepare for the conference. Most other presidents had similar meetings with their staff and other advisers to discuss possible questions and answers. Presidents Johnson and Nixon found the conferences personally agonizing. Johnson felt he did not come across well on television; Nixon hated the relationship with reporters. All Presidents fear that they might make a major misstatement or show embarrassment at a question that probes their political motives. None of these fears have been realized in any noteworthy way, but Presidents Johnson, Nixon, and Ford seemed particularly susceptible to them.

PREPARATIONS FOR THE CONFERENCE

Presidents usually receive a thorough preparation for their news conferences. Probable questions are prepared by the staff along with suggested answers. James Hagerty introduced briefing books during the Eisenhower administration in order to gather information from departments and agencies about issues that might be raised by reporters. Eisenhower would meet with members of his staff at an early morning breakfast on the day of conferences to consider possible questions and appropriate responses. According to Pierre Salinger, the Kennedy staff was able to anticipate almost every question and rehearse its answer with the President.[41] James Shuman of the Ford Press Office staff related that he kept a briefing book current with questions that he and others on the staff knew were on reporters' minds.[42] In the Carter administration briefing books are kept by the Domestic Policy Staff, which coordinates information from the departments for the President.

The staff of the Press Office uses a number of tools to anticipate reporters' questions. First, they analyze the obvious areas of press concern as indicated in print and broadcast media. Second, they review the recurring themes in the questions raised at the press secretary's daily briefing. Third, they note the questions that are asked by reporters who come to their offices. (Some administrations go further and send out staff as scouts into the reporters' area at the White House to find out what seems to be concerning them.) Fourth, the press secretary or his deputy receives reports from department press officers about questions involving the President that have been raised at their briefings and news conferences.

The fact that the President decides which reporters to recognize helps the staff guess what the questions will be. More than two-thirds of the reporters recognized at a typical half-hour televised news conference during the Ford and Carter administrations represented the Associated Press, United Press International, the three television networks, AP Radio, a major national newspaper, a major regional newspaper, a newspaper chain, or a news-weekly. When this group pursues a difficult line of questioning, the President may call on one of the press's backbenchers, who are likely to raise a different type of question.

Sometimes the President will deliberately recognize one of the pariahs of the press corps, either because their rough style of interrogation garners sympathy for the President or because the subject matter of their questions provides comic relief. This tactic can backfire, as President Nixon found when he recognized Sarah McClendon, a longtime nemesis of the White House and some of her fellow reporters. McClendon asked the President a detailed question involving alleged mismanagement of the Veterans Administration. Nixon tried to turn the question aside, but he was caught on the defensive and without the facts.

PLANTED QUESTIONS

Presidents ask their aides to plant questions when they want to make statements on certain subjects. Planting questions was a common tactic during the early years of the public press conference. During the Eisenhower administration reporters knew that the President called on those whose questions had been cleared in advance by Press Secretary Hagerty. The practice was so prevalent that officials discussed it openly once Eisenhower's term was completed. Sherman Adams, Eisenhower's White House chief of staff, recalled how Press Secretary Hagerty arranged the use of planted questions: ''He [Hagerty] got together from the wire services and certain key White House reporters the important questions that were going to be asked the President on press conference day. They were prepared in a list that the press secretary had prepared, and he brought up the questions seriatim, and the consensus of opinion about the nature of what the President's answer might be.''[43]

Hagerty's diary provides several clear examples of planted questions and the uses to which they were put. Hagerty wrote that he "also set up question on Dulles-McLeod-McCarthy with answer from Pres [Eisenhower] that appointment of administrative position within a department, responsibility of Secretary—and no one else."[44] A transcript of President Eisenhower's news conference for that day indicated the following exchange.

Q. Merriman Smith, United Press: Mr. President, this is not closely related, but Senator McCarthy yesterday questioned the wisdom of Secretary Dulles having removed from Mr. McLeod the authority over personnel problems in the State Department. I wonder if you could tell us your feeling on that.

A. The President:. Well, the assignment to duty of any administrative officer in any department of Government is the responsibility of the head of that department, and no one else's whatsoever. I hold the head of department responsible to me for proper operation of that department. He is, in turn, responsible for everything that goes on within it.[45]

The practice of using planted questions continued throughout the 1960s. Lyndon Johnson in particular thoroughly approved of the practice.[46] After an official successfully planted a question for Johnson, the President told him he wanted him to plant all the questions at the next conference. Apparently Johnson was disappointed when he was informed that there were not enough reporters willing to ask the questions the staff gave them. The Nixon administration did not use the technique as often as its predecessors, perhaps because it did not want to get friendly with reporters, as the practice required. By the time of the Ford administration the practice practically had disappeared as a major presidential tool for controlling the press conference. Ronald Nessen recalled that he once tried to get reporters to ask President Ford questions about Solzhenitsyn and the CIA, but was unable to find anyone to ask them. After the conference was over and the cameras were turned off, Ann Compton of ABC News did ask President Ford about Solzhenitsyn, but the President refused to answer at that time.[47]

Planting questions was such a standard practice during the Eisenhower administration that some foreign diplomats operated on the assumption that every question could be a planted one. On one occasion Joseph Harsch of the *Christian Science Monitor* asked the President if a proposed invitation to Marshal Zhukov to visit the United States was still in the works, and Russian diplomats assumed that the question reflected the administration's interest in having him visit. Robert Cutler, the national security adviser, wrote in a memo to the President that a Soviet third secretary had told Harsch that he wanted to meet with him, and that during the course of their meeting "Mr. Harsch gained the impression that the Soviet official assumed that the press conference question was planted and that Mr. Harsch might be able to give him additional information. The Soviet official hinted that he would welcome any information as to whether a U.S. decision to renew the invitation to Marshal Zhukov would be influenced by knowing in advance whether or not it would be turned down by the Marshal."[48]

IV

PORTRAYING THE PRESIDENT

C OVERAGE of the President between 1953 and 1978 in the *New York Times* and *Time* magazine and from 1968 to 1978 on CBS News indicates the increase in the importance of White House stories for these news organizations. The content of stories has changed, as has the tone of stories. Analysis of a sample of several thousand stories from this period provides an indication of how the relationship between the White House and the media affected what actually appeared in this portion of the media. The relationship itself passes through a period of alliance to a period of competition, and finally, to a phase of detachment. What presidents must learn from all of this is that political communications as sent through and by the media play the central role in their struggle for control of political institutions. News organizations must recognize that as the refracting lens for the public, they are a vital ingredient in the political system. The media's critics believe that they contribute greatly to the erosion of presidential power. But the President's difficulties with the media are a symptom of the problems caused by fragmentation of power, not the cause.

TEN

IMAGES OF THE WHITE HOUSE IN THE MEDIA

P RESIDENTS perceive themselves to be in an ongoing war with the news media, a war in which they believe they lose most important battles. Lyndon Johnson believed that this war began immediately after he took the oath of office. "This man [Dan Rather] and CBS [are] out to get us any way Bill Paley can," the President complained after less than six months in office.[1] Like his predecessors, Johnson felt that unfavorable coverage harmed his ability to act as the national steward. When a *New York Times* reporter wanted access to the White House staff for a story he was doing on some of its members, Johnson wrote to his special assistant, Marvin Watson, that he would prefer not to grant the request because "no good can come from it."[2]

The reality was different, as indicated by a survey of White House stories appearing at the time in the *New York Times* and *Time* magazine. During President Johnson's first year in office, when he was complaining of his treatment by the news media, the ratio of favorable over unfavorable articles concerning the White House in the *New York Times* was better than six to one. In *Time* ten favorable articles appeared for each that was unfavorable. Johnson was enjoying the same strongly favorable coverage that his predecessors had received during their first years in office but, like them, he reacted strongly to stories he thought to be negative.

A striking feature emerging from twenty-five years of *Time* and *New York Times* articles and ten years of CBS News broadcasts is the consistent pattern of favorable coverage of the President. The number of negative articles has grown, but the favorable still outnumber the unfavorable. Johnson's successors have not received the same level of favorable coverage that he did early in his term, but in the post-Vietnam and Watergate period, the balance of press coverage of the White House has been favorable. Yet Presidents Ford and Carter, like their predecessors, complained about media treatment of their administrations.

Presidents have tended to blame their inability to achieve desired policy outcomes on the press because of its role in publicizing their administrations' failures. Presidents, George Reedy observed, have political problems, not press problems, but White House fingers continue to point to the press as the creator of problems. Near the end of his life Lyndon Johnson lamented, "From my viewpoint how they twisted and imagined and built and magnified things that I didn't think were true at all. I never thought it was the President's credibility gap, I thought it was their credibility gap. But they owned the papers and networks; I didn't. And they come out every day. And they could talk about my credibility, but there wasn't much I could do about their credibility."[3]

THE CONTENT ANALYSIS

The content analysis of the news sources presented here is based on a sample of White House stories appearing in the *New York Times* and *Time* magazine from Eisenhower's inauguration in 1953 through August, 1978. It also includes analyses of stories from the CBS Evening News during a ten-year period beginning on August 6, 1968, when film was first collected at the Television News Archives at Vanderbilt University. Three coders read and viewed White House stories that appeared at fifteen-day intervals for the entire period. They compiled 8,742 White House stories: 5,270 from the *New York Times*, 2,550 from *Time*, and 922 from CBS News.

This content analysis does not provide a definitive portrait of media coverage of the presidency, but it does produce a clear picture of how the President and the White House were treated by three influential news organizations over a significant period of time. Each of the three organizations attempted as thorough coverage as can be found within that particular medium. The *New York Times* is important as a subject of study because of its role in shaping the opinions of the political and journalistic elite. *Time*, the inventor of the newsweekly format, has the largest national circulation, in addition to the broadest readership among Washington influentials. Of the three networks, CBS has made its White House coverage a top priority item for its evening news program. At times CBS has assigned twice as many correspondents to the White House as the other networks.

An analysis of the stories produced by these three organizations confirms three central points about press coverage of the White House: the favorable tone of the stories; the recurring patterns of the coverage from administration to administration; and the similarities in what the three consider to be a White House story. The continued production by the news media of favorable stories about the President has been mentioned. The study also provides evidence demonstrating the continuing character of the relationship between the White House and the news media. Press coverage tends to follow established patterns. The variations in the tone of stories and the frequency of their appearance demonstrated trends that appeared within and among administrations. Although each president did not start with the same number of stories and the same percentage of stories rated favorable, in almost every case the beginning of a president's term represented a high point for both.

Content analysis demonstrates the degree to which a White House story is a presidential story and the ways in which the coverage of the White House by the different news sources is similar. The similarities in the stories of the three are, in fact, much more obvious than their differences. The prominence of policy stories and the attention paid to personal stories, as well as the tone of different subject categories, are all strikingly alike in the three sources of news.

By studying the frequency of White House stories, their location in their publications, and the development of White House stories on television evening news programs, one can understand the dimensions of the increase in White House press coverage. The increase in the number of reporters assigned to the White House has also increased the types of stories coming from there, but at the same time there has been a tendency for all three news sources to cover the same kind of stories and for these stories to have remarkably similar tones. The importance of the increase in coverage is heightened by the similar trends of coverage in the three. When the White House fails to get a story covered ''its way,'' the chances are that it will fail to do so in all of the news sources, not just in one of them. The similarities in story treatment present the White House with an opportunity to reach a broad audience in the way it wants to be portrayed. There are also substantial risks of which White House officials must be mindful.

COVERAGE OF THE WHITE HOUSE

When all White House stories in the *New York Times* and *Time* are considered for the twenty-five-year period, one is struck by how favorable they are. Each organization presented two favorable stories about the White House for each that was unfavorable. CBS News presented far fewer favorable and more negative stories than the *Times* and *Time*. Because the aggregate number of CBS News stories was tabulated from the ten-year period that includes six years of Vietnam and Watergate, the CBS figures are not comparable to figures for the two print sources, which were based on stories for twenty-five years. Comparison based on a year-by-year analysis shows CBS News following the same trends as the other two.

The positive tone of the stories appears in the same proportions over the twenty-five-year period in the *New York Times* and *Time*. Each story was read by two coders. The figures in table 2 represent, first, articles that both coders found to be favorable to the White House; second, stories one coder found to be positive and the other neutral; third, stories that both coders found to be neutral; fourth, stories ranked by one as neutral and by the other as negative; and fifth, articles judged by both coders to be negative. In our discussion of story tone, we restrict ourselves to those categories on which both coders agree. Thus when we mention a favorable tone, we cite only the positive-positive category, and the same is true when we mention the neutral and negative categories.[4]

Table 2.   Tone of White House Stories in *Time,* the *New York Times,* and CBS News
(Figures express a percentage of stories.)

	Time (N = 2,550)	*New York Times* (N = 5,270)	CBS News (N = 922)
Positive-positive	44.9	39.5	31.6
Positive-neutral	15.1	9.2	6.9
Neutral	11.8	24.1	22.9
Negative-neutral	8.2	4.7	6.0
Negative-negative	20.0	22.5	32.6

By looking at the statistics for each administration one can see the similar favorable ratios in all three sources of news. Figures 1 and 2 are graphs showing the favorable and unfavorable story trends of the three.* The deviations of CBS News from the other two during the period from 1968 to 1978 are not nearly as great as was indicated in table 2, which was based on aggregate figures. We did not prepare a graph to show trends in the neutral category because the figures show little fluctuation. The *Times* began the period with 21.4 percent of its stories having a neutral tone, and ended it with 23.2 percent; *Time* began and ended it with 12 percent neutral, and CBS News ended the period with 19.3 percent of its stories neutral, after a starting record of 31.2 percent. While the number of favorable stories gradually decreased as a percentage of the total number of stories, the number of negative stories increased over the twenty-five-year period.

Even more favorable are the pictures that accompany news stories. There were almost no negative pictures in either the *New York Times* or *Time,* and there were only a few negative films on the CBS News. In contrast to the two print sources, whose pictures were overwhelmingly favorable in tone, the majority of the CBS News film was relatively neutral (see table 3). Pictures often are favorable even when they accompany an unfavorable story. Articles about the relationships between the President and Congress and the President and his administration and among White House staff members were generally among the most negative types of stories that appeared in the *New York Times* and *Time* throughout the twenty-five-year period. As table 4 indicates, the stories in one subject area were favorable in less than 20 percent of the cases, and stories in no area were favorable in more than 42 percent of the cases. Yet of the pictures accompanying the stories, only in one area were the favorable pictures less than 50 percent of the total.

The number of articles about the White House rose markedly in both *Time* and the *New York Times* during the twenty-five-year period. On the other hand, CBS News remained fairly consistent in the attention it paid during the

*The stories from which the data for the tables and figures in this chapter are taken appeared between January, 1953, and August, 1978, in the case of *Time* and the *Times;* CBS News stories covered the period from August, 1968, to August, 1978.

Figure 1. Favorable White House Stories
(Figures represent the percentage of stories coded as positive by both coders. Figures are the
aggregate for each administration.)

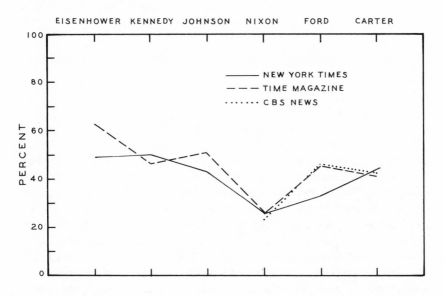

Figure 2. Unfavorable White House Stories
(Figures represent the percentage of stories coded as negative by both coders. Figures are the
aggregate for each administration.)

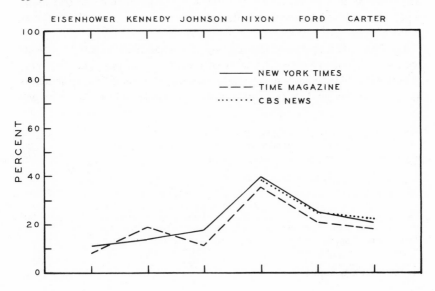

Table 3.   Tone of White House Pictures in *Time* and the *New York Times,* and Films on CBS News
(Figures express a percentage of pictures and films.)

	Time (N = 1,318)	New York *Times* (N = 792)	CBS News (N = 452)
Positive-positive	68.5	65.2	25.7
Positive-neutral	13.8	7.6	13.5
Neutral-neutral	15.0	24.5	52.4
Negative-neutral	0.7	0.8	4.4
Negative-negative	2.0	2.0	4.0

ten years included in this study. Because this twenty-five-year period included an assassination, a resignation, and an unelected president, it might be thought that these aggregate figures are not representative. But a comparison of the first years of each administration, a period that tends to be similar because news organizations report on the same kinds of stories, demonstrates the same trend. The figures also show that a large increase in stories occurred during different administrations for *Time* and the *Times*. The *New York Times* showed an appreciable increase in the Kennedy administration, whereas *Time* showed only a temporary gain then. An examination of tables 5 and 6 indicates that the sustained increase in coverage for *Time* occurred during the Nixon administration and continued for the first year and a half of Carter's term. The two print sources produced almost as many White House articles in the ten years from 1968 to 1978 as they had produced in the preceding fifteen. The average number of articles per issue of *Time* rose from 3.2 during the period from 1953 to 1968 to 5.1 in the last ten years studied. The *Times* reflected a similar increase. In the first period the *Times* averaged 7.6 stories; in the second, 10.2.

The White House stories in each issue or broadcast represented a major portion of the news space or time of each source of stories. The *New York Times*, with almost nine White House articles in each issue (including nearly two on every front page), pays close attention to the President's activities and

Table 4.   Subject Category of Positive Stories and Pictures
(Figures express a percentage of all positive stories and pictures.)

	Stories		Pictures	
	Time (N = 87)	New York *Times* (N = 204)	*Time* (N = 102)	New York *Times* (N = 48)
President and Congress	17.5	25.8	55.1	44.1
President and administration	26.6	22.8	52.5	51.9
White House staff	38.7	42.1	69.4	51.4

Table 5. White House Stories in Each Issue or Broadcast, by Administration

	Time (N = 2,550)	*New York Times* (N = 5,270)	CBS News (N = 895)
Eisenhower	3.2	6.6	n.a.
Kennedy	3.8	9.1	n.a.
Johnson	2.8	8.3	n.a.
Nixon	5.1	11.1	4.2
Ford	4.5	8.8	3.8
Carter	5.9	9.3	3.7

actions. CBS News, with approximately twenty-three minutes to devote to news, devoted almost four stories each night to the White House, 23 percent of which appeared before the first commercial break, television news's equivalent of the front page. The President represents the single most important story that the network follows on a continuing basis. In its advertisements CBS News points to the thoroughness of its coverage. An ad that appeared in newspapers and magazines in 1979 pictured the three CBS White House correspondents standing with the White House in the background. The caption read: ''The President doesn't make a move without them.''

PATTERNS IN WHITE HOUSE COVERAGE

The continuing character of the coverage of the White House can be seen in two important fluctuations that appear in almost every administration: the number of stories and their tone. The largest number of stories and the largest number of favorable stories appear during the first year (see figure 3). Rarely does the tone rise after that first year.

There have been six administrations in the twenty-five-year span from 1953 to 1978. In all of them but two, those of Lyndon Johnson and Richard Nixon, there has been a consistent pattern in the number of White House stories appearing in all of the news sources studied. The pattern has been that the largest number of stories appear during the first year of the administration; the lowest number are found in the final year. In the Nixon administration the

Table 6. White House Stories in Each Issue or Broadcast, by First Year of Administration

	Time	*New York Times*	CBS News
Eisenhower (1953)	3.8	7.6	n.a.
Kennedy (1961)	4.6	10.8	n.a.
Johnson (1964)*	2.7	8.7	n.a.
Nixon (1969)	3.5	9.7	3.6
Ford (1974–1975)*	5.0	9.6	4.3
Carter (1977)	6.3	9.6	3.8

*President Johnson's year runs from November 22, 1963, to November 21, 1964, and Gerald Ford's from August 9, 1974, to August 8, 1975.

Figure 3. Number of White House Stories

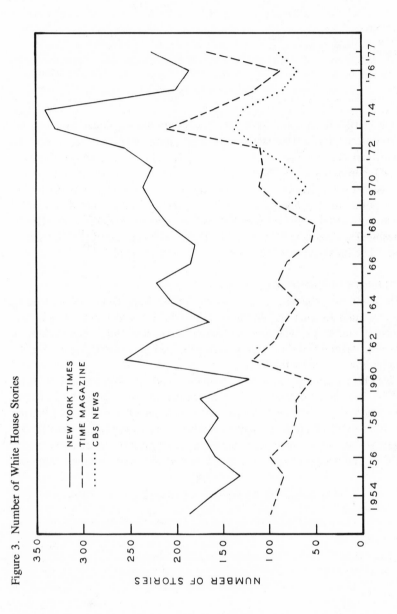

pattern was reversed. In the *New York Times* and *Time*, 1969 was the year in which the Nixon administration had least coverage. Watergate shattered any normal patterns in press coverage in his administration with a tremendous increase in the number of stories in 1973 and 1974. The number decreased in 1975 and then returned to the configurations found earlier, with the high points at the start of an administration and the low points following.

The first year of an administration has received the largest number of stories not because of the high level of activity but because journalists believe that people are keenly interested in learning about the new arrivals. They want to know what the President is like and who his family members are. They want to know what he intends to do during his time in office, even if he is not prepared to bring forth solid proposals in his first month in office. After the media think the public's interest in who the people are in the administration has been satisfied, they turn toward articles on the President's actions. The number of stories declined in the second year, even though the administration might have been more active than it had been in its first year. If a president serves two terms, there probably would be a rise in coverage during his reelection campaign, as there was with President Eisenhower. Presidents tend to be more active and more visible during a campaign, and these activities give rise to an increased number of media contacts with him. The final year of an administration has represented a low point in the number of stories in all media for all presidents in the study except President Nixon and President Johnson in the *New York Times*.

The first year of a president's term in office is also the time when the greatest percentage of favorable White House stories appear. The *New York Times* followed a pattern of having the highest percentage of favorable articles in the first year of an administration in all six administrations, while *Time* deviated from it in the Eisenhower and Kennedy administrations. CBS News followed the same pattern only in the Carter administration. The first year also has the lowest percentage of negative articles appearing in any year of the administrations. The end of the administration does not necessarily represent a low point in the percentage of favorable articles, as it does in the total number of articles written. Some administrations, such as those of Eisenhower and Ford, found that the articles written about them ended on a softer note than was employed at other points in their years in office. Figures 4 and 5 show the patterns of favorable and unfavorable articles in each year of the last six administrations.

While most administrations experience a pattern of decline in the favorable articles throughout their years in office, they have not all started at the same point. Presidents Eisenhower and Johnson started at a high percentage of favorable articles, with 58.6 percent and 63.4 percent respectively, in *Time*, but after the Johnson administration no president got over a 50 percent favorable rating the first year in *Time* and the *New York Times*.

The unfavorable articles follow a pattern fairly consistent with the favor-

Figure 4. Favorable White House Stories
(Figures represent the percentage of stories coded as positive by both coders.)

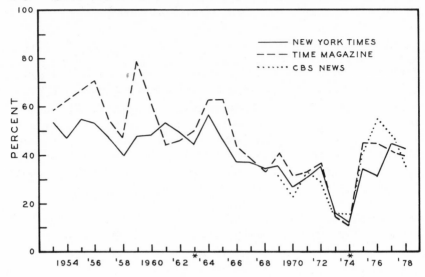

Figure 5. Unfavorable White House Stories
(Figures represent the percentage of stories coded as negative by both coders.)

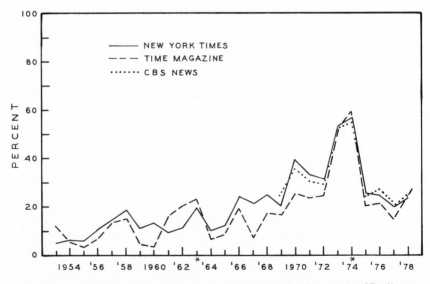

*The first month of Johnson's term is averaged with 1964. The first five months of Ford's term are averaged with 1975.

able. In the administrations of Presidents Kennedy, Nixon, and Carter, the lowest percentage of negative articles appeared in the first year and the highest at the end of the administration in all of the news sources studied.

Just as there is an ebb and flow of articles through the years of an administration, there is one occurring within each year. A look at the monthly figures for the three news sources reveals that the *New York Times* shows a distinct pattern of heavier coverage during the first five months of the year, and *Time* and CBS News show a similar, though less clear, distribution. The *New York Times* has an average of 9.2 stories per issue on the White House during the first five months of the year, while for the remainder of the year the figure is 8.2 per issue. In most administrations the *New York Times* has considerably more articles in the first part of the year than in the second. The figures were fairly close for the year Nixon resigned, since one administration ended and the other, Ford's, began in August (see table 7).

The news media's coverage of the White House has been a response to the President's activities. The budget message, the State of the Union speech, a major legislative initiative, and an occasional foreign trip have occurred in the first part of the year; thus heavy media coverage reflects a full presidential schedule. During the summer and fall the stories tend to revolve around the President's vacation, a foreign policy speech, often at the opening session of the United Nations, and the preparation of the budget. The last seven months of the year have usually been slower than the first five.

When one looks over the full twenty-five-year period of *Time* and the *New York Times* in an effort to assess whether Vietnam and Watergate represented deviations, one can see in the period following the Nixon administration some of the earlier trends. More favorable articles reappeared, and although the percentages do not approach the high points of the Eisenhower and Kennedy administrations, neither do they maintain the lows found in the Vietnam and Watergate years. As the percentage of positive articles has decreased from the first period, the percentage of negative articles has increased (see tables 8 and 9). The percentage of neutral articles has remained fairly constant.

As the number of favorable articles changed over the period, so did the average number of White House stories during the years covered. The Vietnam and Watergate period represented the high point in White House coverage in addition to being the most negative period in recent years. The number of articles per issue or program was higher than the earlier period in all of the news publications, and higher than the later period in all but *Time* (see table 10). White House coverage has lost its relatively negative tone in the last four years, while at the same time there has been only a slight reduction in the attention paid to the White House.

THE WHITE HOUSE STORY

The White House story is the President: who he is, what he does, and what his programs, actions, and goals are. White House media coverage reflects the

Table 7. Average Number of White House Stories in Each Issue or Broadcast, by Parts of the Year

	Time		New York Times		CBS News	
	Jan.–May	June–Dec.	Jan.–May	June–Dec.	Jan.–May	June–Dec.
Eisenhower	3.4	3.0	6.8	6.4	n.a.	n.a.
Kennedy	4.1	3.6	10.6	8.1	n.a.	n.a.
Johnson	3.2	2.4	9.3	7.6	n.a.	n.a.
Nixon	4.5	5.5	11.3	10.9	4.2	4.1
Ford	4.1	4.8	8.7	8.8	3.9	3.7
Carter	6.0	5.6	10.7	7.8	4.4	3.2
All administrations	4.0	3.8	9.2	8.2	4.2	3.8

Table 8. Favorable White House Stories, by Time Period

	Time		*New York Times*		CBS News	
	Percentage	Number	Percentage	Number	Percentage	Number
1953–1965	58.9	655	50.0	1167	n.a.	n.a.
1966–1974	28.7	259	28.5	589	23.5	135
1974–1978	43.3	232	37.5	325	44.8	156

public President. The President is the most important continuing story that the media deal with; he is of interest even when he is not active. Rarely does an issue of the *New York Times* or *Time* go to press or a CBS Evening News program appear without a White House story. In the sample of 656 issues of *Time*, 615 of the *New York Times*, and 236 programs of CBS, there were no White House articles in only 10 *Time* issues, 8 of the *New York Times*, and 8 CBS Evening News programs.

The White House story is a homogenized story. The three news sources show strikingly similar patterns in the types of stories they write and the subjects they cover as well as in the overall tone of their coverage. All three sources concentrate on news in their White House articles. There is some mixture, in varying degrees among the three, of editorials and opinion, analysis, and feature articles, but all focus their attention on news. Table 11 gives the breakdown of types of stories over the twenty-five-year period for *Time* and the *New York Times* and the ten-year period for CBS News.

The similarities between the news sources are more prominent than their differences, with approximately 80 percent of their stories classified as news stories. The other 20 percent is where the variation lies between them. *Time* is a fairly uniform magazine; the tone of its articles varies little. It has no editorials although a *Time* "essay" appears periodically. Its column dealing with the White House is a signed article by their former White House correspondent and present bureau chief, Hugh Sidey. There is almost no presentation of either the text or content of speeches, news conferences, or other documents. *Time*'s articles' function is to present interpretations. The major difference between *Time* and the other two news sources studied is the emphasis it places on feature articles. These are articles dealing with per-

Table 9. Unfavorable White House Stories, by Time Period

	Time		*New York Times*		CBS News	
	Percentage	Number	Percentage	Number	Percentage	Number
1953–1965	10.9	121	11.0	257	n.a.	n.a.
1966–1974	31.6	285	35.2	727	38.2	219
1974–1978	19.4	104	23.4	203	23.6	82

Table 10.   Average Number of White House Stories in Each Issue or Broadcast, by Time Period

	Time	New York Times	CBS News
1953–1965	3.3	7.6	n.a.
1966–1974	4.2	10.0	4.0
1974–1978	5.1	9.0	3.8

sonalities, such as the President's family and perhaps some of his top staff members. The emphasis is on their personal tastes and activities, not their political actions.

The *New York Times* differs from both *Time* magazine and CBS News in the variety of coverage it presents. Both *Time* and the *New York Times* have been moving toward presenting news analysis in addition to their straight news stories, but the *New York Times* has broadened its coverage with columns and editorials. The *New York Times* regards itself as a newspaper of record, and because of that it will often include the texts of speeches and documents, a news story describing them, and interpretation in the form of analysis, commentary, and editorials. The *Times* does not display the same interest in stories about people in the news as *Time*. CBS News has even less emphasis on personal stories than do the other two. Almost 91 percent of its stories are straight news, with editorials, particularly those of Eric Sevareid, being the only other prominent feature dealing with the White House.

In comparing *Time* and the *New York Times* according to the types of stories they print, a time breakdown for the periods 1953 to mid-1968 and mid-1968 to 1978 shows both publications moving toward increasing the

Table 11.   Types of White House Stories
(Figures express number and a percentage of stories.)

	Time (N = 2,550)	New York Times (N = 5,270)	CBS News (N = 922)	Total (N = 8,742)
News	2,052 80.5%	4,159 78.9%	836 90.7%	7,047 80.6%
Analysis	54 2.1%	138 2.6%	1 .1%	193 2.2%
Feature	341 13.4%	165 3.1%	16 1.7%	522 6.0%
Editorial	0	373 7.1%	69 7.5%	442 5.1%
Column	73 2.9%	257 4.9%	0	330 3.8%
Text	8 .3%	178 3.4%	0	186 2.1%
Time Essay	22 .9%	0	0	22 .2%

variety in the types of news stories (see figure 6). In the last ten years there has been an increase in the number of news analysis stories. In a news analysis article the author presents an interpretation of the prospects of a presidential program by pulling together information and opinion from sources outside as well as inside the White House. *Time* now sometimes includes news analysis in its issues.

The breakdown of articles appearing in *Time* and the *New York Times* and on the CBS Evening News shows a similarity in definition of a White House story. Table 12 shows the distribution of stories by subject category. The same general categories of subjects were treated as important by the three news sources, although there was a difference in the amount of coverage they gave to each subject.[5] The category of program and policy stories was the largest during the last ten years. With one exception, the CBS News coverage of Watergate, all of the news sources had the following three subjects behind program and policy in significance: personal, activity, and Congress and administration stories. Program and policy is first because it represents the essence of what it is the President does.

The differences in emphasis given to White House subjects by the news sources depend in great measure upon the type of organization it is. *Time* is published weekly and therefore does not try to build a daily record of what the President does, as do the *New York Times* and, to a lesser extent, CBS News. The *New York Times* closely follows what a president does each day, the speeches he gives, the news conferences he holds, his business trips, ceremonies, and bill signings. *Time* gives an attention to personal stories that neither CBS News nor the *New York Times* gives. As a weekly magazine *Time* can give attention to the newsmakers as people, something that is harder to do in a daily newspaper or television program. The dailies must concentrate on what is going on that day and what will happen the next. CBS News, with severe time constraints, can do little else than cover the basics of what the President is doing and plans to do. CBS News, however, paid proportionately greater attention to Watergate than either the *New York Times* or *Time*. While not a visual story, it was one that interested its viewers, and CBS News probably gave it more attention than the other two networks.

A comparison of the *New York Times* and *Time* magazine over the full twenty-five-year period shows that the same four categories of subjects ranked highest during the whole time period with both publications. *Time* remained consistent in the ranking of the four during the whole time period, but the *New York Times* did change. All top four categories shifted between the two periods. The *New York Times* gave much less attention to activities of the President in the second period, but since the Watergate category does represent an activity (since it took up the President's and the staff's time), this shift may not be significant. Both the *New York Times* and *Time* reduced in relative terms the amount of attention they gave to personal stories about the President.

Figure 6. White House Stories, by Type of Story and Two Time Periods
(Figures express a percentage of stories for *Time* and the *New York Times*.)

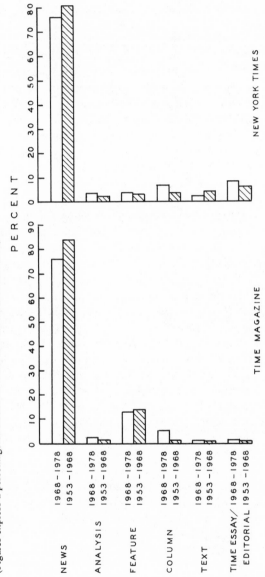

Table 12. Subject Categories of White House Stories, by Two Time Periods
(Figures express a percentage of the total number of stories for each news source.)

	Time			New York Times			CBS News
	(N = 1,279) 1953–68	(N = 1,269) 1968–78	(N = 2,548) Total	(N = 2,824) 1953–68	(N = 2,443) 1968–78	(N = 5,268) Total	(N = 922) 1968–78
Program and policy	30.1	30.6	30.4	24.8	24.7	24.7	32.3
Activity	24.4	15.9	20.2	35.7	24.4	30.5	18.4
Personal	23.7	17.0	20.4	13.7	10.5	12.2	9.9
Vice president	9.2	4.7	6.9	6.4	5.6	6.1	5.6
Congress and administration	7.3	10.3	8.8	10.5	11.5	10.9	10.5
Election	2.5	6.0	4.2	5.2	8.4	6.7	8.1
Staff	1.6	5.8	3.6	2.2	3.4	2.7	1.8
President and press	1.2	2.4	1.8	1.5	1.4	1.4	1.1
Watergate	0	7.2	3.6	0	10.2	4.7	12.2

In each news source, the focus throughout the period of White House stories is the President. Staff stories have increased in both publications, particularly in *Time*, but stories about the vice president have declined over the period. The President, what he is doing and what he hopes to do, are their central concern; next by a wide margin are stories about those close to him and his relations with Congress and the bureaucracy.

The wide variation in the tone of articles and the similarities in the treatment of subjects by the three news sources can be seen in the bar graphs in figure 7. The graphs show the nine subject categories and measure the degree to which each has been treated in a favorable tone.

The similarity of the tone of the different categories in all three news sources means that the White House can predict with some accuracy the response a particular action is going to generate in the media. Two categories, activity and personal, are clearly favorable. While the White House cannot prevent the publication of articles on certain subjects, such as the President's relationship with Congress and the bureaucracy, the predictability of media response to particular subjects does mean that the White House can wage an offensive on negative stories by getting out some favorable ones in areas over which they do have some control.

While the three news sources treat certain kinds of stories in a similar manner, there is a tendency of each to put its own spin on a story. The program and policy area illustrates some of the ways in which each treats the same subject. Table 13 shows the emphasis that each of the news sources gave to the four subjects within the general program and policy area. *Time* paid the greatest amount of attention to general stories that included several policies and gave the reader an idea of what the President was doing in the whole policy area but did not explain individual subjects in detail. The *New York Times* and CBS News, however, gave almost no space to general stories, exploring instead foreign and domestic stories in detail.

While both the *New York Times* and CBS News gave a great deal of attention to specific policy stories, the role of their White House correspondents was different. CBS News imposed stringent limits on the length of a White House story; each generally ran no more than two minutes. In that time the reporter could do little more than tell what it was the President did that day relating to the policy. The *New York Times* correspondent, however, had a different function. While the emphasis on CBS News was on the President and what he did, in the *New York Times* the emphasis was on explaining the policy itself. The White House correspondent would choose subjects based on White House involvement in them. Once a subject was chosen, the correspondent had to look into the policies as legislative and administrative programs.

The *New York Times* is a newspaper of record, and because of that emphasis, its stories reflect an interest in recording presidential events and actions and providing a complete treatment of what happened, who was in-

Figure 7. Positive White House Stories, by Subject Category
(Figures express a percentage of stories.)

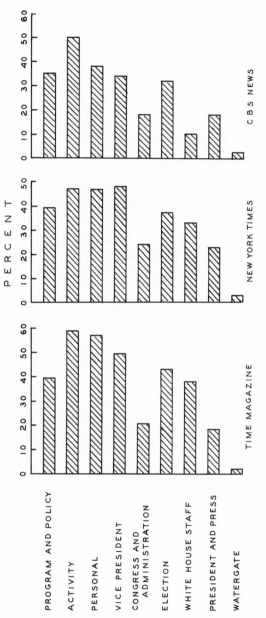

Table 13.   Program and Policy Stories
(Figures express the percentage of all program and policy stories represented by each category.)

	Time	*New York Times*	CBS News
General	11.3	1.8	.9
Foreign	8.5	12.3	17.4
Domestic	9.4	8.5	11.7
Budget	1.2	2.1	2.3
Total program and policy stories as a percentage of total stories	30.4	24.7	32.3

volved, and what it means. CBS News, on the other hand, tries to present the highlights of what happened, but, realizing its own time limitations, does not seek to cover stories completely or give attention to all of the events that its reporters regard as news. *Time* magazine gives a general treatment of the week's events with an emphasis on who was involved in them.

Each of the news sources reflects its own interest, but the most striking finding that a comparison shows is how similar to each other they are. They pay attention to the same general kinds of stories and give their articles a similar tone. While each news source presents different pieces of information on a subject, the overall tone of the articles is quite similar. Knowledge of these patterns over the years has led presidents and their staffs to develop strategies based on the predictability and the uniformity of the press coverage of the White House.

ELEVEN

TRIPLE EXPOSURES

Predictable Phases in the White House–News Media Relationship

E VERY newly elected president promises to be accessible, to speak frankly, and to make available all information that the public needs to form an adequate assessment of his administration. "This will be an open administration," Richard Nixon told his supporters and a national television audience as he celebrated the news of his election victory in 1968. It will be "open to new ideas . . . open to the critics as well as those who support us."[1] Although similar rhetoric still will be heard later in a term, the conduct of the President and his aides will be quite different. Their tactics and strategies, which are intended to influence the way they are portrayed in the media, include managing the flow of news, wooing reporters with ingratiating approaches, using their control over access to avoid reporters, and attacking the credibility of the media.

The way in which a president employs these tactics depends on his view of the press. Presidents who view news organizations as members of another interest group are likely to use tactics of news management or ingratiation. Those who think their responsibility toward the press ends when they release their public communiqués will use the tactics of avoidance or attack. Presidents who want the press to channel the ideas and images of their administration are inclined to use tactics of ingratiation.

These tactics bring about predictable reactions from diverse news organizations that have learned how to protect themselves against the methods used by White House officials. As both the White House publicity apparatus and the organizational structure of publishing and broadcasting enterprises have become more complex, features of cooperation and rivalry seem to have occurred at regular intervals during the history of each new administration. There is a period at the beginning of an administration when the White House and news organizations appear to be allies in producing and disseminating news. This is followed by clashes over news and information so great that the two sides appear to be adversaries. In a third stage the intensity of the competition burns out and is replaced by a relationship that is more structured and less intense than that in either of the first two periods. The second and third periods alternately occur and recur after the initial period of cooperation, and there may be a brief return of the first period if a president is reelected, but the long-term trend through either a four- or an eight-year presidency is for rivalry to be characteristic of the middle portion of an administration and the more formal relationship to dominate at the end. The names given to these periods or phases are "alliance," "competition," and "detachment."

In this chapter the tactics used by the White House to gain the President's objectives are examined in the context of the three phases. The pressures that create each phase and the reasons for their recurrence in new administrations also are discussed.

The Phases

During the alliance phase cooperation is the rule. News organizations communicate the White House line and channel the ideas and image of the President to their audiences. White House officials cooperate with reporters' objectives of obtaining access to everyone in the new administration. Alliance continues as long as both sides present favorable profiles of the personnel and ideas of the administration.

During the second phase, that of competition, both sides use manipulative tactics to present a story "their way." Presidential assistants try to manipulate reporters in order to regain the favorable publicity that existed during the alliance phase. Reporters sharpen their manipulative techniques to extract information from officials, whom they now view as overly circumspect about what and to whom they will talk.

Finally, detachment occurs after most White House officials and reporters have given up some of the more extreme manipulative tactics. White House officials, including the President, are more concerned about preventing reporters from seeing their flaws than in getting them to prepare stories that will be favorable to their policies. Policy-makers have less contact with reporters during this period, while public relations officials become more prominent. Many reporters also stop seeking White House sources and look elsewhere in Washington for information about the presidency.

The changes from phase to phase do not affect equally the routines and relations of individual reporters and officials. For example, during the Nixon administration Herbert Klein, the director of communications, and Gerald Warren, the deputy press secretary who handled daily briefings during the administration's final days, maintained good relations with reporters when the relationship as a whole had become acrimonious. Some reporters are equally well established. David Broder of the *Washington Post* recalled that he had no difficulty maintaining his access to Nixon White House officials even when his own newspaper was under strong attack from the administration and other *Post* reporters were complaining that their White House sources had dried up.[2] Reporters with specialized or regional interests also tend to be less affected by the phases than reporters who have the general assignment of covering the President.

Phase One: Alliance

During the phase of alliance a silent partnership exists between White House officials and representatives of news organizations assigned to cover the presidency. The partnership is based on two elements: the common definition by both parties of newsworthy items; and the willingness of reporters to provide an unfiltered conduit on which the White House can convey messages to the public.

Reporters assigned to cover the presidency on a daily basis need the cooperation of White House officials, particularly those in the Press Office. This is especially true at the beginning of an administration. Reporters are more dependent on White House–sponsored arrangements such as briefings and press releases then than they will be later, when some of them acquire techniques to verify the official line. Because this phase usually coincides with the euphoric early weeks of a new administration, it is commonly but inappropriately referred to as the President's "honeymoon" with the press. The term is inappropriate because it implies the suspension of normal self-interest, thus conveying the impression that the President is being given a chance by reporters to get to know his job and relish the fruits of his newly won office for a few weeks before reporters and White House officials resume their traditional role as adversaries. Although the relationship is more easygoing at this time, neither officials nor reporters would hold back from nonnewlywed treatment of the other if it suited their purpose. The point is that during this period both sides have more to gain by cooperation. They both want to obtain maximum media exposure for the new administration, its people, and its proposed policies. As long as they hold the same definition of news, it makes sense for them to cooperate.

If a president changes his policies and his assistants at the beginning of a second term and provides reporters with easy access to himself and his new aides, there may be a brief reprise of the period of alliance. Since only Eisenhower served two full terms during the era we studied, there is no comparable record by which we can judge. It seems likely, however, that after a four-year term the basic tenor of the relationship between President and press will have been set. The duration of the phase of alliance at the beginning of a second term is likely to be much shorter than that at the beginning of the first term.

NEWSWORTHY ITEMS

The first item on reporters' agendas is to profile interesting personalities—to provide the "people" stories that news editors demand. The most newsworthy person in the new administration is the President. Reporters are interested in three types of stories about the Chief Executive: human interest stories about the man and the people closest to him; stories about the President as policy-maker, focusing on the way he conducts himself while deciding which policy positions he will choose and emphasize; and stories about his goals and plans. All three types of stories are likely to be reported in a manner that is favorable to the President, in large part because of the habits and traditions of reporters in dealing with what they consider to be newsworthy items at this time.

"The President himself is a story, regardless of what he does," said George Reedy, who served as Lyndon Johnson's press secretary.[3] A Ford White House official observing the Carter administration getting ready to take office predicted that reporters would be very interested in "personality" stories about President Carter during the early days of his term. The reporters would want to find out "First, who is Jimmy Carter? What is his personality? Does he get mad? Does he golf? Does he fish in a pond? How do you find out who somebody is? You look at his friends, his habits, his manner, his character, his personality."[4]

The stories that result from these personal glimpses invariably are friendly to the President, as are stories that deal with the new president as he attempts to reach decisions about the direction of his administration. The same Ford administration official explained why he thought reporters would produce favorable stories about Carter at work: "The second story is what is he doing as President? The answer is that he is developing policy. When you develop policy and consult, it is almost universally attractive. That's why there is a honeymoon. It is attractive because you are not making that many decisions. You are pulling together information. You are consulting. You are listening and defining problems. Nothing is as attractive to the country and the press as dealing—or appearing to deal—with problems."[5]

Reporters who covered the new president when he was a candidate have a somewhat different perspective on the new administration from those whose assignment began after the election. They got to know the White House staff during a period when they were especially anxious to be accessible to the press. These reporters may have established a relationship with the candidate, and they can use their campaign experience as a backdrop for their coverage of the administration.

Some of the earliest critical stories of Carter as president were produced by reporters who had covered the Carter campaign. An example of this kind of story—one to which the administration took exception—is a *New York Times* article written by James Wooten that appeared on April 25, 1977, and that seemed to characterize Carter as being "aloof" and a "recluse," terms that brought back unhappy memories of the Nixon administration. But members of this group of reporters are constrained from getting too far in front of their colleagues with critical stories. They too work for news organizations that want personal glimpses of the new leaders. It is a situation that the White House can use to its advantage. "I have seen reporters 'co-opted' by the simple device of giving them private photographs taken by the White House photographer," said George Reedy. "No single one of these pictures could be classified as 'news' in the ordinary sense. Most of them merely show the President strolling through the mansion; drinking a cup of coffee; or playing with his dogs. The reporter who got the pictures, however, received very favorable treatment from his editors thereafter and naturally he reciprocated with stories about the President that actually fawned.'"6

A newly inaugurated president also may receive favorable publicity when he announces such general goals as cutting back unemployment or curbing inflation. Reporters are not likely to prepare critical stories in response to this type of announcement because of two deeply ingrained habits common to most of them in their production of news stories. First, when reporters present criticism, they do so in the form of a comparison between the President's rhetoric and his record. Since the President has no record at this time, his rhetoric is presented as news. Second, critical stories seldom are written by reporters on their own authority—they prefer to pluck critical words from the mouths of public figures. At this early stage of an administration, however, most public figures are unwilling to criticize the President in strong and newsworthy terms because it is not yet clear in which direction he is moving. He may be on their side, and they do not want to antagonize him prematurely. Even columnists and analysts who are not constrained by these habits and practices are likely to hold back at this time because they are still developing their sources. Consequently, in the early months of his term, a president is spared critical news stories of the type that become common later. President Carter, for example, made energy policy a major item on his agenda at the beginning of his administration. The stories about his activities and those of his chief adviser in the Department of Energy were largely supportive until he introduced legislation, lobbied for it, and made compromises.

THE OPEN PRESIDENCY

During the phase of alliance, White House officials provide reporters with the best access that they will have at any time during the administration. The flow of information is least restricted, and reporters have their greatest opportunities to get information about the administration at public interchanges and in interviews. Of course, there are significant differences among administrations as to how available and accessible the information and officials will be. President Kennedy's press secretary, Pierre Salinger, maintains that he did not monitor the contacts between reporters and the White House staff, and the memories of White House reporters from that era bear out his contention.[7] During the Nixon administration both access and information were more difficult from the start, although some reporters recall that the offices of White House aides were opened to them in the early months of the administration.[8]

The promise of an open presidency is an echo of Woodrow Wilson's call for a government "which is all outside and no inside." Although no such sweeping claims have been made by recent presidents, similar, if lesser, assertions are common to all incoming administrations. The new press secretary usually reflects this commitment, especially when he is contrasted against his successors. George Reedy, Herbert Klein, and Jerald terHorst were regarded by reporters as press secretaries who pushed for openness in their administrations.[9]

There is a cordial atmosphere during this period. Most presidents are optimistic about the future when they take office. They forget earlier harsh encounters with the media in the ebullience of their accession to office. Leo Rosten reminded his readers in 1937 that Franklin Roosevelt had had bad press relations before his election. According to Rosten he "offended newsmen" as assistant secretary of the navy, irritated them in his vice-presidential campaign of 1920 "by denying remarks which the newspapermen recalled his having made," and "threatened reporters" as governor of New York on at least one occasion.[10] As a consequence of all of these incidents, in Albany "some reporters avoided his conferences altogether."[11]

In practical terms the open presidency means that reporters are more likely to have their phone calls answered, to be granted interviews, and to get information that has not been specifically restricted. The President is more likely at this time to hold regular and frequent press conferences; important administration officials will be made available for questioning by reporters; and more of the information given to reporters will be on the record.

Some administrations do not move very far in the direction of opening up the White House and providing access. Both the Eisenhower and Nixon administrations never wanted reporters to get close to White House officials. During the Eisenhower administration, which was probably characterized by less variation in its relations with news organizations than any of its successors, most information was channeled through the Press Office or given in interviews scheduled and monitored by James Hagerty, the press secretary. The Nixon administration also conducted formal and detached relations with reporters, although during its first months officials such as Herbert Klein, the director of the Office of Communications, tried to serve as intermediaries for reporters who were trying to find out what was going on.

Most presidents do not regard the media as overly obtrusive, as did President Eisenhower, or as hostile, as did President Nixon. Especially during their first months in office they recognize the tremendous benefits of conducting an open administration. Because in most cases the outgoing administration had developed abrasive relations with some news organizations, reporters are glad to have the opportunity to make contacts with a new group of officials. More important from the administration's point of view, as discussed earlier, most of the stories that reporters prepare at this time are likely to be favorable. Consequently, the "open presidency" is a good tactic. The President's personal relations with reporters tend to be most constant during this period. President Kennedy gave private interviews to reporters most frequently during 1961 and early 1962. By 1963 he saw them less frequently and on a more formal basis.[12] Press conferences also are most likely to be scheduled frequently and regularly during this early period. Lyndon Johnson met with reporters thirty-five times during his first thirteen months in office. In 1965, however, his second full year, he held only sixteen press conferences.

Because of their large audiences, the wires and networks are particularly important to the White House during this phase. The common view in the last five administrations that television is the most important contemporary medium has produced a common thread in them. "You pitch everything you have toward television," said one high-level member of President Ford's White House staff.[13] Jody Powell also commented on the importance of presenting material that can be used by television. Powell remarked that Theodore Roosevelt's appraisal of the presidency as a bully pulpit was essentially true today, "only now the pulpit is CBS, NBC, and to some extent the wires."[14]

Phase Two: Competition

An end comes to the alliance between the White House and the news media when reporters become interested in the administration's involvement in conflicts among personalities and controversies over policies. An activist president who has made clear policy commitments lends himself to stories about conflicts with his adversaries over policy as well as to stories about disputes among his supporters over which tactics should be used to win the policy battle. In the case of less active presidents, reporters are provided with stories leaked by advisers who want the President to take a stand and speak out and stories about which adviser or cabinet official is currently on top of the White House pecking order. The shared definition of newsworthy items that led to stories supportive of the President and his policies during the alliance phase dissolves in the phase of competition. Presidents find that their reaction to press coverage becomes, as Kennedy put it, one of "reading more and enjoying it less."[15]

During this phase, the President and White House officials become unhappy with the media for, from their perspective, focusing on either the wrong aspect of the story or the wrong story entirely. In order to deal with what they see as critical stories, the President and his staff can confront the source of the criticism, its messenger, or both. If the sources have spoken in public, they can be answered; if they are unknown, then the leaks must be traced. "I never saw either president for whom I worked [Kennedy and Johnson] so mad as when they were upset over leaks," Walt Rostow told an interviewer.[16] The most extreme result of such anger occurred during the Nixon administration, when presidential adviser Charles Colson was put in charge of tracking down unofficial disclosures of information, a decision that led to the formation of the plumbers group, which engaged in illegal activities that ultimately led to the downfall of the President.

However, most White House officials feel that tracking down leaks is a no-win situation for the administration. "They're almost impossible to track down because . . . sometimes there isn't just one leaker . . . and sometimes the leak may have been unknowing," a former Press Office official said.[17] Reporters confirmed this view. "I talk to a number of people on a deep background basis and try to piece things together," said columnist Robert Novak, who has based many stories on information that the White House did not wish disclosed. "I almost never have gotten a story from one guy who spilled his guts."[18]

The phase of competition is characterized by the Chief Executive's attempts to manipulate his relations with the news media. There is a retrenchment from the open presidency; the White House specifies the conditions under which officials may talk to reporters and seeks to curb unauthorized disclosures of information. White House officials usually opt for three approaches during this phase: news management, ingratiation, and attack.

NEWS MANAGEMENT

News management involves manipulation by the President and his advisers of the kinds of information that will be made available to reporters and of the forums in which information is given to them. The President and his staff try to recapture through manipulative tactics what the media had done for them without prodding in the period after the inauguration. Manipulation involves strategies of initiation, in order to direct reporters to some people and events, and of reaction, in order to steer them away from others.

Manipulation of access. A major technique of news management is the manipulation of access. During the competition phase White House officials asked to arrange contacts with reporters are more likely to evaluate what they will get out of a story or whether the reporter's news organization is friendly or hostile to them. Lyndon Johnson, who regarded news organizations as either rivals or friends, left evidence of this concern in his files. Marginal notes in Johnson's handwriting appear on a memo from Press Secretary George Reedy that say, "I don't believe I've ever had a fair story in the W. J. I know [Alan] Otten can't be fair. Why should I punish myself—why don't you have the interview?"[19]

Because the President is the official most in demand, officials ration his media contacts in ways that maximize favorable news coverage. "When I came in [as press secretary] I asked President Ford how much time he wanted to spend with the press," Ronald Nessen remembered. "He said two hours." That time constraint, Nessen said, meant they had to limit his contacts, especially interviews, to situations they believed would be favorable to him.[20]

Even celebrated correspondents working for powerful news organizations may accept preconditions when it is important to them to interview the President. On October 12, 1976, during President Ford's campaign trip through

New York and New Jersey, Walter Cronkite appeared on the press bus. Not coincidentally, the President had given an interview to Barbara Walters, who had just begun her new career as a rival anchorperson to Cronkite on ABC News. "I was fairly sure that he wanted to talk to Ford," Ronald Nessen recalled. According to Nessen, when he asked the correspondent why he wanted to see the President, Cronkite replied, "You know the name of the game." Cronkite did get his interview, Nessen said, after he agreed that he was "paying a courtesy call" and would not ask the President substantive questions. In fact, in preliminary negotiations between CBS and Deputy Press Secretary John Carlson, a CBS reporter gave assurances that Cronkite would only ask "softballs." Nessen said that he needed those assurances because he wanted to maintain the momentum of a campaign that was going well for the President. That same day on another news program, John Dean had suggested that Ford had cooperated with the Nixon White House in squelching an early Watergate investigation. Nevertheless, since Cronkite had agreed to the ground rules, the interview was limited to questions that Ford and his staff thought he could handle easily.[21]

Monitoring staff contacts with the media. Since the source of most news about the White House is the staff rather than the President, regulating the contact between officials and reporters is an important technique of news management. This can be done positively in these ways: by fostering contacts between officials and designated reporters and columnists; by coordinating White House publicity resources between the Press Office and the senior staff so that officials at key points will present the same picture to reporters; and by emphasizing indirect resources, such as those provided by Public Liaison or Congressional Liaison, so that when reporters talk to interest groups or congressmen they get the same message they would by talking to the White House staff. These positive techniques were characteristic of the Ford and Carter administrations. In the Ford administration few attempts, if any, were made to shut off reporters from major national or regional news organizations. The "if any" qualification is necessary because some reporters in every administration find it difficult to get interviews. They maintain they are shut out because they are hard-hitting reporters, while White House officials claim they are unprofessional individuals.

The negative techniques characteristic of the Johnson and Nixon administration involved keeping tabs on who spoke to reporters. Johnson asked for and received periodic reports from Marvin Watson of his staff on personal meetings between White House officials and reporters. He demanded that staff and cabinet members provide him with personal reports on which reporters they had seen. He also decided whether someone on the staff would be allowed to appear on television talk programs such as "Meet the Press" and whether someone on the staff could talk on the record to reporters. George Christian, his fourth press secretary, recalled that Johnson sought to avoid staff stories because "he learned that 75 percent of the time press interviews [with the staff] caused him trouble."[22] An aide who served both the Nixon and the Ford administrations agreed with the Johnson-Christian formulation, but added an insight of his own. Recalling that reporters had to go through channels to talk to officials in the Nixon administration, he suggested that Nixon's methods "serve the President's interests better and [Ford's] the nation's."[23]

Planting and plugging leaks. Leaks are unofficial disclosures of information provided by sources who make anonymity part of their price for the story. In a minority of cases, what the White House regards as leaks actually are stories reporters have pieced together after assiduous detective work. Others are obtained by socially well-placed reporters who have access to the table talk and private musings of important or knowledgeable officials, and who pass on the stories through the inadvertent disclosures reporters make while trading information. But the vast majority of leaks are deliberately planted. Joseph Kraft's general comments on newsgathering in Washington are particularly applicable to White House operations: "In the typical Washington situation, news is not nosed out by keen reporters and then purveyed to the public. It is manufactured inside the government, by various interested parties for purposes of their own, and then put out to the press in ways and at times that suit the source. That is how it happens that when the President prepares a message on crime, all the leading columnists suddenly become concerned with crime."[24]

The President and his top aides admit that they give policy information privately to selected reporters as part of a coordinated effort to build policy support. Both authorized and unauthorized leaks flow in profusion in Washington. "It will not be a standard practice for the President's Press Secretary to leak the President's ideas and plans to the press," declared Pierre Salinger after he became press secretary to President Kennedy early in 1961. He would not, however, completely disavow the practice: "The leak had become common Washington occurrence. It generally occurs when Presidents and governments wish to advance a certain viewpoint and pass to newspaper men documents or information of a confidential nature which would advance this point of view. There may be occasions when it may be of some value to test public opinion before arriving at a public decision. But the leak is a device of public information policy to be used most sparingly."[25]

Sparing use can be effective use, however, and not merely use to "test public opinion." When the person who "leaks" is the President himself, the opportunities to control the resulting story are tremendously enhanced. This was the case in 1962, when John Kennedy provided a complete account of the Cuban missile crisis to two reporters who were also his personal friends, Charles Bartlett and Stewart Alsop. The article that the two reporters wrote for the *Saturday Evening Post* depicted the President and his colleagues as great heroes of a major confrontation with America's chief adversary, the Soviet Union. The story, which was disseminated throughout the media, related the events as viewed by the President and his advisers, without a sense of critical detachment. The article included, at Kennedy's insistence, the appraisal of a high-level official that United Nations Ambassador Adlai Stevenson "wanted a Munich."[26] Thus the President was able to provide the script for the major news story about the missile crisis, insist on the details that would appear, and cut down to size an aide and former rival who made him uncomfortable.

Manipulation of settings. News management also involves the attempt to manipulate the settings in which information is given—press conferences, briefings, backgrounders, and interviews—by holding them less frequently, by changing the ground rules, or by providing less information. All of the aforementioned are high-risk forums, which led an associate director of the Ford administration's Office of Communications to predict that President Carter would back away from his implied preinaugural promises to hold twice monthly press conferences and schedule them well in advance:

Carter's going to find exactly what every other president has found, and that is the President's desire to portray his policies accurately and in a positive light invariably runs at cross purposes with the press's cynicism. . . . [Eventually] there's going to be some bad economic news two days before a scheduled press conference or there's going to be some other major story developing over which he has no control and about which he is not going to want to comment. And then the press conferences will stop. It is not a conscious evil decision to evade the press but more a desire to answer those questions that you want to answer in a way that you want to answer them.[27]

The predicted end to regular conferences took place in the summer of 1979, when the President stated he no longer felt bound by any commitment to hold two conferences a month. Even earlier, however, the schedule had been manipulated to avoid embarrassing questions, as in 1977, when the President's budget director and close friend, Bert Lance, was under the public investigation that led to his resignation. For more than two years President Carter did meet his promise to answer questions from the Washington press corps at regularly scheduled intervals. Like his predecessors, however, he eventually decided he wanted to hold conferences when he thought they were necessary rather than at the behest of a prearranged commitment.

INGRATIATION

Ingratiation is the attempt to manipulate reporters by doing favors for them. Sometimes this may involve reporters as a group, as when a White House official provides them with secret information that they are told is usually provided only to those officials who have a need to know. It also may mean looking after the material needs of reporters, both on the job and as they travel with the President. Usually ingratiation involves rewarding some reporters with exclusive information. At times this may take the form of an exclusive interview with the President granted to a reporter who presumably gets stories "straight" from the White House perspective. This undoubtedly was the case with the interview granted to Garnett Horner of the *Washington Star* by President Nixon at the time of his electoral triumph in November, 1972. Such rewards are intended to have the concurrent effect of punishing those reporters who "distort" the White House's position and actions.

The most ingratiating favor that can be done for reporters is to give them information. Its payoff comes because reporters are members of a competitive group that can be divided easily when the members vie for exclusive stories, particularly those concerning the President. Ingratiation as a technique to gain favorable coverage has not been used with the same frequency by all recent administrations. Unlike news management and the open presidency, which have been used by all, ingratiation has been used more frequently by Democratic than by Republican administrations. Reporters were courted as individuals and as a group in the administrations of Roosevelt, Kennedy, and Johnson. Perhaps because Republican administrations do not think of reporters as part of their constituency, Republican presidents have tended to limit their personal efforts to wooing editors, publishers, and network executives. Eisenhower gave few individual interviews. Eisenhower's predecessor, Harry Truman, also gave few on-the-record interviews; but Eisenhower's other contacts with reporters were limited, as well. Ike met informally with publishers, but only infrequently with reporters. Ford did mix with reporters at the beginning of his term, but his contacts became increasingly formal as time went on. Nixon, as is well known, was less interested in developing personal contacts with reporters than any other modern president has been.

Courting the elite. Ingratiation works most effectively with journalists whose status is such that they believe their own message is as important as that of the President and with those who work for highly regarded news organizations that demand that their correspondents obtain access to the President. No individual correspondent had more authority or higher status during his professional career than Walter Lippmann. All presidents were interested in getting Lippmann on their side, but no one cultivated him as assiduously as Lyndon Johnson. The esteem in which Johnson held Lippmann was indicated in a handwritten note to Robert Kintner, the staff and cabinet secretary who had been a colleague of Lippmann's on the *Herald-Tribune*. Kintner had sent Johnson a memorandum telling him that Lippmann had asked to have lunch with him. Johnson replied in the margin of Kintner's note, "I count him my friend and one of America's great citizens. I'm sorry he disagrees with some of my policies and decisions as I'm sorry that Lady Bird does. The lunch will be good for you and him and me."[28] Barely a week after Johnson took office he visited Lippmann at his home. In the next months he sought Lippmann's advice on many occasions. According to one White House official, Johnson asked Lippmann to help him prepare several policy statements; Lippmann wrote major portions of Johnson's major Vietnam address at the Johns Hopkins University in 1964.[29] Top administration officials were told to keep their doors open to Lippmann and to provide him with the help he needed.

Chalmers Roberts, diplomatic correspondent for the *Washington Post* for several administrations, commented that Johnson's ingratiating tactics had a detrimental affect on Lippmann who, Roberts believed, "violated the basic rule that reporters should not get too close to public officials . . . [and should not] become captives. I'm sure Walter feels that he was betrayed because he seemed to be taking his advice or asking for it and listening respectfully. It's something from Lippmann's standpoint which was completely contrary. So he'd been double-crossed in effect. This created a real attitude of bitterness there, that kind of thing. From Johnson's standpoint he thought he was being effective but he was being counterproductive."[30]

Johnson curried favor with other notable journalists who had high status in the profession. Arthur Krock, columnist for the *New York Times*, described a phone call he received from the President shortly after he took office. Johnson told Krock that he had been trying to locate him for three or four days, and then said: " 'I need your help. I need your help particularly. I know I am going to have it.' I said, 'Yes, Mr. President,' and so on and so on, the usual thing. And he said, 'I can count on you; I know I can. I need all the help I can get. And you are in a position to render a great deal to me,' and that was that."[31] Johnson called some journalists regularly, and invited others whom he considered to be important or his friends to lunch at the White House. The President's daily diary shows that in the week of December 1, 1964, he had the following personal contacts with reporters and editors: telephone calls to Katherine Graham, publisher of the *Washington Post*, Frank McGee, correspondent for NBC, Arthur Krock of the *New York Times*, and an unspecified reporter at United Press International. He had meetings in the White House with John Oakes, editor of the *New York Times*, and, later in the week, with the Washington bureau chief of the *Times*, Tom Wicker. He had lunch with his friend Philip Potter of the Washington bureau of the *Baltimore Sun*.[32] A sample of four weeks' of logs of telephone calls and appointments during four different years reveals many meetings between the President and representatives of news organizations. They include a dinner with John Hay Whitney, Richard Wald, and David Wise of the *New York Herald-Tribune;* an evening meeting with Turner Catledge of the *New York Times*; an afternoon meeting in the dining room with Leonard Goldenson and James Hagerty of ABC News; lunch with Garnett Horner of the *Washington Star;* an Oval Office meeting with syndicated columnist Drew Pearson; and a boat cruise with columnist Marianne Means and Mrs. William White.[33] He had other Oval Office meetings with Peter Lisagor of the *Chicago Daily News;* with Henry Luce and Hugh Sidey of *Time* magazine; Cyrus Sulzberger of the *New York Times*; Walker Stone, editor-in-chief of Scripps-Howard Newspapers; and the editor

and the Washington correspondent of the *Manchester Guardian*.[34] Johnson
left the White House to attend a surprise party honoring columnist James
Reston of the *New York Times*.[35]

Presidential friendships. The use or abuse of personal relationships between the President and reporters is an issue that has been raised most frequently about John Kennedy. According to the recollection of aides such as
David Powers, because Kennedy's temperament and interests were compati-
ble with those of many journalists, he had little difficulty striking up friendships with them.[36] These relationships were flattering to reporters and useful
to the administration. "Kennedy was a more subtle operator [than Johnson],"
observed James Reston, columnist for the *New York Times*. "He would see
you when you wanted, but because he had been a reporter he knew it was a
little dicey to play around with being clumsy in the relationship."[37] Kennedy
used selected friends among reporters to channel information, including Benjamin Bradlee of *Newsweek*, Charles Bartlett of the *Chattanooga Times*, the
syndicated columnist Stewart Alsop, and Rowland Evans of the *New York
Herald-Tribune*. Reporters and the President profited. The President got his
version of what was happening into the media, while the news people received
the professional status and public acclaim that comes from being known as
insiders in the administration. Michael Raoul-Duval, an aide in the Ford
administration, explained the benefits to Kennedy: "Look how Kennedy used
Ben Bradlee. He didn't use him because he was a representative of the public,
he used him because he had access to a billboard. Kennedy wanted to effect
the message on the billboard, and the billboard happened to be *Newsweek*."[38]

In his book *Conversations with Kennedy*, Benjamin Bradlee recalled that
Kennedy supplied him with information and met with him on terms that were
ultimately beneficial to the White House. Of course, Bradlee received personal benefits. Because it was known in the Washington and journalistic
communities that Bradlee and Kennedy were friends, Bradlee was thought to
have a clearer picture of Kennedy's plans and thinking than any other journalist. That he was not really privy to important inside information about the
administration was less important than his reputation as an intimate of the
Kennedys.

In exchange for providing Bradlee with status, Kennedy received from
Bradlee useful information about the media. While much of what he received
was professional gossip, it was useful to his overall media strategy. For
example, he would receive advance word on *Newsweek*'s cover story. Occasionally Kennedy received information that was important. On one occasion,
retold in his book, Bradlee brought to a White House dinner plastic arrows
that were part of a newly designed antipersonnel weapon that the *Newsweek*
Pentagon correspondent had gotten. Kennedy was furious that such devices
could be obtained by journalists from military sources, and he moved to
prevent such leaks in the future.[39] Bradlee, by his own account, was eager to

win the favor of President Kennedy, whom he provided with information, including intelligence about the President's rivals that Bradlee could obtain from the network of *Newsweek* correspondents. He sought to ingratiate himself with the President, as have other reporters.

Direct favors. Another technique the President and his staff use involves doing favors for reporters. President Johnson spent more time at this than any other recent president. When Associated Press White House correspondent Frank Cormier's parents took a tour of the White House, they attended a bill-signing ceremony in which President Johnson spotted them and came over to meet them. Johnson invited them to his office, where he served refreshments and discussed their son's importance. Johnson said: "Miz Cormier, your son is in a critical position at a critical time in our nation's history. He's in a job where he could make lots of mistakes—but he doesn't make very many." Cormier recalled: "For myself, I was mindful that it was an election year and that we were being exposed to the vaunted Johnson Treatment. Obviously the President was entertaining us only because I was a White House correspondent whose favor he coveted.... Yet his hospitality and even his excursion into hyperbole were kindnesses that came easy to him."[40]

Throwing them raw meat. While presidents have been direct in their methods of courting reporters and their organizations, they also can proceed in less visible ways. According to his staff, Lyndon Johnson's motto for reporters he felt were critical was "Throw them a piece of raw meat."[41] This meant that Johnson or other White House officials would feed good information to hostile reporters in an effort to win them over and get them to write stories that reflected his interests. It is a bargain that flatters reporters by making them feel that they are trusted and important correspondents.

One event that illustrates this point occurred after an aide to President Johnson successfully planted a question that enabled Johnson to respond at length in a manner of his choosing. According to the aide, because it worked, "it set the tone of the press conference and LBJ came back and said, 'Hey, listen, next time let's plant all of the questions.'" While the staff member thought that the President was joking, he found shortly before the next press conference that indeed he was expected to plant ten questions. The aide asked a reporter he thought he knew well to take a question. The reporter answered: "How dare you try to plant a question with [a prominent newspaper]. I consider this highly unethical." The aide explained to the President that "I went up to _____ and he began to give me a lecture on ethics, and he is very hostile toward your administration, sir." The aide continued to tell his story: "I told you how he handles recalcitrant newsmen: 'When they are nipping at your ass, you throw them a piece of raw meat.' Which he proceeded to do with _____. Every day after that there would be a front page exclusive story by _____."

Later the reporter and the aide had the following exchange. The aide recalled he asked the reporter,

"Do you still feel the same way as you did three or four weeks ago?" And he turned
around, and said, "Is there any doubt in your mind about how I feel? Didn't I make
myself clear at the time?" He started to walk away and I said, "By the way, how do
you feel about planted answers?" And he got red in the face, just flushed. He took the
pipe out of his mouth, and said, "Touché, it has been bothering the hell out of me." I,
of course, now that I had the knife in thought I would turn it around, I said, "You can
get around it by putting an editor's note in the beginning saying the President fed me
this story because he had an ulterior motive, but here is the story. I think your reader
has a right to know that the story is given." He said: "Alright, I deserved that."[42]

The President was using the reporter by providing him with exclusive stories.
Johnson got what he wanted, which was to turn the reporter's attention from
criticism to stories that provided readers with the administration's point of
view. The reporter in turn received front-page exclusive stories.

ATTACK

Attack, the most explosive weapon in the President's arsenal during the
competition phase, is used by White House officials to prevent damage to the
President's ability to lead and persuade that they believe is caused by biased or
unfavorable media reporting. Attack includes efforts to discredit reporters
with their news organizations, to discredit a news organization with the public, and, in the most extreme cases, to challenge the legitimacy of the media's
right to reflect points of view that differ from the administration's and the
public's and to challenge the authenticity of anything that appears in the
media. The attraction that the strategy of attacking the media has had for
presidents and their advisers was explained by a Ford administration official:

Inevitably what they are reporting is what somebody [in the opposition] said [that was]
critical. If the President is going to discount the criticism, he has only two options: He
can say the criticism is wrong, and then say why what he is doing is good for the
country. Or he can imply that it is a critical press that is distorting the President's
position and exploiting the opposition. In some cases the criticism is highly justified.
In that case you have only one option: you have to criticize the press, because you can't
criticize the substance of what was reported.[43]

Some manifestations of attack show up in almost every administration, and
the implied threat of retaliation by the White House may make some reporters
pull in their horns if they see a minor story that is potentially damaging to the
President. Some reporters even profit from the widespread paranoia about
press enemies that has afflicted so many recent administrations: "A few
words of sympathy over the unfair treatment by the 'Eastern press' (or the
liberal press or the conservative press) is an effective method of slamming
doors against competitors. An important leader who can be persuaded that his
journalistic 'friend' is the lone holdout against a 'press conspiracy' can serve
as a meal ticket for many years."[44]

Manners of attack. The form of presidential attack varies considerably according to the styles of particular presidents. Some use words, in speeches or in private comments to well-placed audiences, to attack individual reporters and news organizations. Other presidents have attacked reporters by attempting to destroy their status with their news organizations and in the profession, and to damage news organizations through licensing provisions.

Almost all recent presidents have retaliated against some reporters or news organizations at one time during their term, but Roosevelt, Johnson, and Nixon let their pique rise to the surface most frequently. FDR used his press conferences and private correspondence to vent his feelings and possibly to intimidate his opponents. "I thought he was ill-tempered," Edward Folliard remembered.[45] He objected to a *Washington Post* headline in a letter to the paper's publisher, Eugene Meyer, when he wrote: "I feel confident you want to do nothing which will aid in restoring the old spirit of fear which I mentioned in my Inaugural address. That leads me to call your special attention to the caption over the map which reads: 'UNREST SPREADS IN UNITED STATES AS NEW DEAL FACES ELECTION TEST.' I must tell you honestly that the country must fear those who instill the spirit of fear, and I hope you will agree with me on that."[46]

Memoranda, sometimes with marginal notes by the President, suggest the irritation Lyndon Johnson felt about particular reporters and institutions. When *Newsweek* published an article by correspondent Charles Roberts on Johnson's credibility gap, the President demanded that a report be given to him later that day detailing the facts.[47] Another credibility gap article, this one by James Deakin in the *New Republic,* got a similar response from the President. Johnson regarded certain reporters and institutions as being opposed to him, and he tried to indicate to his staff that he saw no reason to be helpful to them. When Joseph Califano, the President's adviser for domestic policy, wanted to appear on a television program hosted by columnists Evans and Novak, Johnson turned down the request. "*Send* me the favorable columns marked and point up wherein they are favorable," Johnson wrote. "I've never seen *them.*"[48] Columnist Charles Bartlett tried to appease Johnson by writing to the President that he was "chagrined . . . to hear repeatedly from various persons that you are given to saying that I hate you. This is not true, or even close to truth, and I wanted to assert it emphatically."[49] Johnson responded that "I was greatly surprised by the tone of your letter. Now and then I do read your column, and at times I differ with your facts and conclusions, but I have never thought about your writings sufficiently to characterize them."[50]

While Johnson's remarks reflected his strong feelings about his relations with the media, he usually did not go beyond the comment stage to launch direct attacks on reporters. Reporters simply did not get what they wanted from the White House. Interviews and access were withheld. On some occasions he would try to get a reporter in trouble with his superiors. But, like

Franklin Roosevelt, he directed his attack at specific reporters and organizations, not against the media as a whole.

The war against the media. The all-out attack on the media, characteristic of the Nixon administration, was well planned and was successful in intimidating large segments of broadcasting and publishing enterprises.[51] Attack obviously struck positive chords among large numbers of citizens, who indicated that their distrust of the media was nearly as great as their distrust of the political leadership. The ultimate impact of the Nixon administration's efforts to exploit popular dissatisfaction with the news media may be a situation in which large segments of the public believe neither the President nor those who report on and analyze the activities of his administration.

Attacks on the media during the Nixon administration were different in scale from those of previous administrations; they constituted a massive and unprecedented assault on the legitimacy of news organizations' activities. The Nixon administration did not recognize the media's claim to act as a surrogate for the public, nor did it view the media as having a legitimate interest in the operations of government. Because they regarded news organizations as political adversaries, administration officials were willing to use their political, legal, and extralegal resources to reduce the profits, power, and public status of news organizations. White House staff members prepared memoranda that raised the specter of the Federal Communications Commission, the Antitrust Division of the Justice Department, the Internal Revenue Service, and the Republican National Committee. Wiretaps were ordered against newsmen who were publishing or broadcasting stories the White House believed should not have appeared. They harassed reporters they regarded as enemies in the hope that they would leave the White House beat or be fired from their posts.

The core of the strategy was elaborated by Jeb Magruder, deputy director of the Office of Communications, in a memorandum he wrote in October, 1969. In it he suggested some specific responses to what the administration perceived to be unfair press coverage: "The real problem that faces the Administration is to get to this unfair coverage in such a way that we make major impact on a basis which the networks-newspapers and Congress will react to and begin to look at things somewhat differently. It is my opinion that we should begin concentrated efforts in a number of major areas that will have much more impact on the media and other anti-Administration spokesmen and will do more good in the long run."[52] Magruder recommended that the White House use established powers in the Justice Department, the Federal Communications Commission, and the Internal Revenue Service. This choice of institutions was born of a view, shared by the President and his top staff members, that "they [had] won not only the White House but the entire executive branch of the government."[53]

Magruder suggested using the Antitrust Division of the Justice Department to investigate cases where media activities might conflict with the law. "Even the possible threat of anti-trust action I think would be effective in changing their views," he added.[54] For example, the administration considered action against the *Los Angeles Times* for publishing a new regional edition that proclaimed its circulation. In a memorandum to the White House counsel, John Caulfield wrote to John Dean that the new edition "will stifle newspaper competition on the Southern California coast. It is Lyn's [Lyn Nofziger, White House staff assistant] view that this move may be countered by an anti-trust action and strong administration steps designed to limit the number of newspapers which one corporation can own."[55] The *Los Angeles Times* was regarded by the administration as being hostile to it.

The Federal Communications Commission was another executive branch institution that Magruder believed should have been used to combat the administration's media enemies. He suggested that the White House "begin an official monitoring system through the FCC as soon as Dean Burch is officially on board as Chairman. If the monitoring system proves our point, we have then legitimate and legal rights to go to the networks, etc., and make official complaints from the FCC. This will have much more effect than a phone call from Herb Klein or Pat Buchanan."[56] Because the FCC did not provide the kind of support for its plans that the administration wanted, the Office of Telecommunications Policy was reconstructed in the White House to accomplish the same objectives.

OTP had been created to deal with technical developments relating to international satellite communications. The Nixon administration decided to use it to pressure the commercial networks' news programming and to bring public broadcasting into line with the administration's policy views. In December, 1972, OTP's director, Clay Whitehead, went on the attack in a speech on the sensitive subject of broadcast license renewals. Whitehead made it clear that the Nixon administration supported legislation that made local stations responsible for programs produced by the networks. Thus when a local station had to renew its license, it could be questioned, held responsible, and made to defend itself against charges that its license should not be renewed because of "unfair" or "biased" national news programs. Whitehead said:

There is no area where management responsibility is more important than news. The station owners and managers cannot abdicate responsibility for news judgments. When a reporter or disc jockey slips in or passes over information in order to line his pocket, that's plugola, and management would take quick corrective action. ... Just as a newspaper publisher has responsibility for the wire service copy that appears in his newspaper—so television station owners and managers must have full responsibility for what goes out over the public's airwaves—no matter what the origin of the program.[57]

Magruder suggested that the Internal Revenue Service be used to tame recalcitrant news organizations because "just a threat of a IRS investigation will probably turn their approach."[58] Harassment by other investigative agencies, including the Federal Bureau of Investigation, also was considered and, on at least one occasion, used. In 1971 the FBI questioned CBS executives in New York and employees of the network's Washington bureau about Daniel Schorr, who, agents said, was being considered for a job in the Council on Environmental Quality. Schorr, however, had never sought the job, nor had he ever been approached by an administration official. Later a White House assistant admitted that the administration's primary concern was to get Schorr off the air.

In addition to using Executive Office and executive branch institutions in their war against the media, White House officials, including the President, directly confronted their adversaries. President Nixon attacked both the media in general and specific reporters in his news conferences. At the National Association of Broadcaster's meeting in Houston, Nixon traded biting remarks with CBS correspondent Dan Rather. In late 1973 Nixon accused the media of "outrageous, vicious, distorted reporting" that he had never before seen "in 27 years of public life."[59] When Robert Pierpoint of CBS asked whether the President was angry, Nixon replied that this was not the case because "one can only be angry with those he respects."[60] The strongest attacks on the media during the Nixon administration, however, were made by Vice President Agnew and members of the White House staff. Agnew attacked television, the *Washington Post*, and the *New York Times* in speeches in 1970. Nixon aide Daniel P. Moynihan published an article in *Commentary* in which he accused the media of McCarthyite tactics aimed at the destruction of the authority of the President.[61] Charges of unfairness and accusations of bias were hurled from lecterns throughout the administration.

Because many administration attacks were indirect, the press frequently was unaware of their origin. Patrick Buchanan, a White House speechwriter, coordinated a letter-writing and telegram campaign in which he drafted the text of notes from supporters around the country attacking the media and supporting the President. Jeb Magruder described the system in a memorandum to Nixon's chief of staff, H. R. Haldeman. "Ten telegrams have been drafted by Buchanan," Magruder wrote. "They will be sent to *Time* and *Newsweek* today by 20 names around the country from our letter writing system."[62]

A different sort of letter-writing campaign involved a more subtle attempt to influence the recipients. Haldeman directed Magruder to prepare letters to John Osborne, columnist for the *New Republic,* and Hugh Sidey of *Time* magazine. Although the two journalists had written materials the White House considered to be hostile, Magruder said that Haldeman directed that the letters to the two men "were not to be angry or critical." Instead, "the writers were supposed to be anti-Nixon liberals thanking the two columnists for revealing Nixon as the shallow and dangerous man he so obviously was."[63] The letter to Osborne included the statement that "your scathing attacks on President Nixon have delighted me beyond belief."[64] Evidently the tactic worked, because Osborne responded with chagrin and remorse to the charge that he was biased against the President. Magruder noted, "To our delight, not long after this letter was sent, Osborne wrote a troubled, soul-searching column in which he conceded 'a quality of sour and persistent disbelief that I did not like to recognize but had to recognize in my own work and in my own attitude toward the President.'"[65]

The consequences of attack. Six years after the President's resignation, it appeared that the Nixon administration's attack on the media had done little permanent damage. The FBI, the FCC, the Antitrust Division of the Justice Department, and other executive branch agencies proved unwilling to jump at the White House's bidding. The broadcasting networks and most publications resisted the suggestions of aides like John Ehrlichman that they fire reporters the White House viewed as being biased. Ultimately the media did carry the story about the crisis that led to the President's downfall. Indeed, the prestige of journalists was somewhat resurrected because of the part that reporters such as Bob Woodward and Carl Bernstein played in keeping the Watergate story alive.

At the same time, the tactics of attack did provide benefits for the White House. Network reporters stopped reviewing and analyzing presidential addresses after the White House attacked the practice as "instant analysis." Even during Watergate, presidential appeals to "put Watergate behind us" had some affect on the media. After each such speech, the number of Watergate-related stories in most publications dropped from several the day before the speech to a token number in the issues that followed. It is impossible to determine what success the attack strategy may have had if the Nixon administration had not been crippled by Watergate.

REPORTORIAL RESPONSES

To cope with manipulation by the White House, reporters develop manipulative tactics of their own to pry from the White House information that it would prefer to withhold. During the phase of alliance, most reporters adopt the conduit style of reporting. Now, in the competition phase, a reporter may become a friend of the court, an adversary, or a historian-observer. Many reporters do not change their tactics; these more aggressive styles are particularly noticeable on the part of reporters for the major publications.

The friend of the court. This reporter's work depends on information obtained from White House sources in return for supportive articles. In some cases this may involve flattery or ingratiation of a particular official, including the President himself. One correspondent sent President Johnson a picture of his den wall, which contained nine signed pictures of Johnson and the reporter.[66] Not surprisingly, the reporter was regarded as a favorite of the administration.

Most reporters employ the friend-of-the-court technique somewhat less sycophantically. Andrew Glass described it almost as a psychoanalytical tactic for getting news: "Instead of asking them for news, you discuss their problems with them, and eventually they tell you more than they intend."[67] Other reporters who used this technique maintained that it involved writing not favorable stories, but stories that indicated an understanding of the point of view of the officials. Martin Schram, presidential correspondent for the *Washington Post*, used this technique to get stories about the Mideast summit meetings, White House organization, and President Carter's problem with his brother, Billy. White House officials felt they could trust Schram to present their picture of events without distortion.

The adversary. This reporter approaches White House encounters assuming that officials may not be telling the truth or, at the very least, are withholding part of the story. Most White House reporters who take on this role display it only in the combative style with which they question officials in public forums. They argue that this technique pays off because officials do not want to be confronted in public with a lie. A combative style of questioning does not necessarily translate into an accusatory style of writing. One of the best-known practitioners of this style at the White House is Helen Thomas of United Press International. But most readers of Thomas's stories are not aware of how aggressively she questions officials at briefings. Like those of most wire service reporters, her stories report what has happened.

The historian-observer and institutional analyst. Some reporters become historian-observers in response to White House manipulation during the competition phase. Those who adopt this style of reporting interpret both the policies and the personalities who make and administer them in terms of the mood of the times. The advantage of this style for reporters is that, because their stories deal with the character of the administration, they are less influenced by the "hard news" that during this phase often consists of "pseudo-events" staged by the White House.

Related to the historian-observer are the institutional analysts, whose beat includes the entire White House staff and the Executive Office of the President. Officials who have worked at the White House during the last sixteen years suggested to interviewers that in their minds this was the best way of finding out what was going on there.

The single greatest problem reporters have in accurately portraying the presidency, according to these respondents, is that they concentrate almost exclusively on the President and those who have contact with him in the Oval Office. They further suggested that reporters could look more profitably at the whole executive process, including the flow of alternative policies as they are sent from office to office before they finally land on the President's desk. This is the part of the story that reporters miss. The manager of this flow of information in the White House during the Ford administration suggested that the people making these important decisions are virtually unknown to reporters because they seldom are visible in conferences with the President and his top advisers.[68]

The success of individual officials and reporters in getting results from manipulative techniques depends in part on relations established during the early days of the administration. More important to the success of the White House is its ability to place the President in dramatic national and international settings and situations, where news organizations seem compelled to follow the agenda set before them. Ultimately, however, White House officials are faced with the fact that manipulating agendas does not restore favorable publicity. Their problem is that the two sides no longer share a definition of news. Consequently the administration finds it more difficult to prevent the media from producing stories that raise issues in ways it doesn't want them raised.

Phase Three: Detachment

The manipulative tactics used by both sides during the phase of competition create antagonisms between White House reporters and officials that are most visible in settings such as the press secretary's daily briefing, which one White House correspondent referred to as the "bear pit."[69] There appears, however, to be a limit to how far conflict may spread. Each side has such fundamental needs for the other that strong elements of cooperation remain at all times. Consequently, the competition phase is followed by a phase of detachment during which the relationship is carried on in a more structured manner than it was in the previous periods, in almost a formal manner.

The timing of the detachment phase usually is determined by the White House. It occurs soonest in those administrations that have little concern for the need to rally mass support for new policies. Since there is little need to persuade reporters to emphasize the advantages of its policies to a large public, the White House's media policy becomes one of getting maximum exposure with the least risk. It is not surprising to find that in the years since the New Deal detachment has usually occurred sooner and has been employed more successfully in Republican than Democratic administrations.

The most important feature of this period is the tendency of presidents to delegate the management of their relations with the press to surrogates. Although the President may continue to meet reporters regularly, he does so in highly controlled and structured situations. The media strategy that is most characteristic of this phase is avoidance.

AVOIDANCE

Avoidance involves manipulating the schedule so that the President appears only in settings the White House thinks are favorable to him. Other settings might draw questions from reporters that lead the President to say something he does not want to say.

White House officials learn how to ration the President's time by trial and error in the months after a new administration takes office. At the beginning of his term, when the pressures are not as great as they will be later, it is easier for the President to make time for the press. At this stage most presidents want to do so because they like what they read in the press and see on the evening news. It is not long before the President finds better ways to spend his time than on impromptu activities with reporters. Instead, events that communicate the President's message are scheduled.

Tight coordination of the scheduling process is particularly important when a president decides to run for reelection. Because the stakes are now greater, his contacts with reporters are even more likely to be carefully structured and calculated than they were in the middle years of his term. During the 1976 campaign the Office of Communications was converted into a major decision-making office for campaign publicity. "During the campaign we were selective in the occasions in which we provided press access to the President," an aide explained. "There were themes we wanted to focus on. You wouldn't want to publicize another issue. So you scheduled in such a way that you had the major event. You selected what you wanted to emphasize and controlled coverage to the extent that we determined what was treated."[70] During the campaign the President's staff spends large amounts of time arranging formal activities best suited to project his presidential qualities. In 1980 Jimmy Carter was able to employ the avoidance strategy as president; as a candidate four years earlier he had strongly criticized the same strategy.

Another aspect of the detachment phase is the relatively greater emphasis by the White House on contact with the regional press and with interest groups, without the filter of the Washington press corps. For example, in a two-week period during April, 1971, the White House prepared sixteen separate mailings that were sent to 146,000 groups, publications, or individuals. Samples of the mailings indicate that they included environment and reorganization booklets sent to 1,100 reporters and news organizations, a presidential statement opposing abortions sent to 198 Catholic media and organizations, a labor mailing to 1,364 labor and finance writers, a copy of a speech President Nixon made in Williamsburg, Virginia, that was sent in booklet form to 11,094 Republican elected officials, a senior citizens proclamation that was sent to 100,000 groups concerned with issues involving the aged, and a copy of an article by conservative columnist James J. Kilpatrick that was sent to 9,273 academicians and a select group of Republican sympathizers.[71]

The response of some reporters during this phase is to explore the use of independent sources of information in Congress, the Office of Management and Budget, the departments, and among lobbyists. Reporters are also more likely to engage in joint endeavors with other reporters in their own news organizations. They thus reap some of the benefits from the division of labor and specialized expertise in the form of a more thorough analysis of White House plans and actions.

The Phases and the Future

The emphasis in this chapter has been on the permanent and recurring characteristics of the relationship between the White House and the news media. The two sides are locked into a close and cooperative relationship by their mutual needs—and one of these is the need to exploit each other. The rules and habits of the relationship perpetuate themselves because of the importance of the latent functions they perform. The complexity of the organizational worlds of both the White House and news organizations required arrangements that form the basis for the continuation of the major features of the relationship from one administration to the next. In theory it would be possible for a president to alter radically the basis of the relationship, but such efforts were made and failed during the Johnson and Nixon administrations. Thus Presidents Ford and Carter recognized that attempts to effect those sorts of changes not only are undesirable, they are potentially damaging. Reporters' styles of covering the White House today show some residual strains from the era of Vietnam and Watergate. Many correspondents eagerly demonstrate in their conduct at briefings or on television talk shows that they do not trust the White House. Nevertheless, the manner in which reporters go about producing stories at the White House would be familiar to observers of the Eisenhower, Kennedy, or early Johnson years.

The fact that it may be described as a "continuing" relationship does not mean that there have been no changes. Most noteworthy, perhaps, is that the institutional changes brought about during the phases of one administration are carried over to the next. For example, the bureaucratization of both the White House and the media has resulted in the creation of permanent offices in the White House that permit the President to develop relations with editors, publishers, the regional press, and interest groups even while he is still developing his relations with the White House press corps. The structured mode of the period of detachment could be seen early in the Carter administration in, for example, the twice-monthly scheduled meetings with non-Washington-based editors and publishers, the regional town meetings, and the phone-ins.

The assertion of the typical pattern of the phases can be seen if we look at a president's effort to be different and presumably "more open" than his predecessors. When President Carter began his term the Office of Public Liaison, which had been an important vehicle for rallying the support of interest groups and regional political leaders to the White House, was transformed, under Midge Costanza, into an office at the White House where outsiders such as the Gay Liberation Front could get a hearing. By 1978 Costanza had been moved to the White House basement, and shortly thereafter she resigned. Anne Wexler, a solid political organizer with considerable experience, was appointed to the position of representative to interest groups, which marked an evolutionary expansion of the function of the director of the Office of Public Liaison under President Ford.

In sum, it appears that throughout the terms of all recent presidents the relationship between the President and the news media has been characterized by strong elements of continuity. No recent president has been so dominant over Congress, the bureaucracy, his political party, or private sector leaders that he has been able to downgrade media relations. For their part, no major news organization has been able to find ways of covering the presidency without the cooperation of the President and White House officials. When the needs of both sides converge, as they usually do at the beginning of an administration, the cooperative elements are dominant. Later, when the President's need to use the news media to build a basis of support for his administration conflicts with reporters' interests in producing stories that feature conflict and inconsistency, each side uses manipulative tactics to achieve its goals. Yet the level of conflict that might be engendered by some of these tactics is limited by continuing mutual needs. That is why detachment follows competition in the relationship between the White House and the news organizations. This period of detente lasts until a new president takes office and the process begins again.

TWELVE

THE REFRACTING LENS

N EWS ORGANIZATIONS provide the mechanism through which influentials in the Washington community as well as important constituencies throughout the nation take their assessment of the President. News about the White House influences the actions of organized interests both within and without government. Congressmen, bureaucrats, and lobbyists base their decisions to grant or withhold support for the President on perceptions gleaned from the media. National concerns as well as the immediate objectives of these important political actors are at stake. White House news has a major impact on the politically inactive segments of the public included in its general audience. Reality as refracted through the lens of the news media is for most people their only glimpse of what is going on at the White House. It provides them with a basis to judge the person who occupies the Oval Office and suggests the activities that may be needed to secure an individual or a general interest. What the media present to their audience has important consequences for the public as well as for the President, and for political institutions as well as for the individuals and groups who are actors on the national stage.

Until the mid-1960s White House assistants used the media with considerable success to portray a favorable image of presidential leadership. Officials often played on reporters' respect for the office of the President to disguise their man's warts while promoting his image and his issues. Most journalists regarded these activities as part of a harmless game that did not produce significant distortions of reality. Similarly, White House aides seldom stayed angry at news organizations for stories they considered unfair, although deep-seated presidential resentment against unfavorable coverage goes back to the beginning of the republic.

White House–media relations seem to have changed between 1965 and 1974. Especially in the last months before President Nixon resigned, conflict grew between the White House and large segments of the Washington journalism community. Reporters who previously exhibited a high tolerance for White House smoke screens suggested that the President and his chief advisers told lies and withheld information about important events. During the Vietnam War and the Watergate crisis, large groups within news organizations and a substantial portion of their audiences began to suspect that what the White House presented as reality on one day might turn out to be inoperative on the next. Many observers still look back on this period as a decade of deception.

The spillover from this era of conflict continues to affect the relationship. Although most officials responsible for Vietnam policy and Watergate have departed, many reporters remain suspicious of both public White House pronouncements and informal background explanations they are offered. Yet what is striking about the postcrisis era is that by the middle of the 1970s most elements of traditional White House–media relations had reemerged. What goes on today involves a continuing relationship with a high degree of predictability, a stable process of exchanges marked more by cooperation than conflict, and recurring patterns of behavior as the relationship passes through similar phases in each administration during which the interests of officials and journalists merge or divide.

The predictable, stable, and recurring aspects of the relationship are based on permanent and underlying trends that have shaped both sides throughout the period of the modern presidency. For the White House, the main forces affecting its activities are themselves the products of the extensive institutionalization that has taken place in the office of the President. Presidents and their chief assistants have created an enormous apparatus for political communications that consists of press aides, speechwriters, public liaison officials, directors of communications, and many others who influence both what appears in the media and the reaction of the audience. Although reorganizations of these offices may occur, each new administration discovers the existence of traditional functions and routines that the staff is expected to perform. Similarly, the Chief Executive's publics expect him to play the same role as his predecessors as the nation's chief communicator. They expect him to define the nature of national problems and then to propose solutions.

The same type of forces affect the media. Journalists cover and present information about the President for news enterprises that are themselves bureaucratic organizations making decisions and conducting operations according to established routines. What they define as news about the White House depends on limits determined by the form of media in which the story appears, the nature and structure of the particular news organizations, the expectations of editors and producers as to who is in the audience, and the accommodations individual reporters have made with the ethos of their profession.

Even some of the enduring changes brought about by Vietnam and Watergate are exaggerations of trends that have always been part of the ebb and flow of the relationship. For example, presidents and their advisers are tempted to manipulate the media because it is easy to do, especially at the beginning of a term or in the midst of an international crisis, when news is defined as whatever the President says and does. At the same time, the discovery that they have been manipulated leads reporters and editors to become cynical about all White House activities. In the case of Vietnam and

Watergate, this price was paid by subsequent presidents as well as those who were responsible for the policies at the time. Because the Johnson and Nixon administrations succeeded for long periods in their efforts to manipulate both the press and public opinion, many later journalists pursued a more antagonistic style of reporting White House developments than was common prior to 1965. Presidents Ford and Carter were both hampered in their efforts to reap the traditional benefits accrued by the nation's chief communicator.

Although post-Vietnam and post-Watergate reporters expressed doubts about the credibility of the White House in print or on television, the techniques and routines of reporting about the President remain much the same. Reporters find numerous ways to inform their audience that they do not regard the White House as a reliable source. Elite journalists, such as syndicated columnists, frequently suggest to their readers that what the President has said—or what his staff has claimed for him—is prima facie implausible. Although major newspapers such as the *New York Times* and the *Washington Post* reflected their concern about relying on traditional sources of information by increasing institutional coverage of the White House, in much of the media the new antagonism has been expressed in personal terms. In particular, television has been a major arena for the expression of this conflict, both because White House officials believe it is so important to their cause and because its emphasis on the public activities of the President makes it susceptible to manipulation. Television reporters have not chosen to confront the White House directly by changing the manner in which they cover and report the news—the networks' presentation of the presidency has not changed much in the past decade. What has occurred is that reporters now present news about the White House along with an item that casts doubt on the credibility of what has been said or on the reliability of the person who has said it. They indicate to their viewers that a cynical approach is a realistic approach when analyzing the motives of the President and his advisers.

There is one overriding implication of these long-term trends bearing on what the White House can expect to get out of its relations with the media: the President must understand that the way he communicates to his publics affects popular perception of him and his policies. Just as power tends to adhere to those presidents who sense what it is made of, favorable publicity comes to those presidents who have a sense for dramatizing and personalizing issues and policies. Jimmy Carter misunderstood this aspect of presidential roles and thought he could choose whether or not to be a communicator. He did not have such a choice, and he did not understand the consequences of not meeting the expectations of those in Washington and throughout the nation who wanted him to explain himself with force and precision. That he did not perform this role resulted in adverse judgments of his performance as a leader.

In a similar vein, a president woos trouble if he does not understand the appropriate use of White House communications facilities. Chief executives and their staffs have found that the enormous growth of resources available to the White House makes the domination of information received by the public a temptation. This should be resisted, however sweet its immediate fruits, because manipulation ultimately detracts from the President's effectiveness in political communications. The real value of a well-run and effectively organized publicity apparatus is that it enables the President to overcome advantages possessed by Congress, the bureaucracy, and interest groups, all of whom have better channels to communicate with their own group members or with particular segments of the public than does the President. On the whole, White House aides understand the value of using their resources in this manner, although many dream of finding a magic formula that would create a more supportive press. Beginning with the term of Dwight D. Eisenhower, each successive administration's publicity operations have shown some improvement over those of its predecessor once the President sorted out problems with staff assignments and internal White House power conflicts. An administration's failures in political communications seldom have been failures in management. It is not surprising that most presidents have preferred to cite poor management or media hostility as explanations for their poor reception by the public rather than any problems with their performance or the content of their messages.

The central impact of permanent underlying forces on the media is that news organizations have become actors of considerable significance in the American political system. They play a number of important public roles, including influencing the selection and removal of those who hold office, determining the public perception of the importance of many issues, and interpreting the significance of a leader's activities. Nonetheless, news organizations are neither traditional political actors nor a fourth branch of government. They do not have clearly defined objectives, as do interest groups, and they do not seek power in the sense of winning and holding office, as do most politicians. Most media organizations do not seek to determine electoral or policy outcomes, with the exception of a few matters about which their owners and managers care deeply, or about which a few columnists, editors, and elite reporters do have opinions.

What might be said of news organizations is that they strive to become the arbiters of the political system. They legitimize and delegitimize individuals, points of view of issues, and even institutions such as the presidency itself. News enterprises act as if they set the ethical norms for candidates and the criteria by which policies are to be evaluated. In sum, these organizations attempt to establish the criteria of rectitude for political operations in the United States. It is no wonder that the other actors, including the President, resent them.

The Presidency and Political Communications

Critical analyses of the media's coverage of the presidency have focused on two contradictory elements: first, the problems created by the press for the duly elected head of the executive branch; second, the continued domination by the White House of what and how reporters cover the news.[1] To some extent, the type of criticism reflects the partisan or policy positions of whoever is making it at a particular time, as indicated in the following comment attacking the White House for withholding information: "The concept of a return to secrecy in peacetime demonstrates a profound misunderstanding of the role of a free press as opposed to that of a controlled press. The plea for secrecy could become a cloak for errors, misjudgments and other failings of government.''[2] When Richard Nixon made those remarks in 1961 after the failure of the American-backed invasion of Cuba at the Bay of Pigs, he was concerned about a coverup of the affair by the Kennedy administration. Obviously, his perspective had changed considerably by 1972 when his White House staff prepared an official secrets act that would have made the publication of national defense material about the "military capability of the United States or an associate nation'' a criminal action.[3]

Other observers, including most of those interviewed for this study, made similar comments. They suggested that reporters are both too overbearing and too compliant in their relations with White House spokesmen and sources. In spite of the apparent contradiction, both criticisms are relevant. Although White House officials have retained the powers that led them to their traditional position of advantage over the media, many organizational changes and alterations of the rules of reporting have worked in favor of the press. The enlargement and institutionalization of the White House publicity apparatus has provided the President with mechanisms to influence and at times control what news organizations present to the public. At the same time, the increased ability and willingness of news organizations to present an independent and critical version of White House activity to the public is one of the most important recent changes involving the status of the media in national political life.

PERSPECTIVE FOR THE 1980s

Because each president in the modern era has brought different styles, ideals, and tactics to political communications, political observers have tended to emphasize the unfixed, unpredictable, and idiosyncratic elements of White House relations with the news media. We suggest that this always was incorrect. Defining White House–news media relations in terms of what may have been dramatic events when they occurred involves an exclusive concern with the President's personal relations with a small number of people on his staff and with news organizations. A narrow focus, even when placed on important relations, distorts the larger reality.

A more complete portrait of the relationship includes a picture of a highly stratified White House in which the President is the central and most exposed figure, and representatives of the bureaucracies of news organizations of whom reporters are the most visible. While the White House is concerned with the President's problems of sending communications to his various publics and constituencies, the representatives of news organizations are fulfilling institutional goals of keeping the public focus on what they consider to be the newsworthy activities of the President.

In the 1980s it is even more likely that the institutional setting will provide a stage that limits the behavior of an administration toward news organizations. Each new incumbent will discover that his relations with the media are limited by structural constraints, just as they are with Congress, segments of the bureaucracy such as the defense and foreign policy establishments, and bureaucratized lobbies such as those representing labor and business. A president often must do what is expected of him. Although different personal styles provide some opportunities for varied approaches, each new president will discover that he has far less leeway to reshape his relations with news organizations than he anticipated when he ran for the office. Even if he exercises his option to change the format for his contacts with the small group of reporters and media executives who follow him full time, he must fulfill some of their expectations or pay a price. If, for example, the President does not present himself to them on some regular basis, reporters will treat other informants as the authentic sources for accounts of his administration. Accounts by these informants will lack the authority of his own words. Because they may provide varying accounts of his activities, the resulting story may lend credibility to a picture in which he appears to be uncertain of his role or incompetent in command.

In the next decade we can expect the continuing evolution of several major aspects of the contemporary relationship. Presidents will come to need the media more and more; news organizations will continue to move away from cooperation—but not too far; the working relationship between the media and the White House will be part of the story about the President; coverage by the media will continue to be more favorable than unfavorable, although the ratio will decline; and, finally, the publicity operations conducted by and for a chief executive will be an index to his concept of the presidency.

The continuing need for the media. During the 1980s presidents will continue to depend on news organizations as the primary means of sending messages. The relationship between the White House and the news media is vital for a president because of the decline in the layers of institutions that once transmitted news, information, and orders from the President to appropriate audiences throughout the country. As recently as the Eisenhower administration, Congress, the bureaucracy, and interest groups could send their leaders to the White House and then communicate a message from or about the President to an attentive constituency. All of these institutions have been decentralized, and their leadership is no longer in the same position of command or as respected as it once was, with the possible exception of lobbies for major corporations, which appear to be better organized and more effective now than at any time in the recent past. All other indications point to continuing fragmentation in the 1980s. Congressional leaders have neither the same sense of their membership nor the same authority over them as they did in 1960. The bureaucracy continues to grow less susceptible to central control. Most interest groups represent special concerns and single-issue constituencies rather than broad economic and social segments of the society.

Both the White House and the leadership of these groups will increase their dependence on the media. Presidents will continue to be frustrated by what they cannot or will not accomplish through the exercise of their powers of command. The public appears to be the only group capable of helping them overcome their frustrations. News organizations provide a president with a route to the public, including the constituencies of all those leaders in Washington who either cannot or will not cooperate with him. The stakes for the President will grow in proportion to the degree with which information within Washington and among influentials throughout the country funnels through the media. Therefore, it is likely that White House publicity operations will continue to grow in order to permit coordination between direct political communications operations such as Public Liaison and Congressional Liaison. Press operations will be the central channel.

The increasing independence of the media. If there ever was a golden age of partnership between the White House and the news media, it existed during the eight years of the Eisenhower administration. Undoubtedly part of the explanation for the overwhelmingly favorable coverage Eisenhower received is that the President's superb sense of publicity emphasized his almost heroic stature. In addition, the intelligent management of White House–media relations by Press Secretary James Hagerty reinforced the proclivities of news organizations to provide time and space for the administration's message and image. Many reporters shared the admiration of citizens for the wartime leader turned political head, while the top layer of senior editors and publishers found that Eisenhower's policies reflected their views. As they had since Roosevelt's day, the media turned to the White House to supply focus and drama to political news. The close working relationship journalists and officials had established during World War II continued during the cold war of the 1950s. News organizations accepted what they were told by the government, at least until the administration was caught lying in the U-2 incident of 1960.

The decline in the partnership that began after Eisenhower left office scarcely was noticeable during the Kennedy administration because the amount of White House coverage increased. The new president received publicity from a vastly expanded Washington press corps that arrived at about the time of his inauguration. Although Kennedy complained that news organizations provided less support for him than they had for Eisenhower, he later admitted that during crucial episodes, such as the Bay of Pigs invasion, he wished they had been less cooperative. Lyndon Johnson, however, suffered no such ambivalent feelings. He was dismayed after his first months in office when he found that news organizations pursued their separate goals in spite of his courting and cajoling. Later, his and Richard Nixon's demand that news organizations remain loyal during tension over Vietnam ultimately backfired. During the weeks prior to President Nixon's resignation, the White House–media partnership was dissolved.

Although important elements of the partnership have been restored under Ford and Carter, cooperation has continued to decline at approximately its pre-1965 rate. The growing independence of news organizations can be attributed to the size and stability of the major enterprises; to the talents, sophistication, and sheer numbers of journalists who compete to turn up information about blameworthy and therefore newsworthy White House activities; and to the underlying consensus among the media's elite that the failure to resolve national problems should be laid at the White House door. Thus the direction that news organizations have chosen for themselves lessens the likelihood of prolonged periods of partnership during the next decade.

Presidents and their advisers worry about how to reverse this trend, but the usefulness of their concern is questionable, because they can do little to change it. The fact that news organizations follow the beat of their own drummers ought to be, at most, a matter of discomfort, not a subject for dismay. Past performance indicates that news organizations will communicate the essential message and image of a president whose mastery of the arts of political communications includes an ability to formulate and articulate a coherent description of his intention. The pre-Watergate Nixon administration was able to achieve most communications objectives, even though most news organizations always kept their critical distance. Of course major developments distract the media from efforts by any White House persuaders, as Nixon and others have discovered.

White House–media relations as part of the story. Members of the White House staff have applied more energy and have gained more expert knowledge from time applied to learning about the needs and routines of news organizations than they have almost any other subject. There are few people who work as White House aides in the area of political communications who do not understand that the needs of news organizations must be serviced, that reporters should get answers to their questions, and that honesty is the best policy—or at least that outright lying is usually disastrous. In a book about his experiences as press secretary to President Ford, Ronald Nessen described an incident soon after his appointment when he was tempted to mislead his former colleagues in the press. His associates on the White House staff not only were startled at his suggestion, they were also incredulous at his assumption that he would not get caught.[4] They undoubtedly knew that a story about a Nessen lie would become a lead item in what major news organizations, especially television, would present to the public.

Because news organizations have become major participants in the processes of White House politics, conflicts between the media and the White House have become an important part of stories about a presidency. In addition, as White House publicity operations have become institutionalized, they have become personalized and thus a subject for reporters who want to portray the activities of the President's assistants. As these activities have become the focus of White House political communications, they have become items discussed among media people in their forums, in the books and journals on the press that began to appear in the late 1950s, and, slowly, as part of the daily stories. This evolving interest was resisted by important segments of the journalistic community, however, because of the conviction that the internal operations and problems of the press were not a legitimate news story.

White House–media relations became a major story because of three important developments during the 1960s and 1970s. First, the issues of news management and the President's credibility that were raised during Vietnam affected support for the war; second, the Nixon administration's war against the media legitimized the story for all but the most reluctant members of the media's old guard; and finally, the emergence of individual reporters as heroes during Watergate accelerated the public's acceptance of them as being part of the story. The trends stemming from these developments continued during the remaining years of the 1970s, and it seems likely that they will be part of the picture during the 1980s. Presidents can expect to see stories about the relations between the White House and reporters in the extensive feature sections of newspapers and magazines, on talk shows, and in specialized publications such as journalism reviews.

Continuing favorable stories about the President. There is no doubt that trends in the White House–media relationship emphasize its adversary elements; despite this, a large number of stories about any president will continue to be favorable.* At the beginning of a presidential term, both news organizations and their audience can be expected to exhibit a keen interest in the nation's new First Family and its plans for governing. Although these stories become less important when the controversies of the day dominate the news, they continue to be found on the inside pages of newspapers and as feature stories on television. In addition, personal stories are featured by family, home, women's, and "people" magazines throughout a term. These stories invariably are favorable, although officials sometimes view them as negative because they mention family problems such as divorce, drink, or scrapes with the law by members of the younger generation. Stories about presidents' brothers, especially younger brothers, seem to be the one exception to this pattern of positive impact.

Presidents have a number of opportunities to recapture enough positive stories to maintain their favorable impact on their Washington and national

*See chapter 10, "Images of the White House in the Media," figures 4 and 7 and table 8.

audiences. When a president seizes the initiative and appears to take strong measures to resolve or respond to a crisis, news organizations ordinarily line up behind him. At the onset of the Iran and Afghanistan crises during the last months of 1979, major news organizations permitted the President to have almost unlimited access to their columns and broadcasts. Although some nationally syndicated writers demurred, the overall impact was to relegitimize the Carter presidency at a time when it seemed near collapse.

Publicity operations as an index to a presidency. Near the beginning of the twentieth century Woodrow Wilson suggested that a President's relations with his cabinet provided an index to his concept of the presidency.[5] During the last decades, the way in which the Chief Executive has conducted publicity operations and his relations with news organizations has provided the best measure of his understanding of how he expects to fulfill the central role of communicator. The way in which he conducts publicity operations provides an indication of the degree to which he sees himself as an explainer of policy and actions. A president's publicity campaigns thus reflect important aspects of his presidency. A fragmented sense of publicity and communications are products of a fragmented presidency. A president who centralizes publicity in the White House usually centralizes power there. The control that a few White House aides exercise over interviews given throughout the executive branch shows how far the Chief Executive has moved from his promises of an open presidency. Since publicity operations are of such critical importance, it is useful to look at some of the perceptions and misperceptions shared by recent presidents about their relations with the media.

PERCEPTIONS AND MISPERCEPTIONS

Those who work at the White House believe the President's reputation in the Washington community and his public prestige throughout the nation are the key determinants of his influence. Richard Neustadt, who introduced this notion of the basis of presidential power to the public, described the Washington community as an entity that based its judgments on impressions received through multiple conduits of information, including the news media.[6] The contemporary White House looks to its relations with the media as the most important factor determining its reputation and prestige. Officials have a good sense of several important elements of the relationship. Unlike reporters, who often minimize their institutional (although not their personal) roles, White House officials consider news organizations to be important political actors. In both interviews and conversations, officials described to us their relations with news organizations in analytical terms that would indicate that they think about these relations and discuss them among staff members.

There are a great many aspects of their relations with news organizations that presidents and their advisers accurately perceive. They usually know who is important; their sense of the configuration among elite journalists is usually correct. While print media reporters complain about their zealous courting of the electronic media, officials know that although television may not be the basic source of information for elites in Washington, it is essential for the vast majority of citizens, especially those with a low level of attention (not to be confused with interest) to national affairs.

Many reporters complain that the White House is neither responsive nor sensitive to their individual and organizational needs. This is not true. White House officials often understand the operations of news structures such as television networks or newsweeklies better than anyone other than the correspondents who work for the enterprises. With a few infrequent but notable exceptions, they provide all reasonable services required by correspondents. Some reporters, like all presidents, have long memories of every real or imagined grievance. Like a president who can reel off incident after incident of press errors and distortions and irresponsible reporting, these reporters cite a litany of Press Office goof-ups in the form of incomplete information or inaccurate statements. Such complaints, even if accurate, are misleading. Just as a president's activities, character, and style are accurately reflected by the press over the course of his term, the White House does provide most news organizations with the necessary access and information.

Yet, although White House assistants and even most presidents are knowledgeable about the technical aspects of media operations, they continue to misperceive several important features of their relationship with news organizations and their representatives. One set of misperceptions stems from their view that the presidency is the central political institution on which the success of the republic is hinged. From this they conclude that the press ought to be supportive. They believe that at the very least the media should transmit the President's message to the people without amendments, analysis, or interpretations. Another set of misperceptions stems from the view that there is some sort of magic formula that will generate good publicity and favorable coverage. Their search for a publicity elixir stems from their view that the right combination of publicity factors will make news organizations supportive, or at least get them to be "accurate."

Thus presidents and their staffs try to hire alchemists to develop publicity because they confuse strategies for getting political communications across with the substance of the message they send out. Recent presidents have searched for a publicity genius who would ensure that the message news organizations sent out about them would be positive. Lyndon Johnson thought that John Kennedy had that genius in Pierre Salinger. He expected his press secretaries to perform a kind of magic that had no relationship to what he did as president. Richard Nixon tried to be that genius himself, since he could find no one with the required qualities. While he got tremendous mileage from the shrewd use of resources available to him, these tactics could not prevent the true character of his administration from coming through. Publicity cannot change the appearance of an administration for more than a short time. It cannot take someone or something and make it into what it is not. Publicity can be an aid in pulling together the message that an administration wants to communicate when that message is complicated and fragmented. It cannot invent a message; at best, it simply delivers it in the most effective way, at the right time, and to the correct audience.

Perhaps the most common practical application of these misperceptions may be seen in the attempts of the White House to make personal relations between the President and representatives of news organizations into a forum to affect the way the President is portrayed in the media. Because presidents do maintain contacts with a small group of reporters, columnists, editors, bureau chiefs, anchorpersons, and media executives, most of them believe that their personal relations with journalists will be more productive of good publicity than they really can be. The efforts of some presidents in this regard have at times been ludicrous. Lyndon Johnson indicated to reporters that he would put in a good word for them with their "bosses" if they cooperated—not an enticing offer to men who already were near the top of their profession. Most other presidents have shared Johnson's belief in the importance of personal relations. In a number of instances they have tried to rid themselves of a particular journalist by telling his editor or bureau chief that they thought the reporter was hostile and unfair. In a number of instances presidents or their aides have suggested to news executives that their organizations would be better treated if the reporter were replaced.

Although strident language and blatant threats rarely succeed, the more subtle technique of not responding in a timely manner to a reporter's need for information and access has led to problems for correspondents. The fact that the White House seldom employs punishments does not mean that the possibility that they might be imposed does not have an effect on some reporters. Most news organizations want reporters who are well regarded at the White House. Organizations expect their representatives to spend a great deal of time and energy covering the public activities of the President, so reporters need assistance from inside sources so that they will not be caught unaware of important developments and so that they may explain complex activity, such as monetary policy or defense strategy, that is beyond their professional familiarity. Such help is usually an important ingredient in a successful career for reporters assigned to the beat. Thus White House pressures on reporters may succeed in altering the behavior of some and in getting others reassigned, although it would be difficult to prove that the pressures were the direct cause in either case. A reporter who is the victim of a White House freeze-out may be regarded as too abrasive by his or her organization. Reporters are sensitive to this possibility. Few correspondents want to take the chance of being regarded as a failure at what executives at news organizations regard as one of the most prestigious assignments in the media.

A more positive attempt by presidents to exploit the benefits of their personal relations with journalists involves calling meetings in which they talk informally and off the record with reporters and executives of news organizations. Most presidents and their advisers believe that if journalists meet with the President in the White House setting, they will gain and report a positive vision of the Chief Executive's capacities to deal with the nation's problems. Officials expect that reporters will be impressed by the setting as well as by the man. Correspondents may feel awed at their proximity to power. In fact, this technique does provide some short-run benefits. Many reporters who are treated to such meetings do prepare favorable stories about the President that are displayed prominently by their news organizations.

Especially after the initial period of cooperation that exists during the first months of a new administration has been replaced by the competitive phase, White House officials attempt to build on these personal relations between reporters and the President. They hope that what results will enable them to recapture the dominance over the news they enjoyed earlier. However, since what news organizations are interested in at this time are stories about conflict within the administration or between the White House and opponents in Congress or the private sector, the salutary effects of these personal contacts with news organizations are short-lived. In contrast to what presidents believe, the importance of personal relations is marginal. The fact that reporters have been impressed by the President in a meeting, or even that they feel indebted to him for the help he has offered, does provide the White House with an additional benefit, but it will not distract reporters from what they are after.

WHAT A PRESIDENT NEEDS TO KNOW

In a political system in which fragments of power are held by many, a president needs to learn how to use the advantages and resources of his office if he is to pull together his position's potential to command and to persuade. Whether the office is inherently weak or inherently imperial, the notion that the President can gain a monopoly of power at the national level does not fit the experience of chief executives during the post–World War II period. His agenda is often set by others or events. What he needs to know in order to influence the political process is how to distinguish the avenues of power from the dead ends. In the area of political communications, this means that the President and his staff must understand four essential points: first, that even though they may be outsiders who have just arrived in Washington, they do not start off with a clean slate; second, that political communications must be well integrated in the White House, but that the appearance that an administration speaks with several voices reflects the unavoidable reality that they do speak with several voices; third, that there are fixed and malleable aspects to the President's relations with the news media that all who deal with publicity should learn to distinguish; and, finally, that the role of the President as a communicator must be understood by all so that they can adjust the mechanisms of communications to suit his personality and talents.

The election or succession of a new president is, in part, a transfer of power from one leader and his entourage to another and, in part, a transition from one group of office-holders to another. As a transfer, the changes that the new office-holders may bring about are limited only by the forces that impelled them into office and the groups that form the basis of their support. After a clear victory for a side—rather than for a person as in the two Eisenhower wins—as in 1932 and 1936, the President mobilizes his supporters to bring about changes. Of course reading and understanding the nature of a winning coalition's demands and then translating them into policies is not always easy. After a close election, some Presidents have proceeded with considerable caution. Following the 1960 election, John Kennedy stated his goals, but he was reluctant to try to mobilize the power of his office behind them for fear that his support would dissolve. On the other hand, after Richard Nixon won an almost equally close election in 1968, he mobilized his supporters into adversaries without concern that he was polarizing the opposition.

The Washington community regards an election as a transition. The permanent government expects the President and his staff to maintain the status quo. Although its members want to please the new leadership, they expect the new group to move slowly in changing routines. They may be ready to make minimal adjustments to suit the style and personality of the new group, but more dramatic changes must be made gradually, after there is an opportunity to adjust. It is in this area that a new administration has a lesson to learn. It does not start with a clean slate. As the new government, it is expected to perform continuing leadership roles as legislators, bureaucrats, and managers of the national security. As chief communicator, the President must touch base not only with his constituencies, but also with those groups who will implement his ideas by changing them into words and images. In his relations with the media, a new president is supposed to resume the "open presidency" that characterizes the beginning of each administration. News organizations expect he will provide them with at least the same level of accoutrements they already possess, that his staff will keep reporters informed of his smallest movements and the possibilities of major developments, and that officials will be available for both on-the-record and background meetings.

Most presidents know that failure to satisfy these expectations may bring prompt retaliation. In fact, some administrations welcome such conflict. What they should understand is that the real consequences will not come as a result of retaliation—few news organizations really want to go toe-to-toe with the White House or let their reporters do it for them. Instead, they will stem from the efforts news organizations will make to fulfill their institutional goals without help from the White House. If denied traditional avenues of access and information, they will travel along paths that the White House would prefer were off-limits to the press. Most administrations don't recognize this, especially during the early weeks of their term, when everything seems to be going their way anyway. Later, when an administration finds things going less smoothly, the President may relent, and try to establish the traditional pattern.

Reporters may be invited in for "Cocktails with Clawson." A president may bring in an adviser for communications to "Rafshoonize" the process. By that time, it is probably too late. The administration's image in the media has been sculpted in bronze.

A second point an administration should understand when it takes office involves the relations between its press operations and its other efforts to manage the President's political communications. News operations must be well integrated into an apparatus consisting of several elements that are not obviously part of publicity operations. The central business is scheduling. The President and his aides must determine the best use of his time so they can maximize the impact of his meetings with key national leaders, smaller groups of influentials such as members of Congress below the leadership rank, and larger influential groups such as the AFL-CIO or the Foreign Policy Association, as well as his direct appearances before the public at press conferences and in addresses to the nation. Although almost everyone at the White House has become familiar with the importance of these operations—in this sense, at least, an American presidential campaign prepares its participants for what is to come—they don't always see how these activities of the President must be coordinated with the institutionalized White House lobbying and liaison activities with political leaders, Congress, and interest groups. Nor is it clear to them how these activities fit in with those of the White House Press Office in its dealings with the Washington press corps, or of the Media Liaison operation in its relations with news organizations in their home locations throughout the country.

Yet they should recognize that ultimately almost everything of consequence gets into the press. From the White House point of view, many items "appear" at the most awkward time. Obviously, integrating publicity operations will not hide failures or minimize the damage from major political crises. Vietnam and Watergate did not become major political failures because of poor political communications emanating from the White House, any more than they did because of hostile pictures or distortions presented to the public by news organizations. On the other hand, well-run political communications operations will make it more likely that the media will reflect rather than distort what the White House is doing. White House officials often emphasize the desirability of ensuring that all administration officials speak with one voice. They usually give up in despair at the impossibility of this task after a certain amount of internal bloodletting. If they recognized that it is the direction of their activities that becomes the story, they might concentrate on establishing those priorities they want to reinforce through political communications. They would not waste so much time on the counterproductive activity of quieting dissident voices or the voices of those who merely speak out of turn.

A president and his staff must learn what is fixed and what is malleable in their relations with news organizations. In particular, since they invariably are looking for ways to redress the relationship in favor of the White House, they

must learn that what cannot be changed is the determination of what constitutes news. What they need to understand are the ways in which news organizations are likely to present their activities. A president can "squeeze more
juice out of the orange" when he tries to present his messages through activities that are likely to receive favorable coverage in the media.

Sudden shifts from favorable to unfavorable treatment by news organizations often can be foreseen. Clearly many recent presidents failed to learn this
third lesson. For example, when President Carter retreated to Camp David to
plan a major response to the energy crisis during the summer of 1979, his
disappearance from Washington to hold private discussions with national
leaders caught the attention of the media and the public. For the first time in
months, Carter had an audience that was eager to hear what his message
would be. When he finally came down from the mountain to address the
nation, he had succeeded in switching the public agenda to a subject of his
choosing. When he continued the next day to speak virogously on the same
subject, he was portrayed as a man who was in charge. On the second day
after his speech he changed course and engaged in activities that elicited a
predictably negative response from the media: first, he requested wholesale
letters of resignation from his top advisers and cabinet heads; second, he
followed these requests with acceptances that were immediately regarded as
dismissals. The next event was that the dismissals, rather than Carter's renewed drive for an energy program, became the central story. Furthermore,
news organizations portrayed the simultaneous removal of several influential
cabinet officials as the action of an unstable leadership.

What Carter had done was drive from the front pages and evening news
broadcasts the favorable stories about the renaissance of his administration
that had appeared immediately after his television address. Instead of stories
about an administration taking charge of its own house, the media showed a
frightened leadership that was unable to tolerate strong independent associates
in its midst. Members of the White House staff complained bitterly that news
organizations overdramatized the resignation story, and they were right. What
they should have and did not recognize was how predictable it was that all this
would happen.

An administration can set the stage on which its activities will be observed
and reported. But even though a president may dominate the news agenda, he
cannot distract news organizations from what they see as the central questions. Typically, a president thinks that the media deals with the lesser questions of politics while he tries to communicate the important issues of policy.
Whether he or news organizations are right about what ought to be the news
focus, he cannot change it. There is nothing that a president can do to steer
reporters away from conflict, controversy, scandal, or interesting personality
stories. Nor can he change the frame through which news organizations view
these stories.

Finally, a president must understand that he is expected to be the great national explainer. This means that his public must receive a continuous stream of messages through the media explaining what he wants or does not want to do, with reasons for his actions or inactions. There has been a great deal of concern in the White House, particularly since the advent of live national television, with the question of how much public exposure a president can receive without generating public antipathy. This is certainly not a small issue. The question of whether a president becomes less effective if he speaks too often on too many subjects is important. But the President has to communicate his message all the time, in formats other than an address to the nation. He must address elite audiences of the scientific, technological, economic, religious, ethnic, and political communities. He must use the publicity resources of his office to make certain the message gets through the proper channels of news and the direct links of lobbying. In all of this, the President himself must be an active communicator. If he hides from this role his administration will have major problems on this basis alone. It is not merely a question of being a smooth salesman. The whole process by which leadership is glued together is at stake.

The Media as Actors in Presidential Politics

Since the Eisenhower administration, the media have reflected an erosion of support for the institution of the presidency and perhaps have helped to shape the perception that less support is deserved. From the perspective of the White House, their role has shifted from that of cheerleaders to that of demonstrators. The changes that have taken place, however, are more the result of an evolutionary process affecting news organizations and the journalists who work for them than a fundamental shift in loyalties. The growth of the major news enterprises' organizational structures has made it possible for journalists to cover the President in ways that suit their inclinations, ways that previously they had been unable to employ. The large financial resources commanded by the broadcasting industry have permitted the networks to cover the presidency with an immediacy and an intensity that have magnified the faults in the institution and its occupant. Publications use their new technological and human resources to explore dimensions of presidential activities that were not covered in the past.

INFLUENCING AND BEING INFLUENCED

News from the White House alters Washington's political landscape. As actors in presidential politics, news organizations force some decisions and prevent others from being made. They influence what the President does and what others in the Washington community do in response. But there are limits to the ability of news organizations to change the public's assessments. There is no evidence that journalists' efforts could reverse strong currents of opinion. Whether a president is well thought of or has a poor reputation, the media cannot do much to change the public's opinion about him.

The relationship's balance of power, which is still favorable for the presidency, prevents both sides from becoming full-time adversaries. It is true that the corps of journalists have shifted away from their easy alliance with and protection of the White House that characterized an earlier period. Many reporters focus on the problems of the administration from a cynical or even an antagonistic point of view. At the same time, reporters swing back to portraying favorable aspects of a president. Although his problems create the most intense audience interest, news organizations need his successes to reflect the presidency's status as the central political institution of the nation. Without a cycle of successes and failures, the media's coverage of the President would have far less impact. Warts on an ugly person are of far less interest than the appearance of blemishes on someone who is expected to look beautiful.

Contemporary news organizations hire journalists with much better training and more impressive credentials than they did in 1936 when Leo Rosten published his classic study of Washington correspondents. A top reporting or editing position with one of the better organizations today requires an individual to pass standards of employment at least as high as those of the best-run corporations, law firms, or universities. In one important respect, however, little has changed. Although reporters have definite views about the rules of the game, they don't harbor commitments to political causes or policy outcomes. Some White House correspondents indicated that they did not vote in presidential elections. While a few in this group explained their position as an effort to remain uninfluenced by their own desires during a political campaign, others suggested that they just don't care who wins.

In but a few respects are what appear as the media's judgments a product of journalists' own judgments. The shape of stories that news organizations present to the public is molded by such factors as the views of the well-positioned sources who talk to reporters and editors, the trends of public opinion, and the groupthink of the crowd of journalists concerned with the story. With rare exceptions, and these mostly among columnists and commentators, their views are not based on ideological or partisan positions. Personal vendettas, although more frequent, are restrained either by the news organization or by the widespread knowledge that what is appearing is in fact the outcome of a personal vendetta.

The way in which reporters frame their stories about the President to a large extent reflects the opinions of influentials in the Washington community. For example, the evaluation made by many journalists that Jimmy Carter revealed himself to be a bumbler and an incompetent may have been a congressional creation that was moved through the media to the public. Dennis Farney described the process by which this impression was created: "Carter came in as an outsider, and frightened and perplexed members of Congress. . . . He came in as a tough bastard who was going to stop dams. Then he went to a supplicant's position. He started complimenting Congress in the most unconvincing ways. So they talked to journalists and were judging him by the way that other Presidents behaved. It dawned on members that this guy could be had.'"[7]

Because reporters were influenced by their friends on the Hill, they tended to emphasize Carter's words and deeds that showed him alternately as too demanding or too surrendering. They chose for their articles those items that showed Carter to be ill at ease in Washington, as well as those that showed that he was unable to mobilize support behind coherent programs either in the capital or among the people. If an event involved a change of a decision, the emphasis they placed on the change in their story suggested that the President displayed qualities of indecisiveness.

This picture of Carter represented the prevalent view in Washington. At times and in particular stories it was unfair. The story was not, however, a total fabrication. In general terms it reflected the reality that the outsider Jimmy Carter had much on-the-job training to get through before he could gain control of his office. It reflected the reality that in many important areas Carter had difficulty establishing his priorities, that he had difficulty establishing priorities among areas, and that where he had clearly established certain policies as important priorities, he had not succeeded in convincing others to follow his lead. But if the story was a reflection of the reality, it also contributed to the reality of the story. Carter's reputation, as shaped and hardened by the media, contributed to his difficulties in getting control of his office.

Just as news organizations mirror, form, and reinforce the opinions of influentials, they reflect and shape the public perception of the President as a leader. The trends in opinion that indicate the level of support for the President affect the way the media covers him. Stories tend to be supportive of a president for whom things are going well. They accelerate the decline of a man who is perceived to be not up to the job. Walt Rostow suggested that the press reflects inherent public ambivalence toward the presidency: ''When the President leads and successfully rules the nation, there is in the press as in the people, the tendency to be supportive. When things aren't going well, the press both reflects and amplifies the problems of the nation as reflected in the problems of the President. . . . There is an instinct to do this because we had to create this powerful figure [in 1787, and now want] to cut him down to size.''[8]

The judgments of journalists are influenced not only by others in the Washington establishment and by the national consensus, but also by other journalists. When greater numbers of unfavorable stories about the President appear, news organizations will probably produce more stories viewed from an unfavorable perspective until the trend changes. During the summer of 1978 the percentage of unfavorable stories about the Carter presidency climbed to nearly 25 percent in the three sources of news examined in chapter

10, a trend that appeared among most news organizations. Unfavorable stories produced a momentum for continuing unfavorable stories, as the following example illustrates.

The Roper Organization sampled public sentiment on President Carter's proposed tax reforms in 1978. On July 27 Art Pine wrote a story in the *Washington Post* assessing the results, in which he led with the statement that "a new nationwide tax survey brought more bad news for President Carter." The story went on to maintain that the important disagreements between the people and the President found by the survey "mark another blow for the Carter Administration." Ten days later, on August 6, 1978, another story on the survey appeared by Barry Sussman, who conducts and writes about polls for the *Post*. Sussman indicated that economics correspondent Pine had been mistaken. "Surprise: Public Backs Carter on Taxes" read the headline on the second story analyzing the same poll. "If public opinion is to be cited in the tax debate, it seems only fitting to point out what the public really does think," Sussman wrote. "And if polls that show Carter doing poorly are highly publicized, as they are, those that show him in a favorable light ought to be publicized as well."

ESTABLISHING THE CRITERIA FOR RECTITUDE

One way to examine the role news organizations play in presidential politics is to consider what might happen in the absence of their independent activities. The Vietnam War presents a revealing illustration. President Johnson wanted the media to present stories about Vietnam that supported his version of the war. At first a few stories indicated that their authors did not share the President's assumptions. Most of what appeared in the media pictured events as perceived by reporters and editors who did not disagree in any essential way with the official version. Eventually, however, news organizations ran more stories on developments in Vietnam that were based on a different perspective, stories that the White House thought were harmful and distorted. President Nixon wanted to keep news of American involvement in Cambodia away from the public, but the bombings and invasions were continuing subjects in the media, which remained beyond the President's control. News stories did not stop the invasion, however, nor does the evidence indicate that the media can be judged to be an antiwar group. In fact, Presidents Johnson and Nixon continued to receive a large share of favorable stories about their leadership during this period.

What the press did was to focus on news issues involving the conduct of the war—subjects that made it difficult to portray the leadership in a positive manner. In the end, the picture of the war's futility spread to the public and then to official Washington. When it was clear that he could no longer define the war for public opinion, President Johnson withdrew from politics. The war was covered, but not the way the President wanted. President Nixon was forced to accept a legislative restriction on a president's ability to move militarily in Southeast Asia or in "other Vietnams" throughout the world. This act by Congress was their response to the cross pressures of White House demands that it continue to support its Vietnam policies and the wishes of a large segment of public opinion that was war-weary. Congress yielded to the public. The role of the media was indirect but still of great importance. "The press, not Congress, told the truth of Vietnam," James Reston observed. "And made it part of the conscience of the country."[9]

The news stories about Johnson and Nixon's conduct of the Vietnam War were framed by the judgments that some journalists made about presidential behavior. These judgments became the basis on which a large segment of the public evaluated the two presidents' conduct of the war. Reston may be correct when he states that news organizations performed a service to the nation in the case of the Vietnam War. Viewed from other perspectives, however, there are many instances when this role is played for small stakes and in a petty fashion. Rather than contributing to the evolution of a public conscience, news organizations act as the nation's nanny, bustling with demands for their own version of good conduct. Although no single view of the criteria for rectitude is shared among journalists, the selection of news stories by an organization is imbued with these values.

Their view of what a president is supposed to do is reflected in the questions they ask and the stories they compose. A large percentage of both may be summed up in this query: Is he up to the job? During the primaries and the campaign, a period with an opportunity for considerable access to the candidate, they ask him if he's up to winning and if he's qualified for the job. The questions will be somewhat different when asked by a character assessor such as Bill Moyers, a strategy evaluator such as David Broder, or the average reporter who asks, "What makes you think you can carry Texas?" In office, elite journalists and columnists focus on their version of whether he is tough enough to make the hard decisions. The stories of other reporters frame his behavior in the context of their views of such qualities as decisiveness, ability to handle people, effectiveness with Congress, diplomacy, and sympathy with the people. Although their evaluations would be different because their viewpoints are different, they are all asking the same question: Is he the right kind of president?

Journalists are also on the lookout for conflicts of interest and shady behavior. Some elite journalists, especially those with a strong commitment to substantive policy positions, are less concerned with this. Editors and reporters who have a high tolerance for personal shenanigans ignore some of the smaller stories in this area, especially when they involve someone who has been a good source. It may be that it is organizations rather than individual reporters who regard this issue as a personal morality play. It also may be that what is involved is the intense drama of seeing the ground turn to quicksand under the feet of someone who had been a strong public figure. Basically, however, these stories permit journalists to assert their values as to the proper rules of the game in presidential politics or national political life. Their unstated and perhaps unconscious premise is that they should be the judges.

COPING

Although some of the men and women who come to Washington as reporters may dream of covering a story that will blow the lid off the Capitol dome and let in the air of reform, most veteran journalists are uneasy with their role as participants in the political system. Their self-perception is that they cope with the routines of their beat. Although a few deny that they are actors and many suggest that their power is vastly overrated, almost all are aware that public perceptions of them in Washington and in the nation are quite different.

There are a number of political roles that most journalists admit they play: they identify problems that the White House has to deal with; they make interpretations that, especially when accompanied by leaked information, can influence the decisions that are made; they stimulate investigations; they change timetables; they contribute to a separate information channel in Washington that carries some important matters. Finally, their most direct political role involves their relationship with the White House.

News organizations identify problems that require specific governmental or political actions by the White House. Events frequently become problems for the President because they are reported in the media. The unbuttoned remarks of a high official who hadn't realized that he was on the record create problems for the White House, as does an encounter with a legal problem by a member of the staff. This latter situation can be particularly embarrassing because it may lead to the media's reporting previous occasions when the same event had occurred but when the law had not been involved. Sometimes the questions reporters ask at the briefing identify problems the administration can expect to face. Most frequently the press is an actor forcing a response from the White House because the matters raised in news stories would not have surfaced through bureaucratic channels. "The press could provide information that would lead to a policy decision," an aide to President Ford recalled. "I would say that two or three times a week there is a press account that leads [the President] to ask a question."[10]

When stories appear in an influential news source interpreting an event in a manner unfavorable to the President, many White House officials respond with steps to defend the President's image. They are particularly alarmed when stories stress political complications, because they fear that the prediction of problems may become a self-fulfilling prophecy. Thus a story about a vote against a legislative proposal that is interpreted to mean that the President is in trouble in Congress may soften the President's support in Congress among his marginal followers there. They are especially concerned with obtaining a positive interpretation during a political campaign because they (and journalists) believe that an image of success creates its reality. The most damaging result occurs when a story interpreting a controversial decision is accompanied by leaked information. When that happens, as was the case during the Kennedy administration's Skybolt missile crisis, officials have to react quickly to stave off embarrassment. "It [the story] led to some rather hasty decisions," Walt Rostow recalled.[11]

News organizations also influence outcomes by stimulating investigations. Although the media have no legal power to investigate wrongdoing and cannot require that reporters be given information, press reports may create a demand for a government investigation. Once the investigation is underway, news organizations present reports that affect the reputations of those conducting the investigation and those who are the subject of its scrutiny. Sometimes government officials will leak information to the press that they hope will stimulate an investigation that they could not get by going through channels.

What appears in the press can change the White House timetable, particularly on questions involving appointments or dismissals. In 1975 President Ford and his advisers decided to make cabinet changes in a dramatic way in order to put his stamp on the administration he inherited from Richard Nixon. When the press released the story, it had the opposite effect. "It gave the public the appearance that it was a disorderly process," a Ford official explained. "It took several weeks to really get that behind us."[12]

In another political role, the media operate an internal network that provides information to Washington insiders. At one time they passed on personal information of importance about the health or personal activities of prominent political figures. The importance of this network declined during the 1970s because news organizations began publishing hearsay information about people and activities that was previously off limits. Nevertheless, reporters still provide as well as pick up information from their sources. Reporters may inform officials of what they believe to be the story about their counterparts in other organizations, although they are not ready for that story to appear in the media. Some officials want to befriend reporters so they can "cultivate their sources."

Finally, the relationship between news organizations and the White House is itself a form of political activity. Efforts by the White House to shape what appears in the media is a recognition by the President's assistants that it is a basic relationship affecting his reputation, his policies, and the quality of support he receives from the public and influentials in Washington. As we have indicated throughout this book, journalists are not innocent participants in this relationship, although they do chafe at both institutional and conscious manipulation by the White House. They don't like to be channeled, and, of course, they are outraged when they are deceived. Most of the time, however, they are partners, even when they are being used by the White House. "Actually, however, the real strength of government in the communications process comes from . . . its ability to trade on the hunger of the communications media for news about public affairs," Francis Rourke wrote in 1961: "Critics of government information activity often draw a picture of newsmen as the unwilling victims of government propaganda. Often, however, newspapers themselves are so anxious to get the inside story from official sources on a current issue of domestic or international importance that they will become willing if not enthusiastic collaborators in the process by which government influences public opinion.''[13]

White House Reporting: Adequate or Not?

For a brief period after the revelations of Watergate led to the resignation of Richard Nixon, polls showed a public appreciation for the role of news organizations in national politics. Several reporters who pursued the story when the power of the President's office weighed heavily to squash it became heroes. The media, which had been under public attack by the Nixon administration, appeared to be defenders of traditional constitutional values against usurpers who did not think that the safeguards of the system applied to them. The lovefest was short-lived. Doubts about the media's role as the public's sources for information and communications from the White House were reasserted as soon as the glamor of the Watergate achievement faded. Of course much of the criticism of White House reporting can be attributed to the President's aides and supporters, who claim that the unposed, unretouched picture the media present is unfair. Brushing off their criticism as self-serving is also unfair.

White House critics complain that the media distort and misinterpret what happens and thus scramble the President's message on its route to the public. They assert that news organizations fail the public because, instead of providing full explanations of complicated policies, journalists deal with the politics of issues, assessing whether the adoption of a program means that the President is a winner or loser. The real losers, they suggest, are those who need to understand the policy.

Journalistic critics of White House reporting are not more generous. They suggest that elite journalists include both willing recipients of the White House glitter and those who make a career of attacking the President. They find the White House regulars to be alternately too abrasive and too obsequious in their relations with the President and his aides. Critics feel that journalists are often manipulated at the White House because it is so difficult for them to change their routines. Their emphasis on hard news events means that they are too closely tied to the coverage of the ceremonies and major events that take place at the White House. Thus their efforts to explain less visible and harder-to-define activities take second place to the body watch of the President. For these reasons the White House press corps never ''got'' the Watergate story.

Clearly the public has a major stake in whether White House reporting is adequate or not. The President's message, as it is filtered through and interpreted by the news media, often determines the role the public will play in the shaping of policy. The President's conduct, as portrayed and evaluated by news organizations, affects the choices made by the electorate. Some serious critics of the process that provides White House information to the public have been particularly harsh in their evaluation of the role of the media. The gist of their argument may be summarized as follows: News organizations make it difficult to either govern or oppose the government. The media's emphasis on the President's unresolved conflicts, unreached goals, inconsistencies, and personal peccadillos erodes the legitimacy he needs to command and the credibility he requires to persuade. They create major distractions that force his attention from the essential problems of the nation. According to this argument, his opponents are given an equally hard time when they become a large enough target to warrant the media's full attention. Should a critic or opposing candidate become prominent, their receipt of the same media treatment the President gets makes it difficult for the public to evaluate the nature of the alternative they offer.

Behind these criticisms lie some assumptions about the relative positions of the two institutions in the constitutional system. The President is charged with the central role of governing; the media are given the opportunity to assess and criticize the government without fear of punishment. Since the President and the media represent the public in different ways, the media must be held to higher standards of accuracy, while the President is judged by his effectiveness. Because the President is curtailed by the requirements of political life and the day-to-day process of government from engaging in an ongoing pursuit of the public interest, that responsibility is placed on the media. White House reporting requires a delicate balance. The media must portray the President clearly and honestly and alert the public when there are dangerous abuses of power, but not endanger the stability of the presidency.

In assessing the adequacy of White House reporting, it is not difficult to compile a list of areas where the public is not well served. What the media define as news about the President is not always what is important. The organization and routines of reporting discourage the prominent display of stories explaining the institutional structure of the presidency. The public learns more about the style than the substance of developments because of the news values of reporters, and because of the manner in which the White House presents the agenda of the President's activities. The President's message does not get through to the public when its complexities require constant reiteration because those who run news organizations believe their audience doesn't want different versions of the same explanation.

In spite of the demythologizing of the Chief Executive during the 1970s, the mystique of the presidency still overwhelms some reporters. White House aides encourage these tendencies by having the President play symbolic roles on stages that emphasize the charisma of office. A major result of this is overexposure. The heavy investment of both news organizations and the

White House in exploring the drama of the presidency leads to a heightened sense that the achievements are great and the failures abysmal. A surfeit of descriptions and pictures of the President makes it difficult for the public to obtain a clear sense of the realities of the President's capabilities—his power, or powerlessness. An exaggerated public concept of either capability does not help the political system. The media tend to deal in superlatives, however, and thus there are often greater swings in the tone of the coverage of an administration than there are real swings in momentum.

A similar and shorter, but not less important, list can be compiled describing the ways in which the public is well served by White House reporting. It is useful first to remind ourselves that news enterprises are private organizations. The concept of what constitutes news comes from editors and bureau chiefs, who select the areas that are given extensive coverage by reporters. Reporters for mass audience news organizations gravitate toward personal and dramatic items. Those who work for elite publications or programs provide a more sophisticated analysis of White House policies presented from the perspectives of both critics and supporters of the President. The public does get the story in the long run. If there are noteworthy delays, as there were in the general reporting on Watergate developments, there are also circumstances when news organizations bring an important story to an uninterested public. The energy crisis became a prominent story in the media after 1973, but public attention to the reality of the crisis did not occur until the skyrocketing prices and gas lines of 1979.

The media do provide the public with protection against abuses of power by the White House. If they hound suspects rather than pursue wrongdoers, this form of McCarthyism should not be passed over lightly. With few exceptions, however, the media have served as valuable checks on those in the White House who took it for granted that they could use their position for personal gain or to remain immune from the ordinary legal processes governing citizens and officials, or who abused their power in the pursuit of political goals for themselves or for the President.

Finally, what appears in the media does reflect who the President is and what he is doing. Although some stories may be unfair or inaccurate, and a large number present a fuzzy image, the picture that emerges reflects the tone and substance of the administration and the character of the President. In particular, the impact of large numbers of stories has been to leave an impression of presidents' leadership that seems accurate in retrospect. What emerged was a portrait of Johnson as an activist leader with a strong penchant for introducing new programs on which he could place his imprimatur, a wheeler-dealer who knew how to manipulate the political process, and a man given to using pressure tactics; Nixon as a strong partisan who had a penchant for secrecy, little tolerance for his opponents, a vindictive streak, and an opportunist who fronted his positions with rhetoric; Ford as a good man who was not prepared for the job when he took office and who frequently stumbled as he learned the ropes; Carter as a leader who has not established his priorities and who tries to win the support of both sides in a dispute and often loses both, and an intelligent man who does not understand the uses of power.

Most of the time the picture that was presented of each of these presidents was much more favorable. The built-in advantages possessed by chief executives enable them to keep the more critical appraisal in the background as they go about their activities. The fact that the unfavorable undertones become part of the public's assessment does not stop a president from pursuing governmental or electoral objectives. Polls indicate that the public assessment of Nixon in 1972 was not far from the picture just described, but he was reelected by an overwhelming majority.

News organizations have not made it more difficult to govern. What have made the exercise of power more difficult for presidents are the forces that gave to the media their present status—the diffusion of governmental authority and the breakdown of traditional lines of communications. The fact that those who govern seem dependent on news organizations is a symptom of the problem, not the problem.

NOTES

CHAPTER ONE

1. Patrick Anderson, *The President's Men* (Garden City, N.Y.: Doubleday & Co., 1968), p. 187.

2. See Richard E. Neustadt, *Presidential Power: The Politics of Leadership from F.D.R. to Carter* (New York: John Wiley & Sons, 1980), for the classic study of the theory that presidential power rests on the President's ability to persuade.

3. See Elmer E. Cornwell, *Presidential Leadership of Public Opinion* (Bloomington: Indiana University Press, 1965), for an excellent study that puts forth the theory that the President's most important relationship is the one he has with the public.

4. Interview with Richard Cheney, Nixon administration White House assistant and Ford administration chief of staff (White House: MJK & MBG, December 8, 1976). The citation refers to the place the interview was held, which of the authors was present, the initials of the person responsible for the interview being shown first, and the date it was held.

5. Interview with John Herbers, *New York Times* White House correspondent and deputy chief of its Washington bureau (Washington, D.C.: MBG, January 11, 1977).

6. Interview with Gerald Warren, Nixon and Ford administrations deputy press secretary (Executive Office Building: MJK & MBG, July 28, 1975).

7. Interview with Peter Lisagor, *Chicago Daily News* syndicated columnist and reporter (Washington, D.C.: MBG & MJK, February 11, 1976).

8. See George Reedy, *The Twilight of the Presidency* (New York: Mentor, 1970); James David Barber, *The Presidential Character: Predicting Performance in the White House* (Englewood Cliffs, N.J.: Prentice-Hall, 1972); Arthur M. Schlesinger, Jr., *The Imperial Presidency* (Boston: Houghton Mifflin, 1973); Garry Wills, *Nixon Agonistes: The Crisis of the Self-Made Man* (Boston: Houghton Mifflin, 1970); Doris Kearns, *Lyndon Johnson and the American Dream* (New York: Harper & Row, 1976).

9. Criticisms of the media by John Roche and Patrick Buchanan appear frequently in the *TV Guide*. Reed Irvine is the director of AIM (Accuracy in Media). See Edith Efron's *The News Twisters* (Los Angeles: Nash Publishers, 1971).

10. David Truman, *The Governmental Process: Political Interests and Public Opinion* (New York: Knopf, 1951).

11. Robert A. Dahl and Charles E. Lindbloom, *Politics, Economics, and Welfare: Planning Politico-Economic Systems Resolved into Basic Social Processes* (Chicago: University of Chicago Press, 1956).

12. Vermont Royster, "Reflections on the Fourth Estate," *Washington Post,* December 25, 1978.

13. William McGaffin and Erwin Knoll, *Anything But the Truth* (New York: G. P. Putnam's Sons, 1968); David Wise, *The Politics of Lying* (New York: Random House, 1973); Barry Sussman, *The Great Coverup: Nixon and the Scandal of Watergate* (New York: Thomas Y. Crowell Co., 1974); John Herbers, *No Thank You, Mr. President* (New York: W. W. Norton & Co., 1976).

14. Interviews with James Hagerty, Eisenhower administration press secretary (Telephone: MJK, July 1, 1978); Pierre Salinger, Kennedy and Johnson administrations press secretary (New York: MBG: October 12, 1976); Ronald Nessen, Ford administration press secretary (Bethesda, Md.: MJK & MBG, July 26, 1978); and Jody Powell, Carter administration press secretary (White House: MJK & MBG, October 6, 1978).

15. David Halberstam, *The Best and the Brightest* (New York: Random House, 1972).

16. Interview with David Halberstam, *New York Times* correspondent (Baltimore: MBG, October 13, 1978).

17. Interview with Joseph Laitin, Johnson, Nixon, Ford, and Carter administrations White House and executive department press officer (Washington, D.C.: MJK & MBG, January 27, 1976).

18. Interview with Walt Rostow, Johnson administration national security adviser (Austin, Tex.: MJK, July 9, 1976).

19. For a full discussion of this period see William E. Porter, *Assault on the Media: The Nixon Years* (Ann Arbor: University of Michigan Press, 1976).

20. See, for example, James Keogh, *President Nixon and the Press* (New York: Funk & Wagnalls, 1972); Daniel Moynihan, "The Presidency and the Press," *Commentary* 51, no. 3 (March, 1971): 41–52; Victor Lasky, *It Didn't Start with Watergate* (New York: Dial Press, 1977).

21. Interview with Jody Powell (Washington, D.C.: MJK & MBG, January 11, 1977).

22. *Washington Star,* April 25, 1977.

23. *New York Times Magazine,* May 15, 1977.

24. James Deakin, *St. Louis Post-Dispatch* White House correspondent, speaking to a group of students in the White House briefing room, September 11, 1977. Frank Cormier, Associated Press chief White House correspondent, speaking to a group of students in the White House briefing room, September 12, 1977.

25. Hugh Sidey, "But Is He Presidential?" *Washington Star,* August 27, 1978.

26. Interview with Jody Powell, October 6, 1978.

27. Interview with Jody Powell by Martin Agronsky on "Agronsky at Large" (WETA, Washington, D.C.: Public Broadcasting System, June 24, 1977).

28. Quoted by Dom Bonafede in "Powell and the Press—A New Mood in the White House," *National Journal* 9, no. 26 (June 25, 1977): 982.

29. Anderson, *President's Men,* p. 184.

CHAPTER TWO

1. Background interview, Ford administration official (Washington, D.C.: MJK, December, 1976).

2. Elmer E. Cornwell, *Presidential Leadership of Public Opinion* (Bloomington: Indiana University Press, 1965), p. 34.

3. Ibid., pp. 9–61.

4. O. O. Stealey, *Twenty Years in the Press Gallery* (New York: Publishers Printing Co., 1906), p. 34.

5. Quoted by James E. Pollard in *The Presidents and the Press* (New York: Macmillan, 1947), p. 558.

6. Since stenographic records were not kept of press conferences before the Wilson administration, it is difficult to make comparisons. According to interviews with two reporters whose experience began during Theodore Roosevelt's administration, Roosevelt's conferences were informal but regular. Interviews with Louis Brownlow, Washington reporter, author, and presidential adviser (Washington, D.C.: MBG, July, 1963); and Bascom Timmons, Washington correspondent and chief of Timmons News Service (Washington, D.C.: MBG & MJK, January

19, 1976). However, it was Woodrow Wilson who "inaugurated the mass press conference, opened to all correspondents on equal terms, to be held at specified times." Leo C. Rosten, *The Washington Correspondents* (New York: Harcourt, Brace and Co., 1937), p. 24.

7. Cornwell, *Presidential Leadership,* pp. 43–44.

8. Interviews with Louis Brownlow, July, 1963; and Bascom Timmons, January 19, 1976.

9. Interview with Edward Folliard, *Washington Post* White House correspondent (Washington, D.C.: MBG & MJK, January 22, 1976).

10. Interview with Richard Strout, *New Republic* columnist and *Christian Science Monitor* correspondent (Washington, D.C.: MBG & MJK, January 23, 1976).

11. Ibid.

12. Interviews with Edward Folliard, January 22, 1976; Bascom Timmons, January 19, 1976; Louis Brownlow, July, 1963; and Kenneth Crawford, *Newsweek* Washington bureau correspondent and columnist (Washington, D.C.: MBG & MJK, January 21, 1976).

13. Interview with Bascom Timmons, January 19, 1976.

14. Interview with Louis Brownlow, July, 1963. Early's daily meeting with the President and the full range of his activities are described in his diary, which is kept at the Franklin D. Roosevelt Library, Hyde Park, New York (to be noted FDR Library).

15. This information about Early's ability to use changes brought about by technology to Roosevelt's advantage is analyzed by Steven E. Schoenhert in "Selling the New Deal: Stephen T. Early's Role as Press Secretary to Franklin D. Roosevelt" (Ph.D. diss., University of Delaware, 1976).

16. Interview with Gerald Rafshoon, Carter administration assistant for communications (Executive Office Building: MJK & MBG, November 15, 1978).

17. Memo, Fred Panzer to President Johnson, "Background on Presidential Press Relations," February 21, 1967, EX FG 1, White House Central Files (to be noted WHCF), Lyndon B. Johnson Library (to be noted LBJ Library). An example of Johnson's demands for a rebuttal to a news article appeared in four memos Tom Johnson wrote to the staff on December 13, 1966, requesting "facts" in response to a Charles Roberts *Newsweek* article, "LBJ's Credibility Gap" EX PR 18, WHCF, LBJ Library.

18. Jeb Stuart Magruder, *An American Life: One Man's Road to Watergate* (New York: Atheneum, 1974), p. 91.

19. Ibid., p. 101.

20. Interview with James Naughton, *New York Times* White House correspondent (Washington, D.C.: MBG & MJK, September 29, 1976).

21. Interview with John Ehrlichman, Nixon administration domestic adviser (Washington, D.C.: MJK & MBG, October 18, 1976).

22. Interview with Walter Wurfel, Carter administration deputy press secretary (White House: MBG, November 3, 1977).

23. Schoenhert, "Selling the New Deal."

24. Interview with David Kennerly, Ford administration chief White House photographer (White House: MJK & MBG, October 18, 1976).

25. Interview with Walter Rodgers, Associated Press Radio White House correspondent (White House: MBG & MJK, November 15, 1978).

26. Lesley Stahl, CBS Evening News, March 7, 1979.

27. Interview with William Greener, Jr., Ford administration deputy press secretary (Washington, D.C.: MJK & MBG, January 23, 1976).

28. Interviews with Robert Mead, Ford administration television adviser (Executive Office Building: MBG & MJK, January 16, 1976); and Barry Jagoda, Carter administration assistant for media and public affairs (Executive Office Building: MJK & MBG, September 16, 1977). Mead and Jagoda told interviewers that they never had to pressure networks to cover these events and that in fact they were concerned with "overexposure" or angry viewers who have their favorite programs preempted.

29. Interview with Barry Jagoda, September 16, 1977.

30. James Hagerty Diary, March 4, 1954, Hagerty Papers, Dwight D. Eisenhower Library (to be noted DDE Library).

31. Interview with James Fallows, Carter administration chief speechwriter (White House: MJK & MBG, September 16, 1977).

32. Rosten, *Washington Correspondents,* p. 4.

33. Background interview (Washington, D.C.: MBG, January, 1977).

34. Ben H. Bagdikian, *The Effete Conspiracy and Other Crimes by the Press* (New York: Harper & Row, 1972), p. 117.

35. Quoted in Martin Schram, *Running for President, 1976: The Carter Campaign* (New York: Stein & Day, 1977), p. 57.

36. Interview with Joseph Laitin (Washington, D.C.: MJK & MBG, January 27, 1976).

37. Interview with John Ehrlichman, October 18, 1976.

38. Interview with James Reston, *New York Times* correspondent and columnist (Washington, D.C.: MBG & MJK, January 28, 1977).

39. Interview with Jody Powell (Washington, D.C.: MJK & MBG, January 11, 1977).

40. Interview with Martin Schram, *Washington Post* correspondent and *Newsday* Washington bureau chief (Washington, D.C.: MBG & MJK, January 7, 1976).

41. Interview with Dom Bonafede, *National Journal* White House correspondent (Washington, D.C.: MBG & MJK, September 27, 1976).

42. Interview with James Naughton, September 29, 1976.

43. Interview with Edward Walsh, *Washington Post* White House correspondent (White House: MBG, September, 1976).

CHAPTER THREE

1. Transcript, Charles Roberts oral history interview (*Newsweek* White House correspondent), November 20, 1972, pp. 12–13, from the oral history collection of Columbia University (to be noted COHC) and found also in the Eisenhower Library.

2. Interview with Peter Lisagor (Washington, D.C.: MBG & MJK, February 11, 1976).

3. We were observers in the White House press room during the period between December, 1975, and July, 1980. More than seventy interviews were conducted with reporters, including several who had been assigned to the White House at earlier times.

4. Interview with Ralph Harris, Reuters news service White House correspondent (White House: MBG, February 25, 1976).

5. Background interview (Washington, D.C.: MBG, October, 1976).

6. Interview with Ronald Nessen (Bethesda, Md.: MJK & MBG, July 26, 1978).

7. Interview with Ralph Harris, February 25, 1976.

8. Pierre Salinger, *With Kennedy* (Garden City, N.Y.: Doubleday & Co., 1966), pp. 111–12.

9. Interview with Ronald Ziegler, Nixon administration press secretary (New York: MJK & MBG, August 31, 1978).

10. Comment made by Brooks Jackson, Associated Press White House correspondent (White House: MBG, October 6, 1978).

11. Interview with Mel Elfin, *Newsweek* Washington bureau chief (Washington, D.C.: MBG & MJK, December 8, 1976).

12. Interview with Helen Thomas, United Press International chief White House correspondent (White House: MBG & MJK, January 6, 1976).

13. Interview with Frank Cormier (White House: MBG, March 4, 1977).

14. Interview with Martin Tolchin, *New York Times* White House correspondent (Bethesda, Md.: MBG, August 15, 1978).

15. Interview with Ronald Nessen, July 26, 1978.

16. Interview with Frank Cormier, March 4, 1977.

17. Interview with Tom Brokaw, NBC News White House correspondent (White House: MJK, January 19, 1976).

18. Interview with Ronald Nessen, December 12, 1976.

19. Interview with Ronald Ziegler, August 31, 1978.

20. Interview with Barry Jagoda (Executive Office Building: MJK & MBG, September 16, 1977).

21. Interview with George Watson, ABC News Washington bureau chief (Washington, D.C.: MBG, January 6, 1977).

22. Background interview with a White House correspondent (Washington, D.C.: MBG, June, 1977).

23. Interview with Bob Schieffer, CBS News White House correspondent (White House: MBG, July 11, 1977).

24. Interview with George Watson, January 6, 1977.

25. Interview with Robert Pierpoint, CBS News White House correspondent (White House: MJK, January 15, 1976).

26. Ibid.

27. Interview with John Carlson, Ford administration deputy press secretary (Washington, D.C.: MJK & MBG, February 21, 1976).

28. Interview with Tom Brokaw, January 19, 1976.

29. Background interview with a White House correspondent (Washington, D.C.: MBG, June, 1977).

30. Cited by Ben H. Bagdikian, *The Information Machines: Their Impact on Men and the Media* (New York: Harper and Row, 1971), p. 57.

31. Interview with Walter Rodgers (White House: MBG, February 18, 1977).

32. Ibid.

33. Ibid.

34. Interview with Russ Ward, NBC News White House radio correspondent (White House: MJK, January 9, 1976).

35. Interview with Walter Rodgers, February 18, 1977.

36. Interview with Richard Holwill, National Public Radio White House correspondent (Washington, D.C.: MBG & MJK, June 14, 1976).

37. Interview with James Hagerty (Telephone: MJK, July 1, 1978).

38. Interview with Stephen Hess, Eisenhower and Nixon administrations White House assistant (Washington, D.C.: MJK & MBG, March 9, 1978).

39. Interview with Claudia Townsend, Carter administration assistant press secretary and director of White House News Summary (Executive Office Building: MJK & MBG, September 21, 1977).

40. Leon V. Sigal, *Reporters and Officials* (Lexington, Mass: D.C. Heath, 1973), p. 5.

41. Interview with James Naughton (Washington, D.C.: MBG & MJK, September 29, 1976).

42. Interview with Edward Folliard (Washington, D.C.: MBG & MJK, January 22, 1976).

43. Barry Sussman, *The Great Coverup: Nixon and the Scandal of Watergate* (New York: Thomas Y. Crowell Co., 1974), p. 18.

44. Carl Bernstein and Bob Woodward, *All the President's Men* (New York: Simon and Schuster, 1974), p. 220.

45. Interview with Edward Folliard, January 22, 1976.

46. Background interview (Washington, D.C.: MBG, October, 1978).

47. Interview with Edward Walsh (White House: MBG, September, 1976).

48. Gay Talese, *The Kingdom and the Power* (New York: World Publishing Co., 1969).

49. Background interview with a *New York Times* reporter (Washington, D.C.: MBG, October, 1978).

50. Ibid.

51. Background interview (Washington, D.C.: MBG, January, 1978).

52. Ibid.

53. Interview with James Naughton, September 29, 1976.

54. Ibid.

55. Interview with Edward Walsh, September, 1976.

56. Interview with John Osborne, *New Republic* White House correspondent (Washington, D.C.: MBG & MJK, August 29, 1978).

57. Interview with Edward Walsh, September, 1976.

58. Interview with Martin Tolchin, August 15, 1978.

59. Memo, W. Averell Harriman to President Johnson, August 20, 1965, EX PR 18, WHCF, LBJ Library.

60. Interview with Martin Tolchin, August 15, 1978.

61. Interview with John Herbers (Washington, D.C.: MBG, January 11, 1977).

62. Ibid.

63. Philip Shabecoff, "President to Propose Rise in Social Security Tax," *New York Times,* January 17, 1976, p. 1.

64. Philip Shabecoff, "A Vision of America," *New York Times,* January 20, 1976, p. 19.

65. Interview with Martin Tolchin, August 15, 1978.

66. Interview with John Herbers, January 11, 1977.

67. Interview with Hugh Sidey, *Time* Washington bureau chief (Washington, D.C.: MBG, December 6, 1976).

68. Ibid.

69. Interview with Tom DeFrank, *Newsweek* White House correspondent (Washington, D.C.: MBG, March 31, 1976).

70. Interview with John Ehrlichman (Washington, D.C.: MJK & MBG, October 18, 1976).

71. Interview with Hugh Sidey, December 6, 1976.

72. Interview with Mel Elfin, December 8, 1976.

73. Ibid.

74. Interview with Tom DeFrank, March 31, 1976.

75. Interview with Mel Elfin, December 8, 1976.

76. Interview with Hugh Sidey, December 6, 1976.

77. Interview with Mel Elfin, December 8, 1976.

78. Interview with Tom DeFrank, March 31, 1976.

79. Ibid.

80. Interview with Dennis Farney, *Wall Street Journal* White House correspondent (Ford campaign trip through New York and New Jersey: MJK, October 12, 1976).

81. Memo, Fred Panzer to President Johnson, "Background on Presidential Press Relations," February 21, 1967, EX FG 1, WHCF, LBJ Library.

82. Interview with Peter Lisagor, February 11, 1976.

83. Interview with Fred Barnes, *Washington Star* White House correspondent (White House: MBG & MJK, February 11, 1976).

84. Timothy Crouse, *The Boys on the Bus* (New York: Random House, 1973), p. 199.

85. Background interview, Carter administration press official (Washington, D.C.: MBG, September, 1977).

86. Interview with David Halberstam (Baltimore: MBG, October 13, 1978).

87. Interview with Jerald F. terHorst, Ford administration press secretary and *Detroit News* correspondent and syndicated columnist (Washington, D.C.: MBG, November 30, 1978).

88. Interview with Peter Lisagor, February 11, 1976.

89. Interview with Pat Sloyan, *Newsday* White House correspondent (White House: MBG & MJK, February 13, 1978).

90. Background interview with Ford administration official (Washington, D.C.: MJK, January, 1977).

91. Interview with Judy Wiessler, *Houston Chronicle* Washington bureau correspondent (Andrews Air Force Base, Md.: MJK, October 12, 1976).

92. Interview with Joseph Lastelic, *Kansas City Star* Washington bureau chief (Washington, D.C.: MBG & MJK, October 11, 1976).

93. Interview with Robert Boyd, Knight Newspapers Washington bureau chief (Washington, D.C.: MBG, January 10, 1977).

94. Ibid.

95. Interview with Andrew Glass, Cox Newspapers White House correspondent and Washington bureau chief (Washington, D.C.: MBG, June 6, 1977).

96. Interview with Jerald F. terHorst, November 30, 1978.

97. Background interview with a Washington bureau chief (Washington, D.C.: MBG, January, 1977).

98. Background interview with an editor (Washington, D.C.: MBG, January, 1977).

99. The Press Secretary's News Conference (White House: February 13, 1978).

100. Interview with Robert Boyd, January 10, 1977.

101. Background interview with a Washington bureau chief (Washington, D.C.: MBG, January, 1977).

102. Interview with Ronald Nessen, July 26, 1978.

103. Memo, Stephen T. Early to William Hassett, August 27, 1940, Early Papers, FDR Library.

104. Interview with David Kennerly (White House: MJK & MBG, October 18, 1976).

105. Transcript, Merriman Smith oral history interview (United Press International chief White House correspondent), January 3, 1968, p. 35, COHC.

106. Interview with David Kennerly, October 18, 1976.

CHAPTER FOUR

1. Background interview, Ford administration official (Washington, D.C.: MJK, December, 1976).

2. Ibid.

3. Richard E. Neustadt, *Presidential Power: The Politics of Leadership from F.D.R. to Carter* (New York: John Wiley & Sons, 1980).

4. Memo, Bill Moyers to Robert Kintner, April 8, 1966, Confidential Files, FG 11-8-1/ Kintner, Robert, WHCF, LBJ Library.

5. Background interview, Ford administration official (Washington, D.C.: MJK, November, 1976).

6. Background interview, Ford administration official (Washington, D.C.: MJK, December, 1976).

7. Background interview, Ford administration official (Washington, D.C.: MJK, December, 1976).

8. Background interview, a congressional appropriations committee employee (Washington, D.C.: MJK & MBG, February, 1976).

9. "The Big Bucks in the Big House," *National Journal* 9, no. 20 (May 14, 1977): 764.

10. Interview with Jerry Doolittle, Carter administration speechwriter (Telephone: MJK, August, 1976).

11. Background interview, Ford administration official (Washington, D.C.: MJK, December, 1976).

12. Interview with Ronald Nessen (White House: MJK & MBG, December 12, 1976).

13. Interview with George Christian, Johnson administration press secretary (Austin, Tex.: MJK, July 9, 1976).

14. Memo, George Reedy to President Johnson, January 3, 1967, EX PR 18, WHCF, LBJ Library.

15. Interview with Richard Cheney (White House: MJK & MBG, December 8, 1976).

16. Interview with George Christian, July 9, 1976.

17. Ibid.

18. Interview with John Carlson (White House: MJK & MBG, February 21, 1976).

19. Cross Reference, memo, Bill Moyers to President Johnson, January 25, 1966, EX PR 18, WHCF, LBJ Library.

20. Ibid.

21. Interview with David Gergen, Nixon speechwriter and Ford administration director of the Office of Communications (Executive Office Building: MJK, November 29, 1976).

22. Interview with James Connor, Ford administration secretary to the cabinet (White House: MJK & MBG, December 6, 1976).

23. Peter Jay, "Washington Briefly: On Foreign Policy," *Baltimore Sun,* November 2, 1977.

24. Ibid.

25. Interview with William Rhatican, Ford administration deputy director of the Office of Communications (Executive Office Building: MJK, November 19, 1976).

26. Interview with Patricia Bario, Carter administration deputy press secretary (Executive Office Building: MBG, October 5, 1977).

27. Interview with William Rhatican, November 19, 1976.

28. Memo, Charles Goodwin to Pat Bario, "Monthly Mass Mailing Report," September 30, 1978.

29. James Hagerty Diary, July 27, 1954, Hagerty Papers, DDE Library.

30. Interview with Pierre Salinger (Paris, France: MJK, December 5, 1978). Material in the Kennedy Library supports the point.

31. Memo, H. R. Haldeman to Jeb Stuart Magruder, October 16, 1969, Marc Lakritz files, evidence submitted to the U.S. Congress, Senate Select Committee on Presidential Campaign Activities and now held by the Senate Rules Committee.

32. Interview with Ronald Ziegler (New York: MJK & MBG, August 31, 1978).

33. Interview with Jody Powell (White House: MJK & MBG, October 6, 1978).

34. Quoted in Jeb Stuart Magruder, *An American Life: One Man's Road to Watergate* (New York: Atheneum, 1974), p. 79.

35. William Safire, *Before the Fall: An Inside View of the Pre-Watergate White House* (Garden City, N.Y.: Doubleday & Co., 1975), p. 361.

36. Quoted in Magruder, *An American Life,* p. 81.

37. Background interview, Ford administration official (Washington, D.C.: MJK & MBG, December, 1976).

38. Interview with Hamilton Jordan, Carter administration chief of White House staff (White House: MJK & MBG, January 11, 1979).

39. Ibid.

40. Background interview, Ford administration official (Washington, D.C.: MJK & MBG, December, 1976).

41. Interview with Gerald Rafshoon (Executive Office Building: MJK & MBG, November 15, 1978).

42. Interview with Jody Powell (Washington, D.C.: MJK & MBG, January 11, 1977).

43. Interview with James Fallows (White House: MJK & MBG, September 16, 1977).

44. Interview with Joseph Laitin (Washington, D.C.: MJK & MBG, January 27, 1976).

45. Quoted in Magruder, *An American Life,* p. 81.

46. Dom Bonafede, "If the Rafshoon Fits, Wear It," *National Journal* 10, no. 33 (August 19, 1978): 1,331.

47. Dom Bonafede, "Actions Speak Louder Than Words," *National Journal* 10, no. 36 (September 9, 1978): 1,435.

48. Interview with Gerald Rafshoon, November 15, 1978.

49. Terence Smith, "Rafshoon Gathers List of Carter Advocates," *New York Times,* May 3, 1979, p. A20.

50. "A Most Satisfying Victory," *National Journal* 10, no. 48 (December 2, 1978): 1,944.

51. Interview with Gerald Rafshoon, November 15, 1978.

52. Background interview, Ford administration official (Washington, D.C.: MJK, December, 1976).

53. Interview with Claudia Townsend (Executive Office Building: MJK & MBG, September 21, 1977).

54. Ibid.

55. Interview with John Ehrlichman (Washington, D.C.: MJK & MBG, October 18, 1976).

56. Interview with James Shuman, Ford administration associate director of Office of Communications (Executive Office Building: MJK, November 22, 1976).

57. Background interview (Washington, D.C.: MJK & MBG, January, 1976).

58. Interview with Claudia Townsend, September 21, 1977.

59. Interview with William Rhatican, November 19, 1976.

60. Ibid.

61. Memo, Charles Colson to H. R. Haldeman, April 6, 1970, Marc Lakritz files, evidence submitted to the U.S. Congress, Senate Select Committee on Presidential Campaign Activities and now held by the Senate Rules Committee.

62. Memo, H. R. Haldeman to Jeb Stuart Magruder, August 6, 1970, Marc Lakritz files, evidence submitted to the U.S. Congress, Senate Select Committee on Presidential Campaign Activities and now held by the Senate Rules Committee.

63. Interview with William Rhatican, November 19, 1976.

64. Elmer E. Cornwell, *Presidential Leadership of Public Opinion* (Bloomington: Indiana University Press, 1965), p. 70.

65. Interview with Harry Middleton, Johnson administration speechwriter (Austin, Tex.: MJK, July 8, 1976).

66. Interview with James Fallows, September 16, 1977.

67. James Fallows, "The Passionless Presidency," *Atlantic Monthly* 243, no. 5 (May, 1979): 33-48.

68. Transcript, Bryce Harlow oral history interview, February 27, 1967, p. 109, COHC.

69. Interview with David Gergen (Executive Office Building: MJK, December 3, 1976).

70. Interview with Eric Rosenberger, Ford administration assistant for media advance (Executive Office Building: MJK, January 8, 1976).

71. Ibid.

72. Martin Tolchin, "Traveling President Unable to Shun Trappings of Power," *New York Times,* May 4, 1979, p. A14.

73. Transcript, J. Leonard Reinsch oral history interview, March 13-14, 1967, pp. 142-43, Harry S. Truman Library (to be noted HST Library).

74. Interviews with Barry Jagoda (Executive Office Building: MJK & MBG, September 16 and 21, 1977).

75. Interview with Robert Mead (Executive Office Building: MJK & MBG, January 16, 1976).

76. Memo, Pierre Salinger to President Johnson, February 4, 1964, CF FG 11-8-1/Salinger, Pierre, WHCF, LBJ Library.

77. Memo, Jack Valenti to President Johnson, April 1, 1965, EX FG 11-8-1/Okamoto, Yoichi, WHCF, LBJ Library.

78. Interview with Jody Powell (Telephone: MJK, November 19, 1976).

79. James Fallows, "The Passionless Presidency," p. 39.

80. Interview with William J. Baroody, Jr., Ford administration director of the Office of Public Liaison (Executive Office Building: MJK, December 3, 1976).

81. Ibid.

82. Interview with Martin Schram (Washington, D.C.: MBG & MJK, January 7, 1976).

83. Quoted by Dom Bonafede in "Actions Speak Louder Than Words," p. 1,435.

84. "White House and Congress: Why the Troubles" (interview with Anne Wexler, assistant to the President), *U.S. News and World Report* 86, no. 24 (June 18, 1979): 53.

85. Interview with James Connor, December 6, 1976.

86. Memo, Jeb Stuart Magruder to Larry Higby, September 14, 1970, Marc Lakritz files, evidence submitted to the U.S. Congress, Senate Select Committee on Presidential Campaign Activities and now held by the Senate Rules Committee.

87. Lawrence F. O'Brien, "Larry O'Brien Discusses White House Contacts with Capital

Hill,'' in *The Presidency*, edited by Aaron Wildavsky (Boston: Little, Brown & Co., 1969), p. 484.

88. Ibid.

89. Memo, Jack Valenti to Bill Moyers and Horace Busby, April 6, 1964, EX PR 18, WHCF, LBJ Library. The memo includes a list of publications that each could read and be responsible for.

90. Memo, Marvin Watson to President Johnson, May 14, 1965, EX PU 1-2, WHCF, LBJ Library.

91. Interview with Sheila Rabb Weidenfeld, Ford administration secretary to the First Lady (White House: MJK, January 4, 1977).

92. Background interview, Ford administration official (Washington, D.C.: MJK, December, 1976).

93. Interview with James Connor, December 6, 1976.

94. Background interview, Ford administration official (Washington, D.C.: MJK & MBG, December, 1976).

95. Ibid.

96. In 1967 Robert Kintner wrote to John Macy that he wanted an additional writer on the staff to write prefaces for articles submitted to the *Congressional Record*. Memo, Robert Kintner to John Macy, January 6, 1967, CF FG 11-8-1/Shoemaker, Whitney, WHCF, LBJ Library.

97. Interview with Pierre Salinger (New York: MBG, October 12, 1976).

98. Background interview, Ford administration official (Washington, D.C.: MJK, November, 1976).

99. Ibid.

100. Interview with Margie Vanderhye, Ford administration assistant to press liaison for the National Security Council (White House: MBG, January 29, 1976).

101. Interview with Dan Malachuk, Carter administration deputy assistant to Hugh Carter, Jr. (Executive Office Building: MJK, May 16, 1979).

102. Interview with Bryce Harlow, p. 15, COHC.

103. Although members of the support staff are referred to as ''permanent'' or ''career'' employees by many of the President's advisers, they are not. Only the detailees from the Treasury Department's Secret Service, the Army Signal Corps detachment known as the White House Communications Agency, and the clerks have civil service status. Those who work in positions authorized for the White House serve at the pleasure of the President. In practice, most support people who stay on provide valuable services without creating embarrassment for any of the administrations they serve. Some support personnel spend their entire careers in White House posts.

104. *Weekly Compilation of Presidential Documents* 15, no. 20 (Monday, May 16, 1979): 870.

105. Interview with Stephen Selig, deputy assistant to Hamilton Jordan (Executive Office Building: MJK, August 29, 1979).

106. Interview with Dan Malachuk, May 16, 1979.

107. Interview with Landon Kite, director, Presidential Correspondence Office (Executive Office Building: MJK, June 8, 1979).

108. Memo, Chris Camp to George Reedy, April 1, 1964, CF FG 11-8-1/Reedy, George, WHCF, LBJ Library.

109. Interview with William Roberts, Ford administration assistant press secretary (White House: MJK & MBG, November 29, 1976).

110. Memo, Chris Camp to George Reedy, April 1, 1964.

111. Memo, ''Trip to Jasper, Alabama,'' file folder 9/16-18/1940, Hassett Papers, FDR Library.

112. Interview with William Hopkins, chief executive clerk (Silver Spring, Md: MJK, December 20, 1976). Hopkins came to the White House in the Hoover administration, and he stayed there until 1970.

CHAPTER FIVE

1. Inscription on a photograph in the office of George Christian, Austin, Texas.

2. Interview with Fred Barnes (White House: MBG & MJK, February 11, 1976).

3. Interview with Mel Elfin (Washington, D.C.: MBG & MJK, December 8, 1976).

4. Interview with George Reedy, Johnson administration press secretary (Baltimore: MBG & MJK, October 26, 1978).

5. John Dean, *Blind Ambition: The White House Years* (New York: Simon & Schuster, 1976), pp. 130–31.

6. The press secretaries included in our study are: Stephen Early (Roosevelt); Charles Ross and Joseph Short (Truman); James Hagerty (Eisenhower); Pierre Salinger (Kennedy and Johnson); George Reedy, Bill Moyers, and George Christian (Johnson); Ronald Ziegler (Nixon); Ronald Nessen (Ford); Jody Powell (Carter). Not included because of the brevity of their terms are: Jonathan Daniels (Roosevelt); J. Leonard Reinsch and Roger Tubby (Truman); Bob Fleming (Johnson); and Jerald terHorst (Ford).

7. Stephen T. Early Diary, March 4, 1934–December 4, 1939, Early Papers, FDR Library.

8. Eben Ayers Diary, December 22, 1941, Ayers Papers, HST Library.

9. Stephen T. Early Diary, May 8, 1934, Early Papers, FDR Library.

10. Ibid., May 16, 1938.

11. Appointment log: 1/9/76; 1/12/76; 1/13/76; 1/30/76; 2/25/76; 3/4/76; 3/10/76; 3/24/76; 4/1/76; 4/13/76; 5/18/76; 5/28/76. Telephone log: 1/2/76; 1/7/76; 1/28/76; 2/10/76; 2/18/76; 3/8/76; 3/25/76; 4/5/76; 5/4/76.

These logs, said Nessen's staff assistant, Constance Gerrard, "reflect average days, picked at random. The schedule for the afternoons doesn't reflect the ones who called at the last minute. Paper work is not on it." Interview with Constance Gerrard (White House: MJK, July 28, 1976).

12. Nessen logs.

13. Transcript, George Christian oral history interview, December 4, 1969, p. 25, LBJ Library.

14. We have attended briefings at least once or twice each month since December, 1975. During January, 1976, we attended on a daily basis, and during the summers of 1976 and 1977 we attended on a once-a-week basis or oftener. We conducted interviews that included questions about the briefing, but a great deal of our informal conversations with reporters and White House officials also concerned the briefing.

15. Interview with Pierre Salinger (New York: MBG, October 12, 1976).

16. A Carter administration official told us that the press conferences were scheduled well in advance, even though reporters were given the information one, two, or three days before they took place. We asked him if he knew when the next conference would be, and he checked his calendar and gave us a date eight days in the future (when it was in fact held). When we asked why reporters couldn't be given that information so they could include it in their plans, he replied that he didn't think reporters had to be told everything.

17. James Deakin speaking to students at the White House briefing room, October 11, 1976.

18. Interview with Jody Powell (Washington, D.C.: MJK & MBG, January 11, 1977).

19. Interviews with William Roberts (White House: MJK & MBG, December 29, 1975); John Hushen, Ford administration deputy press secretary (White House: MJK & MBG, December 30, 1975); Larry Speakes, Ford administration assistant press secretary (White House: MJK & MBG, January 7, 1976); William Greener, Jr. (White House: MJK & MBG, January 23, 1976); and Ronald Nessen (Bethesda, Md.: MJK & MBG, July 26, 1978).

20. Interview with William Greener, Jr., January 23, 1976.

21. Ibid.

22. Ibid.

23. Even the White House press room has its fun-and-games department. White House correspondents seemed to enjoy bringing Press Secretary Nessen to "his level of ignorance" by asking him questions about economic policy that appeared to be beyond his grasp.

24. James Hagerty Diary, June 30, 1954, Hagerty Papers, DDE Library.

25. Interview with John Ehrlichman (Washington, D.C.: MJK & MBG, October 18, 1976).

26. Information in the President's office files at the Lyndon Baines Johnson and John F. Kennedy libraries.

27. Interviews with: Jody Powell, January 11, 1977; James Fallows (White House: MJK & MBG, September 16, 1977); Barry Jagoda (Executive Office Building: MJK & MBG, September 16 and 21, 1977); Claudia Townsend (Executive Office Building: MJK & MBG, September 21, 1977); Patricia Bario (Executive Office Building: MBG, October 5, 1977); Linda Peek, Carter administration Media Liaison official (Executive Office Building: MBG, October 12, 1977); and James Purks, Carter administration Media Liaison official (Executive Office Building: MBG, October 17, 1977).

28. Interview with James Connor (White House: MJK & MBG, December 6, 1976).

29. Interview with George Christian (Austin, Texas: MJK, July 9, 1976).

30. Transcript, Jack Bell oral history interview (Associated Press correspondent), January 12, 1971, p. 41, HST Library.

31. Eben Ayers Diary, July 21, 1945, Ayers Papers, HST Library.

32. Ibid., August 4, 1945.

33. Letter, an anonymous Washington bureau chief to James E. Pollard, cited in James E. Pollard, *The Presidents and the Press: Truman to Johnson* (Washington, D.C.: Public Affairs Press, 1964), p. 32.

34. Interview with Jody Powell, January 11, 1977.

35. Transcript, George Christian oral history interview, February 27, 1970, p. 12, LBJ Library.

36. Transcript, James Hagerty oral history interview, January 31, 1968, pp. 218-19, COHC.

37. James Hagerty Diary, January 19, 1955, Hagerty Papers, DDE Library.

38. The Press Secretary's News Conference, January 20, 1955, Hagerty Papers, DDE Library.

39. Interview with George Reedy, October 26, 1978.

40. Transcript, William Theis oral history interview (a former Hearst Newspaper White House correspondent), February 8, 1971, p. 36, HST Library.

41. Interview with James Purks, October 17, 1977.

42. Mr. Early's Press Conference, January 19, 1939, Early Papers, FDR Library.

43. Transcript, George Christian oral history interview, December 11, 1968, p. 9, LBJ Library.

44. Interview with George Reedy, October 26, 1978. The presidential logs of visitors and telephone calls support Reedy's memory.

45. Interview with Charles Mohr, *New York Times* White House correspondent (New York: MJK, October 13, 1976.).

46. Quoted in Dom Bonafede, "Powell and the Press—A New Mood in the White House," *National Journal* 9, no. 26 (June 25, 1977): 982.

47. Background interview, White House reporter (Washington, D.C.: MBG & MJK, March, 1977).

48. Stephen T. Early Diary, August 10, 1936, Early Papers, FDR Library.

49. Interview with Frank Cormier (White House: MBG, March 4, 1977).

50. Transcript, James Hagerty oral history interview, March 2, 1967, p. 56, COHC.

51. Interview with James Deakin (Washington, D.C.: MBG & MJK, April 9, 1977).

52. Interview with John Carlson (White House: MJK & MBG, February 21, 1976).

CHAPTER SIX

1. Interview with Joseph Kraft, syndicated columnist (Telephone: MBG, January 9, 1977).

2. Letter, Bill Moyers to Robert Kintner, April 8, 1966, CF FG 11-8-1/Kintner, Robert, filed with Kintner letter to Moyers, 4/12/66, WHCF, LBJ Library.

3. See the following by John Osborne: *The Nixon Watch* (New York: Liveright, 1970); *The*

Second Year of the Nixon Watch (New York: Liveright, 1971); *The Third Year of the Nixon Watch* (New York: Liveright, 1972); *The Fourth Year of the Nixon Watch* (New York: Liveright, 1973); and *The White House Watch: The Ford Years* (New York: New Republic, 1977).

4. Interview with Aldo Beckman, *Chicago Tribune* White House correspondent (New York: MBG, October 12, 1976).

5. See Roger Morris, *Uncertain Greatness* (New York: Harper & Row, 1977), especially pp. 193–99 and 262–65, for a description of Kissinger's techniques of wooing and winning prominent journalists.

6. See Benjamin C. Bradlee, *Conversations with Kennedy* (New York: W. W. Norton & Co., 1975), for a description of the benefits and problems of a social relationship between a president and a reporter.

7. *Maryville-Alcoa Times,* March 1, 1963, "Tennessee Publishers Folder, February 28, 1963," Salinger Papers, JFK Library.

8. Articles found in Tennessee Publishers Folder, Salinger Papers, JFK Library.

9. Memo, Robert Kintner to President Johnson, July 6, 1966, CF PR 18, WHCF, LBJ Library.

10. Memo, Bill Moyers to George Christian, October 6, 1966, EX TR 100, WHCF, LBJ Library.

11. Letter, Paul Martin to Jack Valenti, May 13, 1964, filed with list of bureau chiefs and correspondents, May 19, 1964, EX PR 18, WHCF, LBJ Library.

12. Transcript, Peter Benchley oral history interview (Johnson administration speechwriter), November 20, 1968, p. 28, LBJ Library.

13. Memo, W. Averell Harriman to President Johnson, August 20, 1965, EX PR 18, WHCF, LBJ Library.

14. Memo, Tom Johnson to Bill Moyers, February 26, 1966, EX FG 400/MC, WHCF, LBJ Library.

15. Memo, Robert Kintner to President Johnson, January 18, 1966, EX PR 18, WHCF, LBJ Library.

16. Transcript, Chalmers Roberts oral history interview (foreign affairs correspondent, *Washington Post*), August 29, 1967, p. 6, COHC.

17. Ibid., pp. 4–5.

18. Memo, Horace Busby to Bill Moyers, April 21, 1965, EX PR 18, WHCF, LBJ Library.

19. Memo, George Christian to President Johnson, November 30, 1967, EX FG 1, WHCF, LBJ Library.

20. Memo, Loyd Hackler to George Christian, August 17, 1967, EX PR 18, WHCF, LBJ Library.

21. Interview with Barry Jagoda (Executive Office Building: MJK & MBG, September 16, 1977).

22. Memo, Robert Komer to President Johnson, November 22, 1967, EX PR 18, WHCF, LBJ Library.

23. Transcript, interview with Lyndon Johnson by Walter Cronkite, CBS News Special, "LBJ: Why I Choose Not to Run," December 27, 1969, p. 6, LBJ Library.

24. Interview with John Osborne (Washington, D.C.: MBG & MJK, August 29, 1978).

25. Transcript, William S. White oral history interview (syndicated columnist), tape no. 2, March 10, 1969, p. 11, LBJ Library.

26. Transcript, Robert S. Allen oral history interview (columnist and reporter during 1930s and 1940s), May 30, 1969, p. 22. See also transcripts, oral history interviews: Bascom Timmons, March 6, 1969, p. 21; George Reedy, tape no. 4, December 20, 1968, p. 13; Arthur Krock (*New York Times* columnist and bureau chief), November 21, 1968, p. 28; Edwin Weisl, Jr. (Johnson administration assistant attorney general), tape no. 2, May 23, 1969, p. 17, LBJ Library.

27. Transcript, Chalmers Roberts oral history interview, April 23, 1969, p. 20, LBJ Library.

28. Transcript, Walter Trohan oral history interview (*Chicago Tribune* correspondent), October 7, 1970, p. 73, HST Library.

29. Interview with James Fallows (White House: MJK & MBG, September 16, 1977).

30. Interview with Robert Novak, syndicated columnist (Washington, D.C.: MBG, June 23, 1976).

31. Transcript, Merriman Smith oral history interview, January 3, 1968, p. 57, DDE Library.

32. Ibid., pp. 57–59.

33. Ibid., pp. 61–62.

34. Interview during a Ford presidential campaign trip with Andrew Glass (New York: MBG & MJK, October 13, 1976).

35. Background interview, Washington reporter (Washington, D.C.: MBG, February, 1976).

36. Philip Shabecoff, "Nixon to Visit China Soon: Ford Is Reported Irritated," *New York Times*, February 7, 1976, p. A1.

37. Background interview, Washington reporter (Washington, D.C.: MBG, August, 1978).

38. Jeb Stuart Magruder, *An American Life: One Man's Road to Watergate* (New York: Atheneum, 1974), pp. 70–71.

39. Transcript, DeVier Pierson oral history interview (Johnson administration staff assistant), tape 2, March 20, 1969, p. 31, LBJ Library.

40. Ibid., pp. 31–32.

41. Interview with Ronald Nessen (Bethesda, Md.: MJK & MBG, July 26, 1978).

42. Transcript, Kenneth Crawford oral history interview, June 13, 1967, p. 6, DDE Library.

43. Interview with James Deakin (Washington, D.C.: MBG & MJK, September 20, 1976).

44. Background interview, Ford administration official (Washington, D.C.: MJK, January, 1977).

45. Interview with Robert Novak, June 23, 1976.

46. Interview with George Reedy (Baltimore: MJK & MBG, October 26, 1978).

CHAPTER SEVEN

1. Interview with James Naughton (Washington, D.C.: MBG & MJK, September 29, 1976).

2. Interview with Dom Bonafede (Washington, D.C.: MBG & MJK, September 27, 1976).

3. Interview with Andrew Glass (White House: MBG, June 17, 1977).

4. Interview with Curtis Wilkie, *Boston Globe* White House correspondent (New York: MBG & MJK, October 12, 1976).

5. Interview with Bob Schieffer (White House: MBG, July 11, 1977).

6. Interview with Dennis Farney (Washington, D.C.: MJK, June 25, 1979).

7. Interview with Peter Lisagor (Washington, D.C.: MBG & MJK, February 11, 1976).

8. Interview with John Osborne (Washington, D.C.: MBG & MJK, August 29, 1978).

9. Interview with Martin Tolchin (Washington, D.C.: MBG, August 15, 1978).

10. Timothy Crouse, *The Boys on the Bus* (New York: Random House, 1973), p. 195.

11. Interview with David Halberstam (Baltimore: MBG, October 13, 1978).

12. Interview with Dennis Farney, June 25, 1979.

13. Interview with Martin Tolchin, August 15, 1978.

14. Interview with John Osborne, August 29, 1978.

15. Herbert Gans, *Deciding What's News* (New York: Pantheon Books, 1979), p. 79.

16. Interview with Bob Schieffer, July 11, 1977.

17. James E. Pollard, *The Presidents and the Press* (New York: Macmillan, 1974), p. 558.

18. Interview with James Naughton, September 29, 1976.

19. Interview with Frank Cormier (White House: MBG & MJK, January 21, 1976).

20. John Dean, *Blind Ambition: The White House Years* (New York: Simon & Schuster, 1976), p. 127.

21. Interview with David Halberstam, October 13, 1978.

22. Interview with Peter Lisagor, February 11, 1976.

23. Background interview (Washington, D.C.: MBG, January, 1976).

24. Interview with Peter Lisagor, February 11, 1976.

25. Interview with Frank Cormier (White House: MBG, March 4, 1977).

26. Interview with Jody Powell (White House: MBG & MJK, October 6, 1978).

27. Interview with James Deakin (Washington, D.C.: MBG & MJK, September 20, 1976).

28. Interview with Peter Lisagor, February 11, 1976.

29. The material in the remainder of this chapter comes from interviews in which the nine reporters individually discussed their work. These interviews were conducted as follows: Dom Bonafede, September 27, 1976; Frank Cormier, March 4, 1977; James Deakin, September 20, 1976; Dennis Farney, June 25, 1979; Peter Lisagor, February 11, 1976; James Naughton, September 29, 1976; John Osborne, August 29, 1978; Walter Rodgers, March 2, 1977, and November 15, 1978; Bob Schieffer, July 11, 1977.

CHAPTER EIGHT

1. Interview with Martin Tolchin (Bethesda, Md.: MBG, August 15, 1978).

2. Interview with Jody Powell (White House: MJK & MBG, October 6, 1978).

3. Memo, George Reedy to Jack Valenti, May 13, 1964, filed with list of bureau chiefs and correspondents, May 19, 1964, EX PR 18, WHCF, LBJ Library.

4. Memo, Ben Wattenburg to President Johnson, January 17, 1967, EX PR 18, WHCF, LBJ Library.

5. Memo, President Nixon to H. R. Haldeman, October 28, 1968, evidence submitted to the U.S. Congress, Senate Select Committee on Presidential Campaign Activities and now held by the Senate Rules Committee.

6. Interview with Peter Lisagor (Washington, D.C.: MBG & MJK, February 11, 1976).

7. Interview with Joseph Kraft (Washington, D.C.: MBG & MJK, October 6, 1978).

8. Interview with Robert Novak (Washington, D.C.: MBG, June 23, 1976).

9. Interview with McGeorge Bundy, Johnson administration national security adviser (New York: MJK & MBG, May 1, 1978).

10. Interview with Joseph Kraft (Washington, D.C.: MBG, December 10, 1976).

11. Ibid.

12. Interview with Martin Tolchin, August 15, 1978.

13. Interview with David Broder, *Washington Post* columnist (Washington, D.C.: MBG & MJK, January 11, 1977).

14. Background interviews, *Washington Post* staff (Washington, D.C.: MBG, 1976–1977).

15. Interview with Joseph Kraft, December 10, 1976.

16. Ibid.

17. Interview with Robert Novak, June 23, 1976.

18. Ibid.

19. Ibid.

20. Background interview (Washington, D.C.: MBG, January, 1976).

21. Interview with Robert Novak, June 23, 1976.

22. Philip Nobile, "The Cool and Confident Anchorman," *More*, 6, no. 5 (May, 1976): 11.

23. David Halberstam, *The Powers That Be* (New York: Alfred A. Knopf, 1979), p. 514.

24. The Press Secretary's News Conference, December 19, 1977.

25. Interview with Hugh Sidey (Washington, D.C.: MBG, December 6, 1976).

26. Background interview (Washington, D.C.: MBG, December, 1976).

27. Interview with David Halberstam (Baltimore: MBG, October 13, 1978).

28. Interview with Gerald Rafshoon (Washington, D.C.: MJK & MBG, November 15, 1978).

29. Interview with Hugh Sidey, December 6, 1976.

30. Nobile, *More*, p. 9.

31. Interview with Jack Nelson, Washington bureau chief, *Los Angeles Times*, (Washington, D.C.: MBG & MJK, July 24, 1979).

32. Nora Ephron, "How Politicians Eat Reporters for Breakfast," *Esquire* 87, no. 6 (June, 1977): 26.

33. Interview with Peter Lisagor, February 11, 1976.

34. Interview with Jack Nelson, July 24, 1979.

35. Ibid.

36. Interview with Mel Elfin (Washington, D.C.: MBG & MJK, December 8, 1976).

37. Ibid.

38. Interview with George Watson (Washington, D.C.: MBG, January 6, 1977).

39. Background interview (Washington, D.C.: MBG, July, 1977).

40. Ronald Nessen, *It Sure Looks Different from the Inside* (Chicago: Playboy Press, 1978), pp. 75–76.

41. Interview with Mel Elfin, December 8, 1976.

42. Background interview (Washington, D.C.: MBG, January, 1977).

43. Interview with Hugh Sidey, December 6, 1976.

44. Interview with Mel Elfin, December 8, 1976.

45. Interview with Robert Pierpoint (White House: MJK, January 15, 1976).

CHAPTER NINE

1. Transcript, Chalmers Roberts oral history interview, April 23, 1969, p. 14, LBJ Library.

2. Background interview, Ford administration official (Washington, D.C.: MJK, December, 1976).

3. Letter, Theodore H. White to George Reedy, September 30, 1964, filed with White letter to President Johnson, June 8, 1965, EX FG 1, WHCF, LBJ Library.

4. Interview with Andrew Glass (Washington, D.C.: MBG, June 17, 1977).

5. Edward Walsh, "The Making of a Presidential Trip," *Washington Post,* March 16, 1977.

6. Memo, Horace Busby to President Johnson, January 23, 1964, EX FG 1, WHCF, LBJ Library.

7. Interview with Sheila Rabb Weidenfeld (White House: MJK, January 4, 1977).

8. *The Public Papers of the Presidents of the United States, John F. Kennedy, 1961* (Washington, D.C.: U.S. Government Printing Office, 1962), June 2, 1961, press conference, p. 429.

9. Interview with Andrew Glass, June 17, 1977.

10. Letter, George Reedy to Michael B. Grossman, April 19, 1976.

11. See James David Barber, *The Presidential Character: Predicting Performance in the White House* (Englewood Cliffs, N.J.: Prentice-Hall, 1972).

12. Interview with Joseph Kraft (Telephone: MBG, January 9, 1979).

13. David Halberstam, *The Best and the Brightest* (New York: Random House, 1972), pp. 499–500.

14. *The Public Papers of the Presidents of the United States, Gerald R. Ford, 1975,* vol. 2, November 3, 1975, press conference, pp. 1,791–1,804.

15. Terence Smith, "Bella Abzug's Ouster and the Limits of Dissent," *New York Times,* January 16, 1979, p. A9.

16. Background interview, Ford administration official (Washington, D.C.: MJK, December 1976).

17. Memo, Busby to the President, January 23, 1964.

18. Background interview, Nixon administration official (Washington, D.C.: MBG, February, 1978).

19. Interview with Eric Rosenberger, Ford administration Press Office official in charge of press advance (Executive Office Building: MJK, January 8, 1976).

20. "Son of Egghead," *New Republic* 180, no. 8 (February 24, 1979): 9.

21. Elmer E. Cornwell, *Presidential Leadership of Public Opinion* (Bloomington: Indiana University Press, 1965), p. 97.

22. Background interview, Ford administration official (Washington, D.C.: MJK, December, 1976).

23. Interview with Ronald Nessen (Bethesda, Md.: MJK & MBG, July 26, 1978).

24. Ibid.

25. Cornwell, *Presidential Leadership,* p. 39.

26. Interview with Pierre Salinger (Paris, France: MJK, December 5, 1978).

27. Interview with Robert Mead (Executive Office Building: MJK & MBG, January 16, 1976).

28. Interview with Barry Jagoda (Executive Office Building: MJK & MBG, September 16, 1977).

29. Transcript, Edward Folliard oral history interview, September 7, 1967, p. 7, COHC.

30. Leo C. Rosten, *The Washington Correspondents* (New York: Harcourt, Brace and Co., 1937), pp. 47–60.

31. Eben Ayers Diary, February 19, 1943, Ayers Papers, HST Library.

32. Transcript, Joseph A. Fox oral history interview (*Washington Star* White House correspondent), October 5, 1970, p. 4, HST Library.

33. Eben Ayers Diary, June 8, 1944, Ayers Papers, HST Library.

34. James Hagerty Diary, March 4, 1954, Hagerty Papers, DDE Library.

35. Interview with Barry Jagoda (Executive Office Building: MJK & MBG, September 21, 1979).

36. Interview with James Deakin (Telephone: MBG, March 14, 1979).

37. Interview with McGeorge Bundy (New York: MJK & MBG, May 1, 1978).

38. Interview with Martin Schram (Washington, D.C.: MBG & MJK, January 7, 1976).

39. *The Public Papers of the Presidents of the United States, Lyndon B. Johnson,* 1966, vol. 1, March 12 press conferences, pp. 303–17.

40. Interview with James Deakin, March 14, 1979.

41. Interview with Pierre Salinger (New York: MBG, October 13, 1976).

42. Interview with James Shuman, Ford administration assistant press secretary (Executive Office Building: MJK, November 22, 1976).

43. Transcript, Sherman Adams oral history interview, April 12, 1967, pp. 211–12, COHC.

44. James Hagerty Diary, March 3, 1954, Hagerty Papers, DDE Library.

45. *The Public Papers of the Presidents of the United States, Dwight D. Eisenhower,* 1954, March 3, 1954, press conference, p. 291.

46. Background interview, Johnson administration official (Washington, D.C.: MJK & MBG, January, 1976).

47. Interview with Ronald Nessen, July 26, 1978.

48. Memo, Robert Cutler to President Eisenhower, February 11, 1955, Cutler Files, WHCF, DDE Library.

CHAPTER TEN

1. Memo, Dan Rather to George Reedy, forwarded to President Johnson, marginal notes on the Rather letter are in Johnson's handwriting, April 20, 1964, EX FG 11-8-1, WHCF, LBJ Library.

2. Memo, Marvin Watson to President Johnson, Johnson marginal notes, April 27, 1965, EX PR 18, WHCF, LBJ Library.

3. Transcript, interview with Lyndon Johnson by Walter Cronkite, CBS News Special, "LBJ: Why I Choose Not to Run," December 27, 1969, p. 4, LBJ Library.

4. In order for a story to qualify as a White House story, both coders had to agree that its central focus was on the actions and programs of those physically part of the White House or the Executive Office of the President. Stories about other people with a personal or political connection to the President were not included unless their actions affected the White House in a fundamental way.

The coders were given general instructions relating to story tone. They were asked to categorize a story as favorable, unfavorable, or neutral, based on the overall impression the story gave them. What we (the authors) were looking for was the average reader's or viewer's first response to a story. The favorable and unfavorable categories contained stories that the coders found left a clear impression. The neutral category contains those stories that both found to be neutral and those that contained positive and negative elements that tended to balance each other off. It also contains a small number of cases in which one coder classified a story as negative and the other as positive. Because judgments on tone are subjective, we did not give extensive instructions in order to avoid losing the spontaneous responses of the coders. In spite of the subjective nature of the task, their responses were quite similar and provide a clear impression of the direction of White House press coverage.

The coders working on CBS News had the same evaluation in 87 percent of the stories, while the coders for *Time* agreed on 77 percent of the articles and those for the *New York Times* had the same findings on tone in 86 percent of the stories.

5. The nine subjects contained the following subcategories. Program and policy: general, foreign, domestic, budget. Activity: speech, news conference, ceremony, business trip, meeting, message to Congress, appointments, bill-signing. Personal: personal, philosophy, with family, family, health. Vice President: vice president, vice president during election. Congress and administration: president and Congress, president and administration. The remaining categories—Watergate, staff, president and press, and election—had only one heading. They contained no subcategories.

CHAPTER ELEVEN

1. Quoted in Rowland Evans, Jr., and Robert D. Novak, *Nixon in the White House* (New York: Random House, 1971), pp. 33–34.

2. Interview with David Broder (Washington, D.C.: MBG & MJK, January 11, 1977).

3. Letter, George Reedy to Michael B. Grossman, April 19, 1976.

4. Interview with Michael Raoul-Duval, staff assistant to President Ford (White House: MJK, January 4, 1977).

5. Ibid.

6. Letter, Reedy to Grossman, April 19, 1976.

7. Interview with Pierre Salinger (New York: MBG, October 12, 1976).

8. Interview with Aldo Beckman (New York: MBG, October 12, 1976).

9. Klein never actually served as press secretary. His title was "director of communication," and Ron Ziegler's was "press spokesman." However, in the first months of the Nixon administration, Klein was the top media adviser. His demise from an effective role in determining the media policy of the administration marked the end of whatever aspects of the "open presidency" could be found in the Nixon administration.

10. Leo C. Rosten, *The Washington Correspondents* (New York: Harcourt, Brace and Co., 1937), pp. 47–48.

11. Ibid.

12. Interview with Pierre Salinger, October 12, 1976.

13. Background interview, Ford administration official (Washington, D.C.: MJK, December, 1976).

14. Interview with Jody Powell (Washington, D.C.: MJK & MBG, January 11, 1977).

15. *The Public Papers of the Presidents of the United States, John F. Kennedy, 1962* (Washington, D.C.: U.S. Government Printing Office, 1963), May 9, 1962, press conference, p. 376.

16. Interview with Walt Rostow (Austin, Tex.: MJK, July 9, 1976).

17. Interview with Joseph Laitin (Washington, D.C.: MBG & MJK, January 27, 1976).

18. Interview with Robert Novak (Washington, D.C.: MBG, June 23, 1976).

19. Memo, George Reedy to President Johnson; Johnson marginal notes; February 19, 1965, EX PR 18, WHCF, LBJ Library.

20. Interview with Ronald Nessen (Bethesda, Md.: MJK & MBG, July 26, 1978).

21. Ibid.

22. Interview with George Christian (Austin, Tex.: MJK, July 9, 1976).

23. Interview with Michael Raoul-Duval, January 4, 1977.

24. Joseph Kraft, *Profiles in Power: A Washington Insight* (New York: New American Library, 1966), p. 93.

25. Memo, Pierre Salinger to Theodore Sorenson, undated, Salinger Papers, JFK Library.

26. David Halberstam, *The Best and the Brightest* (New York: Random House, 1972), p. 28.

27. Interview with William Rhatican (White House: MJK, November 19, 1976).

28. Memo, Robert Kintner to President Johnson, Johnson marginal notes; March 21, 1966, CF FG 11-8-1/Kintner, Robert, WHCF, LBJ Library.

29. Interview with Joseph Laitin (Washington, D.C.: MBG & MJK, January 27, 1976).

30. Transcript, Chalmers Roberts oral history interview, April 23, 1969, p. 32, LBJ Library.

31. Transcript, Arthur Krock oral history interview, November 21, 1968, p. 22, LBJ Library.

32. The President's Daily Diary, December 1–7, 1963, LBJ Library.

33. *New York Herald Tribune,* December 3, 1964; *New York Times,* December 5, 1964; ABC News, March 4, 1965; *Washington Star,* June 2, 1965; Drew Pearson, June 3, 1965; Marianne Means, June 4 & 7, 1965; William White, June 4, 1967. The President's Daily Diary, LBJ Library.

34. Peter Lisagor, June 7, 1965; *Time,* September 2, 1965; Cyrus Sulzberger, *New York Times,* March 1, 1966; Scripps-Howard, September 4, 1964; *Manchester Guardian,* December 2, 1964. The President's Daily Diary, LBJ Library.

35. The President's Daily Diary, September 1, 1964, LBJ Library. Comparable material is not available for earlier administrations. Detailed logs of appointments and meetings began with the Eisenhower administration, but telephone records were not kept. There are no such records for the Kennedy administration, and those for the Nixon and Ford administrations are not yet available. The records of President Eisenhower's meetings do not indicate that he had the same kind of meetings with the press.

36. Interview with David Powers, Kennedy administration aide (Waltham, Mass.: MBG, August, 1976).

37. Interview with James Reston (Washington, D.C.: MBG & MJK, January 28, 1977).

38. Interview with Michael Raoul-Duval, January 4, 1977.

39. Benjamin C. Bradlee, *Conversations with Kennedy* (New York: W. W. Norton & Co., 1975), pp. 155–56.

40. Frank Cormier, *LBJ: The Way He Was* (New York: Doubleday & Co., 1976), p. 55.

41. Background interview, Johnson administration official (Washington, D.C.: MJK & MBG, January, 1976).

42. Ibid.

43. Background interview, Ford administration official (Washington, D.C.: MJK & MBG, January, 1977).

44. George Reedy, *The Twilight of the Presidency* (New York: Mentor, 1970), p. 115.

45. Interview with Edward Folliard (Washington, D.C.: MBG & MJK, January 22, 1976).

46. Letter, President Roosevelt to Eugene Meyer, August 14, 1934, PPF 5018, FDR Library.

47. Memo, Tom Johnson to Walt Rostow, Juanita Roberts, Budget Director Shultz, Constance Gerrard, Joseph Califano, Hal Pachios, December 13, 1966, EX PR 18, WHCF, LBJ Library.

48. Memo, Joseph Califano to President Johnson, April 1, 1967, "Press Contacts" folder, (1758), files of Joseph Califano, LBJ Library.

49. Letter, Charles Bartlett to President Johnson, May 12, 1966, EX PR 18, WHCF, LBJ Library.

50. Letter, President Johnson to Charles Bartlett, May 13, 1966, EX PR 18, WHCF, LBJ Library.

51. William Porter, *Assault on the Media: The Nixon Years* (Ann Arbor: University of Michigan Press, 1976).

52. Memo, Jeb Stuart Magruder to H. R. Haldeman, October 17, 1969, as reprinted in "The Shot-gun versus the rifle," Porter, *Assault on the Media,* p. 245.

53. Interview with William Rhatican, November 19, 1976.

54. Memo, Jeb Stuart Magruder to H. R. Haldeman, October 17, 1969, as reprinted in Porter, *Assault on the Media,* p. 245.

55. Memo, John Caulfield to John Dean, November 2, 1971, Marc Lakritz files, evidence submitted to the U. S. Congress, Senate Select Committee on Presidential Campaign Activities and now held by the Senate Rules Committee.

56. Memo, Jeb Stuart Magruder to H. R. Haldeman, October 17, 1969, as reprinted in Porter, *Assault on the Media,* p. 245.

57. Whitehead speech as reprinted in Porter, *Assault on the Media,* pp. 300-304.

58. Memo, Jeb Stuart Magruder to H. R. Haldeman, October 17, 1969, reprinted in Porter, *Assault on the Media,* p. 245.

59. *The Public Papers of the Presidents of the United States, Richard M. Nixon,* 1973 (Washington, D.C.: U.S. Government Printing Office, 1976), October 26, 1973, press conference, p. 901.

60. Ibid., p. 905.

61. Daniel P. Moynihan, "The Presidency and the Press," *Commentary* 51, no. 3 (March, 1971): 41-52.

62. Memo, Jeb Stuart Magruder to H. R. Haldeman, December 11, 1970, U.S. Congress, Senate, Select Committee on Presidential Campaign Activities, 93rd Congress, 1st session, hearings, vol. 10 (Washington, D.C.: U.S. Government Printing Office, 1974), p. 413.

63. Jeb Stuart Magruder, *An American Life: One Man's Road to Watergate* (New York: Atheneum, 1974), pp. 103-4.

64. Ibid., p. 104.

65. Ibid.

66. Letter, Garnett Horner to President Johnson, June 7, 1965, filed with letter from President Johnson to Horner, June 9, 1965, EX PR 18, WHCF, LBJ Library.

67. Interview with Andrew Glass (Washington, D.C.: MBG, October 13, 1976).

68. Interview with James Connor (White House: MJK & MBG, December 6, 1976).

69. Interview with Edward Folliard, January 22, 1976.

70. Background interview, Ford administration official (Washington, D.C.: MJK & MBG, December, 1976).

71. Unsigned memo, "Biweekly Report: Mailings and Distributions," April 12-17, 19-24, 1971. Submitted to the Senate Select Committee on Presidential Campaign Activities and now held by the Senate Rules Committee.

CHAPTER TWELVE

1. Daniel P. Moynihan, "The Presidency and the Press," *Commentary* 51, no. 3 (March, 1971): 41-52. Senator Moynihan, an aide in the Nixon White House, presents a blistering attack on the press for the problems it has caused presidents. *New York Times* White House correspondent John Herbers described the continued manipulatability of reporters in his book, *No Thank You, Mr. President* (New York: W. W. Norton & Co., 1976).

2. *New York Times,* May 10, 1961, cited by Itzhak Galnoor, ed., in *Government Secrecy in Democracies* (New York: New York University Press, 1977), p. vii.

3. John Lengel in the *Washington Post,* August 9, 1974, cited by William E. Porter in *Assault on the Media: The Nixon Years* (Ann Arbor: University of Michigan Press, 1976), p. 192.

4. Ronald Nessen, *It Sure Looks Different from the Inside* (Chicago: Playboy Press, 1978), p. 13.

5. "The character of the cabinet may be made a nice index of the theory of the presidential office, as well as the President's theory of party government; but the one view is, so far as I can see, as constitutional as the other." Woodrow Wilson, *Constitutional Government* (New York: Columbia University Press, 1908), p. 77.

6. Richard E. Neustadt, *Presidential Power: The Politics of Leadership from F.D.R. to Carter* (New York: John Wiley & Sons, 1980).

7. Interview with Dennis Farney (Washington, D.C.: MJK, June 25, 1979).

8. Interview with Walt Rostow (Austin, Tex.: MJK, July 9, 1976).

9. Interview with James Reston (Washington, D.C.: MBG & MJK, January 28, 1977).

10. Background interview, Ford administration official (Washington, D.C.: MJK & MBG, December, 1976).

11. Interview with Walt Rostow, July 9, 1976.

12. Background interview, Ford administration official (Washington, D.C.: MJK & MBG, December, 1976).

13. Francis E. Rourke, *Secrecy and Publicity: Dilemmas of Democracy* (Baltimore: The Johns Hopkins Press, 1961), pp. 197–98.

NAME INDEX

SUBJECT INDEX

The Johns Hopkins University Press

This book was composed in VIP Times Roman text
and VIP Korinna Extra Bold display type by the
Composing Room of Michigan. It was printed
and bound by The Maple Press Company.

DATE DUE

GAYLORD			PRINTED IN U.S.A.